Scott Corrales'

ALIEN BLOOD LUST

Are There Vampires In Space?

By Scott Corrales
With Timothy Green Beckley
Sean Casteel · Tim R. Swartz
Hercules Invictus · Nigel Watson

FREE
Conspiracy
Journal
Included

ALIEN BLOOD LUST
ARE THERE VAMPIRES IN SPACE?

INNER LIGHT/GLOBAL COMMUNICATIONS

ALIEN BLOOD LUST
ARE THERE VAMPIRES IN SPACE?

Scott Corrales With Timothy Green Beckley and Sean Casteel
Additional Material By: Hercules Invictus - Nigel Watson - Tim R. Swartz

Published in the United States of America By Inner Light/Global Communications
PO Box 753 - New Brunswick, NJ 08903

Staff Members
Timothy G. Beckley, Publisher
Carol Ann Rodriguez, Assistant to the Publisher
Sean Casteel, General Associate Editor
Tim R. Swartz, Graphics and Editorial Consultant
William Kern, Editorial and Art Consultant

Sign Up On The Web For Our Free Weekly Newsletter and Mail Order Version of
Conspiracy Journal and Bizarre Bazaar
www.Conspiracy Journal.com
Order Hot Line: 1-732-602-3407
PayPal: MrUFO8@hotmail.com

CONTENTS

SECTION ONE

ARE THERE VAMPIRES IN OUTER SPACE?

SECTION TWO

THE TERROR OF THE CHUPA-CHUPA ALONG THE AMAZON

SECTION THREE

A JOURNEY INTO THE DARKNESS OF CHUPACABRA LAND

BONUS SECTION

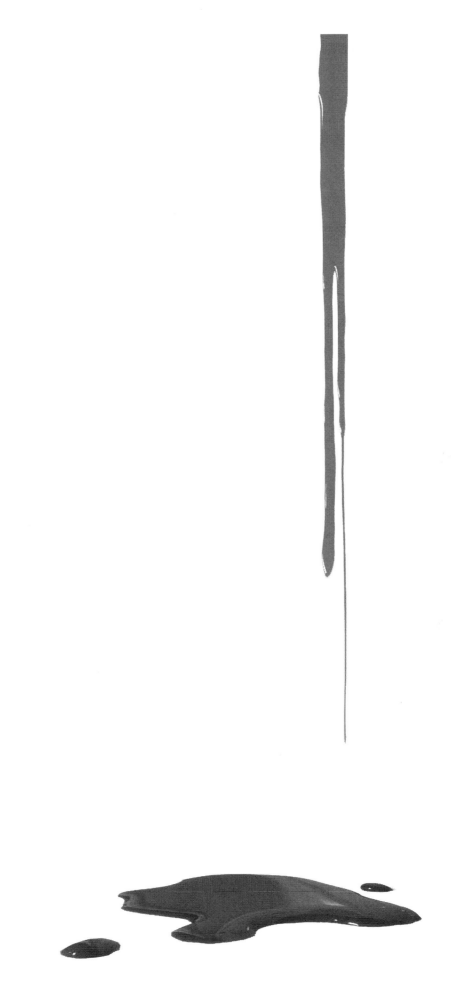

SECTION ONE
ARE THERE VAMPIRES IN OUTER SPACE?

ALIEN BLOOD LUST

PREFACE

SNACK TIME! – FLESH AND BLOOD
MAY BE THE REAL GOLD OF THE GODS
By Timothy Green Beckley

Blood is to some Ultra-Terrestrials what water is to mankind.

The flesh and blood of humans – and animals for that matter, when nothing "more upscale" makes itself available – could be the snack of the gods.

Is there a rationale for such a seemingly bizarre statement?

I would say so, and it is a concept that is after all supported by the evidence presented by our primary author, Scott Corrales, as well as our team of seasoned researchers in what is certain to be considered a provocative volume.

Blood may be necessary for at least some Ultra-terrestrials to drink or to ingest through infusion, in order for them to survive while "adrift" in our physical world. They may be trespassers from a parallel dimension or alternative universe where blood in its various forms has become a requisite to survival while "stationed" here, in effect making them Vampires From Space!

As in the horror classic by Bram Stoker, it could be that blood keeps them forever "young" (whatever that means in the cosmic scheme of things), acting as a necessary source for constant regeneration, or placing them in a state of euphoria like some drugs do to humans. It could be a form of universal dopamine. Dopamine being described as "the molecule behind all our most sinful behaviors and secret cravings. Dopamine is love. Dopamine is lust. Dopamine is adultery. Dopamine is motivation. Dopamine is attention. Dopamine is addiction."

Omitting vegetarians from the equation, most humans crave meat – some like their steaks rare or even in the form of tartar. We think nothing of butchering a steer in order to get to its most succulent cuts, so who is to say that the aliens don't see us in the same light, figuring us for a welcome meal on their journey through the cosmos?

ALIEN BLOOD LUST

I am not a hundred percent certain how I made the connection between blood and saucers. Animal mutilations have been around for a while. So many eye witness accounts exist that say the mutilations on their ranches took place directly after or during the height of a dramatic UFO sighting or flap, mostly at night. Usually, mysterious balls of light were seen over the pastures where the next day the cattle owners would find calfs and full grown cows and bulls missing their vital organs and their blood drained, none of it spilling out onto the ground where it would have flowed had they been butchered in a relatively "normal" manner.

We have not included much on the subject of animal mutilations since it is not the main focus of our activity here, and we highly recommend the works of researcher Chris O' Brien should you want an independent, impartial study of this intriguing phenomena which continues to baffle and perplex.

Putting animal mutes aside, I think I would have to point to what is generally recognized as the worst science fiction movie ever made as an early instigator of my interest in blood sucking freaks from outside realms. Ed Wood's "Plan Nine From Outer Space" had it all. There were grave robbers, ghouls, menacing aliens who warned we were on the verge of destruction, a spectacularly sexy Vampira (who never spoke a word), and a very drugged out Bela Lugosi who shot a couple of scenes before passing away for real this time, never to be resurrected from Dracula's coffin again!

In an offbeat way this movie so impressed me that decades (and I do mean decades) later I produced and "starred" in my Rotten Tomato's version of "Barely Legal Lesbian Vampires – The Curse of Ed Wood" which you might find on the net or in a two dollar DVD bin somewhere out in middle America.

Who could know we would take the general theme of vampires from space and run with it, thanks to the contents offered herein by Scott Corrales and our other most esteemed contributors?

ALIEN BLOOD LUST

THE BLOODMOBILE CHASE
By Timothy Green Beckley

Ok, so who do I legitimately give credit to for bringing the concept of alien blood sucking into my life?

Drum roll please …

The credit has to go to none other than my neighbor and longtime buddy, the late John A. Keel, whose book "The Mothman Prophecies" was adapted for the movies, the film version starring Richard Gere.

It was while in Point Pleasant, West Virginia, home of the huge creature with so much personality that he made it to the big screen, and in the middle of a UFO wave, that John says he heard about the case of a Red Cross bloodmobile being nearly "picked off" by an unidentified craft with claw-like appendages that tried to drag the vehicle along with its horrified passengers into the underbelly of their craft.

The events in Point Pleasant in 1967, at the peak of the Mothman craze and before the collapse of the Silver Bridge spanning West Virginia and Ohio, are best summarized by "Dot Connector Magazine' editor Scott: "While the Mothman sightings were whipping up frenzy among the townsfolk, and focusing all public attention on the TNT area, UFOs and other intelligent lights were making nightly appearances in the surrounding countryside, causing all manner of deviltry. Farmers were reporting poltergeist activity; typical haunting cases were reported from certain backwoods residents. Animals went missing and sometimes turned up dead with the blood sucked out of them and with no visible cause of death. These animal mutilation cases were some of the first connected with the modern UFO phenomenon. Seeing all of this, Keel regarded the Mothman as primarily a distraction from some other activity of unknown origin and motive. It seemed that the gullible townsfolk were busy chasing the Mothman while some insidious snare laid waiting for them in time."

ALIEN BLOOD LUST

Noted another prominent researcher: "The most puzzling aspect of these deaths (of animals) is the absence of blood. Often the carcasses seem drained of all blood. The wounds don't bleed. No blood is in evidence in the grass or dirt where the victims lay."

Returning to the Bloodmobile caper, it went down this way, according to Keel: "On the night of March 5, a Red Cross Bloodmobile was traveling along Route 2, which runs parallel to the Ohio River. Beau Shertzer, twenty-one, and a young nurse had been out all day collecting human blood and now they were heading back to Huntington, West Virginia, with a van filled with fresh blood.

"The road was dark and cold and there was very little traffic. As they moved along a particularly deserted stretch, there was a flash in the woods on a nearby hill and a large white glow appeared. It rose slowly into the air and flew straight for their vehicle. 'My God! What is it?' the nurse cried. 'I'm not going to stick around to find out,' Shertzer answered, pushing his foot down on the gas. The object effortlessly swooped over the van and stayed with it. Shertzer rolled down his window and looked up. He was horrified to see some kind of arm or extension being lowered from the luminous thing cruising only a few feet above the Bloodmobile. 'It's trying to get us!' the nurse yelled, watching another arm reach down on her side. It looked as if the flying object was trying to wrap a pincers-like device around the vehicle.

"Shertzer poured on the horses but the object kept pace with them easily. Apparently they were saved by the sudden appearance of headlights from approaching traffic. As the other cars neared, the object retracted the arms and hastily flew off. Both young people rushed to the police in a state of hysteria. The incident was mentioned briefly on a radio newscast that night but was not picked up by the newspapers."

This was not the last time that Keel found himself dealing with UFOs in relation to blood. There was a talk show host (WBAB), Jay P. Paro from Babylon, Long Island, who professed to having repeated contacts with a group "The Council of Ten Men," who held their meetings in a secret building and whose members all appeared to be androids with Biblical names. One called "Silo" was the leader. It was explained to Jay P. that, while the group appeared menacing at times, they really were on a peaceful mission. One night they sat around arguing in loud voices and drinking a liquid that resembled "very thick, clear glue." The androids all wore white robes and walked like mummies.

The commentator, whose show I had actually been on once – (she was absolutely the worst host in the world, who would ask a question and then turn off her tape recorder to ask me what I wanted her to ask me next) – was given a tour of the group's "meeting hall." Jay P. said there were seven rooms in all, most of them filled with junk, and several bathrooms which housed cabinets filled with pills.

ALIEN BLOOD LUST

She was horrified when they showed her a large, fully equipped laboratory. From John Keel's notes, posted on the only official website JohnKeel.com, we learn in this laboratory were, "Two human bodies on tables with tubes feeding a blue liquid into their arms. Both bodies (a man and a woman) seemed to be dead, but a breathing apparatus covered part of the man's face and a bellows device indicated he was still breathing.

"There were rows of test tubes and bottles filled with blood," Keel's notes—some handwritten—continued. "Each bottle was labeled with names such as 'CHARLES' and 'SUSAN.' The Ten handled some of the bottles and sampled their contents orally and without facial expressions. The whole scene sickened Jay P., and she was disturbed over the experience."

BLOOD BANKS OF THE FUTURE WILL REJUVENATE HUMANS

Just before putting the contents of this book to rest, I came across a press item that seems very apropos to our thirst for knowledge (touche!) Has science taken a page out of the gods of antiquity's playbook and come to the realization that being infused with human blood has the ability to rejuvenate and provide vigorous strength to the person ingesting the plasma of someone much younger than they – like a pubescent virgin let's say?

As we shall see, blood sacrifices were common practice among many "primitive" cultures. The lust for blood throughout antiquity is best made evident by simply thumbing your way through the pages of any academic archaeological study and peering into the dense fog of ancient history to the times in which human sacrifice was widely practiced and the drinking and bathing in of human blood was usually a part of some god-fearing ceremony which was held in order to appease some deity or group of deities seeking immortality in their home somewhere up above the clouds.

In a posting on Science Alert we are informed that blood is likely to be "the next big government approved drug" thanks to a Stanford Medical School graduate named Jessie Karmazin. The founder of Ambrosia Medical has launched his company to fill "the veins of older people with fresh blood from young donors – in the hopes that the procedure will help conquer aging by rejuvenating the body's organs."

The first clinic to offer this radical blood transference procedure (i.e. scientifically approved "ritual") will be opening its doors within the coming months in New York City.

According to the Science Alert article, "In 2017, Ambrosia enrolled people in the first US clinical trial designed to find out what happens when the veins of adults are filled with blood from the young. And while the results of that study have not yet been made public, Karmazin told Business Insider the results were 'really positive.'"

ALIEN BLOOD LUST

The company apparently will not confront any stumbling blocks from the Food and Drug Administration because blood transfusions are already approved by the agency!

We are told, "There appears to be significant interest: since putting up its website last week, the company has received roughly 100 inquiries about how to get the treatment," David Cavalier, Ambrosia's chief operating officer, told Business Insider. In actuality, to date, Ambrosia has "already infused close to 150 patients ranging in age from 35 to 92 with the blood of young donors, of which 81 were participants in their clinical trial. The trial, which involved giving patients 1.5 litres (1.58 quarts) of plasma from a donor between the ages of 16 and 25 over two days, was conducted with physician David Wright, who owns a private intravenous-therapy center in Monterrey, California."Before and after the infusions, participants' blood was tested for a handful of biomarkers, or measurable biological substances and processes that are thought to provide a snapshot of health and disease."People in the trial paid $8,000 to participate. The company hasn't settled on a commercial price tag for the procedure," Karmazin admitted. Karmazin is right about the safety of blood transfusions and their capacity to save lives.The online posting notes that, "An ordinary blood transfusion, which involves hooking up an IV and pumping the plasma of a healthy person into the veins of someone who's undergone surgery or been in a car crash, for example, is one of the safest life-saving procedures available. Every year in the US, nurses perform about 14.6 million of them, which means about 40,000 blood transfusions happen on any given day."There is, however, a controversy swirling about the issue of whether or not such an exchange of blood can actually bring about the physical rejuvenation of someone obtaining the treatment.

The trial studies Karmazin examined turned him into an optimist on the topic. "Some patients got young blood and others got older blood, and I was able to do some statistics on it, and the results looked really awesome," Karmazin told Business Insider last year."And I thought, this is the kind of therapy that I'd want to be available to me."So far, no one knows if young blood transfusions can be reliably linked to a single health benefit in people. Karmazin said, "Many of the roughly 150 people who've received the treatment have noted benefits that include renewed focus, better memory and sleep, and improved appearance and muscle tone."

No doubt the bloodthirsty supernatural beings of antiquity were expecting a lot more than these miniscule benefits as they watched the bloodletting on the stone alters and the bodily fluids of the unfortunate flowed in rivers to the ground below the solid granite temples built for the sole purpose of snuffing out the lives of slaves, captives and, of course, the most beautiful of maidens who would soon find their vital organs gutted in a snuffing frenzy.

ALIEN BLOOD LUST

So far qualifying studies in mice have been made which indicate that the Ambrosia Medical team may be on to something.

Irina Conboy, a bioengineering professor at the University of California at Berkeley who pioneered one of these parabiosis studies in mice in 2005, found evidence that the exchange had done something positive for the health of the older mouse who received the blood of the younger mouse. But the animals weren't simply swapping blood – the older rodent was also reaping the benefits of the younger one's more vibrant internal organs and circulatory system since they had surgically been bound together.In other words, the researchers couldn't say for sure whether it was the blood itself that was doing the apparent reviving or if the fact that the animals were linked in other ways was responsible for those perceived benefits. In 2016, Conboy and her team ran another study to see what would happen if they merely exchanged the rodents' blood without connecting their bodies in any way. They found that while the muscle tissue in the older mice appeared to benefit slightly from the younger blood, they still couldn't say for sure that these modest benefits were coming from the young blood itself.Source: Science Alerthttps://www.sciencealert.com/a-controversial-startup-that-will-inject-you-with-young-blood-is-opening-its-first-clinic

Well, I will be damned if we aren't being peppered with confirmation that the lust for blood is all around us, and that the Ultra-terrestrials may soon have some feeding friends on the ground, especially among the rich who have been accused and are capable of all sorts of atrocities.

In the pages ahead, we have our work cut out for us when we attempt to make a correlation between the nastiest of aliens and their pursuit of blood for whatever cause they deem necessary. By the end of this ledger I think our case will be substantial, though ultimately we leave it up to the reader to decide. Just beware that the possibilities could be categorized as extremely extreme!

Tim Beckley receives the New York "Fortean Award of Merit" from the group's fearless leader, John Keel. It's a rubber frog that didn't fall from the sky. Presented to him over twenty years ago, it still resides in his shower to this very day.

This Red Cross bloodmobile was nearly hauled off into the sky by a UFO during the height of Point Pleasant, West Virginia's struggle with the Mothman and his UFO companions.

Beau Robert Shertzer, bloodmobile driver, who passed away in 2015.

Long Island radio commentator Jay P. Paro saw a group of ten "androids" drink cups of raw blood.

Blood-crazed UFO crew tries to snatch up bloodmobile using claw-like appendages.

Publisher/author Tim Beckley received an early dose of alien blood lust while watching Ed Wood's classic "Plan 9 From Outer Space."

CHAPTER 2

HUMAN SACRIFICE – THE DEADLY DEED
By Sean Casteel

The blood sacrifice of animals and people has been with humankind from our earliest beginnings. While this book concerns itself with the interest in blood as expressed by the UFO occupants, humankind has been led up this blood-soaked path since his infancy, when the UFOs of the present day were seen as the "vehicles of the gods" by indigenous peoples throughout the world.

According to a website called "Occult World," "Ritual blood sacrifice is an ancient custom of propitiation to the gods. Animals, fowl and humans have long been sacrificed in various religious rites to secure bountiful harvests and blessings and protections from deities. Blood consumed in ritual sacrifice is believed to give the drinker the soul and attributes of the blood of the deceased, whether it be human or animal. The Celts and Druids reportedly drank the blood of their sacrificed human victims. The Aztecs cut the hearts out of human sacrifices with flint knives; the still-beating heart was held aloft by the priest and then placed in a ceremonial receptacle. The body was often dismembered and eaten in an act of ritual cannibalism."

THE JEWS, CHRISTIANS AND WITCHES

Other examples of cultures who practiced ritualistic blood sacrifice include the early Hebrews.

"The Book of Leviticus in the Old Testament," the posting continues, "lays out instructions for various forms of sacrifice of animals and fowl. In Genesis, Cain offers the fruits of his harvest, which does not please the Lord, and Abel offers one of his flock, which does please the Lord. Also in Genesis, God tests Abraham by instructing him to sacrifice his son. Abraham is stopped at the last moment, and a ram is substituted. The Paschal Lamb, eaten at Passover, is a sacrifice commemorating the deliverance of the Israelites from Egypt."

ALIEN BLOOD LUST

In the Christian faith, Christ shed his own blood on the cross and thus achieved eternal redemption for humankind. The Eucharist and communion services are "non-bloody" sacrifices in which wine or grape juice substitute for the blood of Christ.

During the witch hunts of the middle ages, witches were said to sacrifice cocks and unbaptized children to the Devil. They were also accused of committing cannibalism on infants and children. These accusations were more likely the result of "confessions" obtained by the Inquisition's use of torture during interrogation. This is also typical of accusations leveled by one religious group against another. For example, the Syrians accused the Jews of human sacrifice and cannibalism, much as the Romans accused the Christians and the Christians accused the Gnostics.

THE UNPRECEDENTED SCALE OF AZTEC BLOODLETTING

But the Aztecs, for one, are a people for whom human sacrifice and bloodletting are all too real and attested to by historians and anthropologists of impeccable credentials. In an internet posting called "Aztec Sacrifice" and written by Mark Cartwright, some of the grisly details are "offered up," so to speak.

"The religion of the Aztec civilization," Cartwright begins, "which flourished in ancient Mesoamerica (1345-1521 CE), has gained an infamous reputation for bloodthirsty human sacrifice with lurid tales of the beating heart being ripped from the still-conscious victim, decapitation, skinning and dismemberment. All of these things did happen, but it is important to remember that for the Aztecs, the act of sacrifice – of which human sacrifice was only a part – was a strictly ritualized process which gave the highest possible honor to the gods and was regarded as necessary to ensure mankind's continued prosperity."

In other words, it was done with the best of intentions. *with no Conscience*

The Aztecs were not the first to civilization in Mesoamerica to practice human sacrifice. They were preceded by the Olmecs, the Mayans and the Toltecs. The Aztecs did however, take sacrifice to an unprecedented scale, thought that scale was doubtlessly exaggerated by early chroniclers during the Spanish Conquest, probably to vindicate the brutal treatment the Spanish were themselves inflicting on the natives.

"Nevertheless," Cartwright writes, "it is thought that hundreds, perhaps even thousands, of victims were sacrificed each year at the great Aztec religious sites, and it cannot be denied that there would also have been a secondary effect of intimidation on visiting ambassadors and the populace in general."

The point in making the sacrifices was to "repay" the gods for the sacrifices made in the creation of the world and the life-giving sun. Sacrifices also compensated the gods for the crime which brought about mankind in Aztec mythology, which declared that a deity called Ehecatl-Quetzalcoatl had stolen bones from the Underworld and used them to make the first humans. Therefore sacrifices were a necessary apology to the gods.

"Gods then were 'fed' and 'nourished' with the sacrificed blood and flesh," Cartwright explains, "which ensured the continued balance and prosperity of Aztec society."

"Feeding the gods" included blood sacrifices made to Tezcatlipoca, the sun god, who had to be well-nourished so that he had enough strength to raise the sun each morning.

OBTAINING THE NECESSARY SACRIFICIAL VICTIMS

"With human sacrifices," Cartwright continues, "the sacrificial victims were most often selected from captive warriors. Indeed, warfare was often conducted for the sole purpose of furnishing candidates for sacrifice. This was the so-called 'flowery war' where indecisive engagements were the result of the Aztecs being satisfied with taking only sufficient captives for sacrifice and where the eastern Tlaxcala state was a favorite hunting ground.

"Those who had fought the most bravely or were the most handsome," he goes on, "were considered the best candidates for sacrifice and more likely to please the gods. Indeed, human sacrifice was particularly reserved for those victims most worthy and was considered a high honor, a direct communion with a god."

Sacrificial victims were also taken from ritual ballgames, where the losing captain or even the entire team paid the ultimate price for defeat. Children, too, would be sacrificed, especially to the rain god, Tlaloc; it was believed the very tears of the child victims would bring forth rain from the gods. Slaves were also a social group from which victims were chosen.

Among the most honored sacrificial victims were the "god impersonators." Specially chosen individuals were dressed as a particular god before the sacrifice. In the case of the Tezcatlipoca impersonator, the victim was treated like royalty for one year prior to the sacrificial ceremony.

"Tutored by priests, given a female entourage and honored with dances and flowers," Cartwright writes, "the victim was the god's manifestation on Earth until that final brutal moment when he met his maker. Perhaps even worse off was the impersonator of Xipe Totec, who, at the climax of the festival of Tlacaxipehualiztli was skinned to honor the god who was himself known as the 'Flayed One.'"

To reiterate, sacrifices were conducted on the top of large pyramids such as at Tenochtitlan, Texcoco, and Tlacopan and were most often carried out by stretching the victim over a special stone, cutting open the chest and removing the heart using an obsidian or flint knife. The heart was then placed in a stone vessel and burnt in offering to the god being sacrificed to. Alternately, the victim could be decapitated or dismembered. Images recorded by the Spanish in various Codex show decapitated bodies being flung down the steps of pyramids. Those sacrificed to Xipe Totec were also skinned, most probably in imitation of seeds shedding their husks.

A single victim could be made to fight a gladiatorial contest against a squad of hand-picked warriors. Obviously the victim could not possibly survive the ordeal or even inflict any injury on his opponents, being tied to a stone platform and given only a feathered club against his opponents' razor-sharp swords.

After the sacrifice, the heads of victims would displayed in racks, depictions of which survive in stone architectural decorations. The flesh of those sacrificed was also sometimes eaten by the priests conducting the sacrifice and by members of the ruling elite or warriors who had themselves captured the victims.

THE DRUIDS DESERVE THEIR BLOODY REPUTATION

According to National Geographic, there is recent evidence that the Druids of ancient Britain committed cannibalism and ritual human sacrifice – perhaps on a massive scale – adding weight to ancient Roman accounts of Druidic savagery, archeologists say.

"After a first century B.C. visit to Britain," writes the National Geographic's James Owen, "the Romans came back with horrific stories about these high-ranking priests of the Celts, who had spread throughout much of Europe over a roughly 2,000 year period. Julius Caesar, who led the first Roman landing in 55 B.C., said the native Celts 'believe that the gods delight in the slaughter of prisoners and criminals, and when the supply of captives runs short, they sacrifice even the innocent.'"

Even worse was claimed by first century historian Pliny the Elder, who suggested that the Celts practiced ritual cannibalism, eating their enemies' flesh as a source of spiritual and physical strength.

But, as Owen explains, with only the Romans' word to go on—the ancient Celts left no record of their own – it's been easy for historians to dismiss such ghoulish tales as wartime propaganda.

But recent gruesome finds appear to confirm the Romans' accounts. Perhaps the most incriminating evidence is the 2,000-year-old, bog-mummified body of "Lindow Man," discovered in England in the 1980s.

"Lindow Man's manicured fingernails and finely trimmed hair," Owen writes, "suggest that he may have been of high status – possibly even a Druid himself. At least one thing appears nearly certain about the ancient twentysomething: He was the victim of a carefully staged sacrifice. Recent studies have revealed that Lindow Man's head had been violently smashed and his neck had been strangled AND slashed."

A DRUID FOUNTAIN OF BLOOD

Owen provides further details on Lindow Man in what the National Geographic piece calls "A Druid Fountain of Blood."

ALIEN BLOOD LUST

"You've got a rope tightened around his neck, and at the moment where the neck was constricted, the throat was cut, which would cause an enormous fountain of blood to rise up," said archeologist Miranda Aldhouse-Green, of Cardiff University in Wales and an expert on the Druids.

Lindow Man's death is dated to around A.D. 60, according to Owen, when the Romans launched a new offensive in the island of Great Britain. He may have been sacrificed to persuade the Celtic gods to halt the Roman advance.

"Something had to be done to stop them in their tracks," said Aldhouse-Green. "And what better way than sacrificing a high-status nobleman?"

The idea jibes with something Julius Caesar wrote: In times of danger, the Celts believed that "unless the life of a man be offered, the mind of immortal gods will not favor them."

Left above: The Aztecs and other Mezoamerican tribes were notoriously infamous for human sacrifices, although there is evidence that some "victims" volunteered.

Right above: Greeks and other Eastern civilizations turned from human sacrifice to offering animals to the "gods."

Left: EarlyMesopotamian civilizations sacrificed human children to "Molech" during soltice rituals to insure good harvests.

14

CHAPTER 3

HUMAN SACRIFICE 101 – A HIDEOUS GLOBAL VIEW
By Timothy Green Beckley

PUBLISHER'S NOTE: — There is some dispute in the academic community as to the validity of human sacrifices and blood rituals in the various cultures and regions of the globe. It is thought by some that, if you go back far enough, no society is immune to such heinous practices. We like to think that the advent of the three major religions put a stop to such barbarism, but scholars admit that doesn't necessarily hold true. Much has been written on the subject and the following is presented as a thumbnail list of the most pertinent information to bring readers who have no background in this rather taboo topic up to current thinking on the matter. Almost always, such sacrifices – human, and later animal – were done to either offer praise or as appeasement to the gods. To ancient societies, the gods were as real as their own mortal selves were, although omnipotent and all powerful. These deities held the power of life and death over their worshippers and their entire society, be it big or small. If they were not presented with blood sacrifices, they might return to their faraway homes, but not before laying waste to the land and its inhabitants as they saw fit.

ANCIENT EGYPT

There is evidence that, upon his death, a King would be accompanied by servants, and possibly high officials, who would continue to serve him in eternal life. The skeletons that were found had no obvious signs of trauma, leading to speculation that the giving up of life to serve the King may have been a voluntary act, possibly carried out in a drug-induced state. At about 2800 BCE, the possible evidence of such practices disappeared, though echoes are perhaps to be seen in the burial of statues of servants in Old Kingdom tombs.

ALIEN BLOOD LUST

MESOPOTAMIA

Retainer sacrifice was practiced within the royal tombs of ancient Mesopotamia. Courtiers, guards, musicians, handmaidens and grooms died, presumed to have taken poison. A new examination of skulls from the royal cemetery at Ur, discovered in Iraq almost a century ago, appears to support a more grisly interpretation of human sacrifices associated with elite burials in ancient Mesopotamia than had previously been recognized, say archaeologists. Palace attendants, as part of royal mortuary ritual, were not dosed with poison to meet death serenely. Instead, a sharp instrument such as a pike was driven into their heads.

THE LEVANT

The Levant is an approximate historical/geographical term referring to a large area in the Eastern Mediterranean. In its narrowest sense, it is equivalent to the historical region of Syria. References in the Bible point to an awareness of human sacrifice in the history of ancient near-eastern practice. During a battle with the Israelites the king of Moab gives his firstborn son and heir as a whole burnt offering (olah, as used of the Temple sacrifice) (2 Kings 3:27)

The binding of Isaac appears in the Book of Genesis (22); the story appears in the Quran but Ismael is the one to be sacrificed. In both the Quranic and Biblical stories, God tests Abraham by asking him to present his son as a sacrifice on Moriah. Abraham agrees to this command without arguing. The story ends with an angel stopping Abraham at the last minute and providing a ram, caught in some nearby bushes, to be sacrificed instead. Many Bible scholars have suggested this story's origin was a remembrance of an era when human sacrifice was abolished in favor of animal sacrifice.

Another possible instance of human sacrifice mentioned in the Bible is the sacrifice of Jephthah's daughter in Judges 11. Jephthah vows to sacrifice to God whatsoever comes to greet him at the door when he returns home if he is victorious. The vow is stated in the Book of Judges, 11:31: "Then it shall be, that whatsoever cometh forth of the doors of my house to meet me, when I return in peace from the children of Ammon, shall surely be the Lord's, and I will offer Him a burnt offering." When he returns from battle, his virgin daughter runs out to greet him. She begs for, and is granted, "two months to roam the hills and weep with my friends," after which "he [Jephthah] did to her as he had vowed." According to some commentators of rabbinic literature, Jepthah's daughter was not sacrificed, but was forbidden to marry and remained a spinster her entire life, fulfilling the vow that she would be devoted to the Lord.

ALIEN BLOOD LUST

PHOENICIA

According to Greek and Roman sources, Phoenicians and Carthaginians sacrificed infants to their gods. The bones of numerous infants have been found in Carthaginian archaeological sites in modern times but the subject of child sacrifice is controversial. In a single child cemetery, called the Tophet by archaeologists, an estimated 20,000 urns were deposited.. Plutarch (c. 46–120 CE) mentions the practice, as do Tertullian, Orosius, Diodorus Siculus and Philo. Livy and Polybius do not. The Bible asserts that children were sacrificed at a place called the tophet ("roasting place") to the god Moloch.

GREEK AND ROMAN ANTIQUITY

References to human sacrifice can be found in Greek historical accounts as well as mythology. The human sacrifice in mythology, the deus ex machina salvation in some versions of Iphigeneia (who was about to be sacrificed by her father Agamemnon) and her replacement with a deer by the goddess Artemis, may be a vestigial memory of the abandonment and discrediting of the practice of human sacrifice among the Greeks in favor of animal sacrifice.

In ancient Rome, human sacrifice was infrequent but documented. Roman authors often contrast their own behavior with that of people who would commit the heinous act of human sacrifice. These authors make it clear that such practices were from a much more uncivilized time in the past, far removed. It is thought that many ritualistic celebrations and dedications to gods used to involve human sacrifice, but have now been replaced with symbolic offerings. Dionysius of Halicarnassus says that the ritual of the Argei, in which straw figures were tossed into the Tiber River, may have been a substitute for an original offering of elderly men. Cicero claims that puppets thrown from the Pons Suplicius by the Vestal Virgins in a processional ceremony were substitutes for the past sacrifice of old men. After the Roman defeat at Cannae, two Gauls and two Greeks in male-female couples were buried under the Forum Boarium, in a stone chamber used for the purpose at least once before. In Livy's description of these sacrifices, he distances the practice from Roman tradition and asserts that the past human sacrifices evident in the same location were "wholly alien to the Roman spirit." The rite was apparently repeated in 113 BCE, preparatory to an invasion of Gaul. They buried both the Greeks and the two Gauls alive as a plea to the Gods to save Rome from destruction at the hands of Hannibal. When the Romans conquered the Celts in Gaul, they tortured the people by cutting off their hands and feet and leaving them to die. The Romans justified their actions by also accusing the Celts of practicing human sacrifice

According to Pliny the Elder, human sacrifice was banned by law during the consulship of Publius Licinius Crassus and Gnaeus Cornelius Lentulus in 97 BCE, although by this time it was so rare that the decree was largely symbolic. The Romans also had traditions that centered on ritual murder, but which they did not consider to be sacrifice. Such practices included burying unchaste Vestal Virgins alive and drowning hermaphroditic children. These were seen as reactions to extraordinary circumstances as opposed to being part of Roman tradition. Vestal Virgins who were accused of being unchaste were put to death, and a special chamber was built to bury them alive. This aim was to please the gods and restore balance to Rome. Human sacrifices, in the form of burying individuals alive, were not uncommon during times of panic in ancient Rome. However, the burial of unchaste Vestal Virgins was also practiced in times of peace. Their chasteness was thought to be a safeguard of the city, and even in punishment the state of their bodies was preserved in order to maintain the peace.

A reconstructed frieze depicts the Vestal Virgin Tarpeia in the center, two soldiers on the left, and a man on the right bringing gifts. It tells the myth of the Sabines suffocating her under the weight of their gifts, and sets the example of punishment for Vestal Virgins who broke their vow of chastity.

Political rumors sometimes centered on sacrifice and, in doing so, aimed to liken individuals to barbarians and show that the individual had become uncivilized. Human sacrifice also became a marker and defining characteristic of magic and bad religion.

CELTS

Celtic Druids engaged extensively in human sacrifice. According to Julius Caesar, the slaves and dependents of Gauls of rank would be burnt along with the body of their master as part of his funerary rites. He also describes how they built wicker figures that were filled with living humans and then burned. According to Cassius Dio, Boudica's forces impaled Roman captives during her rebellion against the Roman occupation, to the accompaniment of revelry and sacrifices in the sacred groves of Andate. Different gods reportedly required different kinds of sacrifices. Victims meant for Esus were hanged, those meant for Taranis and those for Teutates drowned. Some, like the Lindow Man, may have gone to their deaths willingly.

Contradicting the Roman sources, more recent scholarship finds that "there is little archeological evidence" of human sacrifice by the Celts, and suggests the likelihood that Greeks and Romans disseminated negative information out of disdain for the barbarians. There is no evidence of the practices Caesar described, and the stories of human sacrifice appear to derive from a single source, Poseidonius, whose claims are unsupported.

Archaeological evidence from the British Isles seems to indicate that human sacrifice may have been practiced in times long predating any contact with Rome. Human remains have been found at the foundations of structures from the Neolithic time to the Roman era, with injuries and in positions that argue for their being foundation sacrifices.

On the other hand, ritualized decapitation was a major religious and cultural practice which has found copious support in the archaeological record, including the numerous skulls discovered in Londinium's River Walbrook and the 12 headless corpses at the French late Iron Age sanctuary of Gournay-sur-Aronde.

GERMANIC CULTURE

Human sacrifice was not a particularly common occurrence among the Germanic peoples, being resorted to in exceptional situations arising from crises of an environmental (crop failure, drought, famine) or social (war) nature, often thought to derive at least in part from the failure of the king to establish and/or maintain prosperity and peace (árs ok friar) in the lands entrusted to him. In later Scandinavian practice, human sacrifice appears to have become more institutionalized, and was repeated as part of a larger sacrifice on a periodic basis (according to Adam of Bremen, every nine years)

Evidence of Germanic practices of human sacrifice predating the Viking Age depend on archaeology and on a few scattered accounts in Greco-Roman ethnography. For example, Tacitus reports Germanic human sacrifice to (what he interprets as) Mercury, and to Isis, specifically among the Suebians. Jordanes reports how the Goths sacrificed prisoners of war to Mars, suspending the severed arms of the victims from the branches of trees.

By the 10th century, Germanic paganism had become restricted to Scandinavia. One account by Ahmad ibn Fadlan, as part of his account of an embassy to the Volga Bulgars in 921, claims that Norse warriors were sometimes buried with enslaved women with the belief that these women would become their wives in Valhalla. In his description of the funeral of a Scandinavian chieftain, a slave volunteers to die with a Norseman. After ten days of festivities, she is stabbed to death by an old woman, a sort of priestess who is referred to as Völva or "Angel of Death," and burnt together with the dead in his boat. This practice is evidenced archaeologically, with many male warrior burials (such as the ship burial at Balladoole on the Isle of Man, or that at Oseberg in Norway) also containing female remains with signs of trauma.

According to Adémar de Chabannes, just before his death in 932 or 933, Rollo (founder and first ruler of the Viking principality of Normandy) practiced human sacrifices to appease the pagan gods and at the same time made gifts to the churches in Normandy.[49]

Adam von Bremen recorded human sacrifices to Odin in 11th-century Sweden, at the Temple at Uppsala, a tradition which is confirmed by Gesta Danorum and the Norse sagas. According to the Ynglinga saga, King Domalde was sacrificed there in the hope of bringing greater future harvests and the total domination of all future wars. The same saga also relates that Domalde's descendant, King Aun, sacrificed nine of his own sons to Odin in exchange for longer life, until the Swedes stopped him from sacrificing his last son.

CHINA

The ancient Chinese are known to have made sacrifices of young men and women to river deities (Hebo), and to have buried slaves alive with their owners upon death as part of a funeral service. This was especially prevalent during the Shangand Zhou Dynasties. During the Warring States period, Ximen Bao of Wei demonstrated to the villagers that sacrifice to river deities was actually a ploy by crooked priests to pocket money. In Chinese lore, Ximen Bao is regarded as a folk hero who pointed out the absurdity of human sacrifice.

The sacrifice of a high-ranking male's slaves, concubines or servants upon his death (called Xun Zang) was a more common form. The stated purpose was to provide companionship for the dead in the afterlife. In earlier times, the victims were either killed or buried alive, while later they were usually forced to commit suicide.

Funeral human sacrifice was widely practiced in the ancient Chinese state of Qin. According to the Records of the Grand Historian by Han Dynasty historian Sima Qian, the practice was started by Duke Wu, the tenth ruler of Qin, who had 66 people buried with him in 678 BCE. The fourteenth ruler Duke Mu had 177 people buried with him in 621 BCE, including three senior government officials. Afterwards, the people of Qin wrote the famous poem Yellow Bird to condemn this barbaric practice, later compiled in the Confucian Classic of Poetry. The tomb of the eighteenth ruler Duke Jing of Qin, who died in 537 BCE, has been excavated. More than 180 coffins containing the remains of 186 victims were found in the tomb. The practice would continue until Duke Xian of Qin abolished it in 384 BCE. Modern historian Ma Feibai considers the significance of Duke Xian's abolition of human sacrifice to Chinese history comparable to that of Abraham Lincoln's abolition of slavery to American history.

TIBET

Human sacrifice, including cannibalism, was practiced in Tibet prior to the arrival of Buddhism in the 7th century.[62]

The prevalence of human sacrifice in medieval Buddhist Tibet is less clear. The Lamas, as professing Buddhists, could not condone blood sacrifices, and they replaced the human victims with effigies made from dough. This replacement of human victims with effigies is attributed to Padmasambhava, a Tibetan saint of the mid-8th century, in Tibetan tradition.

Nevertheless, there is some evidence that outside of lamaism, there were practices of tantric human sacrifice which survived throughout the medieval period, and possibly into modern times. The 15th-century Blue Annals, a seminal document of Tibetan Buddhism, reports upon how in 13th-century Tibet the so-called "18 robber-monks" slaughtered men and women for their corrupt tantric ceremonies. Such practices of human sacrifice as there were in medieval Tibet were mostly replaced by animal sacrifice, or the self-infliction of wounds in religious ritual, by the 20th century.

INDIA

Fierce goddesses like Chamunda are recorded to have been offered human sacrifice.

In India, human sacrifice is mainly known as "Narabali." Here "nara" means man and "bali" means sacrifice.

Currently human sacrifice is very rare and almost non-existent in modern India. However, there have been at least three cases, through 2003-2013, where three men have been murdered in the name of human sacrifice.

The earliest evidence for human sacrifice in the Indian subcontinent dates back to the Bronze Age Indus Valley Civilization. An Indus seal from Harappa depicts the upside-down nude female figure with legs outspread and a plant issuing from the womb. The reverse side of the seal depicts a man holding a sickle and a woman seated on the ground in a posture of prayer. Many scholars interpret this scene as a human sacrifice in honor of the Mother-Goddess, although many historians doubt it.

Regarding possible Vedic mention of human sacrifice, the prevailing 19th-century view, associated above all with Henry Colebrooke, was that human sacrifice did not actually take place. Those verses which referred to purushamedha were meant to be read symbolically, or as a "priestly fantasy." However, Rajendralal Mitra published a defence of the thesis that human sacrifice, as had been practised inBengal, was a continuation of traditions dating back to Vedic periods.

Human and animal sacrifice became less common during the post-Vedic period, as ahimsa (non-violence) became part of mainstream religious thought. The Chandogya Upanishad (3.17.4) includes ahimsa in its list of virtues. The impact of Sramanic religions such as Buddhism and Jainism also became known in the Indian subcontinent.

Human sacrifices were carried out in connection with the worship of Shakti until approximately the early modern period, and in Bengal perhaps as late as the early 19th century. Although not accepted by the larger section of Hindu culture, certain tantric cults performed human sacrifice until around the same time, both actual and symbolic; it was a highly ritualized act, and on occasion took many months to complete.

The Khonds, an aboriginal tribe of India, inhabiting the tributary states of Odisha and Andhra Pradesh, became notorious, on the British occupation of their district about 1835, from the prevalence and cruelty of the human sacrifices they practiced.

THE MISSISSIPPIAN CULTURE AND OTHER NATIVE AMERICANS

The peoples of the Southeastern United States known as the Mississippian culture (800 to 1600 CE) have been suggested to have practiced human sacrifice, because some artifacts have been interpreted as depicting such acts. Mound 72 at Cahokia (the largest Mississippian site), located near modern St. Louis, Missouri, was found to have numerous pits filled with mass burials thought to have been retainer sacrifices. One of several similar pit burials had the remains of 53 young women who had been strangled and neatly arranged in two layers. Another pit held 39 men, women and children who showed signs of dying a violent death before being unceremoniously dumped into the pit.

Several bodies showed signs of not having been fully dead when buried and of having tried to claw their way to the surface. On top of these people another group had been neatly arranged on litters made of cedar poles and cane matting. Another group of four individuals found in the mound were interred on a low platform, with their arms interlocked. They had had their heads and hands removed. The most spectacular burial at the mound is the "Birdman burial." This was the burial of a tall man in his 40s, now thought to have been an important early Cahokian ruler. He was buried on an elevated platform covered by a bed of more than 20,000 marine-shell disc beads arranged in the shape of a falcon, with the bird's head appearing beneath and beside the man's head, and its wings and tail beneath his arms and legs. Below the birdman was another man, buried facing downward. Surrounding the birdman were several other retainers and groups of elaborate grave goods.

A ritual sacrifice of retainers and commoners upon the death of an elite personage is also attested in the historical record among the last remaining fully Mississippian culture, the Natchez. Upon the death of "Tattooed Serpent" in 1725, the war chief and younger brother of the "Great Sun" or Chief of the Natchez; two of his wives, one of his sisters (nicknamed La Glorieuse by the French), his first warrior, his doctor, his head servant and the servant's wife, his nurse, and a craftsman of war clubs all chose to die and be interred with him, as well as several old women and an infant who was strangled by his parents. Great honor was associated with such a sacrifice, and their kin were held in high esteem.

ALIEN BLOOD LUST

After a funeral procession with the chief's body carried on a litter made of cane matting and cedar poles ended at the temple (which was located on top of a low platform mound), the retainers, with their faces painted red and drugged with large doses of nicotine, were ritually strangled. Tattooed Serpent was then buried in a trench inside the temple floor and the retainers were buried in other locations atop the mound surrounding the temple. After a few months, the bodies were disinterred and their de-fleshed bones were stored as bundle burials in the temple.

The Pawnee practiced an annual Morning Star Ceremony, which included the sacrifice of a young girl. Though the ritual continued, the sacrifice was discontinued in the 19th century. The Iroquois are said to have occasionally sent a maiden to the Great Spirit.

The torture of war captives by the tribes of the Eastern Woodlands cultural region also seems to have had sacrificial motivations.

Mezoamerican civilizations frequently sacrificed warriors captured during regional battles. The hearts and livers of the slain warriors were eaten raw and their bodies were tossed from the platform.

When captured warriors were not available, young boys and girls were sacrificed in their place.

ALIEN BLOOD LUST

IS BLOOD THE TRUE NECTAR AND AMBROSIA OF THE GODS?
By Hercules Invictus

PUBLISHER'S NOTE: There remains a controversy over whether or not the Greeks performed human sacrifices. It's a subject that has been played down because, as Jason Daley reporting for Smithsonian.com duly remarks: "The ancient Greeks are associated with music, philosophy, logic and storytelling. So tales of human sacrifice in the works of ancient writers including Plato are often chalked up as myths. But the discovery of the remains of a male teenager at Mount Lykaion, the spot where some Greeks made animal sacrifices to Zeus, may lend credence to those tall tales."

The story continues crediting several sources, only adding to the mystery surrounding this locale: Mizin Sidahmed at *The Guardian* reports that the 3,000-year-old remains were discovered in an ash altar on the mountain that is the earliest known site of worship for the god Zeus. The area of the altar has been under excavation since 2006, and finds indicate it was used by humans as early as 5,000 years ago, even before the "birth" of Zeus in the Greek world. Archaeologists have discovered lots of animal bones, as well as pottery shards, metal objects and tripods in the area. "Several ancient literary sources mention rumors that human sacrifice took place at the altar [of Zeus, located on the mountain's southern peak] but up until a few weeks ago there has been no trace whatsoever of human bones discovered at the site," David Gilman Romano, professor of Greek archaeology at the University of Arizona, who has worked at the site, tells Nicholas Paphitis at the AP: "Whether it's a sacrifice or not, this is a sacrificial altar ... so it's not a place where you would bury an individual. It's not a cemetery."Not wanting to play down the importance of the Smithsonian, one should note that they almost always go along with conventional "scientific opinion." If they do a UFO or a Bigfoot special on TV, they start out being open-minded, but by the time mid-program rolls around they have planted themselves firmly on the side of the skeptics. Naturally, in order

24

to get all the facts straight from the mouth of the Gods of Olympus, we had to call upon our favorite Greek warrior of the worlds whose research is at once responsible to and inspired by his forefathers. To some, human sacrifice on the Greek Isles might be considered the Achilles Heel of local mythology. Nectar and ambrosia were what the gods normally ate, but they could, of course eat almost anything, including humans, if it satisfied their appetite. As we shall see, the gods did savor sacrificial "lambs" from time to time!

****

O wondrous Muses, daughters of Zeus and blessed Mnemosyne, inspire me to speak truly of Dionysus and his untamed celebrants, partially Human and partially bestial in form.

But first, aid me with dispelling the mists of fear and confusion that obscure the golden-white Light of Olympus from the people of this this time and place, unknowing heirs of our ancient and undying legacy!

For in their ignorance they ask themselves and each other: Are the Olympians evil Powers who mean them harm? Are the Undying truly Celestial intelligences from the star-filled Void? Do the Immortals live off their life-essence like bloodsucking parasites? Who were the first to fall under their divine spell and declare them Gods? Do the Deathless (or their first followers) still walk among them?

THEY GAVE US OUTER SPACE

It is easy to link the Olympian universe to the awe-inspiring light show in the night sky. The planets of our solar system and most of the constellations in the firmaments are named after characters or items from Greek Mythology. This Astral (Starry or Heavenly) lore was explored, explained and continuously expanded by the Hermetic Sciences, which included Astrology (Star Lore). Through the study of Hermeticism (granted to us by the Thrice Great Hermes, aka Mercury and Thoth), Theosophy (the Divine Wisdom) and Theurgy (Divine Practices such as High Magic) we could gain a greater understanding of the Will of the Gods through their places, relationships and interactions in our individual Horoscopes.

The Chariots of the Gods still fly through our skies and the Sun, Moon, planets, comets, meteors, asteroids and other bright aerial phenomena are still credited as their ultimate inspiration. Our Flying Saucer lore continues this tradition, anchoring ancient themes into modern consciousness.

It is also easy to fit the Olympians into the mold of the Ancient Alien (previously Ancient Astronaut) speculations. The Gods of Old descended from the Heavens, lived on mountain tops or deep beneath the waters, had aerial craft and superpowers, mated with us and guided our evolution through selective breeding and taught us the arts of civilization. In the tales they were sometimes assisted by robots and inhuman embodiments. Artifacts such as the Antikythera Mechanism

ALIEN BLOOD LUST

(an actual ancient Astronomical and Astrological computing device), flush toilets, running water, moving statues and even coin-dispensed beverages were known to the Ancients as late as the Hellenistic Age (between the time of Alexander the Great and Cleopatra, plus a handful of Roman Caesars).

DO A LITTLE DANCE, SPILL A LITTLE BLOOD

Was blood sacrifice practiced in Mediterranean antiquity?

Yes, it was. Mostly domesticated animals such as bovines, pigs, sheep, goats and certain birds were routinely sacrificed at festivals and when thanking (or bargaining with) the beings who could be accessed and interacted with through the Olympian World Tree. In most cases the sacrificial act was quick and merciful and the cooked meat was eaten by the celebrants. There is even a tale about how the Gods were tricked into accepting the portion that smelled nicest on the grill but had the least nutritional value and taste-appeal to hungry Humans.

Generally, sacrifices to the Gods faced and floated to the Heavens and sacrifices to the Heroes, aka the Mighty Dead, were spilled on the ground and, in essence, descended to the Underworld. Blood, being the essence of life, restored lost memories in the World Below and allowed those who had passed to answer questions or do favors for those still living.

Animal sacrifice survives, in Greece and elsewhere, when folks raise animals for the express purpose of being eaten during High Holidays. Growing up Greek I saw, time and again, fellow Greeks in New York and New Jersey running afoul of their neighbors, animal activists, government agencies and the local police when "preparing" a lamb for Easter according to the dictates of their time honored traditions.

WASN'T THERE HUMAN SACRIFICE AS WELL?

Yes, there was, most consistently to Kronos during the earliest of times. Echoes of this practice survived during certain festivals in Greece and Rome where a convicted criminal was ritually executed for reasons that were no longer clear.

According to Myth:

Artemis demanded (through Calchas the Seer) that Agamemnon sacrifice his daughter Iphigenia to rouse the winds that would carry his fleet across the Aegean Sea to Troy. The winds were stilled when one of the High King's men slaughtered one of Artemis' sacred deer to feed the troops. Artemis reportedly whisked Iphigenia away before she was sacrificed.

Demeter and, a generation later, Poseidon, demanded that certain royal families sacrifice their daughters to sea monsters for various transgressions. Perseus rescued Andromeda of Ethiopia (this tale was immortalized through various constellations, pottery paintings, literature and the cinematic Clash of the Titans franchise) and his grandson Herakles rescued Hesione of Troy.

There are a few other isolated incidents reported in the lore. By all accounts Human Sacrifice was rare in the lands under Olympian influence and was practiced far more frequently by "barbaric" people in "foreign" lands.

In modern times, those of us who follow the Olympian Heroic Path dedicate our deeds to Mount Olympus. Our daily life and how we live it is thus our prayer, our religious ritual, our song of praise, our heartfelt offering and the sacrifice of our mortal Human self to our Immortal Olympian Self.

VAMPIRE GODS: THE RISEN ONES

Are the Olympians Vampires? Do they drink our blood and/or leech off our energy to continue their existence? A man named William Meyers certainly thought so and in 1993 he published his expose, aptly titled *Gods or Vampires?*

Among the personages he reveals as bona fide Immortals are Cybele, Dionysus, Hercules, Romulus, Caligula, Apollonius and Jesus – all well known to the Greeks of old and their modern day descendants. Meyers quotes ancient sources to support his thesis and convincingly argues that the path to full divinity trod by those who are partially divine may have inspired the legend of the Vampire. Though wary of those who have died and then risen, he reluctantly admits that these Immortals are not necessarily evil and that some of those he's outed are actually remembered for their benevolence and good deeds.

In *Gods or Vampires?* much attention is focused on the symbolism of drinking vessels and the equivalence of wine with blood. Perhaps the Ascended God of the Vine, known to my ancestors as Dionysus, deserves a second look, one that encompasses a wider range of information and focuses on the company he kept.

THE GOD OF WINE: A BEING DIVINE

Before he ascended to Olympus and became one of The Twelve, the Demigod Dionysus was accompanied and served by a retinue of wild and sometimes brutally savage entities. Collectively known as his Thiasos, his followers consisted mostly of rowdy Demihumans such as Satyrs, Centaurs, Sileni and Fauns. He was also served by blood-mad Maenads, who were usually either long-lived Forest Nymphs or mortal-born Human women.

Dionysus, known to the Romans as Bacchus, was a son of Zeus, known to the Romans as Jupiter. Three different mothers are listed in the chronicles (Semele, Persephone and Demeter), leading many to believe that the lives of three distinct incarnations of the Demigod were woven into the final tapestry of his divine hagiography... or that three distinct and separate individuals inspired the legend. Others believe that Dionysus came to Greece from the East, perhaps as far away as India.

He is sometimes depicted as driving a chariot pulled by lions and/or tigers in the fashion of Near Eastern deities. Whatever the case may be regarding his origins, Dionysus became a force to be reckoned with in the Olympian spiritual landscape. Bacchus had his very own Mysteria in Greece and Rome, played a major role in the Eleusinian Mysteries, and was the focus of colorful local cults beyond number. Bacchanalias (uninhibited orgies where the wine flowed freely) were held in his honor. Though clearly a celebrant of Life in its fullness, Dionysus is strongly associated with the cycle of Death and Rebirth, as are many of the other fabled Sons of Jupiter.

As an archetype Dionysus still rules the spontaneous, emotional and sensual aspects of our inner being. Some outwardly equate him with sex, mind-altering drugs, alcoholic beverages and rock & roll. What few realize is that Dionysus speaks through the Delphic Oracle whenever his rational half-brother of Apollo is away. I have met many modern-day avatars, children of, followers and fans of Dionysus during this earthly sojourn. On several occasions I was blessed by a visitation of the God himself. Though still untamed, Bacchus is no longer the wandering adventurer who sought to free his mother from the Underworld. His gift is transcendental ecstasy, the loss of self that leads to a realization of Self.

Phantom lions, tigers and other great cats (some of them long extinct on this plane of being) are still spotted – and sometimes leave footprints and other elusive evidence behind in their wake. Imagine capturing, taming and harnessing two of these feral entities and then having them draw your chariot!

Satyrs are depicted as part goat (lower half) and part Human (upper half). They are horned, extremely randy and sexually aggressive. They inspired the psychological term *satyriasis*, a condition of insatiable sexual appetite in human males.

Centaurs are usually portrayed as Human from the belly up and fully horse (sans head and neck) in all other respects. Though there are Wise Ones like Cheiron among them, most are wild and become wilder still when intoxicated or provoked.

Silenii look a lot like Satyrs but are hornless and possess longer and larger ears. They have horsey bottom halves, but – unlike Centaurs – only two legs (which are considerably smaller than those of a horse as well).

Fauns appear similar to Satyrs and Silenii. They are horned or antlered, and are mostly Human-like in their upper bodies and akin to mini-deer below their torso.

Nymphs often appear in the guise of ethereal young Human women with angular features. They present themselves nude or scantily clad and retreat into their tree, stone, body of water or other physical anchor whenever they feel threatened. The term *nymphomania* is used to describe Human women with insatiable sexual appetites.

ALIEN BLOOD LUST

As the days of myth and legend passed and Human history began the Demihumans slowly faded from the scene and were replaced in the fired-clay art of the ancients by depictions of Human followers who are clearly wearing costumes.

However, some inhuman stragglers remain and can be encountered to this day.

SHADOWY HALF-HUMANS AND FALLEN GODS

Satyr sightings never entirely ceased in Greece and I have heard numerous modern accounts over the years. Typically Satyrs are sighted at night, casually perched atop boulders and seemingly lost in thought. Almost without exception the encounters occur on or near dirt paths on the sides of mountains. The Satyr, initially caught unawares, invariably attacks by radiating waves of fear and panic that immediately drive the human intruder away.

Humans in Satyr costumes can also still be seen in rural Greece. As a child I witnessed a modern-day folk-ritual in Lemnos where youths with painted faces, wearing horns and fur leggings, paraded down the main street of my town brandishing clubs, knotted rope and torches, angrily chanting *"Pa-loo-kah."* They menaced and humiliated all who dared cross their path and chased those who, knowing better, fled the area of the rowdy procession.

There is a belief among Hellenes (Greeks) that when the Satyrs and their ilk (Silenii, Centaurs, Fauns) left Gaia, many entered the Realm of Shadows, where some remain to this day as Kallikantzaroi (usually translated as Goblins in English). They remain Shades until they finally fade from our world. Some of the more powerful Shades are actually lesser Nature Gods who were consigned to Shadow. Their leader in Greece is called the Koutsodaimonas (literal meaning: Lame Daimon. Please note that the term Daimon denotes an in-between spirit and not necessarily something evil). Most Kallikantzaroi avoid human contact and others can best be described as mischievous or playful in their interactions with people. Kallikantzaroi are said to be most disruptive in human affairs during the numinous time between late December and early January when one year transitions into the next. They like to tear down Christmas decorations and defile holiday meals lovingly prepared for family gatherings with their dung, urine and other fluid secretions.

Beyond the borders of Greece (but still most often encountered near mountains or desolate areas) are the Peering Shades, also known as the Bedroom Visitors. In the Olympian paradigm they are Kallikantzaroi pure and simple – a hodgepodge of former Greco-Roman elementals and devas that have yet to fade into nothingness. They have also, in the greater human community over time, been equated with sex demons (the incubus and succubus), the Djinn (who are very much like us – you can even marry one in certain parts of the world), horny UFO Aliens, amorous Ultra-terrestrials and even Bigfoot on occasion (note that in Olympian lore the Kallikantzaroi can also appear as shaggy apes – or sometimes dogs).

Peering Shades are perceived as patches of darkness substantially darker than the surrounding night. You can actually feel them looking at you. When you focus your attention upon them one of their number will reassure you that all is well then suggest you go to sleep. This always seems like a reasonable request and usually, unless you train yourself not to, you will immediately enter the Realm of Hypnos. Peering Shades will sometimes sit near you or lie down next to you on a bed. They are known to sometimes touch, hold, caress or molest the objects of their affection, who usually – if conscious - find themselves unable to move.

DEER WOMAN: A MODERN DAY FAUN

She is drawn to nocturnal celebrations. She loves to dance. Her face has been described as sweet and innocent, almost angelic. Yet her body is mature and sensual: most definitely a woman's, not a girl's. She is adept at directing, and misdirecting, attention. Unless she has specifically targeted you, you probably wouldn't register her presence at all.

She's the mistress of getting lost in a crowd, practically invisible in the midst of a typical night-out's countless distractions. Poncan legend has it that this entity is a Unique Creature, though there may be several of them presently roaming the continent. The indigenous people of Wisconsin, who knew her of old, described her as having raven-black hair and dark, hypnotic eyes. She invariably wore soft white leather buckskins and, back then, took subtle precautions to divert attention away from her feet.

Assuming that this is a third-density being, which is unlikely, her superficial features can easily be camouflaged in these decadent days of over-the-counter hair dyes, mail-order prosthetics and color-change contact lenses. And there is no guarantee that she still accentuates dramatic contrasts through her attire. The Deer Woman has long-since abandoned her remote, aboriginal haunts and now wanders white-man's America. She gravitates toward large urban centers. They are ideal hunting grounds with their busy night-lifes, ever-shifting crowds of anonymous strangers looking for a good time, and reputations for tragic misadventures culminating in gory death.

She usually targets attractive and athletic males. Her movements and gestures draw the attention of her prey. If she's dancing, her dance is for him, and him alone; alluring and inviting. Her potential lover feels chosen, special, singled out. Once mutual attraction, and interest, is established, she will discreetly lure her victim away from the herd with the promise of immediate sexual gratification, no strings attached. Once alone with the lucky guy, in a dark and inaccessible place, she delivers: passionate, animalistic ecstasy. If you find yourself in this situation, be prepared to get your mind blown, literally. In the afterglow, while you're spent, disoriented and grinning like an idiot, she will strike.

The Deer Woman will ruthlessly brutalize your head. She will stomp on your face, crack open your skull, splatter your gray matter and slash your throat. And she won't stop until your blood flows freely. In days of yore she did this with her sharpened hooves (which is why she carefully hid her feet from horny Poncan braves). She can reportedly run fast, leap high and telepathically command various herd animals, which makes her especially dangerous if encountered in rural or forested areas.

THE DANCING MAIDENS

Like modern-day Satyr sightings, the Dancing Maidens are usually encountered at night on the slopes of mountains. The moon, most often full, also figures into the story. I've heard more than a handful of personal and second hand accounts over the years.

Typically a man traveling alone (or in the company of friends) will hear female laughter and merriment in a remote location on a large hill or mountain far from town. Seeking out the source of the sounds, he spies a small group of women (usually three) dancing in the moonlight. Sometimes there is music and sometimes they are drinking.

The dances are Greek style and they are joined together by their bare arms.

Described as young and beautiful, they seem more like Human women than the fey Nymphs that are sometimes encountered in out-of-the-way places. As they appear uninhibited in their interactions and there are occasional glimpses of naked flesh, the witness remains, usually hidden behind nearby trees or boulders.

As their dancing becomes more frenzied, their garments (usually thin white fabric – long like the ancients wore) become loose, revealing increasingly more of their anatomies. The witness is mesmerized and enthralled by the show until... a donkey leg is suddenly revealed. Yes, the Dancing Maidens each have one or two donkey legs, marking them as Strighles (usually translated Witches) and inhumans!

At that point the witness runs back to town without stopping or looking back. They are fueled by the fear of what the Dancing Maidens may do if they are caught. No one I have met who has shared this tale with me could articulate exactly what they feared that these entities would do to them. Stomp them like Deer Woman? Turn them into prey and loose a pack of predators on them (the Olympian Artemis reportedly did this to Actaeon, who spied upon her while she bathed with her Companions)?

Could the Strighles be the Maenads of old, few in number but still dedicated to

ALIEN BLOOD LUST

the Lord of Frenzied Trance? In the days of Myth they sought privacy, disrobed and performed blood rites in honor of Dionysus. They reportedly tore their living victims (animal and human) into tiny pieces with their nails and teeth. Whilst doing so they bathed in the blood and gore of their sacrifice and consumed its quivering flesh before consciousness could flee.

Orpheus, musician son of bright Apollo, was torn apart by Maenads for mourning lost love instead of embracing and living life in its fullness. Pentheus, King of Thebes, suffered a similar fate for dissing Dionysus and spying on the secret rites of the Bacchae.

IN CONCLUSION

There are many ways to approach and reach Mount Olympus. Though you may be booted out when you arrive, if you truly don't belong there, or humbled if you approach in a spirit of arrogance or overweening pride, the Olympians are overall a welcoming and hospitable pantheon and treat their guests quite well before sending them back to Gaia – with plenty of gifts of course.

The Olympians have been viewed in a variety of ways and each perspective leads to a much greater understanding of their totality. Are they Ancient Aliens? Returning Astronauts from lost Atlantis? Immortal Sylphs? Crypto-terrestrials? Ultra-terrestrials? Vampires? Ascended Beings? Sure, why not? They don't seem to mind our various attempts to comprehend what they are and are sometimes amused by how they are portrayed in our popular culture.

Since entering our awareness it has been known that they walk among us, sometimes in disguise. They have joined their essences and entwined their destinies with our own and are still extremely interested in our daily doings, which they enjoy guiding (or interfering with, depending on your point of view).

Are the Olympians a bloodthirsty bunch? Perhaps, but certainly not more than we ourselves are, or any other divine pantheon on Gaia for that matter. Even the most benevolent of Space Brothers often confess to having colorful (and often bloody) incarnational histories. Perhaps it is, indeed, as many assert, that the Olympians (and other Celestials) are merely us writ large. To me that is not a bad thing to be. And certainly something worth striving for.

Thank you O awesome Muses, who dwell eternally upon the slopes of Mount Helicon yet are forever whispering in our ear, for inspiring me during the composition of this work! May those who have Awoken, those who are Awakening, those who still Sleep and the Sons of Men all gain a more panoramic perspective by contemplating this tapestry of words!

Onwards!

Hercules Invictus

ALIEN BLOOD LUST

Postscript: Synchronistically, after I completed the first draft of this work I learned about and started reading *Last Clash of the Titans* by Derek P. Gilbert. It spans some of the same territory I've touched upon above yet offers a fresh Bible-based understanding. I am enjoying the journey of reading it, have learned a thing or three that broadened my perspective and I am looking forward to writing a review and interviewing the author on my *Voice of Olympus* podcast. In the promotions and on the cover *Last Clash of the Titans* promises to reveal how the Second Coming of Hercules (which is a cool yet extremely accurate way of describing my life-work and reason for being) will rekindle the flames that lead to the Final Confrontation. I haven't gotten to that part of the book yet, but I'm certainly curious about what he has to say!

© Hercules Invictus

Ancient Greeks believed their "gods" were real, living beings, all of whom had come from the stars.

Above: Mount Olympus, where the "gods" are wont to retire for a little R and R.

Right: Remains of a young man found with a stone in his mouth, indicating the community believed he was a vampire.

CHAPTER 5

BEWARE OF THE GODS AND THEIR BLOODLUST
By Sean Casteel

PUBLISHER'S NOTE: One has to pace the floor and search far and wide to find someone who has an adequate knowledge of the alien blood lust situation and who is able to articulate the possible purposes of such a driving thirst along with its deep-rooted heritage in the dark side of the occult. I don't believe you will find anyone – outside of the researcher who is the subject of this chapter – who could qualify for such a position. It is without a doubt a macabre topic that is both intriguing but at the same time frightening. It's like Halloween on steroids.

****

Salvador Freixedo is a former Catholic priest and a former member of the Jesuit Order who has worked as a UFOlogist and paranormal researcher beginning in the 1970s and 80s. Perhaps his best known work is the book "Beware of the Gods," translated from the original Spanish by our very own Scott Corrales.

THE GODS AND THEIR UNENDING NEED FOR BLOOD

In "Beware of the Gods," Freixedo declares that, "What the gods have always demanded in antiquity and continue to demand today is nothing other than BLOOD, the blood of both humans and animals. Why? I do not know for sure. Do they extract some product out of blood that is of some use to them? I don't know that either. The only thing which I know with exactness, and that is well known to all of us who are dedicated to the investigation of UFOs and the paranormal, is that blood and certain entrails are the common denominator between the gods of antiquity – including the Biblical god – and the UFOs of modern times."

The former priest paints a portrait of Moses as likely being disappointed that Yahweh, who claimed to be the "one and only" God, demanded of Moses the same repugnant animal sacrifices as the "false" gods of the Egyptians and the Mesopotamians.

ALIEN BLOOD LUST

"What does the death of a lamb and the dissection of its guts in a certain way," Freixedo asks, "or the spilling of its blood in one place or another, have to do with demonstrating the love of God and obedience to his commandments? What does the slaying of a cow have to do with sincere repentance and the acknowledgement of one's shortcomings?"

Freixedo quotes German author Wilhelm Ziehr thusly: "In this way was the offering of victims explained: the gods do not appreciate gratitude by way of prayer or in the moral change of life, or in the acceptance of certain commandments, but only by sacrifice; and the greatest sacrifice that can be offered is human blood."

Returning to Freixedo's negative assessment of the Biblical God, he continues by saying, "To Yahweh, the blood and entrails were a fixation and an obsession. But the bad thing is that Baal, Moloch, Dagon, etc., demanded the very same from the Mesopotamian peoples, and Jupiter-Zeus asked the very same sacrifices from Romans and Greeks; and, if we jump to the Americas, we discover that Huitzilopochtili asked the same of the Aztecs, and with the aggravating condition that the blood had to be human on certain occasions. The majority of the African tribes that have not accepted Islam or Christianity continue offering their gods blood sacrifices to this very day."

THE MODERN DAY GUISE OF SPACEMEN

Freixedo links the UFO phenomenon to the "gods" he refers to above, writing that, "Those who appear to us today under the guise of spacemen are the very same who appeared as gods to our forebears – sometimes in flying machines, as many ancient chronicles tell us – demanding adoration and sacrifice."

That the UFO occupants continue in their desire for blood is made manifest by the countless cases of cattle, sheep and goats who have been mutilated and drained of blood. Freixedo has traveled on many occasions to see firsthand the carcasses cut with a surgical precision that leaves no blood behind.

"This butchery," he writes, "which always takes place at night, has occurred practically everywhere in the world and the authorities of some countries, having been notified by ranchers and damaged parties, have intervened to find the source of these slayings, without having ever found a satisfactory explanation. Readers new to this strange facet of UFO activity, which likens them to the legendary Dracula, will be inclined to dismiss it as another legend. Putting Dracula aside – and much could be said about him – we are left with events whose investigation has no need of oral traditions or old books. All that one has to do is take the trouble to read certain articles that modern news agencies publish in newspapers now and then."

There is no doubt, according to Freixedo, that the UFOnauts, much like the gods of antiquity, have a strange predilection for animal entrails and cannot disguise their interest in the blood of both animals and humans.

"John Keel mentions a case," Freixedo writes, "in which a blood mobile in

ALIEN BLOOD LUST

Ohio was repeatedly assaulted by a UFO which was trying to lift it into the air by means of large, pincer-like appendages. Amid the hysterical cries of a terrified nurse, the driver evaded it as best he could until the presence of other vehicles along the road caused the UFO to cease and desist."

In ages past, according to Freixedo, it would seem that both Yahweh and the rest of Elohim managed to convince those primitive tribes to offer them animal sacrifices. In our own time, faced with the impossibility of telling civilized societies to continue to offer them sacrifices – out of which they probably obtained some kind of benefit – it would appear they are handling the sacrifices themselves. They find their animal victims on farms and ranches and take from them blood and certain entrails out of which they extract some vital substance, some pleasant drug, and some energy which they need to maintain their physical form.

AND HUMAN BLOOD AS WELL

"If the mutilations and bleedings of animals are interesting, those of human beings are all the more so," Freixedo writes.

He recounts the story of his first encounter with the taking of human blood. In 1977, he was in the city of San Luis Potosi, some three hundred kilometers north of Mexico City. The local media reported that a newborn child had been found lifeless and entirely devoid of blood. When Freixedo investigated the bizarre circumstances surrounding the case, he quickly realized it was but one case among many similar ones.

"The general circumstances were these: the victims were usually newborns or very young babies; hematomas or blemishes on their skins were apparent, as if blood had been sucked through them. The common denominator in all cases was that they were entirely bloodless. In some cases, it appeared as if the blood had been sucked out through their mouths, as there were no wounds or marks of any kind on their flesh.

"It is also common," Freixedo continues, "for the mothers of these children to be found in a deep, lethargic state of sleep beside their dead offspring, as if they had been drugged by someone while the bleeding of their children was being carried out. There are also adults who claim – or suppose – that they have been attacked in their sleep, because they awaken to find themselves covered in bruises and also feel a great lassitude."

In one case, reported on by a newspaper in San Luis Potosi, a seven-year-old girl found in the morning that her mother was in a deep sleep, hugging her two-day-old baby. When she wouldn't wake up, the girl ran to tell her aunt. They discovered that the baby was dead, and the mother did not become completely conscious until two days later."

ALIEN BLOOD LUST

TALK OF VAMPIRES QUICKLY SPREADS

When these events occurred in various localities in Mexico, naturally the people began to talk about vampires, and panic spread throughout the poor inhabitants of the region. The cases were reported to the authorities, who conducted an investigation but were unable to reach a satisfactory conclusion and preferred that the matter be forgotten.

One could attribute the strange deaths to some kind of natural causes, but there are still circumstances that make the events similar to animal mutilations. Inhabitants of the parts of Mexico that endured the vampire-like attacks were constantly seeing lights moving slowly across the sky at night, around the time when the bloodletting incidents occurred. The lights would stop on nearby hills, or even in the treetops, and execute very strange maneuvers. The humble villagers call these lights "brujas" (witches) and are in fact quite afraid of them. To defend themselves, they have certain magic rituals.

Freixedo writes that he has investigated numerous other cases in which entirely bloodless human corpses have been found in the wilderness, coinciding with the sightings of mysterious lights flying at low altitude over the countryside at night.

WHAT MAKES BLOOD SO SOUGHT AFTER?

Why do the aliens need and seek out blood? Freixedo writes that he does not know, nor do other UFO investigators, nor do contactees and abductees.

But an essential element in the matter is the fact that "blood liberates the type of energy that the gods find pleasing in a very easy and natural way. To obtain such energies from a living body, the gods must kill it violently and then burn it, while the blood flows freely, releasing this energy in an entirely spontaneous manner. Black sorcerers use the vapors of blood to summon astral entities, which find the necessary plasma to materialize in this element. The priests of Baal wounded their bodies to produce tangible apparitions with their blood."

There is also a religious sect in what used to be Persia, near the Russian border, whose members form a circle and dance themselves into a frenzy, wounding one another with knives until they are drenched in blood. Then each of the dancers sees himself accompanied by an astral being. Different forms of sorcery around the world require the spilling of human and animal blood.

The former priest defines the gods as "creatures of the cosmos more highly evolved than ourselves," and believes they are able to receive the energy and waves that blood gives off.

"This energy apparently gives them a great source of pleasure, which is why they seek it today and have sought it always, employing a thousand different ruses to obtain it."

ALIEN BLOOD LUST

SUGGESTED READING

Starting in 1970, after his break with the church, Freixedo devoted himself to studying paranormal phenomenology, considering it to be a window onto other realities or other dimensions of existence. The fruit of his many trips, investigations and reflections are more than thirty books. Most are available only in Spanish, with the exception of BEWARE OF THE GODS, translated by Scott Corrales, from which the quotations in this chapter were taken, and another book called VISIONARIES, MYSTICS AND CONTACTEES, also translated by Corrales.

EXTRATERRESTRIALS AND RELIGIOUS BELIEFS

THE DIABOLIC UNCONSCIOUS

SIXTY CASES OF UFOs

WHY CHRISTIANITY IS AGONIZING

 THE APPEARANCE OF EL ESCORIAL (THE MARIAN APPARITIONS)

THE HEALERS

THE HUMAN FARM ✗ In English

IN THE LIMITS OF THE UNIVERSE

ALIEN BLOOD LUST

CHAPTER 6

DO WE HAVE BLOODTHIRSTY VAMPIRES FROM SPACE?
By Timothy Green Beckley

The material in this chapter has been assembled and edited by editor/publisher Timothy Green Beckley based on the actual words of Alvin Moore as put forth in his "Diary of a CIA Operative," which was published in a very limited edition by Tim's Inner Light/Global Communications. This section has been greatly updated for purposes of this book.

WHO WAS COMMANDER ALVIN E. MOORE?

Of all investigators of UFOs, the late Commander Moore has one of the most impressive backgrounds. His skill in engineering and other sciences, his expertise in history, law and intelligence work, uniquely qualified him to evaluate the mass of data about the alien presence, which he defined as Sky-men, or extraterrestrials. Educated at the U.S. Navy Academy, plus the American University, George Washington School of Law and Louisiana State University, Moore held both B.S. and M.A. degrees. As part of his extensive contribution to his country, Moore specialized in aeronautical engineering and was the patent engineer and attorney for the Werner von Braun team of space scientists. He also served as a U.S. Patent Office Examiner specializing in aeronautics and propulsion; an assistant nautical scientist with the Navy Oceanographic Office; a CIA intelligence officer and an American Vice Consul. He was granted more than 50 U.S. patents on his own inventions, mostly on aircraft, marine craft and automobiles. He also authored numerous technical and historical articles and books.

BLOOD OF THE HOSTS

Probably the biggest influence on Alvin E. Moore's thinking in relation to the UFO phenomena and its connection to the dripping of blood from a cloudless sky came about because one day the Commander picked up a copy of either Charles

39

ALIEN BLOOD LUST

Fort's "Lo" or "The Book of the Damned," we have no way of knowing which, and almost immediately he found his philosophy on life and the universe altered forever.

For more than three decades, Albany-born Charles Fort visited libraries in New York City and London, reviewing scientific journals, newspapers, and magazines and taking notes on slips of paper and file cards on unexplained phenomena, which to this day can still be found in Manhattan's Public Library. Mainly written in a "cramped shorthand" style, they cover everything science finds impossible to explain, from people who seemingly vanished into thin air to the mystery teleportation of objects (he coined the term teleportation!), but above all else he had a fixation on objects that fell from the sky, often of the bloody variety. In fact, he collected widespread reports of blood rain, which go back centuries, as well as fish, frogs and fresh meat that smacked many an unsuspecting individual on the head as they went along doing their daily routines not expecting to be pummeled by – let's say for the hell of it — space aliens taking a lunch break.

While having been deceased since May 3, 1932, Fort's legacy includes a slick monthly magazine, "Fortean Times," a number of national and regional organizations, such as the one founded here in NYC by John Keel and which I served on the board of directors of, as well as numerous reprints .of Fort's four books – The Book of the Damned (1919), New Lands (1923), Lo! (1931) and Wild Talents (1932).

Historically, blood rain is not that rare, though the source may well be, be it animal or human.

Though not easily verifiable, as far back as the 12th Century King Arthur admirer Geoffrey of Monmouth penned the following:

"In the same time here came a strange token, such as before never came, nor never hitherto since. From heaven here came a marvelous flood; three days it rained blood, three days and three nights. That was exceeding great harm! When the rain was gone, here came another token anon. Here came black flies, and flew in men's eyes; in their mouth; in their nose; their lives went all to destruction; such multitude of flies here was that they ate the corn and the grass. Woe was all the folk that dwelt in the land! Thereafter came such a mortality that few here remained alive. Afterward here came an evil hap, that king Riwald died."

An academic with many degrees, Dr. Jacques Vallee notes that unexplained phenomena such as the type we are discussing has had a deep impact on many cultures.

"Celestial phenomena seem to have been so commonplace in the Japanese skies during the Middle Ages that they influenced human events in a direct way. Panics, riots and disruptive social movements were often linked to celestial apparitions. The Japanese peasants had the disagreeable tendency to interpret the 'signs from heaven' as strong indications that their revolts and demands against the feudal system or against foreign invaders were just, and as assurance that their rebellions would be crowned with success."

Commander Alvin E. Moore believed that without a doubt the sky-men as he identified the Ultra-terrestrials, were either stationed on invisible islands in the sky or perhaps in underground locations. He thought it a grim conclusion, but one based on facts! He cites several references made by Charles Fort to support his contention.

"For example, on 15 May, 1890, stuff that looked like fresh red blood fell from the sky on Messiquadi, Italy. Public health scientists examined it in a Roman laboratory and determined that it was in fact blood. And Fort cites a reported fall of blood in 1860 in Morocco and then stated: 'I have about a dozen other records of showers of red fluids that were not rains colored by dusts. Upon several of these occasions the substance was identified as blood.' And on 1 August, 1869, in Los Neton Township, California, a shower of flesh and blood, witnessed by clergymen and many others fell for three minutes – enough of it to cover two acres! The flesh was in strips and particles – some as long as six inches. The sky was clear, and there was no wind. Two months before, there had been a similar fall in Santa Clara County, California."

There are many other such grisly sky falls about which Fort and others entertained numerous possible causes.

One source says that, "The approach of some to red rain places this phenomenon in the context of belief in the Little People. Lewis Spence, in 'The Fairy Tradition in Britain' (Rider, London, 1948, pp. 60-1) talks about the Sluagh, or hosts of Little People that engage in midair battles. The sounds of their fighting, including their shouts and the noise of clashing armor, could be heard by witnesses on the ground below. . .

Spence cites A. A. Macgregor ('The Peat-Fire Flame,' p. 88) concerning the belief of the people of the northern Outer Hebrides off Scotland that "after one of these conflicts the rocks and boulders are stained as with blood, and that the red crotal used for dying cloth, and taken from lichened rocks after a spell of hard frost, is called 'the blood of the hosts.'"

In 1850, a strange package arrived at the office of The North Carolinian. It contained a letter and what appeared to be the rotting organ of an animal. "The piece which was left with us," the editors wrote in March, "has been examined with two of the best microscopes in the place," and certainly contained blood. "It has the smell," their article continued, "both in its dry state and when macerated in water, of putrid flesh; and there can be scarcely a doubt that it is such."

Thomas Clarkson, who lived on a farm about thirteen miles southwest of Clinton, wrote the accompanying letter. "On the 15th of Feb'y, 1850," he wrote, "there fell

ALIEN BLOOD LUST

within 100 yards of the residence of Thos. M. Clarkson in Sampson county, a shower of Flesh and Blood, about 50 feet wide, and as far as it was traced, about 250 or 300 yards in length."

"The pieces appeared to be flesh, liver, lights, brains and blood," the newspaper wrote. "Some of the blood ran on the leaves, apparently very fresh. Three of his (T.M.C's) children were in it, and ran to their mother, exclaiming 'Mother there is meat falling!'"

A neighbor's child was nearby and came running, claiming to smell blood. A red cloud hung over the scene.

In April 1861, Clarkson, then 49, enlisted as a musician in Company A of the 30th North Carolina Infantry Regiment. His son, Thomas N., also served, dying of pneumonia in 1862. No doubt he was one of the terrified children who ran for their mother on that awful day twelve years before.

In a strange twist, rotting meat "the size of a pigeon's egg to that of an orange" fell on Fort Benicia near San Francisco in 1851. A piece struck brevet major Robert Allen, who would go on to command all quartermaster operations west of the Mississippi River for the Union Army during the Civil War. It's strange to think that meat raining from the sky could be the commonality between men who would stand on either side of a divided nation.

The Clarkson family were not the only witnesses to this strange phenomenon in North Carolina. It was reported to have rained flesh on a farm near Gastonia in 1876, and a shower of blood in Chatham County in 1884 was investigated by none other than F. P. Venable, a young chemist who went on to become president of the University of North Carolina.

These are only a few of the two dozen reported such cases occurring in 19th-century America. Blood and meat were claimed to rain down on slave and soldier, adult and child. Even if all the events were hoaxes, it remains one of the strangest and most obscure artifacts of our cultural psyche.

Sources:

A shower of Flesh and Blood in Sampson County (NC) by Lew Powell

The News and Observer (Raleigh), Thursday, April 17, 1884

Georgia Weekly Telegraph and Georgia Journal & Messenger (Macon, Georgia), Tuesday, November 14, 1876

Missouri Courier (Hannibal, Missouri), Thursday, September 18, 1851

North Carolinian, March 9, 1850

ALIEN BLOOD LUST

A SKY FALL AND A PUTRID SMELL

Some of the reports are just plain disquieting

Here is one as a prime example that appeared in an academic publication and not in some local broadsheet.

In the American Journal of Science, 1-2-335, is Prof. Graves' account, communicated by Professor Dewey. That upon the evening of August 13, 1819, a light was seen in Amherst – a falling object – and the sound as if of an explosion. "In the home of Prof. Dewey, this light was reflected upon a wall of a room in which were several members of Prof. Dewey's family. The next morning, in Prof. Dewey's front yard, in what is said to have been the only position from which the light that had been seen in the room, the night before, could have been reflected, was found a substance 'unlike anything before observed by anyone who saw it.' It was a bowl-shaped object, about 8 inches in diameter, and one inch thick. Bright buff-colored, and having upon it a 'fine nap.' Upon removing this covering, a buff-colored, pulpy substance of the consistency of soft-soap was found – 'of an offensive, suffocating smell.'

"A few minutes of exposure to the air changed the buff color to 'a livid color resembling venous blood.' It absorbed moisture quickly from the air and liquefied. For some of the chemical reactions, see the Journal."

Some researchers profess that the fall of flesh, meat and blood often repeatedly occurs in the same approximate spot, as if our Ultra-terrestrial "friends" have set up a dining room table above our heads in the invisible ether.

Naturalist Philip Henry Gosse also accepted that real red rain sometimes falls, although not necessary blood-red rain. He cites the case published in the London Times on January 24, 1861, by Mr. Giovanni Campani, a professor of chemistry at the University of Siena. Mr. Campani describes a red rain that fell on December 28, 1860, at 7:00 a.m. In the northwestern part of the city, the locals watched as there was a great two-hour long shower of reddish rain. At 11:00 a.m. there was a second shower of the red rain and a third at 2:00 p.m. On December 31st and January 1st the phenomenon was again recorded. Gosse comments that the strangeness of the event was added to by the fact that every shower of red rain fell only in the northeastern quarter of town. The area in which the red rain fell could be determined fairly accurately, so much so that it was known that the red colored rain stopped at approximately 200 meters from the meteorological observatory, which collected only colorless rain at the same time that the red rain fell so nearby.

KENTUCKY MEAT FALL

As the tale is usually told, it was a clear and sunny afternoon when meat rained down in a thick shower onto a field in Kentucky, sticking to trees and fences and only covering a 100-yard by 50-yard patch of land. When scientists were forced to

ALIEN BLOOD LUST

admit it was, in fact, meat, they came up with a ludicrous theory about vulture vomit to explain it away... which sums up Charles Fort's summary of the "Kentucky Meat Shower" as presented in his infamous 1919 volume, The Book of the Damned. Later authors included more details, largely taken from just two contemporary articles in the New York Times... the event had been witnessed by a woman, and two men had eaten some of the meat and identified it as mutton, which implied the meat was relatively fresh.

I start with Fort's summary and the two New York Times articles for a simple reason: most modern versions of this event start with these as well. But Charles Fort always had a simple way of making a strange story even more mystifying... he left out unwanted details. Knowing this, I dug for original sources on the matter; and now I'd like to re-tell the tale of the Kentucky Meat Shower, which most definitely did occur, except with all the details on display.

Friday, March 3, 1876

It was a clear and sunny day. Mrs. Allen Crouch was making soap and her 11-year-old grandson Allen was playing, both in the yard of her house near the Olympian Springs in the state of Kentucky, USA, when strange flakes started to shower down around them. Allen commented that it was snowing, and so it seemed... until a large chunk of what was unmistakably meat slapped into the ground behind Mrs. Crouch. She and her grandson ran indoors as the strange shower continued.

The odd downpour covered an area about one-hundred yards long by fifty yards wide near the house (nothing landed on the house) with flakes and chunks of tissue generally the size of snowflakes. It happened sometime between 11am and noon, and the whole shower only lasted for about a minute or two. "The largest piece that I saw was as long as my hand, and about a half an inch wide," Mrs. Crouch offered in a later interview.

While Mrs. Crouch and Allen were the only witnesses to the actual fall of the material, two other people were in the house at the time... Miss Sallie Crouch, an ailing daughter who did not leave her room, and Miss Sadie Robertson, a schoolmistress who was boarding with the Crouches. Robertson had rushed outside as soon as Mrs. Crouch had told her about the fall, but it had already stopped by the time she got out. She saw the meat in strips and chunks hanging from briars and sticking to the fence, as well as scattered about the ground.

The meat lay untouched by the people in the house until later that afternoon, when Mr. Crouch and his son arrived back from their trip; but in the meantime the hogs, chickens, cat, and dog at the farm had "been eating of it freely, and seemed to like it well." When asked if any of these animals had shown signs of "any peculiar effect on them," Mrs. Crouch said that the dog had since gotten sick... but she wasn't sure if the meat was necessarily involved with that.

Mr. Crouch said that on the chips and on the fence where chunks had fallen there appeared to be stains by something resembling blood, but Mrs. Crouch had not observed any blood falling. The matter was sparsely scattered, with some patches in the affected area having no meat at all, so it could not be described as covering the ground. Nonetheless, samples were gathered and preserved in alcohol and glycerin, and later dispersed to various authorities and scientists. By the time a reporter from the New York Herald arrived to interview people around ten days after the fall, about a half-bushel worth of chunks (about 4 gallons) remained in the town of Mount Sterling near the Olympian Springs; an unknown amount more had been sent off and left at the farm.

Harrison Gill, owner of the Olympian Springs, heard of the fall and visited the Crouch farm on Sunday afternoon, March 5. At the time of his visit, Gill also saw and examined the chunks on the fence. The bits of matter appeared to be a variety of tissues. Gill carried samples back to the Olympian Springs to show people there, among whom was L.C. Frisbe, a local butcher, who took some of the samples and passed them on... but he also tasted one of the samples while at the springs. Frisbe had intended to just eat the chunk, but after chewing it a little he spit it out; despite having eaten many types of meat, he could think of nothing that resembled the flavor or scent of the odd piece. Visually, Frisbe said it resembled mutton. There was no blood, but a "milky, watery fluid oozed out of it" while he was handling the meat. It was tender and easily torn apart, which revealed stringy fiber running through the matter.

Another man named Joe Jordan, who also passed samples on to authorities, had also attempted to eat a small piece of the meat; he spat it out very quickly after biting off a bit, before he could even taste it. In his defense, however, it should be noted that the meat was just over a week old by then and smelled "like a dead body," so it probably was not very edible at that point (assuming it had been edible before). Jordan stated that brown mucous came from the pieces when he squeezed them; some resembled dried beef, and he described other bits as elastic and thin with a "fine, wool-like fiber running through it in all directions."

Every person the New York Herald reporter interviewed that personally knew Mrs. Crouch – and that was most of the people he interviewed – stated that Mrs. Crouch was as trustworthy as a person could be, and they believed her account of the strange fall. Mrs. Crouch herself remained mystified by the whole matter.

Also among the accounts of the incident reported by the New York Herald was that of Benjamin Franklin Elington, who claimed to identify the meat as positively bear flesh... but this claim was made in a bar after drinks, and Elington also stated that he essentially fought bears to the death on a regular basis (and that this was easy for him). Elington's claims were likely only included in the article because his rough storytelling made good copy for the newspaper. The same can be said of the reporter's attempt to dare a man named Jimmy Welsh into eating a piece of

ALIEN BLOOD LUST

the strange meat while he was "interviewing" people in the bar, which ended in Welsh finding a variety of excuses why he could not go through with the dare.

SCIENTIFIC GUESSWORK

Most of the samples were sent to various authorities rather than scientists; but of the samples that went to scientists, the first to express a theory was Prof. J. Lawrence Smith. In a March 12 New York Times article, Smith claimed the sample he looked at had to have been "the dried spawn of bahcachian reptiles, doubtless that of the frog [Garth Note: the author of the article misspelled the word 'batrachian', the Latin term for frogs and toads]." Smith further claimed the spawn had been picked up by wind from ponds and swamplands and thus transported to where they were dropped. He further claimed to have several examples of this odd event having happened before, yet only had one he could state the date for, a fall recorded by 'Muschonbroeck' – a reference to Pieter van Musschenbroek, a Dutch scientist – in Ireland in 1675.

When the New York Herald reporter arrived in Mount Sterling, he asked the locals what they felt about Smith's theory. Every person who had actually seen and/or handled the meat disagreed with Smith's assessment, and felt a second opinion was needed. The New York Herald reported that, apparently, the sample sent to Smith had the appearance of being just animal fat. It was also noted that, since some of the matter had landed in the Crouches' well, the Crouches would probably have seen frogs in their well by that time. The New York Herald article also passed on two others theories that had been generally proposed by men the reporter had talked to in Mount Sterling. The first thought it might have been a balloonist's lunch that got dropped – which must have been a very hungry person – or that a flock of vultures flying high above the farm had vomited up the contents of their stomachs all at the same time.

The next attempt at a scientific explanation came from a Mr. L. Brandeis, who shared his ideas in a May issue of Sanitarium magazine. He proclaimed the substance to be "Nostoc," a cyanobacteria that forms as large gelatinous clumps in moist environments and at the bottom of lakes and ponds. Brandeis explained that the spore of this odd growth was carried by the wind and, once deposited on the ground, would quickly grow to cover large areas; this fact had led to a belief in the past that the matter just fell out of the sky, since people were of the impression it appeared very suddenly over a short time. He further declared the Nostoc that was found in Kentucky was of the type N. carneum, which was well known for looking like meat and tasting like frog or chicken... which sounds like a great theory, if you ignore that Mrs. Crouch saw the stuff falling.

By June and July, some better analysis was coming from several people and labs, and it was clear that the samples that had been sent actually contained various differing types of tissue. The consensus agreed there were examples of animal muscle, connective tissue, and fat, likely from sheep, and the sample of "Nostoc" was specifically re-labeled as lung tissue. Given the fact that at least five separate investigators confirmed this – Dr. L.D. Kastenbine, Mr. A.T. Parker, a Mr. Walmsey of Philadelphia, Prof. J.W.S. Arnold, and Prof. A. Mead Edwards – the only real problem left was the key one: why did bits of sheep rain down over a hundred by fifty yard patch of Kentucky land?

The experts had no good explanation. One of them, Kastenbine, once again brought up the New York Herald's mention of a flock of vultures at an extremely high altitude – high enough they wouldn't be seen by Mrs. Crouch looking up – all suddenly disgorging the contents of their stomachs for unstated reasons. The meat would then, theoretically, spread out before hitting the ground, explaining why it would be small bits of sheep over a large area... and this is what has been reported as the cause ever since by people who want a stative explanation, though it sounds like imaginative guesswork.

As far as the theory of vulture vomit goes, it depends on the idea that a group of vultures would all vent their stomachs at the same time. While vultures can vomit food up purposely, this is generally as a defensive maneuver... to reduce the animal's weight for a quick take off when under attack, or to project (up to ten feet!) as an acidic and foul-smelling attack that drives predators away by either the sheer odor or causing stinging in the eyes if unlucky enough to get hit in the face. But if vultures vomit defensively, what high up in the air would scare a group of them into vomiting all at the same time?

There are many other episodes we could select, the list may be endless. It takes time to research the matter thoroughly. It would take a person like Charles Fort to do the immense work necessary, or someone like the late Mark Chorvinsky, who did a great job of editing "Strange Magazine," which we used as a reference, before his unfortunate demise at a very early age.

THE STRANGE CONCLUSIONS REACHED BY COMMANDER MOORE

Aliens known as "skymen" have been coming to Earth and exploiting it for many years. Some of them have homes in caverns on the moon, Mars and its satellite Phoebus, Jupiter, as well as the Asteroids. Many more originate much nearer to the Earth's surface, from "Sky Islands," or even from within the hollows of our planet, and possibly underwater hangers! Sky chemicals and electrostatic gravity-like force of the alien sky islands and skycraft have caused legions of accidents. Skymen have kidnapped a multitude of people and have long extracted blood from animals and men, as well as committed mysterious murders!

During his life, Commander Alvin E, Moore (of Naval Intelligence and with close ties to the CIA) spent nearly a quarter of a century researching the possible association of mysterious events attributed to UFOs and extraterrestrials. His conclusions are utterly shocking and certainly deserve further investigation despite attempts by so-called "serious UFOlogists" to sweep this aspect of the phenomenon under the cosmic rug.

There was a report on a New Orleans television news program the evening of 10 September 1977 of a woman who had been found dead with "punctures in her abdomen." And the next morning's New Orleans Times-Picayune gave a few more details of her strange death. She was an "unidentified black woman in her early twenties found dead in bushes of a hedge. Her blouse had been pulled up over her face and her jeans had been unzipped. Police stated she had apparently died of a penetrating wound to the vagina, although they were unsure what kind of instrument had been used to inflict the fatal wounds."

I note that the plural word "wounds" was used – tying in with the plurality of "punctures" in the abdomen referred to in the television report; and I wonder if one of those wounds was made by an instrument that penetrated the womb of the young woman. As apparently was done in the case of Betty Hill, and might have been done in the case of Pat Price. Also blood might have been extracted via one or more of the "punctures." The police would easily recognize a slit made by a knife or dagger. Was the puncturing instrument round or triangular?

On the night of May 10th, 1951, police found a young woman screaming on a street corner in Manila, crying out that she was being bitten by something, and seemed to be fighting something in the air. She was eighteen years old and her name was Clarita Villanueva. The police arrested her. She said she was being bitten by something that looked like a man with big bulging eyes, wearing a black cape, and able to float in the air.

After she was locked up in a cell, she began screaming that the thing was coming at her through the prison bars. A policeman unlocked the door and brought her out, still screaming. And then he was astounded to see punctures that looked like teeth marks being formed on her arms and shoulders. The next morning in the presence of policemen and Medical Examiner Dr. Mariana Lara, the screaming girl was again attacked by a being or object, invisible to the men. For five minutes the punctures appeared on her arms, back of the shoulders, and back of the neck. Then she fainted.

Reporters and the Mayor of Manila Lascon came. The Mayor and Medical Examiner went with her in a car to the prison hospital. On the way she began screaming again, and the horrified men saw what looked like teeth punctures appear on both sides of her throat, on a finger; and while the Mayor held one of her hands it was deeply punctured by an invisible wound-making instrument.

They saw that her arms and hands were badly swollen from previous punctures. Obviously, this was a case of blood extraction by a floating being or object – probably object – that could be made invisible.

Concerning invisibility of alien sky objects: In 1953, Associate Editor John

ALIEN BLOOD LUST

DuBarry of True Magazine showed me a photograph that a woman had taken of her rose bush. There was a little object in the air near the plant that looked like a swastika. The woman who sent the picture to True had not seen the swastika, but the camera had pictured it. If it had whirled fast enough – with the speed of a bullet in flight – she would not have seen it. This ancient-earth symbol, the swastika, was one of the characters in the strange writing on the footprint casts of the skyman that George Adamski reportedly saw in 1952.

A number of persons who have been captured by alien skymen have reported their extraction of "blood samples." This taking of blood probably involves more than mere samples.

Some earlier examples of mysterious, blood extraction wounds: In June and July 1899, in the eastern United States, an outbreak in many cities of a large number of so-called "bug bites" – for instance, eleven persons in New York were said to be "bitten" on 8 July; and children in Iowa, New Jersey and New York were "bitten" and one died; and on 10 July on a woman in Chicago: "the marks of two small incisors could be seen." About 16 September 1910, in Portugal, a child was found dead. Her body was bloodless. The last man seen with her was arrested. Somehow, the police got a confession from him; he said he was a vampire. On 7 May 1909, on Broadway, New York City, at least six persons reported being jabbed by something like a hat pin. In March 1901, at Cambridge, England, Lavinia Farrar was mysteriously killed. Her body, fully dressed, was found on her kitchen floor. There were no signs of robbery. Near her, on the floor, there were some "drops" of blood and a blood-stained knife. Policemen could see no connection between the knife and her death. But in the coroner's examination, her clothing was removed, and on the innermost garment the examiners saw a very slight blood stain. They removed this and found that the woman had been "stabbed to the heart." But the wound and her body were almost entirely bloodless! Her dress was not punctured and had no fastenings opposite the wound. Obviously, it had been replaced after the stabbing. What had happened to the blood? In my opinion, a skyman of the evil type had killed her and taken her blood.

On 19 July 1975, Charles D. Savelie, 21 years old, was in his truck on North Beach Road, Bay St. Louis, Mississippi, when, according to his later report, something bit his neck, puncturing an artery. "Savelie jammed a finger into the wound to halt the bleeding," and drove to a hospital. After an operation his condition, in spite of blood loss, was satisfactory. Deputy Sheriff Lethon Garriga said apparently he was stabbed. Probably he was – by an invisible blood-extraction device.

Our maid, Mrs. Leona Toomey, cleaned a room where a man of Waveland, Mississippi, allegedly shot himself and died. She said she was puzzled by the very small amount of blood on the carpet where he fell.

An extract from an entry in my UFO journal, dated 29 February 1972, at

ALIEN BLOOD LUST

Waveland, Mississippi: On Saturday night, February 19th, as we were returning at about 11 PM from playing Canasta, Laura received one of the strange, slightly bloody, small cuts she gets from time to time. She was unaware of the cut until we got home. On the 21st Laura again was mysteriously cut – in a small cut, with blood, on one of her fingers. (In an entry I also referred to several of her mysterious occurrences on the 18th to 21st.)

On the morning of 31 December 1930, 19-year-old Beulah Limerick of Washington, D. C. was found dead on a mattress in her bedroom. No blood was seen on or near the body; and a hospital intern reported her to have died of natural causes. But the undertaker who was preparing the body for burial found that a lock of her hair had been compactly placed in a hole in the back of her head. A news item of about fourteen years later concerning this strange murder stated that the hole marked the path of a small-caliber bullet into her brain.

But I wonder if a bullet actually was found. For: a small hole was discovered in one corner of her mattress, and a small blood stain was by it; and the body obviously was bloodless. For: when it was found, no blood was seen; the intern saw none; and apparently no hair was matted with blood near the hole in her head. The instrument that neatly punctured her skull probably went through the corner of her mattress and into the back of her head, as she slept – probably paralyzed by an alien skyman's power. The police made a long, intensive investigation; but no one guilty of the murder ever was found. I refer back to my account of the three mysterious 1953 wounds of the dog "Molly", which looked like .22-caliber bullet holes, but no bullet was found. According to my memory, I saw only a little blood around those holes.

On 24 March 1955, at Green Meadows, Maryland, the rather happy family of Mr. and Mrs. Cecil Harp ate supper. The children, 15-year-old Ken William, his 14-year-old sister Lois and their younger brothers Charles and Robert, were in high spirits. After supper, Charles went out to buy ice cream and Ken went upstairs to his room. About twenty minutes later, Lois went to Ken's room to call him to come down for ice cream. She found him on the bed unconscious. An emergency team arrived and tried to revive him, but he was pronounced dead. One of the volunteers noticed a small hole in his sweater just over his chest, with a corresponding hole in his chest. No bullet was found then or later.

Ken's father had given him a .22 caliber rifle with instructions not to use it until he wanted to go hunting. It was stored securely in a nearby closet. No one downstairs had heard a shot.

The sweater and Ken's body had no blood on them or it would have been noticed by the emergency volunteers. What happened to the blood? Was it sucked out by a skyman's blood-extraction apparatus, including a small, round, body-puncturing instrument?

ALIEN BLOOD LUST

On 26 September 1954, a mystery arose at Alexandria, Virginia, as to who or what killed 25-year-old Mrs. Grace Smith, a beautiful blonde dancing instructor. She was found dead in her locked, combined home and studio; and her 2-1/2 year-old son, Sergoff, was also in the locked upstairs bedroom, where his mother's body lay on the floor. Obviously, the woman had been killed, for on her bed there was a blood-stained sheet, and there were other blood stains in the room. But how had she been killed? There was no visible mark of violence on her body. Was this a mysterious blood-extraction death?

About 9 P.M., 6 August 1954, at Bonner Springs, Kansas, 44-year-old Mrs. Eva A. Wagenknecht, lay down on her bed, removing her clothes. In another room her husband Henry, son Henry, Jr. and two others were playing cards. The card game ended about 10:30 P. M., and Henry, Sr., turned on the television for a while. But Henry, Jr. said that soon after he went to bed he heard a noise like the house was vibrating. Thinking a storm had come up, he went to the window to check outside, but seeing no sign of stormy weather, returned to bed.

According to Henry, Sr.'s account (and he said he was willing to take a lie detector test in support of it): He quit watching television about midnight and went into the kitchen to see about some plum preserves cooking there. Uncertain that they were done, he went toward the bedroom, calling to Eva to come and taste them. Unanswered, he went into the bedroom; and he found his wife gone. Horrified, he saw blood spots where she had lain.

Policemen were summoned, and a little after midnight Marshals Alva Kerby and Elbert Woolf found Eva Wagenknecht's body in weeds, nude, face upward. An 18-inch, two-by-four piece of lumber was found, but it was about fifty feet from the corpse. In a nearby culvert Eva's blouse had been stuffed. Her slacks were found in the house. The blood spots apparently were few – on the bed, an adjacent curtain, and below the window. A window screen had been moved. Why was the dead or nearly dead body taken outside? Did murderous skymen quickly remove it, before extracting blood, in view of what happened in the later-described mysterious murder of Marilyn Shepard near Cleveland, during the month before this August, 1954?

The following circumstances indicate that this murder of Eva Wagenknecht might have been by an alien skyman or skyman-controlled device: (1) the vibratory noise and apparent brief motion of the house; (2) the fact that there was no sign at all of struggle in the bedroom; (3) the fact that the husband in a neighboring room heard no noise of the killing and removal of the body, apparently through the window; (4) the stripping of the body, possibly for blood extraction; (5) the fact that Eva, mother of seven children, apparently was not raped, and doubtless had no ruthless enemies; (6) the face-upward position of the body – a position convenient for extraction of blood, probably left unchanged in a hasty getaway.

51

ALIEN BLOOD LUST

In the morning of 8 September 1974, at Kennett, Missouri, the body of Mrs. Lee Ann Garrison was found in her home. She had been beaten, presumably shot, and was dead. On that morning and the night before, her husband was with seven persons on Pickwick Lake in northeastern Mississippi, including Ronald Windsor, prosecuting attorney of Alcorn County, Mississippi. Nevertheless, Missouri authorities tried to extradite Dr. Garrison from Mississippi to be tried for the murder. Dr. Garrison opposed the extradition; and the testimony at his hearing by Melvin Duckworth, Missouri Highway Patrol investigator, not only further established that the physician was not guilty, but indicates that a collector of various types of blood killed Lee Ann Garrison, for: (1) a surgical glove was found near her home with type-O blood on it; (2) type-A blood was in a footprint at the base of the stairs of the ill-fated home; (3) type-B blood was on the murdered woman's leg; and (4) apparently blood on her body was type-AB. She had type-A blood; and the only type-A blood found was in the footprint. Four types of blood at the murder scene! If a skyman had killed her and was taking her blood, the blood-holding device must have been leaking.

I have long been suspicious of some of the reportedly accidental deaths as a result of mishandling firearms. I have numerous reports and clippings concerning several deaths of this type during that hot, dangerous 1954 and early part of 1955. Early October 1954 was particularly hot around Maryland, Washington, D. C. and further westward. The hottest September 30th in Washington since 1861 had occurred, and on October 5th, a writer at the Washington Post stated:

"Since Friday we have had a sense of being constantly in a Turkish bath." And on the 6th, the Post included an Associated Press item that during the first three days of West Virginia's hunting season seven men had been shot to death or had succumbed to fatal illnesses while hunting.

Early in the morning of 1 January, 1955, Michael A. Kendall of Bethesda, Maryland, thought he heard a prowler in or outside of his home. He got out of bed, loaded his .22 rifle and started across the room. Something caused the rifle to discharge and the bullet went through the flesh of his right shoulder. Police stated the rifle did not have a trigger guard. With such a rifle, Mister Kendall must have been very careful. But he was shot. This, of course, might have merely been an accident, but what of the prowler?

On the same New Year's Day in the same town, 17-year-old Douglas Shae Hutton left his family downstairs and went up to his room, which contained his .22 rifle and a number of National Rifle Association trophies he had won in competition. No one in the family heard a shot, but they later found Douglas dead, shot between the eyes.

Twenty days before these bizarre events, on a Sunday night, 12th December, 1954, in her apartment at Arlington Towers, across the river from Washing-

ALIEN BLOOD LUST

ton, D. C., 23-year-old Sallie Wood of the National Security Agency, was wrapping Christmas presents. In the room was a 12 gauge shotgun with the price tag still on it, which she had bought a day or two earlier as a present. Her door was locked and chained and the windows were locked.

On Monday, she and her fiancé, Herbert Gallegly, were to select an engagement ring. Instead, he and apartment officials broke into her room and found her shot to death. She was lying on her side and her shoulder had a gaping wound, apparently from a shotgun blast. The new gun had the butt on the floor leaning against and on the far side of a table.

How could she have been shot by a gun whose barrel was pointed toward the ceiling? An intensive investigation finally resulted in a freakish report supposing that she loaded the gun, placed it on the table, got back down on the floor to wrap more presents, and jarred the table, dislodging the gun which then tumbled off the table and discharged, then flung itself back against the wall on the far side of the table where it was found. This, clearly, was not possible.

The following events cause me to suspect alien skymen influence in Sallie Wood's murder. 1) The neighbors in the apartment across the hall heard no shot (and shotguns make very loud noises when they are discharged). 2) Her apartment was on a high upper floor and thoroughly locked and chained. 3) The new apartment complex was at the riverside. 4) There was a "blackened indentation" on the adjacent door. (Blackened by sky chemicals?)

During an evening of March, 1929, Isidor Fink, owner and operator of the Fifth Avenue Laundry, New York City, was ironing clothes. Numerous robberies had occurred in the neighborhood, so Isidor had bolted his doors and locked the windows. Only the transom was unlocked. Outside the laundry, a woman heard him screaming and other noises, but heard no shots. She called the police.

Isidor Fink was found dead on the floor with wounds that appeared to be bullet holes in his chest and in his left wrist. There were powder burns on the left wrist. Later, New York Police Commissioner Mulrooney said the killing, in a locked room, was an "insoluble mystery."

About 8 November 1954, Peter Pivaroff of Los Angeles began having severe pain in his heart. After about a day of the pain, he went to a hospital, thinking he had a heart attack. X-ray pictures were taken, but he died before he could see them. They showed a darning needle that had been inserted between the fourth and fifth ribs and into his heart. But this wasn't his only puncture. There was another, between his seventh and eighth ribs. The darning needle was identified as one his daughter Diana had borrowed, which had disappeared.

On 4 December 1913, Mrs. Wesley Graff, sitting in a theater box, felt a thing "scratching her hand," and pain there like a wasp sting. She rose to her feet. There was a man near her, the only person, she thought, who could have harmed her, so she accused him, and fainted. Policemen came. On the floor they found a pricking instrument – a darning needle. But the marks they saw on Mrs. Graff apparently were not made by the needle. Was this darning needle put on the floor as a cover-up for blood-extraction? Was the darning needle of Peter Pivaroff's daughter also such a cover-up?

Late in the night of 2 February 1913, the body of Maud Frances Davies was found on tracks of the London Underground Railway. Her head had been cut off by train wheels. At the inquest someone said that she probably committed suicide. But a Dr. Townsend (apparently the coroner) testified that, while living, she had been punctured more than a dozen times by a hat-pin-like instrument, and that in one of the thrusts it had penetrated to the heart. I say: Probably, while rendered immobile, blood had been extracted from Miss Davies. And then, in cover-up, probably a skyman or skymen, carefully placed her body on the rails with her head positioned to be run over by the next train.

In January, 1975, nine men, mostly middle-aged drifters, were killed in the Los Angeles area in similar mysterious murders. The murderer came to be called the "Skid Row Slasher," because, with a surgeon's or skilled butcher's type of precision, and in one powerful cutting-instrument stroke, he slashed the victim's throat all the way to the spinal cord, nearly cutting off the head, in each of the nine murders of that month. Someone theorized that the murderer was a very powerful man who could hold an attacked man while he neatly nearly beheaded him. If the victim was conscious and in possession of his full strength, such a slashing would not be possible. But he could be made immobile, temporarily paralyzed, as so many victims of skymen have been, and his blood extracted, and then his head nearly cut off as a cover-up

SUGGESTED READING

THE COLLECTED WORKS OF CHARLES FORT: Large print edition. Four volumes. Available only from this publisher mrufo8@hotmail.com
STRANGE MAGAZINE X
THE SECRET UFO DIARY OF CIA OPERATIVE COMM. ALVIN E. MOORE
UFO HOSTILITIES – AND THE EVIL ALIEN AGENDA, by Beckley, Casteel and others
PASSPORT TO MAGONIA, by Dr. Jacques Vallee

ALIEN BLOOD LUST

Admiral Moore believed there are unusual planets in orbit above Earth and that they are inhabited by "skymen."

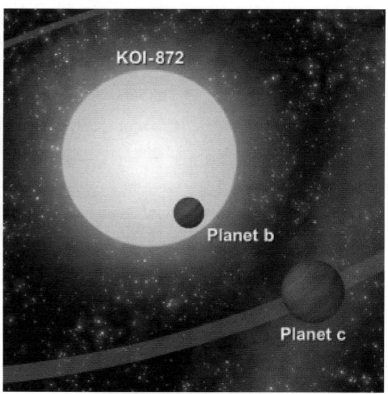

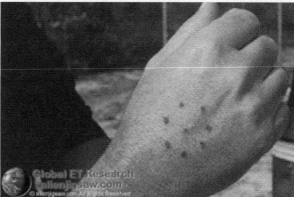

Center left: A quantity of blood fell on Benicia Barracks.

Center right: These odd marks have been reported by several abductees. A center puncture wound surrounded by seven others in a circular pattern.

Bottom left: Rachael Madow usually does not comment on paranormal events, however, she had plenty to say about the showers of meat that fell in Kentucky.

ALIEN BLOOD LUST

Above: Tim Beckley and the "MIB Lady" Claudia Cunningham at the grave of Charles Fort in the rural Albany cemetery where he is interred.

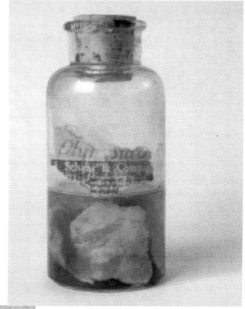

Above: Sample of meat that fell in Kentucky still lays on a museum shelf.

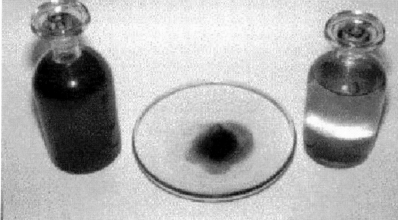

Left: Samples of the "blood rain" that fell in India. Analysis showed that the liquid contained unknown viruses which were presumed to have originated in space.

It seems the "skymen" tossed away fish they might have caught. A great quantity of whole fish fell from the heavens in a single day.

HIS THIRD CLASSIC STUDY OF FORTEAN PHENOMENA

Charles Fort's book, "LO!" turned Commander Moore on to such phenomena as the showers of fish and blood from the sky.

Charles Fort, the father of the supernatural, coined the term "teleportation."

Weird Wires
price = #6.41

ALIEN BLOOD LUST

WAS DRACULA AN ALIEN?
By Nigel Watson

PUBLISHER'S NOTE: At first glance, this chapter's title rings of absurdity — of course Dracula, Vlad the Impaler, was not an alien you might be indignantly saying. But then why is there proof in the form of a painting that hangs in his one-time residence which clearly shows a UFO, a distinctly saucer-like object, hovering in the sky? It's not absolute proof of course, but our UK associate Nigel Watson has put together all the "facts" for us to ponder. Now you really have something to worry about. Drac might still be out there, hiding in the rafters, acting as a go-between for those bloodsucking vampires from space. Food for thought — hopefully WE'RE not the food, dear friends!

****

The depiction of a strange disc-like craft emitting smoke as it hovers over buildings on the wall of the 14th century Church of the Dominican Monastery in Sighisoara, Romania, has continually excited the imagination of UFO fans and investigators.

If one acknowledges the fact that this is thought to be the birthplace of "Vlad the Impaler, whom the blood-sucking Dracula legend is based on, then it is a short leap to the idea that he was brought to our planet by the polluting spacecraft featured in the Church.

Never one short of a theory or sensational "revelation" about alien visitations to our planet, UFO detective Scott C. Waring of the "UFO Sightings Daily" website says,

"This UFO does explain a lot. What if the stories of Dracula drinking blood to stay alive are true? Then his being an alien would make sense. I have heard that there are a few alien species that feed off humans. Every story has a grain of truth...especially if it stands the test of time."

ALIEN BLOOD LUST

The caption under the fresco, written in German, says, "Israel, put your hope in the Lord. Psalm 130.7" and is thought to date from just after 1534, when the Bible was first translated into German.

Another Dracula connection concerns a UFO sighting by Sorin Neacu, a history student at the University of Bucharest, and his girlfriend on 12 August 1978. They decided to spend the night on the mountain close to the ruins of the Poenari stronghold that was rebuilt in 1459 by Vlad the Impaler. Sorin said that as they admired the view:

"At around 23:00, from the lake rose suddenly a giant disc with an approximate diameter of 30-40 meters. We were in front of it at a distance not greater than 500 meters. I could see it perfectly and I followed its movement with my eyes wide with terror. But it did not come towards us. After it vertically rose up and gave the impression that it would head in our direction, the disc tilted sharply backwards and shot skyward at an incredible speed. In five seconds it was only one bright spot in the sky, moving away to the north, towards Transylvania. After another few seconds, it totally disappeared from view beyond the mountain tops. The object was shaped like a basin turned upside down and had an undefined color, in any case a dark one; and in the central dome were several portholes with green lights. I did not see beings on board, but I'm sure they were there. I must mention that throughout the period of observation I did not hear any noise coming from this giant object. Once it was gone, I noticed that the lake's waters were very rough, quite large waves were smashing into the side of the dams, which I think does not happen often in inland waters. I have visited the area several times since then but we have never again seen such occurrences."

This account was collected by journalist Gabriel Tudor, and recorded in "UFOs Over Romania," by Dan D. Farcas (Flying Disk Press, 2016). The same book mentions that Gili Schechter and Hannan Sabbath, from the Israeli Extraterrestrials and UFOs Research Association, examined the Sighisoara painting, noting that, "...in the image is a large building, possibly a church, above which floats, slightly oblique, a large disc-shaped object, divided into about 10 large sections. From the center of the disc, pointing down, is a sort of spike. Above the bright object is a short column on which you see other objects that are hard to identify."

They were unable to find out who painted the fresco but they did find it was very similar in style to medals that were used as gambling chips in the 17th Century. They concluded that in all probability it depicted Ezekiel's vision rather than an alien spaceship piloted by Dracula.

However, Dan Farcas says that:

"As an academic and a UFO researcher, I must admit that the images in these paintings are certainly worth a second look and we should not rule out the possibility that they do depict something that today would be described as a UFO."

ALIEN BLOOD LUST

UFO experts have drawn a comparison with other well-known paintings which seem to depict flying saucers, such as the 1710 painting of the Baptism of Christ by Aert de Gelder. Nicolae Tescula, the manager of the museum, says, "There is a painting in the sacristy of the church with a religious scene that represents a cloud – perhaps Elijah's assumption to Heaven – which looks like a dome, but can lead to a more modern representation that might make us think of a UFO."

Flying saucers, UFOs and other weird objects in the sky have been depicted throughout the history of humanity.

What seem to be UFOs and aliens appear in the cave paintings of ancient man, the religious paintings of the Renaissance period and in the works of chroniclers and storytellers.

Some of the most striking UFO images appear in Renaissance art. As an example, a painting titled "The Crucifixion" depicts two spherical flying craft that plainly have a pilot inside them. It is of 1350 vintage and hangs over the altar in the Visoki Decani Monastery, Yugoslavia.

In the 15th Century, in "The Madonna with Saint Giovannio," the artist Domenico Ghirlandaio depicts a disc-like craft with rays shooting out of it over the left shoulder of Mary. A man with a dog behind Mary are shown looking at this aerial object.

"The Baptism of Christ," painted by Aert De Gelder in 1710, is a stunning vision of a circular craft beaming rays of light that illuminate Jesus and John the Baptist. It can be viewed at the Fitzwilliam Museum, Cambridge.

An explanation for these Biblical paintings is that they are symbolic representations of angels and that the beams of light from them represent the Holy Spirit. These beams of light can also represent the miraculous impregnation of Mary that led to the birth of Jesus. Ironically, people today are literally seeing objects like this in the sky and associate their activities with the concept of ancient astronauts that, it is speculated, we worshipped as Gods in the past.

Certainly, symbolism and artistic license is at work, but whether or not they are based on "real" sightings or belief in UFOs from other realms, they still give us a sense of wonder and have a powerful impact on our psyche.

Scientists became fascinated with the folklore stories concerning blood sucking vampires in the 18th Century and wondered whether such creatures were real. Even though there were witness testimonies supporting their reality, across Europe scientists tried explaining this phenomenon in terms of mass hysteria, the product of bad diets, disease and drug usage. Whatever the possible solution, it did make scientists speculate as to whether the dead really could come back to life or not.

This background of history, art and politics helped fuel Gothic fiction that used the fascination with the macabre, darkness, the supernatural, wild nature, mythology, folklore and the nature of reality to drive their narratives. The first Gothic novel, "The Castle of Otranto," was penned by Horace Walpole in 1764. Mary Shelley's "Frankenstein: Or The Modern Prometheus," in 1818, established much of the trappings and concerns of Gothic fiction with her examination of what it takes to be truly human. Another significant milestone was Bram Stoker's "Dracula," in 1897, that heavily draws on vampire legends and has the aristocratic villain originating from Transylvania.

This Gothic ethos went on to inspire the Hollywood, Universal Studios portrayals of Frankenstein's Monster and Dracula in the 1930s and 1940s, and by the British, Hammer Film studios in the 1950s to 1970s.

Gothic fiction does not just look back at the past, it is also very much concerned with the price of progress. In this manner, Ridley Scott's "Blade Runner" is very much in the Gothic tradition with replicants (bioengineered beings) that are modern-day versions of Shelley's "monstrous" creation, who grapple with understanding whether they are human or not.

The rise of the flying saucer mythology acts as a similarly gothic framework to deal with the worries and problems of our time that are integrated and expressed in a dynamic and dramatic fashion. In this sense they stimulate an unconscious artistic "need to create an external, concrete experience in order to identify or communicate a nebulous, and in many cases almost totally non-understood, emotional or philosophical feeling," as John Rimmer put it in "Facts, Fraud and Fairytales" in MUFOB magazine, New Series No. 9.

Today, the vampire and Dracula have morphed into the abducting greys, who are the latest representation of the alien "other" that follows the gothic tradition. Abductees have been promised immortality, drained of physical energy and have had their blood taken from them by the extraterrestrial greys in their laboratory/ spacecraft. Like the vampire of old, the alien vampires entrance and horrify us.

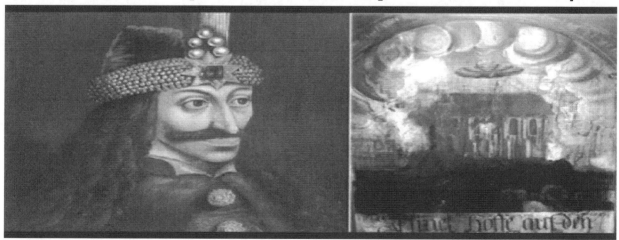

Vlad, the Impaler, from whose legacy the monster "Count Dracula" was created. At right is a painting of church with a huge UFO spewing great clouds of fire and smoke, an image that has piqued the interest of several UFO researchers.

ALIEN BLOOD LUST

Paintings found in an ancient church depicting the crucifixion of Jesus and two manned craft believed to be UFOs in attendance.

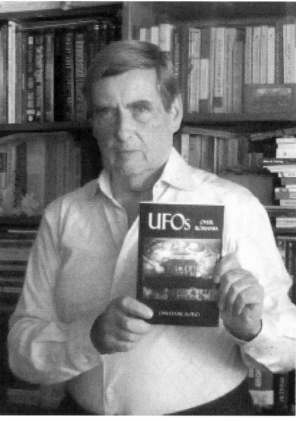

Author Dan Farcas was the first to publicize the fresco of Vlad in his book, "UFOs Over Romania," published by Flying Disk Press

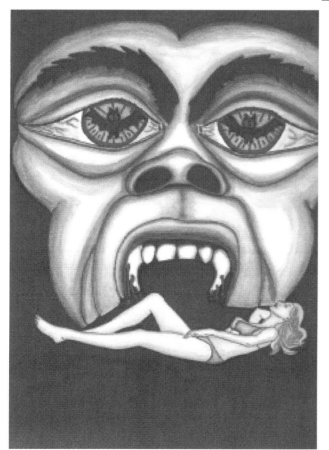

Was Vlad, the Impaler—the real Dracula—driven by his thirst for human blood?
Art by Carol Ann Rodriguez

CHAPTER 8

BLOOD IS THE LIFE FOR THE MONSTERS THAT SEEK IT
By Tim R. Swartz

There are monsters. Ask any child who has lain awake in the dark of night, certain that some unknown horror lurks in the shadows under their bed. Ask anyone who has walked through a dark forest, aware that inhuman eyes are following their every move. Ask anyone who has heard a strange noise where there should only be silence. They will tell you. There are monsters.

Perhaps there is some place deep within our brains that remembers a far off time when we huddled together in the cracks and crevices of rocks, listening for the black things of the night. And they hungered; always hungered.

We like to think that things are different now, that we have tamed the things that used to hunt us in the night. It is comforting to think that our bright lights and big cities offer a refuge from those that would slake their thirst with our blood. However, are things really so different? Are we really as safe as we think we are?

Are there still monsters?

TALES OF MUTILATIONS IN THE DARKNESS

Researchers of the UFO phenomenon have openly speculated over the years that if UFOs do represent extraterrestrial visitors, why do they operate in such secrecy? Alleged UFO contactees say that the aliens are friendly and are here to help mankind. However, evidence that extraterrestrials have a sinister, hidden agenda when dealing with Earth's inhabitants tells a different story. The most obvious example of nefarious UFO activity has to be the mutilation of cattle. The evidence is mostly anecdotal that UFOs are involved with cattle mutilations, but the unusual circumstances surrounding this mystery seem to point to UFOs, or at least UFO-like activity.

Over the years, strange attacks on animals and humans have been recorded and attributed to predators, other humans and even vampires. What makes these

ALIEN BLOOD LUST

incidents similar is the general lack of blood found on the bodies. Primitive man believed that blood was sacred, the source of life in all creatures. When you lost your blood, you lost your life. So it made sense that the life force must be contained in blood. The Old Testament is a good example of ancient beliefs regarding blood. Leviticus 17:14 states, that "the life of every living creature is its blood." The verse goes on to say that it is forbidden for anyone to eat blood because it is the source of all life.

Because of these early beliefs, man has always had a superstitious horror when dealing with unusual attacks that involve the loss of blood. Throughout history, there have been numerous reports of strange attacks and mutilations that seem to go beyond normal animal predators. In 1874 near Cavan, Ireland, for several months something killed as many as thirty sheep a night, biting their throats and draining the blood. In 1905 at Great Badminton, Avon, sheep were again the target for attacks. A police sergeant in Gloucestershire was quoted in the London Daily Mail, "I have seen two of the carcasses myself and can say definitely that it is impossible for it to be the work of a dog. Dogs are not vampires, and do not suck the blood of a sheep, and leave the flesh almost untouched." In a single night in March of 1906, near the town of Guildford, Great Britain, fifty-one sheep were killed when their blood was drained from bite wounds to the throats. Local residents formed posses to hunt down whatever was killing their livestock, but nothing was ever caught, and the killings remain a mystery. Events of this kind have probably occurred regularly throughout history. The cases that have received media attention, are those involving a large number of deaths, but there are probably hundreds of smaller attacks that have gone unnoticed over the years.

These strange livestock attacks are eerily similar to the recent attacks by the so-called Chupacabra, which means "goat sucker." Confining itself chiefly to the southern hemisphere, the Chupacabra has been blamed for numerous attacks on small animals. The animals have had their throats bitten and their blood sucked out by the creature that reportedly stands on two legs, has large black or red eyes and is about four feet tall. Unlike past killings, the Chupacabra has been seen by shocked eyewitnesses whose descriptions seem to describe an animal that superficially resembles the "Grays" of flying saucer lore. As in past cases, attempts to track down the Chupacabra have met with failure. If history is any indication, the Chupacabra will never be caught, and the strange events will remain a mystery. It is as if the mystery mutilators appear out of thin air, do their damage, and then, just as quickly, disappear again.

MUTILATED CATTLE IN SCARY NUMBERS

The mutilation of cattle seems to involve a different set of circumstances than past vampire-like attacks on livestock. While cattle mutilations almost always involve the complete draining of blood, physical mutilation of the flesh is so apparent that seasoned ranchers are shocked by the unusual nature of the deaths. No one really knows when the first unusual cattle mutilations began. Records show that in the middle of 1963, a series of livestock attacks occurred in Haskell County, Texas. In a typical case, an Angus bull was found with its throat slashed and a saucer-sized wound in its stomach. The attacks were attributed to a wild beast of some sort, a "vanishing varmint." As the attacks continued through the Haskell County area, the unknown attacker assumed mythic proportions and a new name was created, "The Haskell Rascal." Whatever was responsible for the mutilations was never caught, and the attacks slowly stopped. Throughout the following decade though, there would be similar reports of attacks on livestock. The most prominent of these infrequent reports was the mutilation death of a horse named Lady, in 1967. Area residents of southern Colorado reported UFO activity the night before Lady was found dead, and the consensus was that the unknown craft were somehow responsible.

In 1973 the modern cattle mutilation wave can be said to have begun in earnest. It is interesting to note that a huge UFO flap was occurring across the country in 1973, with many sightings taking place in the same areas that cattle mutilations were happening. In November of 1974, rumors began to connect the sighting of UFOs with mutilated cows that were being found in large numbers in various Minnesota counties. Dozens of UFOs were reported in Minnesota and dozens of cattle were found dead and mutilated. Although the sightings and mutilations were never correlated, many felt that the number of sightings was added proof that the UFOs were somehow involved.

In 1975, an unprecedented onslaught of strange deaths spread across the western two-thirds of the United States. Mutilation reports peaked in that year, accompanied by accounts of UFOs and unidentified helicopters. By 1979, numerous livestock mutilations were also being reported in Canada, primarily in Alberta and Saskatchewan. In 1980, there was an increase in activity in the United States. Mutilations have been reported less frequently since that year, though this may be due in part to an increased reluctance to report mutilations on the part of ranchers and farmers. In the 1990's the mutilations have continued. In the United States, over ten thousand animals have reportedly died under unusual circumstances.

Because of the strange nature of the killings, wild stories and rumors have surfaced over the years in an attempt to explain what is really going on. Chief among these are stories that aliens are harvesting cattle at night for their evil purposes. The extraterrestrials' preoccupation with cattle is apparently due to the fact that the ET's absorb nutrients through the skin. The blood that they acquire from the cattle is mixed with hydrogen peroxide, which kills the foreign bacteria in the mixture, and is "painted" on their skin, allowing absorption of the required nutrients. Supposedly human blood is preferred by the aliens, but cattle blood can be altered to serve the same purpose.

ALIEN BLOOD LUST

While it may seem far-fetched that animal blood could be used in place of human blood, recent scientific discoveries seem to confirm that animal blood can be altered for human transfusions. According to The Observer, a respected weekly paper in Great Britain. The scientists who helped engineer the first cloned sheep are reportedly close to generating human blood plasma from animals. PPL Therapeutics, the Scottish firm that helped Edinburgh's Roslin Institute clone a sheep, is developing the means to replace the plasma genes of sheep and cows with the human equivalent. PPL told the paper it plans to raise herds of the animals and manufacture plasma from the proteins extracted from the animals. The Observer quoted Dr. Ron James, the firm's managing director, as saying, "Only 5 percent of Britain's population regularly gives blood. Genetically modified animals could produce 10,000 times more plasma a year than a human donor."

In 1991 DNX Corp., a Princeton-based biotechnology firm, announced that it had developed genetically engineered, transgenic pigs that produce large quantities of recombinant human hemoglobin. When commercialized, DNX's blood substitute could provide a cost-effective, virtually unlimited alternative to the human blood supply that is entirely free from the threat of contamination by infectious agents that cause diseases such as AIDS and hepatitis. In addition, DNX's recombinant hemoglobin-based transfusion product will be universally compatible with all blood types, eliminating the need for blood typing and cross matching, and will have improved shelf-life and storage characteristics. DNX's announcement was made to the 1991 World Congress on Cell and Tissue Culture in Anaheim, Calif., by John Logan, vice president of research at DNX. Perhaps the wild stories are not so far-fetched after all.

THE COVER-UP OF HUMAN MUTILATIONS

If the stories are true, some would ask why aren't the aliens catching and mutilating humans instead of animals? The truth could be that human mutilations and deaths are occurring on a regular basis, but that the stories are too horrible to contemplate. If murderous, UFO-related human mutilations have taken place, they have either gone unrecognized for what they really are, or have been adeptly covered up by official intervention. Thousands of people worldwide disappear every year, never to be seen again. A majority of these disappearances can be attributed to homicides or other more common situations.

However, some disappearances are so unusual and unexplained that more disturbing scenarios must be examined. In 1956 at the White Sands Missile Test Range, an Air Force major reported that he had witnessed a disk shaped flying object kidnap Sgt. Jonathan P. Louette. Louette was missing for three days when his mutilated body was found in the desert near the test range. Louette's genitals had been removed and his rectum cored out with surgical precision. Like many cattle mutilations, Louette's eyes had been removed and all of his blood was missing. The Air Force filed a report stating that Sgt. Louette had died of exposure after being lost in the desert.

S.S. XX

The late Leonard H. Stringfield, a former Air Force intelligence officer wrote in his self-published book, UFO Crash/Retrievals, Status Report No. 6, about the testimony given by a "high ranking Army officer" whom Stringfield says he has known for several years and who is allegedly a "straight shooter." The officer claimed that while he was in Cambodia during the Vietnam war, his Special Operations group was involved in a fire fight with aliens, whom the soldiers came across sorting human body parts and sealing them into large bins. Subsequently the unit was held for several days and interrogated under hypnosis. The officer claimed that he and his men were given cover memories which only began to surface years later. The implications here are staggering. If this story is true, then the possibility exists that military and government officials are aware of the aliens' interests in the physiological makeup of the human body.

In 1989, the mysterious death of a man a decade earlier came to the attention of the MUFON State Director of Idaho, Don Mason. According to the report, in 1979, two hunters in the Bliss and Jerome area of Idaho stumbled across the almost nude body of a man that had been hideously mutilated. The body's sexual organs had been removed, its lips were sliced off, and the blood had been drained. Although the body was found in very rugged country, its bare feet were not marked, and no other tracks, animal or human were evident. After the police were notified, an intensive search was mounted and the man's possessions were recovered miles from where the body was found. No one knows how the body ended up where it was found, or even more importantly, what happened to him. It should be noted that this area over the years, has had many unexplained UFO reports and cattle mutilations.

In Westchester county New York, in 1988, several morgues were broken into late at night. Fresh human bodies had undergone mutilations involving partial removal of the face and total removal of the eyes, stomach, thyroid gland and genitals. An assistant medical examiner who had broken the silence concerning the case, stated that checks were immediately run on the employees who were on duty at the morgues. No links connecting morgue employees with the crimes were found. While there is no evidence that UFOs were responsible for the bizarre incidents, once again we see human bodies being mutilated in the same ways that cattle and other animals are being mutilated.

Another interesting case that has received little publicity in the United States is the Brazilian Guarapiranga reservoir case. Brazilian ufologist Encarnacion Zapata Garcia and Dr. Rubens Goes uncovered a series of sensational photographs obtained from police files. The photos are of a dead man whose injuries are similar to the wounds of countless UFO-related animal mutilation cases. The body had been

ALIEN BLOOD LUST

found near Guarapiranga reservoir on September 29, 1988. The name of the man has been withheld from the media and UFO investigators at the request of his relatives. After studying the photos, Encarnacion Garcia was impressed with how similar the wounds of the body were to those found on the carcasses of so many mutilated animals. The initial police report noted that the body, although extremely mutilated, showed no signs of struggle or the application of bondage of any kind.

The body appeared to be in good condition. Rigor mortis had not set in and it was estimated that the victim had been killed approximately 48 to 72 hours previously. There were no signs of animal predation or decay which might be expected. Strangely, there was no odor to the body. Bleeding from the wounds had been minimal. In fact, it was noted that there was a general lack of blood found in the body or on the ground around the body. Police photos show that the flesh and lips had been removed from around the mouth, as is common in cattle and other animal mutilations. An autopsy report stated that "the eyes and ears were also removed and the mouth cavity was emptied." Removal of these body parts, including the tongue as here, is common enough in animal mutilation cases.

The "surgery" appeared to have been done by someone familiar with surgical procedures. The lack of profuse bleeding suggested the use of a laser-like instrument producing heat, thus immediately cauterizing the edge of the wounds. The autopsy report states that, "The axillary regions on both sides showed soft spots where organs had been removed. Incisions were made on the face, internal thorax, abdomen, legs, arms, and chest. Shoulders and arms have perforations of 1 to 1.5 inches in diameter where tissue and muscles were extracted. The edges of the perforations were uniform and so was their size. The chest had shrunk due to the removal of internal organs." The autopsy report continues, "You also find the removal of the belly button leaving a 1.5 inch hole in the abdomen and a depressed abdominal cavity showing the removal of the intestines." The report also noted the victims scrotum had been removed, and that the anal orifice had been extracted with a large incision about 3 to 6 inches in diameter.

It is significant that the police and medical examiners were convinced the holes found in the head, arms, stomach, anus and legs were not produced by bullet wounds. What is most disturbing about the anal incision and the extraction of anal and digestive tract tissue is that it is a carbon copy of the surgery seen in so many UFO-related animal mutilation cases. While no evidence linking the Guarapiranga reservoir mutilation case with UFOs has been found, Brazilian ufologists and police have hinted that there may be at least a dozen or more cases similar to this one. In fact, Brazil has had past incidents where UFOs have reportedly attacked people, and possibly taking blood from them. The July 12, 1977 edition of the JORNAL DA BAHIA reported that, "A fantastic story of a flying object emitting a strong light and sucking blood from people, circulated from mouth to mouth among the population of the counties of Braganca, Vizeu and Augusto Correa in Para',

ALIEN BLOOD LUST

where many people fear leaving their homes during the night so they won't get caught by the vampire-like light from the strange object which, according to information, already has caused the death of two men. No one knows how the story started, but the truth is that it reached Bele'm and grabbed headlines in the local newspapers."

Months later, on October 8, the newspaper O LIBERAL launched the first in a series of reports, about the Chupa-Chupa (suck-suck) phenomenon. "Sucking animal attacks men and women in the village of Vigia: A strange phenomenon has been occurring for several weeks in the village of Vigia, more exactly in the Vila Santo Antonio do Imbituba about 7 kilometers from highway PA-140, with the appearance of an object which focus a white light over people, immobilizing them for around an hour, and sucks the breasts of the women leaving them bleeding. The object, known by the locals as "Bicho Voador" (Flying Animal), or "Bicho Sugador" (Sucking Animal), has the shape of a rounded ship and attacks people in isolation. One of the victims, among many in the area, was Mrs. Rosita Ferreira, married, 46 years old, resident of Ramal do Triunfo, who a few days ago was sucked by the light on the left breast, and passed out. Increasingly it looked like she was dealing with a nightmare, feeling as if there were some claws trying to hold her. She was attacked around 3:30 in the morning. Another victim was the lady known as "Chiquita," who was also sucked by the strange object with her breast becoming bloody, but without leaving any marks."

Compared to reports of mysterious animal attacks and mutilations, reports involving humans are somewhat rare. The probable reason is that many such incidents involving people are not recognized for what they are. The possibility is that a massive cover-up by officials worldwide exists to hide the fact that something is preying on humans. If we consider that extraterrestrials are visiting Earth, the likely reason for such visitations is scientific exploration. Consider that with billions of galaxies and the likelihood that there are multitudes of different kinds of life scattered across the universe, the Earth is just another source of specimens for extraterrestrial scientists to gather and study. While man's ego would like to think that we are special in the universe, the hard reality could be that we are just curiosities to be collected, studied, and possibly exploited, and then finally pickled in a jar someplace with the notation: *HUMAN, MOSTLY HARMLESS.*

BLOODSUCKERS DOWN THROUGH THE AGES

Vampires and vampire-like creatures have been found in the folklore of every civilization, every culture, and every religion since the beginning of recorded time. In ancient Babylonia there was Lilitu, (in Hebrew Lilith or Adam's first wife in Talmudic lore); after her rejection of Adam's dominance, she becomes a demon that attacks infants and children in the night.

ALIEN BLOOD LUST

In India, tales of the Vetalas, ghoul-like beings that inhabit corpses, are found in old Sanskrit folklore. The Vetala is an undead creature, who, like the bat associated with the modern day vampire, is associated with hanging upside down on the trees found in cremation grounds and cemeteries.

The Chinese have the Ch'Iang (or Chiang-Shih), irrational creatures that are driven by bloodlust. They have difficulty walking because of the pain and stiffness of being dead, so they hop instead. Some even will sexually assault their victims in addition to their bloodsucking.

The Malaysian Langsuitis is a woman who wears a gown, has long nails and long jet black hair. This vampire has a hole in the back of her neck which she uses to suck the blood from children.

The Scots tell of the Baobham sith, which takes the form of groups of beautiful girls who lure their victims into the woods and marshes to drain victims of blood.

MYSTERIOUS MUTILATING CREATURES

One mysterious creature that seemed to appear out of nowhere was the notorious "Killer Kangaroo" of South Pittsburg, Tennessee. In mid-January of 1934, something described as looking like a giant kangaroo terrorized rural Marion County, along the Tennessee, Alabama border.

According to the local newspaper, the Reverend W.J. Hancock saw the animal and said it was "as fast as lightning" as it ran and leapt across a field. This beast was reported to have killed and partially devoured geese, ducks, and several large dogs.

One witness named Frank Cobb claimed the kangaroo attacked and ate a German shepherd dog, leaving only its head and shoulders behind. A tracking party followed the kangaroo's prints to a mountainside cave, where the trail ran out. The creature disappeared and was never found.

Perhaps the bloodthirsty kangaroo left Tennessee for warmer climates because in 1975, Puerto Rico was invaded by the so-called "Moca Vampire," an entity whose activities began in the town of Moca's Barrio Rocha, where it killed a number of animals in a grisly fashion never before seen. Fifteen cows, three goats, two geese and a pig were found dead with strange puncture marks on their bodies, indicating that some sharp object – natural or artificial – had been inserted into them.

Autopsy reports showed that the blood had been drained from the animals, and local police officers were mystified as to how a wild predator could have scaled the fences surrounding the dead animals' pens.

After killing more than ninety animals in a two-week period, the vampire then went after larger prey on March 25, 1975. When Juan Muñiz was returning home to Moca's Barrio Pulido, he was attacked by a "horrible creature covered in feathers." The laborer threw rocks at the creature to frighten it away, but it flew at him, scratching his face and neck. An armed group of locals sought to find the strange being, but no trace was found.

The vampire continued to kill on and off for the next several months before finally tapering off. Like the Chupacabras killings twenty years later, the majority of the Moca Vampire's attacks occurred at night or in the early pre-dawn hours. Those cases in which eyewitnesses managed to see the perpetrator usually described it as a weird bird or as a kangaroo-like creature.

CATTLE MUTILATIONS BLAMED ON UFOs

Throughout the 1970s and 80s there was an unprecedented onslaught of strange livestock deaths that left ranchers and law enforcement officials baffled. Even though mutilations have been reported less frequently, due in part to an increased reluctance to report mutilations on the part of ranchers and farmers, the odd killings have continued into the 21st century. In the United States alone, over ten thousand animals have reportedly died under unusual circumstances.

There is no hard evidence that these rumors are anything other than "urban legends" (or in these cases "rural legends"). The only differences between the old vampire stories and the modern mutilation reports are the proposed identity of the attackers. Cultural conditioning can play an important role in how such mysterious attacks are understood. If a society believes in supernatural entities that thirst for the blood of the living, then any mysterious deaths where blood is noticeably absent would be attributed to a vampire.

However, in the modern age of science, supernatural creatures have been relegated to the realm of fairy tales and superstition. So when any unusual deaths occur that involve the loss of blood, the attackers are no longer seen as undead vampires, but instead blame is laid at the feet of beings from another planet.

The only real truth is that we have no idea who, or what, is responsible.

So, as you try to sleep tonight, wondering what that noise was in your closet, or what strange thing is moving in the shadows just beyond the headstones in the cemetery, remember that we are not that far removed from our distant ancestors whose blood and flesh nourished unseen horrors. For even safely behind our locks and security cameras, we still cannot hide from the monsters.

ALIEN BLOOD LUST

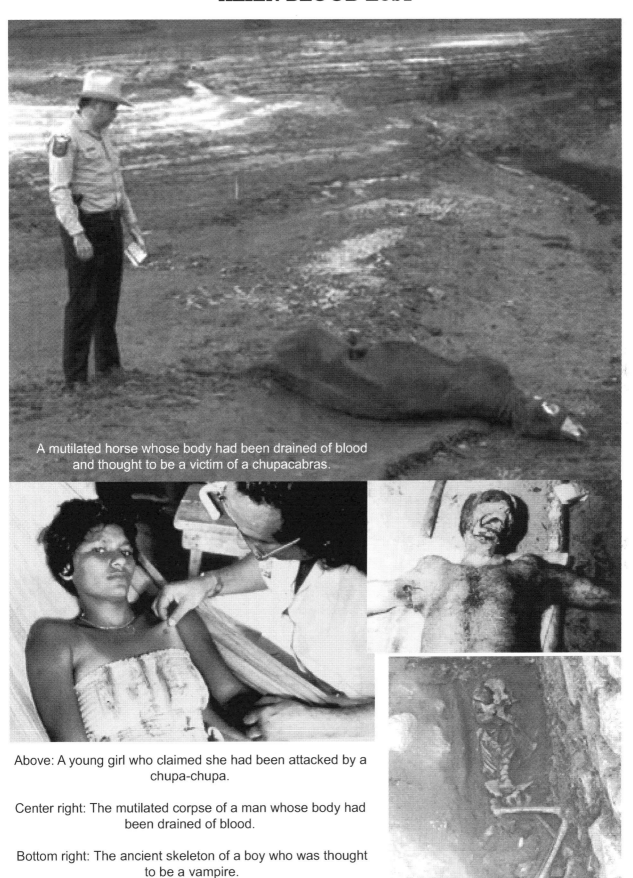

A mutilated horse whose body had been drained of blood and thought to be a victim of a chupacabras.

Above: A young girl who claimed she had been attacked by a chupa-chupa.

Center right: The mutilated corpse of a man whose body had been drained of blood.

Bottom right: The ancient skeleton of a boy who was thought to be a vampire.

SECTION TWO:
THE TERROR OF THE CHUPA-CHUPA ALONG THE AMAZON

ALIEN BLOOD LUST

CHAPTER 9

ULTRA-TERRESTRIAL VAMPIRES ALONG THE AMAZON
By Sean Casteel, and Timothy Green Beckley
With Major Contributions by A.J. Gevaerd

They were for the most part "refrigerator-shaped." They came out of the sky or up out of the ocean attacking their victims – many hundreds in all – with a horizontal beam of light out of which projected a pincer type device, like a "cannula," used by physicians to extract fluids. The strange device penetrated human flesh and extracted a quantity of blood from the horrified victim, the end results of which were almost always the same. One health official summarized the victim's condition thus: "They did not have a fever, but they had a drop in their immune resistance because they were very sick, with no appetite or willingness to do routine tasks. They began to have the slowest reflexes. They had been burned severely on the right or left side, and it became routine to look for holes in their neck, markings similar to those suffered by a vampire's prey!"

****

Dr. Daniel Rebisso Giese spent five years researching a 1977 Brazilian UFO sightings wave that had locals claiming that not only had they seen terrifying

A.J. Gevaerd is the editor and publisher of Brazil's prestigious "UFO Magazine, "one of the longest-running UFO publications in the world. (Photo International UFO Congress)

74

lights in the sky they had also been attacked by a vampire-like creature they called a "chupa-chupa," which translates from the original Portuguese as "suck-suck." Giese's research became a well-known book on the subject called "Extraterrestrial Vampires in the Amazon."

In 1977, strange happenings began to cause unrest in several villages and settlements in Northern Brazil. Unknown lights and unknown creatures were roaming the skies over the Bay of Sao Marcos, in the State of Maranhao, spreading terror throughout the region known as the Lowland Belt.

Extraterrestrial Vampires in the Amazon By Dr. Daniel Rebisso Giese.

The people of the backwoods – called Caboclos, the local word for half-breed Brazilian – believed that beings from another world were at large in the area, searching for human blood. The victims were struck by a mysterious light which could penetrate anything and let none escape.

The situation was taken seriously by the Brazilian Air Force, who sent teams into the region and secretly documented everything. They heard the same testimony from hundreds of people, all of whom talked about a "vampire light," or "a luz chupa-chupa."

As you will come to see, there are many testimonials of a dramatic nature that show the unparalleled horror the witnesses experienced, such as in the case of Ana Célia Oliveira, a teacher in Colares who was 6 years old at the time:

"I will never forget him," she said. "People and animals were attacked. There was nothing to eat. We were terribly lacking in food. Nobody was fishing. People did not want to go outside to harvest.

"Everyone was trying to move in large groups," she continued. "Nobody wanted to be alone. All Colares had stopped. At 6 pm it was dark and we went to bed. Groups as numerous as 50 or 60 women and children gathered in a house. The men remained awake all night. They lit fires and tapped pots and pans to make noise to frighten and scare away UFOs. People started shooting in the sky to scare them away.

"We had just heard from our fathers and other men what was happening. We

ALIEN BLOOD LUST

did not know why we went to other people's houses at night to sleep. At night, people saw many UFOs flying in formation.

"Once I heard a man shoot and I ran to the door and opened it," Oliveira recalled, "and saw many UFOs in formation. And suddenly they went in all directions. The objects moved very fast. People started shooting in the sky to frighten them. One came over the village, just 15 meters high."

The chupa-chupa was seen on many occasions floating and darting across the heavens on its way to cause panic in the hearts and minds of the residents of Colares, Brazil.

THE NIGHTMARE SIEGE BEGINS

Giese's book constitutes impressive evidence furnished by doctors, journalists, soldiers and rural Caboclos all describing unbelievable facts that challenge the limits of our "reality."

It was July of 1977, a sunny day after the long rainy season of winter, in the little Brazilian town of Viseu. Normally the families would be seated outdoors in the evening, with the children running to and fro. But on this night strange lights were seen moving across the sky, lights of various colors, not ordinary lights or aircraft lights. These lights were completely silent. Some of the more religious-minded locals thought the lights were "signs of the end times."

ALIEN BLOOD LUST

The next morning, people arriving from nearby villages had news of a powerful sort of light which, coming down from space, could paralyze you and "suck out" your blood and your energy.

These reports of the "Vampire Light" came to the ears of the man in charge of the local police post, Sergeant Sabino do Nascimento Costa, who considered them of no importance. The mayor of the town, Carlos Cardoso Santos, laughed and gave his verdict that it was all "just fantasy." Even the priest, who was alarmed that his parishioners were talking about prayers to ward off the evil force, took the same view, calling the reports "the wild imagination of the rural folk. Nothing to it!"

However, the next day, there arrived in town a fisherman and his son. According to the son: "About ten days ago, we were fishing near Ilha Nova. Suddenly we saw a star moving. Its brightness was very strong, stronger than the rest of the stars, and it seemed to be flashing and it came straight toward us. We remembered what we'd heard about the 'chupa-chupa,' so we paddled for the river bank and hid in the bushes. We just managed to escape being touched by the light. It was hanging a few meters above our boat and sweeping the whole area with a sort of searchlight, as though probing, seeking."

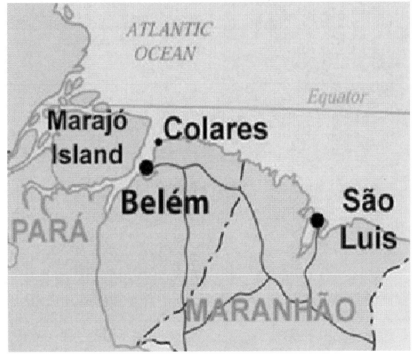

A "blood map" of where the sightings transpired in Colares.

In the end the light or object flew off towards the farm of a neighbor.

Another local resident was not so lucky. A hunter was sitting quietly in the thick bushes, awaiting game. An animal appeared, but something in the sky threw down a beam of light onto the animal and made off with it. Meanwhile, the hunter himself could not escape the light, which he felt bearing down on his body and sucking the strength out of him. He was sure he was going to die.

The flying object was shaped like a cylinder and he could hear voices coming from it, speaking in an unknown language. The object departed, but left him powerless. He seemed to have absolutely no strength whatsoever and was hospitalized.

ALIEN BLOOD LUST

A cylindrical craft was also seen by a woman schoolteacher, who said it shone its beam down on her house. She reported the incident to the same scoffing police sergeant mentioned earlier. He felt that given such testimony from an educated woman, he could not simply ignore her report.

THE FEAR SPREADS AND THE MEDIA RESPONDS   *July 1977*

"By now, nobody in the whole area was venturing out at night," writes Dr. Giese, "no children were playing out of doors, and fishermen were wary about putting out in their boats."

The phenomenon began spreading to nearby villages and once again the local authorities there at first refused to believe the reports.

"In due course," Giese writes, "the wave of cases of 'vampire lights' over the region turned out to be the greatest 'UFO Wave' ever recorded in the whole of Brazil."

Giese then quotes an area newspaper: "The appearance of an Unidentified Flying Object in the skies over Pinheiro is producing suspense and panic among the population and has stimulated imaginations to such an extent that some are even saying that the object approaches people and then stuns them with a beam of light and extracts their blood. The presence of the craft has been here has been established as certain. There is general terror throughout the region, folk fear to go outside at night, because of rumors that when the UFO comes down near the ground it emits an extremely hot luminous beam that burns people's skins."

From the mass of reports at the time, it was evident that the UFO's beam would first immobilize the victim. Then he would feel intense heat and would collapse, some fainting totally. In general, small rural settlements were mainly targeted, and the victims were single, isolated persons or small groups of people.

The panic continued into October-December of 1977, again with no one venturing forth alone at night "for fear of the blood-seeking 'vampires.'" By that time, some of the rumors and popular theories had grown to be more fantastic than ever. It was even believed by some that the UFOs were part of a secret Japanese plan for contraband trafficking in human blood. There was of course the belief that the UFOs came from other planets and there was the occasional unsubstantiated rumor that a ship had crashed in North East Brazil. But in all his years researching the area, Giese never found any proof for the crash-related rumors.

Local men began to band together into patrols at night equipped with firearms as well as fireworks to frighten off the intruders. With the 1977 Ceremony of the Procession of Our Lady of Nazareth, held the second Sunday in October in the city of Belem (the Portuguese form of the name Bethlehem), there came many folks from throughout the Amazon region to take part, bringing with them fresh stories about the chupa-chupa. Many of the stories were now perhaps a bit exaggerated, but people were talking about "vampires that came down sucking human blood, and especially from women's breasts."

As the tales ran like wildfire through Belem, women were all growing hysterical; immediate action was needed. And the authorities indeed took action.

Instantly, the local newspapers, which up until then had been reporting very objectively everything about the sightings of the chupa-chupa and their victims, changed their tune overnight. While one newspaper had proclaimed in November that "The Interplanetary Vampire Only Likes Women," the very next day that same paper ran the headline "The Chupa-Chupa Is Mere Fantasy."

But the testimony of the witnesses told another tale – a tale of intense bewilderment, frustration in not knowing what was going on, and, in some cases, a sense of panic due to the nature of the events.

The "Vampire Lights" created a wave of terror around the town of Colares. No one ventured outside and alone at night for fear of the blood-seeking vampires.

A MEDICAL PSYCHIATRIST INVESTIGATES
THE "VAMPIRE" PHENOMENA:
DR. WELLAIDE CECIM CARVALHO
Interview conducted by A.J. Gevaerd
Introduction

A modern and courageous lady, independent and generous, determined and fearless. These are just a few adjectives to define the medical psychiatrist Wellaide Cecim Carvalho, whom I had the privilege of meeting and the pleasure of interviewing in Belém. But perhaps the introduction is not very appropriate because of just one word: lady. Wellaide, despite having an enviable curriculum, is a person of absolutely young spirit who started medical school at age 16 and completed it at 21. She had numerous functions in her professional life and was nothing less than the municipal secretary of Health in Belém and State Undersecretary of Health in Pará.

Wellaide also accumulated many other titles and at the time of this interview worked simultaneously in several medical institutions of the capital of Pará and in other cities. She lives at a frenetic pace – has five cell phones and reserves very little leisure time for herself. Still, she does not neglect her family or passion for fast cars. "My dream as a teenager was to be a mechanical engineer," she said as she disembarked from a convertible and powerful Japanese vehicle at the door of the hotel we were staying in.

In the midst of such a rush, she found time – soon after arriving from her weekend job in Paragominas (more than 300 km from Bethlehem) – to give a long interview to the staff of The History Channel of the United States. And on the same evening, she sat with this editor for another five hours, describing in detail her fantastic experiences on Colares Island during the height of the UFO wave.

It was her first job, and Dr. Wellaide found an indescribable scenario ahead of her, having never imagined what the situation would consist of. She attended to no less than 80 victims of the attacks, lived in an ever greater fear of being attacked herself and also ended, fortunately without violence, having several close personal experiences with the aggressors. This interview shows the gravity of the government's attempts to hide information and how this newly trained physician had to almost single-handedly help the population to endure their suffering.

What was your first impression when you became aware of what Colares Island was like?

I arrived there in a rather tragic way, because the tide was low and the ferry could not cross the river that separates the island from the mainland [Rio Guajará-Mirim]. I was accompanied by a friend of the family, native to the place, in a green Fusca that I kept for a long time and in which I had a terrible

It was on this spot that the military set up Operation Plate.

experience. Not being able to cross the river, we had to use a canoe. Near the other side, just in time to get off, the canoe turned and I almost drowned because I could not swim. My friend helped. When we got close to the edge of the island, we realized it was a mangrove swamp and we got stuck in the mud up to the knees. That put me in pain which lasted about six months. So I'd already been "shipwrecked" on my first day at my new job.

What was the specialty you had to practice at the Colares Sanitary Unit? General practice or psychiatry?

I was a sanitarist, because public health is the only specialty that encompasses all health care and assistance programs, such as pediatrics, general practice, medical, gynecology, dermatology, and pneumology. This was my first job. I had never even heard of Colares. I did not know anything about the region.

As Colares Island is a very small place to this day, we would like to know what it was like back then?

The whole island had approximately six thousand inhabitants, and in the head-quarters of the municipality there were two thousand people. But, from the edge of the island to the village of Colares, on the opposite side, there was a very precarious road with beaten ground. And since my green Fusca could not cross the river, we had to catch a bus there. I was introduced to the mayor at the time, Alfredo Ribeiro Bastos. He took me to view the sanitary unit, which was a very basic establishment. In his technical composition he had a top-level nurse, an odontologist and a dozen nursing technicians. I was undertaking the functions of doctor and director of the institution. The village was very small and had electric light coming from diesel oil, which was only maintained from 6:00 p.m. to 9:00 p.m. From that time, we had to go with a lamp, or candles.

It should be a challenge for you. What were the cases you saw most often at the health clinic?

Generally, they were accidents with stingrays, very common in the island. For that reason, I became a specialist in them and their methods of attack. The beaches around Colares are infested by these critters, causing many injuries to people. I met people who had been stung up to 80 times by them.

Besides the stingray accidents, were there other health problems on the island?

Yes, we also had a lot of polyps, caused by the ingestion of raw fish, and some cases of malnutrition, perhaps because people did not know how to feed them-selves properly. Almost all of the food came from the sea or the rivers of the region, and people ate a lot of manioc flour. But despite this, there were no cases of anemia. Other diseases we had were the dermatological ones, such as scabies, impinges and rheumatism. Many people in Colares had problems with migraine and high blood pressure. In short, the clinical picture of the island's residents was normal and comparable to that of any other small town in the interior of the Amazon.

And in cases of UFO observation and attacks by supposed extraterrestrial beings, did you attend to any victims?

No, before the so-called "chupa-chupa" wave, almost no one commented on these things or sought help at the Sanitary Unit of Colares. What happened, usually at night, was that I had to attend pregnant women in the countryside, because most of them liked having their children in their own homes, some in the hammocks, on the floor, some in the chair. I got tired of doing this till dawn. It seems that children only like to be born at night ... I would leave at this time, often alone, carrying a lantern down the dirt road. And no one has ever told me a history of anything, no sightings, no attacks or hauntings. This was an island of quiet and extremely Catholic people, but without reaching fanaticism. But, about six months

One can only imagine if the chupa-chupa candy is, pardon the expression, in good taste.

after I arrived on the island, in July or August 1977, the chupa-chupa cases began to occur.

How was your first case?

It happened in the second half of 1977, in July. The first victim was a young girl who lived in the countryside. She was taken to the Sanitary Unit of Colares extremely apathetic and with great muscular weakness. She arrived at the hospital and thought she had been affected by some disease, such as malaria or hepatitis. I asked her relatives what had happened and if she had any serious previous ill-

ALIEN BLOOD LUST

ness, and they told me no. They said she was attacked by a "light" when she was lying in the hammock on the porch of her house. What light could that be, I wondered?

How did the case happen and how did the family react when they saw the light attack the girl?

Everyone was terrified, but they did not even have time to help her. This happened at dawn. It was almost dawn, it must have been 5 o'clock, when the family members arrived at the health unit and the attendants on duty came to call

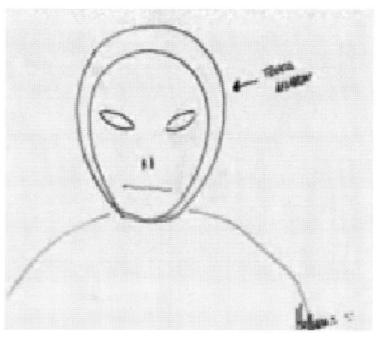

Illustrations drawn by Hollanda depicting the alien entity.

me at home. Towards the end of the afternoon I was told my services were needed so I went to ask her directly what had happened, for until then I only had information from the family. I thought the girl's relatives were crazy. I even asked if they had had a party and gotten drunk —something common in that region. I did not ask if they were drugged, because at that time no drugs were being used, like today. Everyone told me that they had not drunk anything and did not have any party. I was amazed. That's when the victim described what happened to her. She said she was lying in the hammock when she felt something heavy, intensely heavy, on top of her. She described that when she opened her eyes, she saw a bundle of thick light that burned her and paralyzed her at the same time. When she tried to get help from her close family members, she could no longer move her mouth and no muscle, no hand or leg - the only thing she kept was her eyes open.

How long did it take before the relatives began to realize what was really going on?

It was not long, since they were sleeping in nets around this girl. They described that early in the attack they felt a near and intense heat. She repeated exactly what the relatives had said. Only she told me the full details of what they had seen. At the time, the girl was fully conscious, but she had none of her reflexes working. She was inept, but lucid, so much so that her eyes remained open, but with few movements. One thing I noticed is that even though it was day, when I examined her, her pupils were dilated.

Of the whole family, only she was attacked?

ALIEN BLOOD LUST

At that moment, yes. But they all witnessed the attack. They saw that a beam of light had struck the hammock in which she slept, and when they awoke, they perceived that there was strong heat from the place. As soon as they saw the lightning bolts on the girl, they ran terrified to see what it was about. She managed to scream for the last time, for she was catatonic. The bundle focused on the right side of her chest. When I went to examine her, I was told not to touch her because she was burned very badly. I opened her clothes and saw that there was an extensive black burn on her chest that ran from the neck to the diaphragm. She had no fever. I asked how many days ago since that had happened and the family members said that it was only a short time, less than an hour. Then I said: "But it can't be! This injury could not have happened so soon. This is a four to five days burn." The skin was already necrotic and this only happens after at least 96 hours.

Besides the burn, were there any stitches or even punctures in the victim's body?

Yes, I found on the right side of the neck two parallel, high, reddish holes similar to insect bites. They were palpable and visible.

What did you think of what you were witnessing for the first time?

Well, that impressed me a lot, but I did not believe the story of that family, especially since no burn could have that feature in just an hour. It was a surreal story. At the end of the afternoon, after taking some energy medications, the girl began to improve. The only thing I did all day was to try to increase the victim's energy so that she would come out of that state of incompetence. I used syringes with high doses of B-complex. When she spoke again, she said that the burned place ached terribly. I noticed that it was not a burn caused by any chemical substance, thermal effect or radiation, because the wounds from these elements are totally different, very reddish. Hers were in a state of necrosis, that is, as if they were already healing. Out of curiosity, I put an anesthetic ointment on top of the burn, like Xylocaine, to relieve some of its pain, since Dipirona injected had no effect. With a surgical tweezers, I pulled the skin from the burned area, which separated from the entire body. I've never seen anything like it in all the years I've been working as a doctor.

Have you seen that girl again or followed her case?

Yes, just like all the cases I've been called in on. I made a point of visiting these individuals later on. Her hair did not grow back. She had irreversible loss of hair. But the problem was not all over her body, only in the region affected by the chupa-chupa. The light not only burned but destroyed the hair follicle, the root of the hair, in the first layer of the skin, the epidermis. So it was not simply a shallow burn, but something that even reached deep layers of skin. In addition, the victims were ill and many were unable to recover their health. As for the girl I attended, as far as I know, she was not attacked again, but became very depressed

85

ALIEN BLOOD LUST

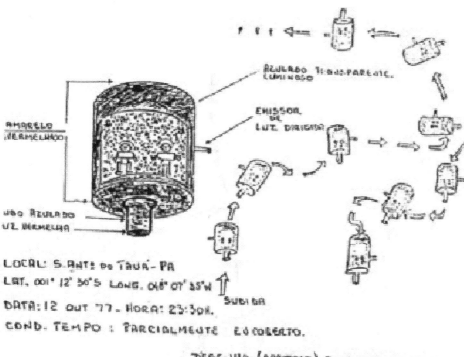

Colares Brazil, the size and shape of object depicted along with path it took.

and weak after the fact, as if she had lost her immune resistance.

Doctor, when the burned skin came out, how long did it take for the place to recover?

The skin looked like it was raw. In fact, it was already in immediate healing process. When you pulled it, it would turn red and burn for days, as if you had taken the bark out of a wound. The victims, on their own, went from their wounds: butter, cocoa fat, sheep's fat, and copaiba oil. Some substances alleviated the pain a little, since the analgesics had no effect, not even Dipirone injectable. I usually used Xylocaine to ease the pain of the patients, which took an average of 15 to 30 days to heal. After the fact, the skin looked white, without pigmentation.

Please describe how the piercings you found on the victims looked?

These took months to disappear, because they were not only visible but palpable. Even after the burn had healed, there were two holes at the level of people's necks. I passed my hand and felt it. Everyone saw. In reality, the perforations did not heal because they were not wounds, but holes, which then closed and became flat. From then on nothing else was seen.

How often have people burned by these lights registered?

Initially, we received one occurrence every three days. Then the cases became daily; sometimes we served three to four people in one day. In a little more than a month, we had attended more than 40 victims. It was a growing thing and people began to leave the island. The emptying of Colares reached 60-70% and the local population was reduced to about two thousand inhabitants. In the village of Colares, in the center of the island, there were no more than 800 inhabitants. Many fled in fear, for the attacks were no longer concentrated at night, as before. They were happening in the afternoon, too. The situation was so terrible that no one else fished or hunted. Everything closed: schools, forum, notary and even the police station. The whole city stopped.

Where were the attacks most frequent, in the countryside, on the island or on the coast?

Generally inside the island, even more so than on the beaches. The attacks began to become frequent and intense, especially in the countryside and near the forests. There was a region called Santo Antonio das Mucuras, a place where many people attacked by the vampire light came to the Sanitary Unit of Colares. According to the testimony of the victims, the objects descended and were under the canopy of the trees. Maybe that was their way of camouflaging themselves.

Did the authorities take any action in the face of what was happening?

At first, no. Anyway, I still continued to think that this was some kind of visual hallucination, simultaneous collective delusions, and self-mutilation. I thought it was the victims themselves who somehow did this, but I did not understand why. The situation even "knotted" in my head and I often wondered how someone could mutilate himself with the same kind of delirium, with the same visual and synesthetic hallucination. What intrigued me most was the fact that the cases were identical, even though they occurred in places very distant from each other. The difference in the time of the attacks was very small and prevented a combined action of the people, not to mention that the victims did not even know each other. This does not exist in any literature, not even in psychiatry. Nobody hallucinates like that. I cannot have a hallucination like that, like yours, me being here and you in Mato Grosso Sul, for example. This is impossible!

What was your opinion of these facts back then, and how did you handle your conclusion that they could not be hallucinations?

In fact, I did not have a concrete opinion about the cases, but I thought they might be some kind of visual hallucination combined with self-flagellation. I really did not know what the attacks were, and I had many doubts. It took me a long time to realize that they could not be delusions, even because of my skepticism and I being a newly informed doctor. If this were to happen now, it would never have taken so long to understand the facts and I would not miss the opportunity to gather important data, which today would greatly enrich Ufologists' research. My immaturity and, perhaps, lack of professional humility, because I was new to the profession, made a lot of difference.

And you decided to stay on the Island of Colares even knowing that the situation worsened every day and you could be attacked?

Yes. But it was not easy. As everyone was leaving, I also thought about leaving the region, but Mayor Bastos and Father Alfredo de Lá Ó convinced me to stay. People panicked and did not know what was really happening, not even us, from the health unit.

You were fully aware of the risk you were running while staying?

Yes, I knew all the risks. But the mayor made a deal with me – he would have people watch my house at night, so I could sleep and be able to help the victims the next day. The local government distributed, both in the county seat and in the rural area – which was made up of eight localities – pistols, cans, pieces of wood, fireworks and thermal bottles with very strong coffee, so that the population did not sleep and could let loose fires every 10 minutes. The remaining residents would have to beat cans all night to chase away the lights.

From PDF CENDOC 10-1978 **Page 40**

Documents from Operation Plate were released in 2009.

And the mayor's method worked?

It worked for some time, but the attacks continued. The objects did not descend, but continued to victimize the people from above. Then, neither letting go of fires, nor strong coffee, nor anything prevented the attacks, which returned to normal and full force. The events began in July 1977 and the 40 or so cases I referred to were recorded mainly at night and at dawn, especially in the countryside. It was from the month of October of that year that the occurrences began to be also in the late afternoon and early evening. And they no longer reached the rural area, but they reached the county seat. The following month, the cases occurred all afternoon, especially after 4:00 p.m. At this stage of the lollipop phenomenon, I came to believe that "they" — whatever the pilots of those machines were – were filled with much despair, to the point of doing everything to reach the victims. I do not know why. I do not believe they were there for pure and simple evil. They needed something those people had.

When you say "they," to whom exactly are you referring?

"They" means the extraterrestrial beings, who are believed to be behind the attacks. Today I refer to them this way. In my opinion, at that time there was a squadron of ships lost in the Amazon and desperately needing fuel or something else to return to their place of origin. Who are we mere mortals to know what fuel they used? Ours comes from alcohol and oil, but what about them, did not they come from humans? I think they were taking people's vital energy and turning it into something. I began to realize this from the first 40 cases I attended. I tried to elucidate my doubts and give an answer to the population, because they all changed my thinking a lot.

People asked me what it was, and I began to stop thinking like a doctor and began to reason as a human being. We wanted to know why the victims weakened so much and so quickly after the attacks. They had diarrhea, screamed and had joint pains that lasted for months. Many became apathetic, fearful, depressed, and irritable. Little did they speak, but when I visited them in their houses, I always asked if they felt better. They often responded in a monosyllabic way. "More or less. I never saw any health again, Doctor. I do not know what I have," some said. "It's as if something had sucked me," others had remarked.

Was the precarious state of health of the victims' visible even months after the attacks? Did they ever get better?

Yes, visibly. It seemed that someone or something had extracted their vital energy, which was why they usually got sick. It was when I started searching the archives of the Colares Sanitary Unit for data on the previous blood and urine tests of the people who had been attacked, since many of them regularly checked the post, since they lived in a region where the incidence of diseases was big. Luckily, there was a large file several years before my performance there, containing patient data.

What did you have in mind?

My idea was to compare this information with current information and see what had changed. I discovered one thing incredible: 100% of those who had had laboratory tests before the attacks were struck by a sudden anemia, in which the number of red blood cells had reduced to almost 50%. I also found that the staining of patients' blood cells had changed.

Was that a constant pattern in the people who were attacked?

Yes. For example, a patient who had had an examination in March 1977, which accounted for 4,600 million red cells and a rate of 12.5 g / dL hemoglobin, presented only 3 million red blood cells and 9 g / DL of hemoglobin. Many people

Anywhere from 6 to 8 different types of UFOs were sighted during the wave. One type of craft even had occupants peering out at startled residents.

even had even more striking variations, losing up to 50% of red blood cells. Now it was impossible for this to happen to so many people at the same time, and only in that region. Of the 80 people who attended the whole, about 80% had severe anemia. [The normal values for the hemoglobin concentration defined by the World Health Organization (WHO) are 13 g / dL for men, 12 g / dL for women and 11 g / dL for pregnant women and children between six months and six years. Below these data, the individual is considered anemic].

And what about the attacks themselves, how did they happen, according to the description of the countless victims that you attended to?

I heard many reports, almost all the same. First, it was not a ray of light coming from the sky, but an object descending down, close to the treetops and camouflaged between them. It made a loud noise and glowed, and all were cylindrical, no victim described artifacts as discoids (or "plates") to me. Therefore, I do not understand the name given to the military expedition made in the region, Operation Prato [Operation Plate], which presumes that the objects had this disk format. Writer Daniel rebisso, author of "Extraterrestrial Vampires in the Amazon" [Private Edition, 1991], described the UFOs as being metallic and silvery, with several bright lights shining from the top and bottom. They stood on top of the trees and when they moved they did not do it in a straight line. This fact I even witnessed: they moved in an elliptical way.

Were the cases very similar?

Yes, there was no disagreements; the reports were all the same. When a person came to the health unit with a large burn in the hemi-thorax, on the right or left side, I was already looking for the holes in the neck, because I knew I would find them. I was referring to them as similar to the marks made by vampires on their prey.

Has any case of those who came to your notice escaped the pattern already described of attacks and consecutive burn?

The only case that escaped a bit of the pattern of burn in the chest and perforations in the neck happened with a patient who was staying in someone else's house to take care of their children in the terreiro. Turns out, she was attacked, she raised her hands to protect herself, suffered the burns there, in her hands. In addition, people had all the same symptoms after the attacks. They did not have a fever, but they had a drop in their immune resistance because they were very sick, with no appetite or willingness to do their routine tasks. I realized later that they began to have the slowest reasoning. Using a popular Amazonian term, they became "lesos" (translates as dumb or "stupid").

Let's go back a little in our conversation. I wonder how the people attacked came to the health unit?

They never came alone, were always supported or carried by relatives, friends, compadres or neighbors, because they could not walk. These people, in general, witnessed what had happened to the victims, but were left unharmed. Curious thing is that when the attacks occurred, the victims were never alone. Sometimes they were dating couples or people who still insisted on going to parties. Then, with the repetition of the cases, all the festivities ended and everything stopped. And look, this is a difficult thing here in Pará, where the people are really very festive and excited.

Do you have case information where more than one person was hit simultaneously?

Sure! For example, people were usually attacked together. In one large group, many were stung. Those who got away came back to help their colleagues. Later on, people stopped leaving and even the fishermen did not dare to continue their activities, as several of them were attacked at sea. No one else dared to leave their homes because, in the course of time, the lights began to become more audacious, making victims in broad daylight and in the streets of the Village of Colares.

You attended to about 80 people who were attacked, but how many victims in all do you estimate that the suck suck did?

ALIEN BLOOD LUST

I believe that the number of people attacked was very large, but many did not have easy access to the county seat, living in the rural area of Colares, and never sought medical help. So they did not make it into the statistics. At that time, it took several hours by boat to cross the Laura Tunnel, a region that separates the coast from the island. Many people were carried in hammocks, others were even afraid to bring them and be attacked along the way. I was also afraid of going to see them in their homes, and I was constantly receiving news that more and more residents were being attacked by the light. Even the employees of the unit did not want to take drugs to the farthest regions, in fear for their safety.

Was there a pattern in the sex or age of the victims?

Well, more men were attacked

Brazil's long-running "UFO Magazine."

than women, more young adults than old people. Few cases of children were registered, and none with children under 10 years. I did not take care of anyone so young or old at old age. It was as if there was respect for such age groups. The oldest patient who I attended, and who even died, was 72 years old. She was attacked inside her kitchen, which had no window, protected from the sun or rain only by a plastic curtain. This happened between 5:00 p.m. and 6:00 p.m.

Now, please describe if there was any physical patterns among the victims?

It is interesting to note that all the victims were thin and none were overweight or obese. Besides, they were all pardos or caboclos. I did not take care of any white or blonde people, even though there were only a half dozen of them on the whole island, still counting on the laboratory technique of the Sanitary Unit of Colares and myself. The vast majority of the victims were farmers, fishermen and housewives, married and not using alcohol. I know this because I made a point of asking the circumstances of their lives, since at the beginning of the cases I thought they were hallucinating and could be provoked by alcohol. I was wrong.

ALIEN BLOOD LUST

Was there any incidence of attacks within the same families, i.e., members of the same family group were attacked?

No. There were several cases where the husband was first attacked, and after four to six weeks, his wife or children. But not simultaneously or immediately.

Was it possible to identify when the lollipop was near the city, through sounds?

We all knew when they were on the way, for they made a buzzing-like noise. When people heard this sound, they would soon find a place to hide. Thankfully the objects were not silent, because if they had been they would have attacked many more people. These artifacts, always of cylindrical shape, reached an extreme of audacity when they emitted their rays of light through the cracks of the houses of wood and straw of the island that generally did not have lining. The lights actually penetrated through the gaps with extreme skill and aim. To protect themselves, people covered these spaces with papers, newspapers or magazines, even covering the keyhole, which solved the situation somewhat.

Were rays emitted from flying objects always linearly or curved to reach people?

They held linearly, never curved. Sometimes they were emanated obliquely, but always straight and never horizontal. I realized this because, in order to have better communication with the patients, I would draw on a paper what they described to me, asking them to check if they were correctly representing the cases. Residents reported that the lights usually came through the windows and doors.

Did any of the patients you attended in Colares ever die due to their encounters?

Three cases, all women. The first one happened in a hospital in Belém. This lady arrived at the Colares Sanitary Unit and received the necessary energy medication, at the same time we controlled her blood pressure. She was a bit old, she was 72 years old, had heart problems and hypertension. I waited 36 hours and saw no results in the treatment. We did not even have a patient reaction. So I decided to talk to the mayor to take that lady to the State Servants Hospital in Belém. We had difficulty even putting her in the car, because she had muscle spasms [Exaggerated and permanent contraction of a muscle]. But she lay in the backseat of the car, with her legs out the window. It was almost cadaverous, just as the animals that were attacked were completely dry and stiff. As soon as she arrived at the hospital, she died.

What happened after that first death?

I asked the relatives of the deceased to follow all the procedures and to demand an autopsy. They asked but they were not taken care of. It was a time of repression and the military dictatorship was effective, with Constitutional Act No. 5 in force. At a time like this we could not ask for much. When the relatives of the

ALIEN BLOOD LUST

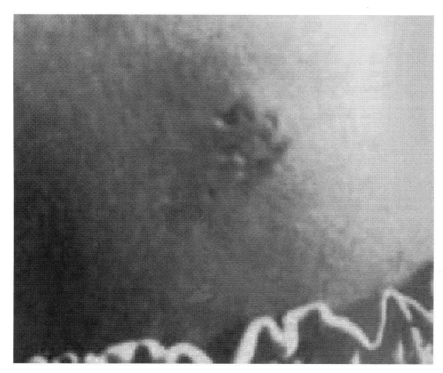

Close up of puncture wound found on many of those who came under attack by the chupa-chupa.

deceased returned, I asked them for a copy of the death certificate, and it was written that the cause of death was given as unknown.

And the other deaths?

The second case was a younger patient, around age 44, who also had hypertension. She was attacked at her house by a light that came in through the window. The victim had the same characteristics as the first and the cause of death was not clear either. These two incidents happened in October. The third one was in November or December. The woman was taken to my house by her comadre. She was in a deplorable state and spoke with difficulty. She was attacked in the same way as the others, but died six years after contact with light. She was affected by red spots on the skin [Systemic erythematous nuclei] and renal insufficiency.

Was there any involvement of any other Parana health institution with the deaths, either in the treatment of the victims or in the analysis of their bodies?

Well, in addition to the State Servants Hospital, the victims could have been taken to the Renato Chaves Legal Medical Institute, which was supposed to carry out an autopsy on the corpses. But, they never did because the law said they would only do so if the deaths took place on a public road.

One more frustration, is it not? But you had the case of a victim you personally accompanied to the hospital . . .

It was the last case. I took the victim to the hospital, left her there and returned to Colares. I had promised the mayor that I would return, that I would not stay in Bethlehem. That was his fear. On that occasion, I called the State Department of Public Health (SESPA) and asked the staff to answer my appeals to the institution, asking for help, supervision, explanation and support. No one from SESPA answered me, either out of fear, because no team wanted to go to the island, the technicians were afraid of being attacked or for fear of defying the military dictatorship, wanting to expose, to get involved or to have to agree with something that at that time did not allow that was known. And so, SESPA was left out of the lollipop phenomenon.

What was the consequence of those deaths among the population, more panic than before?

Yes, they provoked more panic in everyone. So much so that many people fled the island after the first two cases. Those who stayed began to press the mayor to call the Public Health Department and the Armed Forces to take action, and he did so by calling the Aeronautics military.

Have there been cases of animals being attacked and their owners not?

Yes, there were, but others where their owners were also victims. Of course, animals were more frequently victimized than humans. Generally, we found dead animals that had more hair or feathers. At dawn they had compulsive crises and died. When they had not been recently attacked, they were burned, dried and stoned, with wide, open eyes, as if they were placed alive inside an oven. The locations around the scenes of the attacks had burnt-fur odor. No one had the courage to eat them, even if we had hunger and nothing to eat. No one even tried because everyone was terrified.

Were you aware of any cases in which animals and humans were attacked simultaneously?

Not that I know of. Take, for example, the case of that 72-year-old cardiac lady I mentioned. She was feeding her animals when she was attacked, but they suffered nothing.

And the objects that attacked humans were the same ones that victimized animals?

Yes, they were the same. I think a lot of people did not see that happen, even though the attacks happened more at night. The locals listened to a strange noise and some thought that they were people wanting to steal their animals, since there was lack of food in the region. When they ran into the yard to scare away the supposed thief, they found no one. They saw only the light emanating from the lollipop and returned quickly into the house. Sometimes they even tried to call for help.

What species of animals were most attacked during the suck-suck wave?

Usually they were ducks, chickens, pigs, and cows, as well as dogs headed toward the light to see what was happening. The form of death was always the same: the next day, everyone was dry and wide-eyed. I estimate that a much larger number of animals were attacked, much more than people. This is perhaps information the Ufologists did not know, because I never thought it was interesting.

In fact, animal attacks during the suck-suck wave were unknown. This information is very important and gives a larger dimension to the phenomenon. Now,

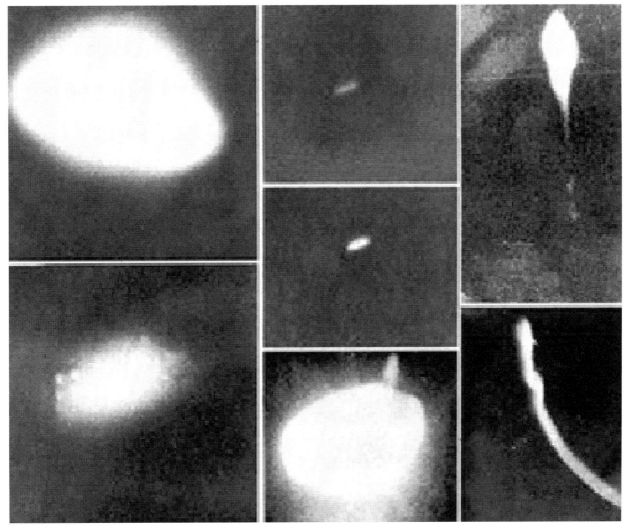

Official Operation Plate photographs, which were taken at different times, show strange objects over the area. (Credit Brazilian Govt.)

as for your personal encounters, when was your first sighting of a flying object in Colares?

It was in October 1977. At that time, the Aeronautics had already set up two observation posts there, one mounted on the beach that is in front of the Village of Colares and another, 50 m from my house in the middle of a football field. They surrounded the city with their observation equipment. Then, from 4:00 p.m., we were all attentive. I was going to meet some people and I was going home quickly, because the attacks had started earlier and earlier.

What kind of equipment did the military have at that time? Were there many?

Many and of very high technology. This story that they had no technology was a lie [As reported by some members of Operation Plate]. The military's radar was very powerful, it blew frantically whenever "they" were approaching. I had to snoop around every time the radar went off, because after I saw the flying saucer for the first time and realized that the beings did not want anything to do with me,

ALIEN BLOOD LUST

I was audacious. I had a Lieutenant from the state of Espírito Santo who admonished me every time I did this. He would say, "Go home and stop being irresponsible, because your safety is our responsibility." And I, being rebellious, said: "I am not a soldier, nor a corporal, and I do not have to obey your orders."

Tell us about your first remark?

One day I was called at 4:00 p.m. to meet a child who had broken his collarbone, exactly the youngest son of the only patient who had his hands burned to protect himself from the light that terrified people. So I went with the three secretaries of the unit to her house. It was about 5:00 p.m., when I finished making all the dressings and immobilizing the wound site. I thought I could have done it in just 20 minutes, but it took me an hour. The child was very nervous and screamed a lot. When I finished the service, the family immediately took the boy home and I closed the unit with the three secretaries - Loló, an 88-year-old woman full of stingrays, Jucemar and a 16-year-old boy. At that time there was no one else on the street and we were striding. When we arrived in front of the house of the president of the Fishermen's Union, whose nickname was Compadre Caneco, I heard a noise of something falling – his house was next to mine. I looked down and saw my escort Jucemar fainting, lying on the floor.

When that happened you were almost home?

Yes, it was a few yards away. Then Loló started pushing me, tapping my arm and pointing my finger up, wanting to show me something. She did not look, only showed something, but I was busy giving care to Mrs. Jucemar. Meanwhile the people shouted in the windows of the houses to get us out of there. But I could not run – I do not know why. It was a mixture of three distinct feelings: curiosity, ecstasy, and awe. And should anything happen to me there, it would be definitive proof that the population was not delusional, hysterical or hallucinatory.

What happened next?

I looked up and saw something cylindrical, with the appearance of metal and a supreme beauty. It was not silver or stainless and had a glow I have never seen, with lights at the bottom and top, blue, pink, and yellow, one in each color. I can roughly compare the colors of that object with those of the rainbow. And the metal may be like a class-A stainless steel, extremely polished and well treated, but it was not quite the type we know. I never saw similar material again. The object must have been approximately 4 m in diameter, super low and gigantic. I live in a 13-story building and the artifact was at a height of a building of 10 floors.

How was the movement of that object?

It was going towards the bay, coming back again and passing over my head. At that moment, I thought it might fall on me. Then he would pass quietly back. Its movement was elliptical, always moving toward the bay. It was not a light but something metallic, even though it was late, the day was clear and the sky was cloudless. I saw the artifact clearly.

Did you see if there was anything inside that object?

Yes. As he began to lower, I could see something in the front, like a transparent window. I saw beings inside the artifact, just from the waist up, and they had a humanoid shape. What struck me was their long, bulky yellow hair. Everything they say in comic books is a lie, they have human forms! They were two silhouettes of human-like creatures. They did not have a green color as some attribute to the aliens, but the color of ordinary people. The front of the artifact was transparent and had a panoramic window. I could clearly see the silhouette of the creatures as they descended and reached the height of a five-story building. I saw them from the chest up, so I did not identify them as women or men. I only know they were not the same height – one was a little taller than the other.

Did you have any idea what that might look like?

Of course, because you only believe in what your eyes see. Such an object stood almost 15 minutes under my head and I did not know what "they" were going to do to me. I stood there. I even thought of running, but if I had done as Loló did, flee with fear, they could attack Jucimar, who was fainting. Besides, I wanted to see and know what that really was. I had to keep seeing to believe once and for all that the population was not crazy. Many residents shouted for me to leave, but I did not move. Those few minutes lasted an eternity, but it was one of the most beautiful things I've ever seen.

What was the attitude of the Aeronautics military when they saw this happening to you and your companions?

They rushed to the beach where the radars and other equipment and the high-range machines they had set up was located. A military team went to the soccer field, where another base of observation was set up. But the objects only went back and forth to the bay. All this was short-lived, but the military nevertheless observed the aerial activity. Their radar whistled frantically, while the soldiers photographed everything. Then, the artifact went towards the bay and disappeared.

After this fact did you feel pressured by the military?

After the officers saw that they could no longer hide the facts and it was true that "they" existed, they began to make worse proposals for me to say that they were Russian squadrons studying the Brazilian population. That's because they could no longer claim that they were just the delusions of the residents. The entire population of the island was already seeing everything with the naked eye and during the day. I did not receive this order directly from Colonel Uyrangê Hollanda, but from his subordinates. He, Hollanda, never came to tell me anything, I suppose out of fear of being reprimanded.

How was your contact with the military at this point?

ALIEN BLOOD LUST

It was hostile. The first people they visited were the mayor, me, and the priest. All the military had the same proposal: to make the mayor persuade me to obey them and that the priest, being a doctor, persuaded the population to believe that everyone was part of a collective hysteria. The lieutenants of the Aeronautics asked me to apply the tranquilizers Idsedin (which is now known as Psicosedin], Diazepam and Benzodiazepam) to the victims. I was asked to convince the witnesses that they were hallucinating. They even gave me boxes of these medicines, but I did not minister to people. And I said to them, "But how could you do that? So I'm hysterical too, just like you! Because I saw them, and all of you ran to photograph the UFO when it was on me. Why don't you take the medicine too if you think it will scare the chupa-chupa away?"

Did they threaten you?

Yes. They told me: "If you continue to believe what the people say, you will suffer severe punishment. You will be punished by the institution and by the Armed Forces." I realized that I ran the risk of being arrested, punished and transferred, besides having my registration revoked by the Medical Council of Pará. The military knew that my word in the community was very important, even more than that of the mayor and priest. They went so far as to say that if I told the locals that it was all hallucination, they would believe. And that's exactly what they wanted! "We know that you are very dear to the people and the only one on the island who has a higher level than the priest. Convince your patients that they are having hallucinations, delusions and visions," they told me.

When the military gave you the medicines they wanted you to minister to the people, did they speak like an order?

Well, as an order I do not know, but I'm sure it was not a mere request. They asked me that with conviction. And they said, "We brought these medicines. Give a card to each of the people who say they have been attacked by this light. You will be responsible for administering the remedies." Until that time I had attended more than 50 cases and said that I would not prescribe medication to anyone. First, because those were drugs and can only be indicated for patients who have a need and still have a blue color prescription. Benzodiazepam, for example, is a black-striped medication indicated for the symptomatic relief of anxiety, agitation, and tension due to psychoneurotic states and transient disorders caused by a stressful situation. It may also be useful as a coadjuvant in the treatment of certain psychic and organic disorders. But since I did not want to medicate anyone with these drugs, the military began to treat me with hostility.

Was Colonel Uyrangê Hollanda among the lieutenants who took the drugs?

No, it was usually his commanders who came to the Sanitary Unit of Colares. Hollanda kept a polite distance, greeted me, but he never approached me to give me any orders. Even because, I think deep down he knew that every-

ALIEN BLOOD LUST

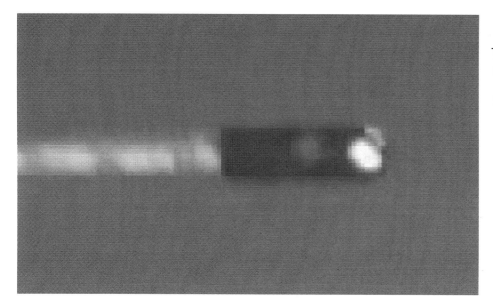

The chupa-chupa, who seemed to inflict most of the pain and drew blood was shaped like a flying refrigerator.

thing that was happening on the island was true. Perhaps he was the most upright of all the military, but he took orders from his superiors and had to comply. The military wore official Aeronautical uniforms but had no identification. They had an accent from the southern region of the country, not being a Pará. Many even identified themselves as biologists and geologists, except that one of them, who drove a jeep, was a sergeant and had no upper level.

Were the soldiers who were looking for you at the health center always the same?

No, but there were usually between three and four soldiers talking to me. They never came alone. The total number of them in the Island of Colares was of 33 or 34 people, between officers and soldiers. Usually, there was always someone watching me. Once a military man, referring to my sighting, told me that "It was nothing, it must have been some plane crash, that's all." Then I said, "What do you mean, accident? So it was an accident to you? If it is not to explain to the people what really happened, what have you come here to do? Put those drugs down the throat of the people? "

Did the military have a rough or crude attitude toward the population?

Yes, a lot. That lady who was burned in her hand, for example, was being treated at the mayor's house when they arrived, opened the door and shouted, "Stop your hysterical attacks, go home and take care of your family." The mayor was very divided on these occasions, because I think he was afraid to face them. He would say to me, "Doctor, do not argue with them because if they leave, it will be worse for us." I would answer and say, "But I cannot dope a whole population."

Do you have any bad feelings about the military?

Yes, I grieve the tyranny of those soldiers. At that time, despite being a doctor and having studied so much time, I was forming my personality. What has happened has meant that, to this day, I do not like the military. I was a woman, professional and young, who was trying to protect a population for which she was responsible and whose work was paid – very well paid, by the way.

Was the pressure you received from the military always the same, constant?

When the equipment was set off, I would go out without a candle or lamp in my hand so nobody would identify me and I would see what was happening. But there were always two or three military men watching me, to take me back home. I did not let them touch me, but I was always angry and they ended up taking me to the police station. I remember even one time when I said to them, "How are you going to arrest me, if you do not have a special prison here on the island?" One of them then replied: "We ordered a cell and put in front a sign written 'special cell' for you." (Publisher's Note: Damn rude — must be related to our president!)

Did Hollanda personally make any proposal or pressure for you not to reveal what was happening in the region?

No, never. He was always very kind to me, but his orders always came through the commander, of course. And when I had to say something myself, I'd send someone. He never came in person. I identified those sent by stripes and embroidered stars on uniforms, for none had name identification. Since I was a medical intern at Aeronautics, I knew who each patent was.

How would you describe the commander of Operation Plate, Colonel Uyrangê Hollanda?

He was an introspective person, shy and quiet. A reserved soldier who did not treat his staff with hostility and never raised his voice. I have never heard a cry from him, nor in moments of agony amid so many apparitions. Hollanda always kept his distance, but he watched me a lot. I even knew that the military was watching me with binoculars and following my every step. And I knew all the orders came from him. When we met, he would just greet me and ask, "Have you taken care of many patients, Doctor?" Nothing more.

Did you ever see any foreign military officers participating in any activity on Colares Island?

No, not at all. All I knew were Capixabas, Miners, Goianos, Pernambucans, and a very few people from Parana. They were always Aeronautics military men, without camouflage clothes. They wore the same official uniform, blue pants and white shirt. But it was strange that they should not wear their name on the chest, because they are obliged to do so. Every time I asked the name of a soldier, they would say, "Call me only as a lieutenant." They never said anything personal about it. To get an idea, I just came to know the name of Captain Hollanda after I had left Colares in 1978.

At that time, when you were not in Colares, were there still attacks?

101

ALIEN BLOOD LUST

They occurred sparingly, once every 30 days. At that time, the Aeronautics had already been withdrawn from the site and sent a report to the State Secretary, so that I was transferred immediately for "insubordination and rebellion." If this were to happen today, I would surely be arrested, because it would be even more rebellious. Now I have more insight than I used to.

Did you ever get transferred to another unit, far from the events of Colares?

It was for me to be transferred to the city of Juruti, on the border of Pará and Amazonas, in March 1978, to serve as director of the State Health Secretariat. Everything was ready, I just needed to approve the state ordinance, but I did not want to go. I went to talk to the secretary of Health of Pará, Dr. Manoel Ayres, and say that I was not going to leave. "Then you'll have to be fired for insubordination," he told me. I left his office and went back home. Two days later, I was received by the governor of the State, Aluízio Chaves, who listened to everything but promised nothing. Shortly after, the same secretary called me again, said that I would no longer go to Juruti and that he was going to cancel the transfer order to that location. But even so, I could not return to Colares. He wanted me to head a unit in the interior of Maranhão.

Did the authorities know the gravity of the events and do nothing?

They knew yes, because the local press reported it. The people who fled Colares passed on the information to the journalists, so much so that the reporter Carlos Mendes published detailed articles on the subject in the newspaper in which he worked. Mendes is one of the bravest people I know, and deserves that title. He has much to reveal about this subject.

How do you feel about the suck-suck attacks?

This should be my hundredth interview on the subject, and maybe the last one, because it never helped me, just messed me up. I give this information with the provision that the people who receive it only divulge what is true and not use Ufology for the deviant acts, which only makes the researchers demoralized. I am not a Ufologist and I am sure that I will never be, even for lack of time, but I am fully convinced that we are not the only intelligent beings in the midst of millions of galaxies, especially after reading so much about Ufology,

By the way, describe the other observations you had in that region.

Well, my second experience with those unidentified flying objects was on the football field, when "they" tried to do – according to what UFO researchers say – third degree contact. That is, they wanted to communicate with us. Until then I did not even know what that was. But that day it seemed as if they wanted to land and get in touch.

How did this happen?

The Aeronautics still remained in the area with their radar devices because of something strange in the sky, around 6:00 p.m., between November 15 and 25,

Colonel Hollanda, who later took his own life, was Commander of Operation Plate.

1977. I ran off and went to the main road that gives access to the island. There was already a crowd of people, even in the water, wanting to hit the object with stones and slingshots. But the military tried to stop the residents from doing so because they believed the object was intending to land. It was difficult because about 200 people were running down the road to prevent the ship from descending. Many believed that the population would be massacred. The military wanted the object to land, but the population did not.

Was the object the same as you saw it before?

It was another great thing, some three or four times bigger than the first, both in breadth and height. That's why I think that first one could be some small aircraft, and this one would be the mother ship. Both had the same metallic characteristics, shape and color. Only I could not see silhouettes of beings, because there were so many people screaming, beating cans, throwing rocks and rockets that it became a mess. The villagers did not obey the military and I tried to persuade them not to continue that mess because it was dangerous. "They" could retaliate. So from that, the Aeronautics had no way of hiding anything else.

What do you think that object was doing there, an unsuccessful landing attempt?

After a long time of thinking, I came to the conclusion that those objects might just be lost in that part of the Amazon, perhaps straying from a larger group and intending only to return to their place of origin. I do not know how, but "they" seemed to be storing some form of fuel to be able to return to their world, and perhaps the energy and fuel they needed was just our synthesized vital energy.

One always had the idea that the lollipop drew blood, besides the vital energy of the people. Do you think the loss of energy is due to the loss of blood?

For sure. Why exactly the blood was sucked from these people, I cannot tell you. I did several laboratory tests and did not notice extreme changes. I believe that "they" did both, take the energy of people and tinker in their hematological part.

The victims had no bleeding, but where was the blood?

They had no vomiting, no bloody diarrhea, no gum bleeding or pores. Curiously, women had up to three menstrual cycles in a single month, because when they are anemic a woman menstruates with more intensity.

Anyway, how did your third and last sighting happen?

It happened when I had to leave the island to get some medicines in the capital, Belém. I planned to leave Colares at 4:00 p.m., because the tide was low at this time, and would return to the city before the end of the day, as the rivers would rise again. We had to think about everything, especially the crossing of the raft. I was alone in my green beetle, scared to death. I took the road that connects the village of Colares to the port where the ferry was anchored, which is about 6 km, and when I was halfway there, my car stopped inexplicably. The engine had completely collapsed, even though the key was still in the ignition. That was when I realized that this situation was not normal. I began to hear a strange noise, which I thought was from the vehicle. Then I saw a glow immensely larger than my car, just above the vehicle. It was as if I had entered a tube of light. It was huge, about four cars in a row.

What happened next? Did you see the object?

The first thing I did was lie down on the bench and throw myself down on the steering wheel. I had the impression that "they" were angry with me and that they were going to take me. I kept my eyes closed for a shock, a blow or whatever happened. But as I opened my eyes, the beam of light subsided and drifted away. I could not see right what it was, because my car had no sunroof. I was paralyzed because I knew I could not ask for help from anyone. Where I was, it was bush everywhere. I decided to be quiet, hoping that everything would be over soon. When I could no longer see the object, I decided to try to start the car again. I pumped the gas and I left at breakneck speed, not caring about the many holes in the road. When I got on the ferry, I asked the operator if he had seen anything strange, and he, as frightened as I, answered yes. We were traumatized.

How did you feel after this experience?

I was shaking and I was all creepy, super nervous. I could not get on the raft with the Fusca, and I had difficulty even stopping the car in my maneuvers. I hit the bumper on the ramp, making the car stop. So I got out of the car and asked for the ferry owner to board the vehicle. I took advantage of it and asked him if I was burned, because I could not feel anything. But there was nothing, still good!

It's strange that you were not attacked in any of the three contacts, including in this case, when you would have been simple prey.

Yeah, they had opportunities to attack me and they did not. But I can confess something to you, that I even talked to Ufologist Daniel Rebisso [UFO consultant and author of the book Alien Vampires in the Amazon, private edition, 1991]. I think I was spared because of the color of my hair, which at the time was natural blond. Daniel says it has nothing to do with it, but I still think so. Why, my hair was the same color as the beings' hair, and maybe that stopped them. In addition, there

Dr. Wellaide Carvalho holds drawing of the "lollipop" drawn by one of the witnesses.

105

were only six blond people in all of Colares, since the majority of the population was cabocla, with dark hair and eyes. No blond person was victimized. None! When I saw the beings inside the object, on my first date, I realized that they had long, bulky, yellow hair. So I still question this and I think there must be some relationship. Why did they not attack blond people?

What did your family think of you being at the center of all these events?

My father said I was crazy. He said that I should have gone to Lebanon to do specialization, or to any other place, because at the time we had money for these trips. He said, "You see, you went to stay in a place like that, where there's a lot of weird stuff going on. There's something going on with you." My father was also believing in what the Aeronautics was spreading in the state, that all this was being caused by the Russians or the Americans. My mother was much more desperate than my father, for she was always super-protective. It's always like this: when we were young, we always tried to show our parents that everything they invested in us was worth it. This was how I felt working at Colares, helping those humble people and being totally useful to society.

Are you still going to Colares? Any news of what's going on there?

No. It's been years since I've been there. My life is very rushed and I have not had more time. But I do not think there's anything else going on there. Now the chupa chupa stories are almost like beliefs, told and misrepresented. Like legends that go from father to son, that each counts in a different way. There are still people there who want to appear anyway in the press, even if it's with lies.

Were you ridiculed at the time for defending the reality of the cases?

I am not ashamed to be ridiculed, nor am I afraid or afraid to talk about it, for I am quite sure of what I have seen and lived with those people. I have been harassed by many skeptics, both today and in the old days. But I never shut up, because I do not care about people's opinions. I'm not here to convince anyone, just to report my experiences. Each one draws their own conclusions. In reality, the one who harasses is actually the layman, the one who has neither the notion nor the knowledge of the facts, the one who thinks that the Supreme Being is the human, only because he does not crawl.

****

ALIEN BLOOD LUST

CHAPTER 11

WITNESSES REMAIN TERRORIZED TO THIS DAY

Though numerous years and long decades have passed since the height of the activity in the northern region of Brazil, the recollections among the witnesses still living – and a few presumed deceased because of age and other "ordinary circumstances" – showed that the aerial atrocities of 1977 were to be construed as the most terrifying of the participants' lives. Bruises on their body, weakness, the forcible loss of blood, some found unconscious, others not knowing what really happened, all indicate why they would have undergone severe and dramatic levels of panic.

Here are stories and comments made by the witnesses as recorded by a number of independent sources:

Inácio Rodrigues, Fisherman And Witness To The Chupa-chupa:

"I was fishing with my friend Genésio Silva one night in April. It was about 01:00 am, when we saw a small fire in the sky to the north. It was very small. I was a little worried and asked Genésio to put out his cigar as the fire was getting bigger and bigger and I could see that it was spinning. We jumped out of the boat into the water and tried to find some hiding place. The fire grew bigger and closer. We hid underneath big shrubs so we would not be seen.

"The object stopped about a hundred yards from us and stayed there until about five in the morning. We were hidden all the time because we were afraid to leave. The light was bluish, but when it first appeared, it was a small red ball. It was beautiful, but it shone so bright I could not look at it much. Just before dawn, it disappeared, the way someone turns out a light, but where it was, you could see a kind of shadow, the shape of a refrigerator. When the sun came up, the dark form disappeared as well. I had dysentery and was sick all day. "

Witness Begs For Help

"I asked for help, but I could not hear people," Newton de Oliveira Cardoso told diarioonline.com.br

ALIEN BLOOD LUST

Even today Cordoso cannot hide the trauma of the attack in September, 1977.

His report is similar to that of other people who are victims of the phenomenon: the body is paralyzed by light, the heat is intense and the body is pierced with the person who is unconscious.

"I was 21 at the time. The exact day of the attack I do not remember, but I assure you that the phenomenon was already happening. The military was already in town," he said.

Known by the nickname of "lieutenant," Newton is one of the few victims still living. He remembers that he suffered the attack because he did not want to sleep in his house in the center of Colares because he was afraid and it was already night. He decided to stay at his girlfriend's house in the community of Mucajatuba, which is about 3 kilometers from the city. "They gave me a hammock to sleep in and I set it up in the hallway of the house." he reports.

That night, a luminous object flew over the property. The light was seen by several witnesses in the street, who began to shout. Inside the house, lying in the hammock, the lieutenant felt a strong "warmth" covering his body and then he was "hooked" in the neck. "I was asking for help, but I could not hear people... When I woke up the house was full of neighbors and they said it was the 'sucks-sucks' because they saw the light on the house." Because of the distance to the health center, he did not seek immediate medical attention. He said for a long time he continued to sleep under a balcony, figuring the chupa chupa would not find him hiding there. As a "tribute" to the memories he must endure, he had constructed a small "monument" to the beings and in the center a miniature of a ship in the form of a globe. "I get people here from all over the world who seek to know the story, but no one has any answers!"

Cinaldo de Oliveira,
A Reporter Who Spent Two Weeks In The "Danger Zone."

"About 90 percent of the people we talked to had seen UFOs, and a lot of fishermen got burned. One night, we filmed a strange thing passing through the sky in a wavy motion. And then it suddenly disappeared.

"This thing we shot flew in a triangular motion. It came from Caranguejo Island, in the Bay of São Marcos, and continued to Anajatuba, then to São Bento and Pinheiro. It looked like a star, but as it grew in size, it changed color from yellow, to blue, and then to red.

"The next day, about 3 km from where we had been, we talked to a man with burns on the back. He told us that the night before, when the light went out and lit again, well above him, that he had suffered the burns. I do not know how many fishermen were burned, but the men were so afraid they did not want to go out to work. We talked to some people on a farm that had a building where all the workers live and sleep. This guy in question ran as fast as he could to the building, and the light flew around the building for about 20 minutes. "

Carlos Mendes, Reporter

"The people were terrified that this beam of night light had assaulted several of them. The whole community gathered together in only three houses for safety's sake. They were praying, sometimes they sang some religious songs, people in a state of panic ... The Colares health unit, it almost became a courtyard of miracles. I was really amazed to see what I saw in those people, which was the result of the activity of these lights they called a 'lollipop.'"

Benedito, Fisherman

"We were on the boat and the UFO went over the river several times. It followed us and fired a light into the river for 10 or 15 meters. 80 meters away. Then the UFO flew over the bush and disappeared."

Claudomira Paixão, A Resident Of Colares, Another Victim

"The light was first green, it touched my head and it crossed my face, I woke up (from a deep sleep) and when the light turned red, I could see a creature like a man wearing a jumpsuit just like a diver. He pointed an object at me, and the object flashed three times, striking my chest during the three occasions, almost in the same place: it was hot, it hurt, and it seemed that I had needles pierced at all three points. I was terrified, I could not move my legs. I screamed and I screamed. My cousin, Maria Isaete, was sleeping in the same room. She woke up and saw the light, and also started screaming. "

Manoel Paiva, Former Mayor Of Pinheiro

"What most impressed people was that the UFO rose to such a high point in the sky that it looked like a star. In fact, it could not be distinguished from a star, and suddenly it descended quickly to the earth again. If this is something of this world, then we have reached perfection, because the object does not emit any sound, it has an enormous speed, it stops at whatever point it wants and follows in any direction.

"The object used to come at a great speed and stop. Suddenly the UFO would rise or fall with the same speed. Many people fishing in boats were chased by this fireball, which left many people sick. They had a fever and their eyes were burning. The UFO light was so strong that the night looked like day.

"The intensity (of the attack) left the witnesses dumb. Everyone was afraid because they did not know if the object was radioactive. I was myself scared, too. Some people were attacked by UFOs and persecuted, and some were burned. The fishermen were so afraid that they did not go fishing for three or four months. Many people did not even go to the yard at night to do their chores, because they were so afraid. You never knew when the objects were going to show up. Sometimes they were seen around 6 pm and other times, only around 4 o'clock. Generally, this fire reaches about 300 or 400m off the ground.

"On one occasion, there were 26 people working some 6 kilometers from the city, building fences. One of the workers went fishing so that the others could eat a good dinner. While he was fishing, the object suddenly appeared well above his head. He ran to the camp, exhausted, and told everyone that a fireball was chasing him. Then everyone at the camp also saw the object. It had a bluish light that illuminated the area for about a mile around, waking up all the horses and cows, startling them.

"The next day, they moved the camp to another location because they were very scared. In the new place, they decorated a piece of wood as if it were a scarecrow and placed a lantern with kerosene on top. They wanted to see if the strange object would return, and hid in the woods to observe. Later that night, the object suddenly appeared, coming close to the lamp. It stayed there for about 45 minutes. The workers said the light was so strong they could not see its shape."

Ana Célia Oliveira, Resident Of Places Of Incidents

"I'll never forget, people and animals were attacked, there was no food, no one was fishing, no one went to the vegetable gardens to harvest the vegetables, everyone tried to go out in large groups, nobody wanted to be alone. And nobody was sleeping. Groups of 50-60 women and children gathered in a single house, while the men stayed up all night, lighting fires and pounding pots and pans to scare the chupa-chupa away. The children did not know what was going on. "

Wellaide Cecim de Carvalho
(More from Dr. Carvalho later in this chapter.)

"What struck me is that when I was attending a person from a locality called Airi, and one from a locality called Candeúba, they were more than 100 kilometers away. And people would tell me the same story, without knowing each other, without ever having spoken and on the same night and at the same time or even at different times.

"There were always, always, always two parallel holes, which did not disappear and were raised as if two needles had penetrated the skin.

"Burns on a person normally require about 96 hours for the skin to blacken and go into necrosis. But the burns that were done to these people, necrosis was immediate.

ALIEN BLOOD LUST

"The population of Colares was taken over by a crisis and the city went into a process of emptying. The fear got to the point that we no longer had medicines, or food. Everything was in real chaos.

"I had never seen anything strange when suddenly, in broad daylight, there was this huge thing, a few feet above of my head, humming and emitting a brightness of great intensity and beautiful colors."

Emidio Campos de Oliveira

"It happened when I was looking at the roof and then I saw like a light bulb burning on the inside of my thigh."

Newton de Oliveira Cardoso - Victim

"I slept even under a counter in the house, afraid of that light.

"I was very weak and moody for several days and I still felt a strong dizziness and headache (for a long time)."

José Moacir da Rocha, witnesses

"Whatever it was that made little holes in people's skin, it happened when that light passed and hit them. Our weapons here (were limited to) sticks, rocks, and a shotgun."

Alceu Marcílio de Souza, Former Police Officer

"We have been several times in Umbituba, doing police diligence. On the nights we spent there, it was possible to observe the uneasiness of the people. At that time, an Aeronautics team walked around the area and some of its members even talked to me about the apparitions. "

Aurora Nascimento Fernandes, Victim

"I was terrified. I called my mother, and before she came, a red light enveloped me, leaving me stunned. At the same time, I felt very thin holes being borne in my womb, and I fell to the ground unconscious."

Jonas Ferreira Godim, Witness

"At that time we did not sleep properly. I and other colleagues went out for vigils in the house of compadres. One night, I saw that device on the treetop, on St. John Street. The UFO stood for a moment and let out a clear light over the trees and then disappeared at a great speed to another corner of the village. "

ALIEN BLOOD LUST

Zacarias dos Santos Barata, Witness

"I saw this device twice. The first time it came into town from the direction of Souré (island of Marajó) crossing over the village very fast. The other time, I saw from the house when it was a luminous ball clearing all the tops of the forest trees of Luzio. The object made no noise and I could not see straight because the light was very strong and bluish. "

Carlos Cardoso de Paula, Witness

"In chupa's time, I often go out at night to visit the homes of compadres and colleagues. Most of them were in the street making a bonfire and roasting fish. From time to time, they made a noise with pistols and cans to scare away the chupa ... Once, when leaving the house, around 9:00 pm, we heard the cry of the people: 'There goes the sucks;' from the house I only saw when a ball of fire was coming towards us, but soon changed course, entering another street. "

"We were all sleeping at home and I was smoking my last cigarette when suddenly a ball of fire came in to the corner of the house and began to wander around the room until it came to my hammock. I looked at all this with great curiosity and I began to feel weak and sleepy. The cigarette fell from my hand and, frightened by the situation, I screamed, at which time the ball disappeared and everyone woke up. That creature was looking for a vein in my body, but had no luck ... When it brightened up, I could feel a kind of heat coming from it."

Although the Air Force would eventually investigate the strange events in the region, responding to much public outcry and outraged demands, whatever the military discovered was never made public.

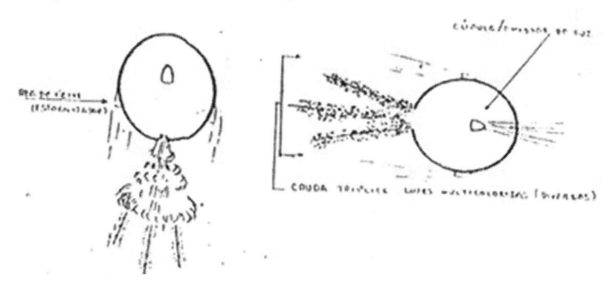

The beams of light from the craft were described as being so bright that they resembled those used to illuminate night sporting events. They were "always sharply defined, directed with perfect precision towards any target – houses, people, boats, trees, even the Brazilian Air Force's helicopters deployed over the island during the investigations.

ALIEN BLOOD LUST

CHAPTER 12

OUR BOY "LOLLIPOP": DR. DANIEL REBISSO GIESES

The sightings around Colares were thoroughly investigated by UFO sleuths, the military and those in the medical profession. All conclude that the "suck-suck" phenomena was legitimate, despite what they might have thought when initially getting involved in the case. Before there were the American researchers Bob Pratt and Jacques Vallee, there was Daniel Rebisso Giese, a biologist and professor, currently working in the state system of health of the State of Para' in Belem. President of the Centro de Investigacion de Pesquisas Exolo'gicas (CIPEX) since its foundation, he currently serves as a director of Grupo Ufologico da Amazonia (GUA), Caixa Postal 624, 66000 Belem (PA).

In 1991, the book "Extraterrestrial Vampires in the Amazon" appeared in a privately-issued edition and it has long been in the process of being updated and re-released. However, many years have passed, making it less likely that the reissued book will actually appear as time goes on. Dr. Giese has apparently retired from UFO research but is active in the biomedical field, working in hospitals and blood banks around Pará,.

The following material was translated from the original Portuguese by Edward G. Steward and is taken from material appearing originally in the Brazilian "UFO Magazine," No. 7, Vol. 2, and in a sit-down interview conducted on August 13, 2005. The magazine's editor/publisher, A.J. Gevaerd, said the translation is fairly accurate and has no objections to it being disseminated.

In his research, Giese found that there were several types of objects present in the area during the "attack phase." The same fact was reported by the late Colonel Uyrangê Hollanda, who even described a UFO "sport model," which was always seen and caused great frustration to the military, as they could not register it in photos or on film. On this, the ex-Ufologist Giese is clear: "The ufological casuistry of the time was intense and many facts were recorded, involving several types of ships. But the ones that attacked people were cylindrical ones, like those described by Dr. Carvalho."

ALIEN BLOOD LUST

You were the first Ufologist to raise the issue of the chupa-chupa or the "lolli-pop," bringing to the attention of the population the gravity of the events that were taking place in Belem. Looking back, what is your impression of these events to-day?

Well, that is an issue that is still a subject of reflection, and sometimes I feel powerless to find a definite and definitive answer to the phenomenon. But what is observed is that, in recent years, information, sources, witnesses and reporters have begun to migrate to other forms of performance. Many important characters (i.e. witnesses and informants) from the lollipop period have passed away, which limits us in our evaluations on the subject. I have always wondered why this wave of sightings appeared and how it would be articulated in the national UFO sce-nario, because I have always understood that the UFO phenomenon is something global and that it interacts with all areas of research.

What do you think was behind the phenomena in Colares and other regions of Pará?

I believe they were objects that came here for a reason, to have some kind of contact with the local people. Sometimes I meditate and try to find an answer. Operation Plate, which had a mega structure to investigate the mystery, came close to finding out some answers. It was the military who saw the events more closely and were perplexed by everything that happened. Interestingly, they started with a militarized thinking. They observed the facts as a true official mis-sion; they discovered that they were in front of a fleet of ships and beings with an advanced intelligence and also a military agenda – mainly because of what the artifacts did to the people. "Military intelligence" is a well-suited expression to describe the lollipop.

Is this an expression of Colonel Uyrangê Hollanda or some other official at the time that had that same thought?

It was also from another soldier, Sergeant Flávio [João Flávio de Freitas Costa, first sergeant and member of Aeronautical intelligence, A-2] who observed the facts a lot, especially the way the aircraft had entered in the night in the river val-leys, as well as the structure to support their action, such as sightings of objects large and small that together flew over the regions. They were probes being col-lected or sometimes simply disappearing. What attracted the most attention was that there was no lollipop activity during the morning hours.

From what hour did the phenomenon manifest itself and in what way did this happen in the day-to-day life of the inhabitants of the region?

Cases usually occurred in the early evening hours, around 6:30 p.m. or 7:00 p.m. At that time the first probes were seen, which moved slowly, as if they were satellites. The attacks began around 10:00 p.m. or later when people were still asleep. The reason for this really should be investigated in more depth. Another interesting point is that many witnesses reported seeing in the lights that a kind of catheter descended from the sky, like a catheter or endoscopy device that, coupled to the person's skin, removed the plasma, blood or something. Then there was the lightning which would only be to paralyze the victim. This was also agreed upon by Colonel Hollanda himself.

Do you have data that this was also seen by other people?

Yes. I have a report from a driver in Belém who claims to have seen a tube in the light, such as the one through which hospital patients receive serum. There is also the experience of Mrs. Claudomira, a resident of the region, who presented a fantastic testimony to me and to Hollanda. However, he diverged on numerous points, so I did not publish in the book I wrote. This situation was also confirmed by US UFO researcher Bob Pratt. According to the testimony of the witness, the alien who attacked him had clothes similar to that of a diver and when he was seen he began firing shots or lightning with a kind of pistol. It was from within these bundles of rays that there was something like a cannula (a thin tube inserted into a vein or body cavity to administer medicine, drain off fluid, or insert a surgical instrument}, where the blood of the victims could possibly be taken. Then there is a suspicion that the luminous focus had a paralyzing function and that a second object, smaller and with properties to remove the skin or to extract blood samples, would migrate from within.

In this case, is it possible to assume that to be able to strike lightning the aggressors would need to be close to the victims?

Exactly. And this is interesting because during Operation Plate, when there were several lights in the sky and people reported having had contact with the lollipop, there were no photos of burned witnesses and there was only one man taken to the hospital to get first aid. He was subjected to an analysis and found that his testimony was true; the man was not crazy. He revealed that he had seen a creature of damp skin emitting light from the palm of his hand. As we do not have many reports of humanoids in the observations of the military expedition of the time, this needs to be checked in detail.

In the period of the phenomena you lived in Belem and then went to Paraná. What made you come back and write a book?

When I got back, I still had no idea of the size of the suck-suck phenomenon. At that time, that mixture of panic, popular belief, and collective paranoia remained in the air, since nobody imagined how serious the extent of this phenomenology was. That's when I became aware of the magnitude of the UFO Phenomenon.

You had a little time with Colonel Uyrangê Hollanda in the 1980s, and you were able to discuss these manifestations with him. What were the conversations about events witnessed on the coast like?

By the time I met Hollanda, I realized that he was a very enthusiastic person in

Ufology. He even had contact with researcher Rafael Sempere Durá [UFO consultant who died two years ago]. They presented some things in common, and it was Durá who showed the military several Ufological mysteries. Hollanda had a vision of his own about the lollipop. For him, beings would be collecting biological material and human plasma for an immunological research. He thought that ETs – yes, he believed they were extraterrestrial beings – collected antibodies and searched for lymphocytes or cells for future contact.

Is your impression of Hollanda the same as that prevailing today in the Brazilian UFO Society, a person sincerely dedicated to understanding the phenomenon and who was frustrated when Operation Plate was prematurely closed in December 1977?

Exactly. Colonel Hollanda, at the time, showed great interest in how to regain or recover the UFO material recorded during Operation Plate, which had been dispatched by the commander of the First Regional Air Command (Comar) to Brasilia. He also thought of writing his memoirs, recounting this whole process and presenting his opinion on the wave. Of course he was annoyed, but since he was very loyal to the Armed Forces, he accepted their decisions. He was also very open-minded, so much so that he even submitted much of the reports of the operation to Bob Pratt,

Do you believe that the other members of Operation Plate, especially the Brigadier Protásio Lopes de Oliveira and the higher hierarchy of the I Comar, shared the ideas of Hollanda?

I once interviewed Brigadier Protasius, who said he had seen the films, reports and photos resulting from the mission in the jungle, but I do not know if he shared the ideas of Hollanda. What I know is that his opinion was that it did not convince anyone in the military at all. Everyone in the Comar thought they were just lights or something, and that there was nothing conclusive. I believe that they might find the document prepared by Hollanda weak, with no concrete or palpable evidence of the existence of ships in the region, and that it would be ridiculous to expose it to the public.

Do you think that if such a report had a better or more substantial content, would the authorities open it up to the population?

I remember an episode presented by Sergeant Flavio, who because of the desire to get a more concrete proof of the phenomena, almost led a team of soldiers into an extremely dangerous situation in which they would be true human guinea pigs for the extraterrestrial beings. They wanted closer contact and it was suggested by the military that one group be on a beach and another, hidden in the bush – both to wait for the flying saucers to attack them.

Did such action occur during Operation Plate and with the consent of Colonel Hollanda? Could this attitude have been motivated by a feeling of frustration at not having something concrete about the manifestations?

This happened during the military mission, but Colonel Hollanda refused to accompany the men and did not allow them to commit such madness. There was a sense of frustration, yes, and I even think they underestimated the human injuries, not photographing the details of the victims and even making a more technical report on the phenomenon. I even asked Hollanda if there was a parallel document from the team's medical committee, for example, but he said there was nothing more than what they were doing.

Does it mean, then, that there was a certain resistance within the Comar around the research activities of Operation Plate? Was there a group that did not think it was right to conduct such research?

What I learned later is that the investigations started, in fact, as an incentive toward the mayors from the interior, from the areas hit by the lollipop, especially from the municipality of Vigia. Jose Ildone Favacho, who sent a letter to the command saying that the population was scared. Favacho asked the military for help, as there were objects flying over the region and urgent steps should be taken. It was then Brigadier Protasius ordered that such a matter be investigated. The city of Vigia is located 93 km from Belém and is a place almost hidden in the edges of the Bay of Marajó, behind the Island of Colares.

Was there, then, concern of the Aeronautics on the subject, to the point of having the phenomena analyzed?

Yes, but at first there was a suspicion by the I Comar that the aerial demonstrations were in actuality guerrilla maneuvers. It was thought that a new outbreak of communist guerrillas was emerging in the area and that they were using military apparatus to drive the population from its base. The Aeronautics never thought that they were UFOs, ships of non-terrestrial origin. Initially, they thought that they were sophisticated warfare devices to foil the people, for the clandestine landing of armaments or ammunition, which had already ended the military repression in 1977. But such a theory was soon dismissed as officials began to look at inner cities and saw the fantastic things that were in the sky.

Do you believe that the higher-up military personnel of the Armed Forces, especially Brigadier Protasius, personally went to the affected places to witness the events?

Yes, because there was an episode in which ships were mobilized to make tests and see what was really happening in the region. Such maneuvers of recognition are also described in the report of Operation Plate. They used a helicopter, with which they made a nocturnal flight on the Island of Colares, coming from the Bay of the Guajará towards the village, in a silent way. They intended to see the reaction of the population to the device, since they were maneuvering about with the spotlights of the aircraft on. But people soon realized that it was a military mission and did not overly react. They saw only one plane, unlike the lights that attacked them. They were very different. That was in October or November of 1977. The officers of Operation Plate never imagined that they would come across UFOs, and did not even think to investigate such a subject. That was when a certain skepticism began to emerge within the I Comar itself. The subject became a joke and I think that was why the colonel chose to silence the report on the expedition.

Other academic or research institutions were consulted on the demonstrations taking place on the islands?

No. As far as I know, none of them got involved. At times I even wondered why the scientific community, the biologists, geologists, physicists and engineers of the Federal University of Pará (UFPA), for example, were not consulted by the Brazilian Air Force (FAB). And simply there was no interest from any state institution. The chupa-chupa subject was treated as a collective hysteria or popular belief within colleges. Not even the civilian scientific community organized itself to see what it was about. Then things were right in our noses and we were not able to get any cooperation from anyone it seems.

Thus the contacts that happened in the region went unnoticed, but many reports heard in Colares are like the films of Steven Spielberg, stupefying. A resident of the locality told me an interesting episode about a ship that parked near Guajará Bay. They were probes that were almost 2 m in diameter. Such objects made low flights over the village, through the streets and alleys, and stayed close to the trees. They moved like the Smoke Squadron aircraft and then drove away. The witness, last we heard, is a teacher in Colares, but at the time she witnessed such a fact, she was a young girl and would have been 14 years old. I do not know if such a story could be invented, but the fact was confirmed by the father and other people who also saw the lights. There were many such cases.

Of all the cases you have followed, investigated, or just heard, which do you consider the most notorious or impressive?

Of all these episodes, I think there are three very important ones. A fact observed by Colonel Hollanda himself on the Rio Guajará-Mirim, which flows near the region of Mosqueiro Island, is one of them. In this locality there was a pottery and a shop of photographic material of a certain Paulo Coefer, where the soldiers bought their equipment. The merchant advised one of the military that a victim of the lollipop was nearby and a team was detached to investigate the fact. The boy said that he went to the edge of the creek to get clay to make bricks and tiles. When he arrived at the place, he decided to hunt inside the woods, since the tide was low, with no danger of being caught by surprise by the waters.

What time of day was this fact and what happened then?

It was late afternoon, at about 6:00 pm, when the boy took his shotgun and set up a kind of mutá observation post built in tall trees, where the hunters wait for the passage of animals in the woods. As soon as it darkened he noticed a very intense light coming from the forest, and inside he observed a floating humanoid. It was when he jumped from where he was and ran into the bush. He panicked and ran, especially when he realized the light was on him. Looking back, he saw that the creature was following. He arrived panting by the river, got into the boat, and left. Because of this episode the military established an observation point at this location.

And how were the other cases?

In that same area, Colonel Hollanda told me something had struck him. He saw at night a cylindrical object the size of a Boeing, which silently crossed the river, about 1,000 m away. It was just above the treetops, horizontally. He prepared his camcorder to record the demonstration and minutes later the same artifact was already upright. At first, it fired something like a lightning bolt that flashed into the sky.

And the last case of an attack that most impressed you?

It was the story of Mr. Manuel Noronha, who saw a ship flying over his house in the city of Santo Antonio do Tauá, some 30 km from Colares. He observed a cylindrical shaped object with two beings inside, who looked at him. The villager was willing to shoot at the creatures to get them to leave, but when he thought about it the object cast a light on him. Noronha felt numb all over his body, as if paralyzed. Then he screamed for help and the ship just disappeared. This story is very interesting, since it was the first one that involved a contact with humanoid creatures.

Do you believe that the local population changed their habits after the investigations of researchers, the action of the military authorities and the press?

It's interesting, but it did. Before the intervention of the press, the researchers and even the police, the population presented faithful, simple accounts. But then people started to get scared. I remember that when I interviewed a gentleman named Manuel, he gave me some information about his experience. Later I learned from a neighbor that he thought I was from the federal or civil police, so I did not want to go into details. The villager had a gun and tried to shoot a flying saucer, and I believe he omitted this information for fear. At that time, how many other people were afraid to talk to the police?

Have you re-interviewed the victims of the lollipop attacks after these events, to see if anything has changed in their lives?

Yes. I met again two people who were burned by the lightning bolts and they told me that their health was never the same. They used to get sick a lot, they had severe headaches and they always had a bad headache. Maybe it was just a coincidence, but after the end of Operation Plate all the people involved with the lollipop had to wear glasses. It was Sergeant Flavio who called my attention to this, which made everyone think about it. Of one thing I am sure: we are all more open to the Ufological question, because the facts have shifted, along with the psychological world of each one of us.

You were the person who initiated the spread of these phenomena, causing many Ufologists to engage in this research. In your opinion, what has been missing? What is there left to reveal about the lollipop, and what can be done so many years after the closing of the wave?

First, a more exhaustive field survey, because I think we covered only 20% of the area hit, or less even, reaping 10% of the total data that can be revealed. That is, the demonstrations happened from the Baixada Maranhense, passing through the municipalities of Bequimão, Bragança and Maracanã. There are areas in the Lower Amazon that we never visited. So we would have to have support to involve researchers from various regions to analyze these sites and collect reports in a more technical way.

Do you believe that there is still evidence or people that can be researched and that would present important new data?

I think so. It seems that there are some sensitive points, because still today there are activities, especially in Colares. Colonel Hollanda even suggested that there might be submarine bases in this region, for the ships mysteriously disappeared. Thus, there were two possibilities: either they were at the bottom of the Atlantic Ocean or in Earth orbit. The choice was made for the belief that flying saucers were hidden in the water, because objects always came in the direction of the sea to the mainland, not the other way around, or the rivers to land. It would be interesting also if we could analyze and evaluate the documents of Operation Plate, so that the data of the researchers and military were complete. The mission investigated basically the region of Vigia, Colares and some localities near Belém, such as São Miguel do Guamá, Santo Antonio do Tauá and Benevides, but did not analyze the Baixada Maranhense or the Low Amazon, such as the Strait of Breves and Monte Alegre. No military activity was carried out in these places.

Do you intend to meet the insistent claims of many UFO researchers to supplement, update and relaunch your book, which is a very important document about this phenomenon?

If we can get resources, it will be possible to reissue the publication, since at the time of launch we had many difficulties. No one financed the book, not even the State Government. We made a private issue and because of that many photos and maps were not included. I still have this stuff, but I need to update it.

What message would you leave to UFO readers who still have many questions about Operation Plate?

I think we were privileged with the possibility of contemplating the cases of the lollipop. I have no news of a UFO wave as intense and disturbing as was this

ALIEN BLOOD LUST

wave, nowhere in the world. It was an ugly mega-event, behind which there were extraterrestrial logistics. This led the military to understand that they were dealing not with a military organization, but with an alien force, which also had ships and objects of various forms. The involvement of the Armed Forces was also crucial. So we had the perfect wedding – social and Ufological events – an odd file on the UFO Phenomenon in national and worldwide casuistry.

Above: Daniel Rebisso Giese.

Below: UFOs were seen flying over the Amazon, shooting beams of light that would paralyze people caught in the horrifying glare.
Credits: Daniel Rebisso Giese

ALIEN BLOOD LUST

CHAPTER 13

> Light Blinds Better in the Dark

THE PHENOMENON "CHUPA-CHUPA" IN AMAZONIA, INCLUDING AN OVERVIEW OF MEDIA ACCOUNTS OF THE PHENOMENON AND MORE RELEVANT DETAILS FROM DR. GIESE

In Amazonia, UFOs are called "aparelhos" (machines) by victims and the violence by these extraterrestrials, principally in their attacks on women, have characterized an odd phenomenon: "chupa-chupa." [Suck-Suck]

Daniel Rebisso Giese—Grupo Ufologico da Amazonia (GUA)

INTRODUCTION

In the decade of the 1970s, strange phenomena began to occur on the coast and interior of the states of Para' and Maranhao. News came from all parts and the depositions were unanimous: mysterious light beams, projected from unidentified flying objects, which in the majority of cases appeared at night, were burning men and women. Chasing people, taking blood from its victims, originating the expression "CHUPA-CHUPA," a name by which the phenomenon became popularly known. In other regions, principally in Maranhao, the phenomenon became known by the name "APARELHO."

The phenomenon, in spite of a long hatching period, manifested itself with a force and consistency never before seen in the history of the national Ufology. In a few short weeks, the news ran throughout the entire States of Para' and Maranhao, taking the population by surprise, generating a climate of terror and collective panic. Motivated by curiosity, and with the objective to shed light on the chupa-chupa mystery, we undertook a research which took us to several counties of Para'. But, due to our modest financial resources and available time, it was not possible for us to cover all of Para' and Maranhao. We hope that in the near future someone will be able to complete this research.

What we will be exposing in this article won't consist of fables created by backwoodsmen or diverse residents of the interior and coast of Para'. We will be faithful to the facts and rendered depositions. Each interview was taken with attention and care. This way, we selected the most coherent reports, whose rela-

Inspired mind Imprints create impressive, Expressive Especially
when Generated By Invisible, Intelligent, Interdimensional, Beings who are people
a write
Legal
ALIEN BLOOD LUST without Bodies -

tionships with other depositions, added to the competence of the testimonials and constituted bearing elements. The objective of this work is to trace a real picture and an historical outline of one of the most impressive Ufological manifestations which we could know.

NEWSPAPER ANNOUNCEMENTS:

The first part of this research constitutes a bibliographical survey of all articles and reports published in the periodicals of Para' such as A PROVINCIA DO PARA', O LIBERAL, and ESTADO DO PARA'. However, the same was not possible, for the reasons previously described, with the press of Maranhao. We read all the articles of the cited periodicals and feel that the press of Para' related in a very interesting form the development of the chupa-chupa phenomenon. All of the articles were heavily illustrated and taken at the locations of incidence, together with the testimonials... If today we are able to reconstitute this Ufological wave, it is due to the press and the care of the Public Library of Bele'm.

Several ufological news forecasted the Chupa-Chupa wave, but the most significant article was in O LIBERAL, 7-16-77, where we read: "The UFO photographed in Montevideo, spherical shape, compares in detail with the strange objects seen at several locations in Para', along the Maranhao side of the Gurupi River and along the entire Para'-Maranhao border. Just yesterday, these objects were observed at several locations in the interior of Maranhao, frightening the population, similar to what occurs in the area of Vizeu in Para'."

A few days before, precisely on 7-12-77, the JORNAL DA BAHIA reported in a clear manner what would become the phenomenon Chupa-Chupa:

"Flying object which emits fantastic light frightens Para': Bele'm (AJB) — A fantastic story of a flying object emitting a strong light and sucking blood from people, circulated from mouth to mouth among the population of the counties of Braganca, Vizeu and Augusto Correa in Para', where many people fear leaving their homes during the night so they won't get caught by the vampire-like light from the strange object which, according to information, already has caused the death of two men. No one knows how the story started, but the truth is that it reached Bele'm and grabbed headlines in the local newspapers."

Months later, on October 8, O LIBERAL launched the first in a series of reports, giving the population knowledge of what was the chupa-chupa phenomenon. The report begins in a taxing manner: "Sucking animal attacks men and women in the village of Vigia: A strange phenomenon has been occurring for several weeks in the village of Vigia, more exactly in the Vila Santo Antonio do Imbituba about 7 kilometers from highway PA-140, with the appearance of an object which focuses a white light over people, immobilizing them for around an hour, and sucks the breasts of the women leaving them bleeding. The object, known by the locals as "Bicho Voador" [Flying Animal], or "Bicho Sugador" [Sucking Animal], has the shape of a rounded ship and attacks people (principally women) in isolation, in spite of it also having attacked some men... One of the victims, among many in the area, was Mrs. Rosita Ferreira, married, 46 years old, resident of Ramal do Triunfo, who a few days ago was sucked by the light on the left breast, and passed out. Increasingly it looked like dealing with a nightmare, feeling as if there were some claws trying to hold her. She was attacked around 3:30 in the morning. Another victim was the lady known as 'Chiquita,' who was also sucked by the strange object with her breast becoming bloody, but without leaving any marks."

CHUPA-CHUPA:

It was then on 10-16-77, that O LIBERAL launched for the first time the expression "Chupa-Chupa," as we read in the first paragraph of this report: "Chupa-Chupa: That was the denomination given by the population of Vigia to an unidentified flying object, which has brought to panic the dwellers of Imbituba, Camaru and Km-25, as well as other localities situated in the vicinity of those cities."

Henceforth, until the end of mid-November 1977, the newspapers of Para' did not hesitate to bring to the public articles on the chupa-chupa. The newspaper A PROVINCIA DO PARA' brought, on 10-20-77, 11-19-77 and 11-20-77, valuable reports for Ufological investigation. On October 20 there were two full pages with popular depositions, graphics of UFO evolution in the skies of Vigia and the strange CI 2 [Hynek's CE-I] occurrence with colonist Manoel Matos de Souza (known as Coronha), registered in the small village of Monte Serrado, county of Santo Antonio de Taua' (PA).

This farmer, 44 years old, was awakened around 2 to 3 am by a strong light which circled his area and penetrated his shack. On opening the door, he met with a flying object with two creatures in its interior. He returned to this room, and now armed with ammunition, he tried to fire in the vehicle's direction. To his surprise, the weapon did not fire and, feeling paralysis overcoming his body by the light from the UFO, screamed for help.

On 11-19-77, A PROVINCIA DO PARA' published, for the first time, photographs of possible lesions of chupa-chupa, registered on the young Aurora Nascimento Fernandes, 18 years old, resident at Passagem Tabatinga, in the Jurunas neighborhood (Bele'm). Aurora found herself washing dishes around 9 p.m. on 11-18-77 in her home when a strong gush of cold air surprised her in conjunction with a strong, reddish light. The young lady relates: "I became frightened. I called my mother and before she arrived, a strong red light enveloped me, making me dazed. At the same time, I felt really fine piercings striking my breast, and fell to the floor, having fainted."

Afterwards, Dr. Orlando Zoghbi, after seeing the patient, said her case was an episode of hysteria and panic produced by the collective psychosis around the chupa-chupa phenomenon. According to Dr. Zoghbi, by the configuration of the marks, the wounds present on Aurora's right breast were caused by the contraction of her hands clutching (over the breast), in an instinctive act of protection at the possible chupa-chupa attack. We loudly disagree, because the same appeared to be concentrated and deep (like biopsies) within a small area; no traces of scratches and the wounds did not possess a fingernail configuration.

In conversation with UFO phenomenon researcher and student, Professor Fabio Zerpa (ONIFE)1, he observed similar facts, ahead of the described picture by Aurora and other women of Para' who said they were chupa-chupa victims, occurring in southern Argentina in the 70s where one women was attacked by an entity which took blood. It is interesting to note that the described events occurred in cities and villages in proximity to rivers, lakes or seas. This makes us recall the Japanese mythological entities called the "kappas," which, according to legend, came from a distant star and populated the rivers (or seas) of Japan.

Researchers Scornaux and Piens, in their excellent work "A Descoberta dos OVNIs" [The Discovery of UFOs], relate: "Kappas appear to use a submarine, or something of the like, provisioned with a respiratory device as well as some strange helmet with antennas. The ears are abnormally large. The skin is copper-colored (see the men of bronze who appeared at the Utinga reservoir, county of Bele'm, during the chupa-chupa period) and the hands and feet are hook-like. This description reminds us of some humanoid ETs observed in our day, and the reputation which the Kappas had, of making ill the people who came in proximity to them, makes us think of the physiological effects experimented on some current witnesses."

THE PHENOMENON IN COLARES:

The island of Colares is located around 70 kilometers northeast the city of Bele'm. It bounds the county of Vigia, another region rich in apparitions and Ufological cases. To its front is the Bay of Marajo~ which finds itself separated from the continent by the river Guajara'-Mirim. Colares comprises an area 600 square kilometers, approximately, and harbors several communities, such as Vila de Colares (the county seat), Fazenda, Mocajatuba, Ariri and others. Its population, in great part, is dedicated to fishing and agriculture.

During the chupa-chupa period, Colares was the target of intense UFO apparitions and several victims of the mysterious rays were detected. The fear was so much that a good part of the island residents abandoned their homes and temporarily went to reside with their parents in other counties.

CIPEX2 located several witnesses to the phenomenon during the days which it stayed in Colares. We look at a few cases:

1. (a) Jonas Ferreira Gondim, 60 years old, a married fisherman, confesses that in that time his house was illuminated by the chupa light. Taken with courage, he went outside to the yard and fired a June firecracker to scare away the

"aparelho." His son, Claudio Gondin, related to us: "During that time, we did not sleep right. I and some other colleagues went out for vigils at the home of friends. One night, I saw that machine over the treetops, there on S. Joa~o street. It suddenly stopped and emitted a clear light on top of the trees and right away climbed at great velocity towards another side of the village."

2. (b) Mr. Zacarias dos Santos Barata, 74 years old, married, confesses: "I saw this machine around two times. The first time, it came from the direction of Soure' (Marajo' Island) and cruised the village really fast. On the other time, I saw here from the house when a luminous ball came lighting up all of the Luzio countryside. It wasn't making any noise and it was not enough to see how it was correctly, for the light was very strong and of a bluish color." The same was observed by his neighbor, Julio de Brito Correia, 70 years old, adding solely that the ship flew low and at great speed.

3. (c) The carpenter Carlos Cardoso de Paula, 45 years old, married, describes two curious events. We see: "In the time of the chupa, many times I left at night to visit the homes of friends and colleagues. The majority of them would meet on the street making a bonfire and frying fish. Once in a while, they would make noise with guns and cans to scare the chupa... One time, at leaving the house around 21:00 hours, we heard the people yell: "There goes the chupa"; here from the house I only saw when a ball of fire came running in our direction, but soon it changed headings, entering into another street. A strange thing occurred another time, second account: "We were all asleep in the house and I was still smoking the last cigarette when all of a sudden, through the house's roof ridge, entered a small ball of fire. That thing started to ride around the room until it came next to my hammock. It climbed up my right leg up to the knee. I regarded all of this with much curiosity when that small ball passed to the other leg and I started to feel weak and sleepy. The cigarette fell from my hand and, scared of that situation, I screamed. The small ball disappeared and everyone woke up. I think it was looking for a vein in my body, but it didn't have any luck... When it would increase in brightness, I would feel a kind of heat..."

PROBES:

The account of Mr. Carlos de Paula, besides the bizarre, indicates to us that that small ball, in reality, could be a matter of a probe, for the described characteristics by the witness so indicate. During our research, we located two people in the Vila de Colares who were victims of the chupa-chupa. The clinical picture of this phenomenon will be better detailed with the description of the accounts which we gathered there.

The first one was of the merchant Neuton de Oliveira Cardoso, 27 years old, married and who, at the time, resided in the Vila de Mocajatuba. One night, he woke up ill, feeling a "heat" throughout the body and, frightened, noticed that he was burned to the height of the neck on the left side. Family members took him on the following day to the Vila dos Colares for the medical appointment owed. Neuton comments: "I became very weak and without courage during various days and still feel a strong torture and headache." The second victim was Mrs. Claudomira Rogrigues da Paixã~o, 43 years old, married, popularly known as "Mirota." She was hit in the breast by the chupa-chupa light when sleeping at her parents' house. It was around midnight and she slept in the hammock next to the window. She was surprised by an intense glare; quickly, she felt a heat over her body that paralyzed her, after which a focused beam of greenish light was projected over her thorax and then quickly withdrawn.

During the next several days, she felt a great weakness and strong headaches which occasionally still return to bother her. Later, she was led to the Instituto Medico Legal Renato Chaves (Bele'm) for complimentary exams. Years ago, inclusive, she had the visit of two foreign researchers who arrived together with an interpreter at the island in a single-engine plane. Mrs. Claudomira certifies: "During the instant the fire struck me, I felt holes like from needles over my chest. Later, I did not feel any pain, unless you count headaches and a great laziness which kept me in the hammock for several days..."

SECRET ACCOUNTS:

At the start of the rumors of curious Ufological apparitions in the interior of Para' and in Maranhao, increased by the panic of the population about the phenomenon, the 1st Regional Aerial Command (1st COMAR) 3, located in Bele'm, activated an exhaustive field operation with the intent of clearing up the chupa-chupa phenomenon enigma. The command's order was the following:

1. The UFO phenomenon merits a deep and objective study;

2. All relevant information on the phenomenon needs to be gathered;

3. Public announcements and commentary about the subject need to be avoided.

During the time, the Air Force sent researchers to several counties where the presence of UFOs was detected, in such a way that hundreds of reports of the first and second degrees and around 200 photographs of strange objects, UFOs, were gathered. The most rich locations were Baia do Sol (Ilha de Mosqueiro) and the Ilha de Colares (Para'). In these regions several UFO photographs were obtained, mostly nocturnal, and some films of short duration registering the ships' evolution.

The majority of the photographs were taken with professional cameras (Cannon, Nikon) coupled and tele-aimed, utilizing Kodak 1000 ASA film, black and white, with the equipment belonging to the military. At the end of the field investigation, the second phase of the operation was initiated which included the elaboration of a report and analysis of the recognized data. This report, around 500 pages, including photographs of UFOs, drawings, maps, records of interviews and clippings of local newspapers, was sent to the military high command (EMFA), together with all the existing photographic documentation (films, negatives, photograph copies).

The obtained results of this far away work demonstrates that the chupa-chupa phenomenon was genuine and of a Ufological nature, being difficult to specify with objectivity the origin and purpose of the same.

EVIDENCE:

In Ufological research, it is not sufficient to gather and archive cases. It is necessary to test them, compare them with others and submit them to several criticisms (both internally and externally).

The climate that the 1977 Para' wave generated in the breast of the population is complex and rich in data; all of society's sectors were hit and the divulged opinions are the most diverse possible. The press effected an excellent job, addressing on one side the skepticism of the higher authorities; and, on the other side, the inexperienced groping of the Ufological camp. However, these small flaws are understandable and natural. But, the same judgment is not valid when we denounce the scientific, political and military community's position, which still insists on hiding themselves under old anti-Ufological pretexts. This omission was expected, being in part deliberate.

Tactics of this nature are well-recognized among researchers and publicists of the UFO reality, as were the Air Force's secret research, the ridicule, the "prophets" announcing the arrival of the Martians and, as always, the confusion tactic of the prejudiced affirmations of some liberal professionals with their "famous" convenient explanations.

CONCLUSIONS:

This research, despite its limitations, allowed us an adequate sampling of the 70s Ufological wave in Para'. We emphasize some points:

1. The zone of action was the north of Brazil, being frequent the sightings on the edges of rivers and of the Atlantic Ocean;

2. The UFOs surfaced, in the majority of times, at night, being rare the sightings during the day;

3. The depositions confirm the presence of ships – not always coming from high and disappearing in the sky;

4. Whatever the small ships, everything indicates they were about probes, due to their aerodynamic and behavioral profile, such as round extremely luminous objects, rapid movements, low altitude flying, emission of luminous beams and chasing people;

5. The burns produced by the UFOs were not accidental, but demonstrated an

ALIEN BLOOD LUST

objective. Men and women were the aim, preferably targeted when they slept;

6. There is no complete proof that the UFOs removed blood from their victims; on the other hand, the biochemical and clinical exams performed by Dr. Wellaide Carvalho and C.C. de Oliveira attest to the lower numbers of hemoglobin in the hemogram from the victims, besides the quite peculiar clinical picture of people who have lost considerable blood (fainting, chronic headaches, body weaknesses, preventing the victims from standing on their feet) including the presence of diminutive "prick marks" in the regions hit by the beams from the UFOs;

7. Informational references about the occupants of the ships were few, but they point to the presence of beings of below/medium stature, greenish and wrinkled skin;

8. There is a specific objective of great importance which precipitated the UFOs invasion of coastal Para' and Maranhao.

Everything leads us to believe that the global phenomenon was a mission of great scope, not only by the frequency of sightings, but by the great number of sighted objects. The zones incidental were chosen due to their strategic positions and by the security which they gave to the action of the UFOs (geographic isolation, far apart and small population centers). The objective of that invasion was related (possibly) with the research and biological manipulation of man on the part of the aliens, whose purpose in the meantime we are unable to elucidate.

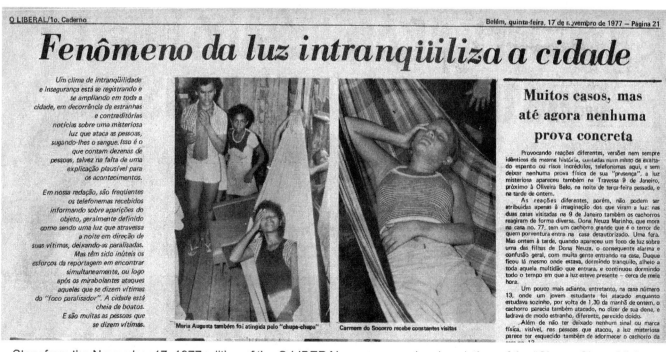

Story from the November 17, 1977 edition of the *O LIBERAL* newspaper showing victims of the "Chupa-Chupa" lights. The headline literally translates as "Light Phenomenon Makes the City Uneasy."

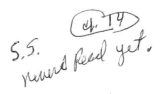

CHAPTER 14

COLONEL HOLLANDA BRAVELY SPEAKS OUT

In 1997, Colonel Uyrange Hollanda bravely chose to speak out in an interview with the Brazilian "UFO Magazine." A partial transcript follows.

UFO Magazine - If you have created a file, then it tells us that there has already been some progresses in the investigation?

Hollanda - Yes, when I arrived from Brasilia I already had agents who had been sent to investigate occurrences of UFOs, because this thing was already happening so often in the area of Colares, which belongs to the city of Vigia, on the coast of Pará.

The mayor of the city sent an officer to the commander of COMAR to inform him that the UFOs were bothering the fishing very much. Some of them could not conduct the routine fishing activity anymore, because the objects navigated under their boats. At times, some objects even dived near to them, in the rivers and in the sea. The local population spent the night outside. The people set up fires and used firecrackers to try to drive the invaders away. It was the panic that made the mayor contact the command of COMAR, asking for instructions, and the Brigadier General ordered that I was to investigate the sightings.

UFO Magazine - Was there at some point a participation or instruction from Brasilia (Ed.: the capital; i.e. the government) so that the situation is inquired?

Hollanda - At the time, it did not participate in the discussions. There was only one captain and he received only orders. I was no part of this proceeding and I do not know with certainty as of the decisions that had been taken. But, for the little that I know, the decision was in the hands of the command of COMAR. If it had the involvement of Brasilia, I do not know about it.

UFO Magazine - How did you organize Operation Plate? How many sections, how many people, how many missions etc.? And did you organize all the tasks?

Hollanda - Well, we were a team. I was at the head of it. We had five agents, all sergeants, that worked in the second division of COMAR. Moreover, we had in-

ALIEN BLOOD LUST

formers on location, people in the places where the lights appeared, on the field that helped them. At the time I divided the team in two or three different positions in the country. Clearly, we were constantly in contact with one another, through radio.

UFO Magazine - What was the immediate objective of Operation Plate? To observe flying disks, to photograph them and to contact them?

Hollanda - As a matter of fact I wanted to test this thing off exactly and completely. I wanted to explain it and clear it out. Because everybody spoke of the lights and objects and had even nicknamed them with popular names, such as "chupa-chupa" (Ed.: "suck-suck" or "absorb-absorb"). And, the Brazilian Air Forces needed to know what was really happening, since this occurred in the Brazilian airspace. The responsibility to inquire was ours. But in the beginning of Operation Plate, what I really wanted was a confirmation that the events were happening.

Drain

UFO Magazine - What motivated the local population to call the lights "chupa-chupa?"

Hollanda - There was a series of stories of people who had been touched by a light ray. All judged that the effect of the ray was to suck blood out of them. And actually we verified some cases and we discovered that several of them, mainly women, had the strangest marks on their left breast, and there were two needle punctures around a brown spot. It looked like iodine burning. And those people had their blood sucked out, in small amounts, by those lights.

Therefore they had started to nickname them "chupa-chupa." It was always the same thing: a light came out of nothing and followed somebody, generally a woman, who was hit on the left breast. At some times they were men who were hit, with marks in the arms and (pemas.) To tell you the truth, in ten cases, there were more or less eight women and two men.

UFO Magazine - And you have recorded and checked the marks on the people?

Hollanda - Yes, it was all checked and analyzed by doctors, who went with us to the locations at the time. Sincerely, I entered in this as the devil's advocate. What I exactly wanted was to demystify this story and to say to my commander that this thing did not exist, that it was a collective hallucination. I found that some things were being seen, but that it was not extraterrestrial.

UFO Magazine - What did you think it was, then, that was being seen and attacked the people?

Hollanda - I do not know. Perhaps the plumage of an owl reflecting the light of the moon or some other thing of this sort. It was thought it might be extraterrestrial, but I did not think so. I went there to verify that this thing was really happening. I spent at least two months trying to get an answer for my commander, but when I came back from the mission, I had discovered nothing.

During the first two months of Operation Plate, I saw nothing that could change my opinion. At one point we spent one week in the weeds and came back on Sunday. We lived a little bit like a family. At each report, my commander asked:

"Did you see something?" And my response was always: "We saw strange lights, at least, but nothing extraterrestrial." In fact, we saw lights that never blinked, that passed at a low altitude, but nothing very strange.

UFO Magazine - This was during the night. What happened during the day? Were there other activities during Operation Plate?

Hollanda - Yes, we had other things to do, that were part of the objectives of the operation. We conducted interviews with people who had had experiences, we prepared the places to spend the night and searched "hot" spots for night watches. We made a survey of the situation, and we always registered the names of the people involved in a proper form.

UFO Magazine - What procedure or methodology was used to collect information?

Hollanda - We always recorded the name of the person who had the experience, the place where it occurred, the date and time, etc. We made a description of each fact that occurred in the same locality. Thus, if three cases in a night happened, people heard three witnesses. Some of the descriptions were common, the others were stranger. At times, we received stories about things that we could not prove to be authentic, as in the dematerialization of entire walls or roofs, for example.

UFO Magazine - What do you mean? Do you have some example to illustrate this type of event?

Hollanda - Yes. The first lady that I interviewed in Colares, for example, told me absurd things. We came by the helicopter from Belém just to hear a woman who had been attacked by the chupa-chupa. We really did see that she had a mark in the left breast. It was brown, as if it was a burn, and had a series of holes in a line. When we talked, she told me that she was seated in a net trying to put a child to sleep when, suddenly, the environment started to change its temperature. She found it rather pleasant, but she could not imagine what happened next. Then, lying in the net, she saw that the roofing tiles had started to be colored, in a coal-like color. After that, they became transparent, and she could see the sky through the roof. It was as if the roofing tiles had turned into glass. She saw the sky and even the stars.

UFO Magazine - Were strange stories such as this very common during Operation Plate?

Hollanda - Very common, and it scared me a lot, because I had never heard anyone speak about such things. When I heard of such cases, I was both worried and even more curious. These people seemed to be sincere. For example, through the hole that the woman described she saw a green light shining in the sky. The

ALIEN BLOOD LUST

lady was half asleep, until, after that, a red ray that left the UFO reached her left breast. It was strange that in the majority of the cases the people were hit at their left side. There was more: exactly at the time where we were speaking of this, a girl came to us and said:

"Look at the thing that is passing above." When I left the house, I saw the light that the young girl was pointing at, flying at a reasonable speed. It was not very quick and it blinked as it was going to the North. It looked like a satellite, except that this light turned back on its route – and satellites do not do this!

Soon after that, there was something even stranger. But I could not exactly say if it was an extraterrestrial ship. By the way, I was not there to cover up anything that appeared to be a flying disk.

UFO Magazine - Did you use some type of radar equipment that could confirm or follow these phenomena?

Hollanda - No. All the airports have fixed radars. We did not carry anything of this type.

UFO Magazine - Were the attacks that were happening with a certain frequency communicated to the Government, to the state or municipal authorities?

Hollanda - Yes, clearly. Some doctors of the Ministry of Public Health of Pará had been sent by the government to examine the people. They analyzed the burnt skins and took the patients statements, but they did not do anything more than that – never. Some victims recovered easily. Others were very terrified. Some were nauseated or fell asleep for days. A citizen once came to look for me and said that next to his house a light had appeared, that focused a shining ray towards him. He told me that he had been so terrified that he ran inside his house, grabbed a weapon and pointed it to the light. Then stronger rays came and caused him to fall. The poor men spent two weeks with locomotion problems (Ed.: Because he fell), but did not have anything more serious.

He had not been hit by anything solid, as a gunshot, for example. It seems that the nature of this light was that of a very strong energy that left people paralyzed. I believe that the federal authorities were informed that this type of attack on human beings were happening in the region, but I am unaware of any tests. I only received orders from my commander, nothing more.

UFO Magazine - If these depositions had been collected since the beginning of Operation Plate, when did the first close encounters with UFOS in that region begin?

Hollanda - It was sufficiently significant. On a certain night, our team was searching the Island of Mosqueiro, in a place called Bahia do Sol (Ed.: Sun Bay) (Publisher: a well-known health-resort of Belém, near Colares), therefore we had information that these things were happening there. And as we were investigating any and all indications of Ufological occurrences, we settled ourselves in the place.

ALIEN BLOOD LUST

In this period, the agents who had more time than I to devote to this operation – since "I caught the train when it was already started" – they questioned me all the time, after they saw some lights, as if I was already convinced of the existence of the phenomenon. As I was still undecided, they said to me: "But captain, do you still not believe?" I answered that I didn't, that we needed more tests to believe that those things were flying disks. I had not seen any ships at that time. Only lights, many and varied. I was still not satisfied

****

Less than two months after this interview, Hollanda was found hanged inside his home. While the official investigation declared his death to be a suicide, there are some who suspect that the incident involved much more than that.

Documents from the infamous Operation Plate were released by the Brazilian military in late 2009, and four years later officials from the Brazilian Air Force, Navy and Army joined forces with civilian UFO researchers to further investigate the UFO phenomenon.

SUGGESTED READING

UFO DANGER ZONE by Bob Pratt

UFO HOSTILITIES AND THE EVIL ALIEN AGENDA by Beckley, Casteel, Swartz (others)

UFOS AT CLOSE SIGHT: https://ufologie.patrickgross.org

FLYING SAUCER REVIEW: http://www.fsr.org.uk/

VIDEO AND AUDIO (Mostly in Spanish): https://bataklagu.com

REVISTA UFO MAGAZINE (BRAZIL): https://ufo.com.br/

Live Broadcast with Tim Swartz and Tim Beckley

Exploring The Bizarre - Live Thursdays at 10 PM Eastern/7 Pacific

www.KCORradio.com

Our YouTube channel - "Mr. UFO's Secret Files"

Over 400 interviews and videos posted.

SECTION THREE
A JOURNEY INTO THE DARKNESS OF CHUPACABRAS LAND

Scott Corrales—Blood Oath Of The Chupacabras
by Tim Beckley

ALIEN BLOOD LUST

INTRODUCTION

SCOTT CORRALES – BLOOD OATH OF THE CHUPACABRAS
By Timothy Green Beckley

One of the benefits of editing nationally-distributed magazines in the field, like "UFO Universe" (which I did for eleven years), is that I got to read the articles submitted by our regular contributors ahead of anyone else.

I always looked forward to receiving something new and original in the mail (no internet) from a Pennsylvania writer who knew UFOs inside out when it came to the appearance of the OVNI phenomenon in Latin American culture, from South America to the Caribbean to Spain.

Scott Corrales was right on the ball.

He had correspondents in every Hispanic community it seemed and he was able to give a very accurate translation of the material filtered through him from all over the world. And in addition his articles were well written with few grammatical errors and entertaining to boot. Something you don't often find with a lot of UFO writers, who may be good researchers but are not amongst the top notch authors in the country.

As a bit of background, Scott Corrales became interested in the UFO phenomenon as a result of the heavy UFO activity taking place while he lived in both Mexico and Puerto Rico. He was also influenced by Mexican Ufologists Pedro Ferriz and Salvador Freixedo, the latter a former Jesuit priest who advocated a paranormal, interdimensional interpretation of the phenomenon.

In 1990, Scott began translating the works of Freixedo into English, making the literature and research of experts and journalists available to English-reading audiences everywhere. This led to the creation of the SAMIZDAT journal in 1993 and his collaboration with Mexico's CEFP group, Puerto Rico's PRRG, and the foremost researchers of Spain's so-called third generation of UFO researchers.

In 1995, Corrales documented the manifestations of the entity popularly known as the Chupacabras in three works: "The Chupacabras Diaries," "Nemesis: The Chupacabras at Large," and "Chupacabras and Other Mysteries." In 1998, the

ALIEN BLOOD LUST

SAMIZDAT bulletin was replaced by "Inexplicata: The Journal of Hispanic Ufology," as the official publication of the nascent Institute of Hispanic Ufology. In addition, Scott has been a guest on numerous radio shows and his articles have been featured in numerous English and Spanish publications, in and out of the UFO field.

Scott knows the obvious interest that the aliens or Ultra-Terrestrials have in blood. When the wave of Chupacabra sightings started to garner attention, he investigated many of these cases first hand and came to realize that the witnesses were mostly sincere, though some might have misidentified the blood sucker.

In the pages to follow you will read Scott Corrales' "Chupacabras Diary" notes. The end result is that, while you may have a different opinion as to the cause of the phenomena, you will have to admit that Scott's investigation has been as thorough as is humanly possible.

Timothy Green Beckley

mrufo8@hotmail.com

Author Scott Corrales with friend.

ALIEN BLOOD LUST

DEDICATION

The 1996 original did not feature a dedication. It is only fitting that this re-issue have a dedication to someone whose encouragement (and distribution) helped to make it possible:

To Robert C. ("Bob") Girard of Arcturus Books, Inc., and his timeless words of advice: ***"Mystics never have any money. Price it accordingly."***

Robert C. Girard of Arcturus Books

ALIEN BLOOD LUST

CHAPTER 15

CHUPACABRAS: A STUDY IN DARKNESS

No one knew the darkness as well as they did, these desert shamans responsible for supplying the sacrifices. They would stand in the cold desert night, the skies above filled with stars, waiting at a distance for the gods to appear. Generation after generation had learned the ritual and carried it out. Sometimes a dog, sometimes a young llama, the animal would be sacrificed and left out in the desert for the gods.

At sunrise, when it was no longer a sacrilege to approach the patches of desert where the gods had made their presence felt, the shamans would check to see if their offering had been accepted, and it always was: the carcass was now completely drained of blood, with the tell-tale puncture mark visible somewhere on the body—neck, hindquarters, stomach—indicating that the gods' thirst had been slaked. It was now time for the priests and the tribe to share the meal with the gods by eating the sacrifice's flesh, whose remains would ultimately be buried under a cairn as reminder of the bond between mortals and their deities.

Anthropologist Juan Schobinger has written that the northern coast of Chile faces the one of the richest seas in the world and one of the world's most barren deserts. This characteristic has granted a special archaeological value to the region's organic and ceramic deposits, causing experts to marvel at preservation of so many fragile and perishable cultural elements, such as basketry, textiles and food remains.1

It has been further possible to reconstruct the rituals of the inhabitants of the Atacama Desert from chronicles kept by the conquering Spaniards or from oral traditions that still survive to this day. Dr. Virgilio Sanchez-Ocejo has noted that the museum of the city of Calama boasts an exhibit of one of the desert cairns, called apachecta, and the remains of a desiccated dog employed in a sacrifice...perhaps the only tangible link of a trade between gods and men that has gone on since the dawn of history.

ALIEN BLOOD LUST

Chupacabras in the Southern Cone

Chile, the longest nation on earth, is pinned between the Pacific Ocean and the towering Andes. The verdant rainforests of its southern islands, which number in the thousands, stand in stark contrast to the northern deserts and salt flats bordering Perú and Argentina. Known for its fine wines and fruit, this country first came to the attention of U.S. audiences following the violent overthrow of Socialist leader Salvador Allende in 1973 and the brutal dictatorship that followed under Gen. Augusto Pinochet. Chile had always been of special importance to UFO researches given its reputation as a "proven producer" of high-quality UFO sightings, due in great measure to the clarity of its nocturnal skies, a feature which had led a number of research facilities to build important optical telescopes along the Andean cordillera.

A world emerging from the threat of Y2K and facing the dawn of a new millennium barely gave little notice to the news stories which indicated that northern Chile was in the midst of a strange wave of animal deaths. On April 20, 2000, Chile's prestigious El Mercurio newspaper told its readers that a multi-agency meeting had been convened to look into the bizarre sheep and goat deaths occurring in the northern province of El Loa. The task force's goals were simple: determine what had caused 135 animals to die under mysterious circumstances and put down the perpetrators, which officialdom had a priori identified as dogs, dismissing all the talk among the locals that the dreaded Chupacabras might be to blame.

Lucas Burchard, chief of Environmental Hygiene and Food Control in Calama, posited the theory that dogs developed a taste for blood by biting each other during fights. Therefore it followed that packs of blood-addicted canines would go on cattle-killing sprees, after discovering that it was easier to drink their prey's blood than eating its flesh. Another agency, the Cattle Farming Service (SAG, by its Spanish acronym), informed the concerned locals that it would install baited traps to capture the predators and removed them, while the country's national police force, the Carabineros (who had played a major role in President Allende's overthrow) promised to use its infrared gear to conduct nocturnal patrols.3

Yet even as these agencies took a pro-active stance regarding the mutilations, reports continued streaming in from all over El Loa province to the provincial seat at Calama. Dozens of dogs, hogs and chickens were now added to the roster of mutilated animals, even as reports of an outlandish predator were being brought before the authorities. Jose Ismael Pino, a farm laborer from the village of Huepil, told the state police and the media that a creature he called "The Bird" had been responsible for the deaths of four sheep and a cow in the area; on April 29, 2000, Pino had gone to fetch a bucket of water at around at ten o'clock p.m. under a moonlit sky when a shadow caught his attention. At first he thought it was a bulls belonging to the ranch he worked for, but "that's when I saw it. It hardly moved. It just stood there, looking at me. It stood about 1.50 meters, like a big monkey, with long, clawed arms and enormous fangs protruding from its mouth, as well as a pair of wings." The farmhand ran back to the ranch house for his hounds, whom he sent after the monstrous intruder. One of the hounds "returned with a bloodstained neck." 4

Local schoolteacher Carlos Villalobos did not hesitate to remark upon the strangeness of the attacks: "I think its linked in some fashion to an unknown life form, probably alien in origin, but the problem is that the authorities do not wish to acknowledge it, and this course of action may probably be justified, since a collective panic situation may be unleashed."5

There were clear signs that the attacks were waxing in strangeness. On May 3, 2000, professor Liliana Romero was enjoying a good night's sleep in her apartment in the town of Concepción when she was wakened by the howling of five stray puppies she had adopted and kept in the building's courtyard as company for Black, her large mastiff. Fearing that a burglar might be at work, Romero carefully looked through the window and was startled by what she saw. The mastiff was huddled in fear against the wall as the puppies continued to whine. "I could see the back of what appeared to be an immense man, standing some two meters tall. It's shoulder blades were split, as though it had wings," she would later tell reporters.6 Professor Romero made an unsuccessful effort to get her husband to take a look, and by the time she'd returned to her vantage point, the entity had vanished.

The following day, Professor Romero went about her business and gave the matter no further thought until her children informed her that they'd found a dead dog near where the strange sighting took place. Her husband agreed to take a look at the carcass, which had "two deep holes in its jugular [vein], about as wide as a BIC pen, separated by 5 centimeters. What impressed me most was that [the carcass] was completely bloodless and light as a feather. The dog was incredibly wooly and in fact, I had to move its fur to see the wounds."7

Within hours, three Carabineros officers reported to the Romeros' home to collect the mutilated dog, remarking on the similarity between the attacks on the canid and the animals found at other locations. The state policemen asked the Romeros for trash bags in which to carry their grisly find and then curtly ordered them to keep quiet about the event.

The dog was brought to the precinct and left in an office near the local prefecture, where many local functionaries were able to get a good look of the carcass, some of them even confirming Prof. Romero's remarks about the puncture marks and the dead animal's near-weightless condition.

On May 8, 2000, Jorge Torrejón, writing for the Estrella del Loa newspaper, reported that three young men travelling aboard a refrigerator van transporting 20 tons of fish from Lebu to Arica had a close encounter with the creature. Mauricio

ALIEN BLOOD LUST

Correa, an experienced articulated trailer driver, was trying to park his rig not far from the María Elena salt mines assisted by Oscar Robles and Ricardo, an anonymous hitchhiker he'd picked up along the route. After parking the truck at 5:00 am, he turned off the engine and the lights and became aware that the vehicle's cab was tilting toward the right, where Oscar was sitting. The vehicle's lights inexplicably began turning themselves on and off. To their horror they noticed that a "very ugly animal, very hairy and black, having a long oval head, fangs and slanted, goggling yellow eyes" was staring at them through the side window. The apparition had pointed ears and "whiskers similar to those of a boar. It was something awful that was stuck to the glass for several seconds."

Recovering from the shock, the driver managed to get the truck going to make a report to the authorities. Oscar, his co-pilot, checked his wristwatch to ascertain the time for the report, but discovered that the digital timepiece had stopped, and later resumed functioning in a haphazard manner.

The drivers did not stop until they reached the vicinity of Victoria, where the frightened men waited for daybreak before getting out of their vehicle at a truck stop, where they had coffee and resumed their journey to the town of Pozo Almonte, presenting their report at the local Carabineros headquarters at 7:00 a.m.

The only evidence of their experience were the prints apparently left by the creature on the back and side of the trailer cab.

Ghastly encounters aside, the number of mutilated animals was increasing almost exponentially, prompting Judge Flora Sepúlveda of the Third Criminal Court to open an inquest into the strange deaths on May 10, 2000, ordering that the University of Concepción's Department of Pathology conduct an analysis to determine the causes of the events, if necessary by exhuming the remains of the animal slain to date.

The phenomenon itself was clearly unimpressed by all of officialdom's fussing and flapping: Twenty-four hens were exsanguinated in the commune of Lebu on May 14, and 30 more on the following night in the vicinity of Concepción, but these numbers would pale in significance when compared to the 500 hens slain on July 3, 2000 in a single farmstead—the Chilean Chupacabras was obviously playing for keeps.8

Conspiracy in the Wasteland

It is conceivable that the Chilean animal mutilations may have been completely overlooked outside the country had it not been for a development which catapulted them to worldwide prominence.

On May 15, 2000, the Crónica newspaper told its startled readership that Pablo Aguilera, an on-air talk show personality with Radio Pudhauel 90.5 FM, had received a series of telephone messages from Calama and other points in northern Chile indicating that a family of strange animals, "possible Chupacabrases", as the paper put it, had been captured by the Chilean armed forces near the Radomiro Tomic copper mine. The male, female and cub were allegedly handed over to FBI agents who arrived in Calama from the U.S Embassy in Santiago de Chile.9

The newspaper story made no mention of the creature's taxonomy nor if they had been taken dead or alive. "Police sources told Crónica that the capture of the specimens was real and that everything had transpired as originally told. Pure paranoia?" asked the unsigned journalist.

Chilean researcher Jaime Ferrer notes that the military stood fast by its "neither confirm nor deny" stance, but sources were able to determine that the three creatures were provisionally held in the stockade of the 15th Infantry Regiment based in Calama, but that an Army lieutenant was forced to kill the male specimen "because it was causing them too much trouble."10

Adding conspiracy-enriched fuel to the fire, a retired air traffic supervisor named Patricio Borlone claimed that all flights arriving or departing Santiago's international airport had been put on hold while a cargo plane loaded two cargo containers with the NASA seal, allegedly containing the rare specimens in question. Borlone provided the flight numbers and departure times to substantiate his theory.

Transmitted via the Internet to the remotest corners of the world, the belief that the U.S. and Chilean governments might possibly be in collusion regarding these improbable creatures prompted a firestorm of speculation. Was the Chilean Chupacabras a American genetic experiment run amok in the barren salt deserts of Chile, as some believed? Or, given the area's history of animal predation, were the creatures natural inhabitants of the deep caves and passages under the dusty desert towns, perhaps brought to the surface by the mining companies' copper production? Even more disturbing were rumors that a security guard for the SOQUIMICH conglomerate had been clawed in the back by one of these hairy beasts, and that a Chilean soldier had allegedly been killed by one of the "Chupacabras" creatures during the operation that took them captive. If the U.S. was somehow involved, as many believed, the superpower saw nothing wrong with paying the price for its covert operations in Chilean blood.

Almost a month later, on June 10, 2000, Chile's largest UFO research group, OVNIVISION, spearheaded by researcher Cristián Riffo, announced that it would formally petition the Chilean Ministry of Defense to look into allegations of NASA involvement with the Chupacabras and the deaths of hundreds of animals in the country. During the press conference, Riffo noted that the belief that NASA had lost control "of at least three genetic experiments in Chile" was becoming increasingly widespread, and that the specimens in question would be the creatures responsible for the massacres. "Many persons agree that they have seen a kind of ape or mandrill with human features but with very large eyes," added OVNIVISON's leader. "An animal having these characteristics was hunted down by the Chilean military in the vicinity of the Radomiro Tomic mine near Calama, an operation in which one soldier allegedly died." 11

Riffo was not being overly dramatic in his statements to the media. Residents of Calama and its encircling towns and villages openly blamed NASA for the Chupacabras's apparitions and attacks. "The gringos had at least three genetic experiments run away from them and they've only be able to capture two," was the belief expressed by architect Dagoberto Corante, a respected citizen of Calama who informed Spain's EFE news agency that one of the captured specimens was kept "all day at the regiment's barracks until the NASA experts arrived to take it away."12

Perhaps the most curious twist in the chronicles of the Chilean Chupacabras came when the Antofagasta Diario La Estrella newspaper featured a story on the discovery of "Chupacabras eggs", which suggested that the predator might be oviparous. A caller to the aforementioned Pablo Aguilera radio show claimed that Chilean soldiers had returned to their base near Calama— after having encountered as strange creature during their nightly patrols— carrying several of these "eggs", which were obtained the same day that NASA personnel allegedly came to collect the creatures.13

The story involving the "eggs" came to a spectacular, if not downright explosive, end when the Chilean Air Force's fighter/bombers dropped an unspecified number of bombs between 8:30 and 9:45 a.m. on July 20, 2000, causing the earth to shake and creating a good deal of consternation, something that isn't exactly easy to do in a region accustomed to underground mining detonations.

The military aircraft allegedly took out a "Chupacabras nest" located in an area filled with small hills and mounds located between the town of María Elena and the abandoned Pedro de Alvarado mining camp. According to copper miners, erosion had eroded many of these hills into ideal locations for the creatures to hide. 14

Researchers suggested that an unknown number of breeding pairs of this creature may have entered their reproductive phase, and the government had seen this as the most opportune time for getting rid of them.

The forces behind the conspiracy to destroy the creature and silence any further stories coming out of Calama employed a variety of tactics, including an all-out effort to purchase the silence of individual witnesses, ostensibly to keep the panic from spreading and perhaps causing unrest among the mining industry workers who may suddenly have felt threatened by the entity. One of the most unusual events involved a promise made by unspecified "authorities" to the owners of an automobile destroyed by a hairy, simian entity with bat-like wings. In exchange for their absolute silence in this matter, they were promised a brand new vehicle of the same make and model.15 However, human nature being what it is, the victims could not resist telling their story to a friend, who in turn told the entire world on "The Pablo Aguilera Show". As the show's host noted, it was unlikely that the unidentified agency would make good on its offer after that.

A New, Improved Goatsucker?

In the monograph Chupacabras Rising: The Paranormal Predator Returns, this author stressed the physical differences between the creature commonly identified as the Chupacabras (small head, wraparound red eyes, kangaroo-like body, small arms and spines running down its back) during the Puerto Rican events of 1995-1996, the Mexican events of 1996-1997 (a huge bat-winged entity), the 1997 events in Spain (conflicting descriptions involving a mandrill-like entity and another with more canid characteristics) and the one seen in Chile during 2000.

Most of the Chilean reports agreed that the mystery predator had large, self-luminous yellow eyes that can mesmerize its prey, as occurred in some of the Puerto Rican cases. On July 14, 2000, two motorists were unwilling participants in a case which illustrates the strange properties of the creature's eyes. As they drove toward Calama on their way back from a civic organization meeting, the two anonymous women saw two bright yellow lights up ahead. Thinking it might be a driver heading toward them, the driver flashed her high beams. But as they got closer, they realized that the "thing" standing in the middle of the road wasn't a car: it resembled a very large, earless dog with long grey hair and a pair of immense, slanted yellow eyes.

The women and the "thing" exchanged looks for some five to ten seconds, after which the car drove off along the left lane. The "animal" followed their departure with its headan extremity capable of 180 degree turns.

"I felt a terrible panic," the driver told journalists. "I wanted to get out of the car but she [the companion] calmed me down. We saw the two yellow lights again, but this time they lit up the entire road before disappearing. I hit the accelerator and kept up speed until we reached Calama."

Researcher Liliana Núñez Orellana mentions a case in which a Calama witness was able to take a good look at the creature, describing it as very similar to a mandrill with black and grey fur, two very long eyeteeth and the curious detail of a nose similar to that of a pig or bat, and a hyperkinetic, nervous attitude as it darted around. The witness frankly admitted having nearly lost control of his bowels during this sighting. "It is known," writes Núñez, "that males and females of this species exist and that they appear to reproduce sexually." She points out a case involving a fire fighter who noticed that their genitalia was quite similar to that of humans.

Yet, as the old saying goes, the scariest monster is the one you can't see. This was certainly the case in the early morning hours on June 9, 2000 when residents of the town of Maria Elena felt the presence of a strange entity that they identified as "dense air" falling over the town. "It was as if something went past pushing against the walls, but without making any noise," according to a nervous local.

The Paranormal Possibility

Since the Chupacabras made itself known in 1995, three probable origins for its existence have been suggested: believers in extraterrestrial life consider it either part of the cargo manifest of an itinerant UFO that got left behind on our lonely planet, or else a cunning E.T. experiment whose ultimate purpose we cannot fathom; scorning any non-terrestrial considerations, others have successfully managed to weave the Chupacabras into the vast quilt of conspiracy theory by identifying it as either "a genetic experiment gone astray" or as a biological robot dropped off in the Third World by the New World Order's minions for equally unfathomable reasons.

But the Chupacabras' penchant for that sticky vital fluid called blood appears not to have made much of an impact among either of these two factions. Thus, a third faction composed of believers in the paranormal origin of the creature has paid closer attention to the blood factor.

Civilizations around the globe since the beginning of recorded history have considered blood as a sign of invulnerability and potency, a substance to be sacrificed to gods in exchange for divine favor. Looking back from our own century, we are understandably repulsed by the hideous blood orgies of the Aztecs and Mayas, whose high priests' hair was "caked with human blood" according to chronicler Bernal Díaz del Castillo. The demand for blood sacrifice by the God of the Old Testament is no less bewildering; yet we read of the mythical Roman king Servius, who thwarted Jupiter's request for the sacrifice a living creature by throwing in a small fish into the offering. The immolation of animals or humans for propitiatory purposes, according to German scholar Wilhelm Ziehr, stems from the fact that deities do not accept gratitude expressed through prayer or the acceptance of commandments — only sacrifice, and the greatest sacrifice that can be offered is, of course, human blood.16

In many traditions, deities both good and evil have craved for blood, or will perform services for a human sorcerer in exchange for it. In the Odyssey, brave Ulysses summoned the grim shades of the dead with an outpouring of blood from freshly slaughtered black sheep, and must the hold the howling revenants at bay with his sword so that only one of them — the specter of the dead seer Tiresias — can feast on the blood's energy and foretell the circumstances of his return to Ithaca. The ancients believed that the spirits of the dead lusted after blood, as did other beings belonging to the spirit world, which could be appeased with nothing less. As a result, the sight of blood created was highly disturbing, particularly among the old Middle Eastern cultures.

ALIEN BLOOD LUST

A number of contemporary authors — Salvador Freixedo, John Keel, Anthony Roberts — have done their level best to explain the seemingly insatiable need for vital fluids. Freixedo, for one, has noted that the entities crave not the substance, but the vital energy associated to it. Therefore, the manner in which the blood is released from the body becomes supremely important—the unwilling donor's pain and shock amplify the release of this energy, which — observes Freixedo — appears not to be necessary for the existence of these forces, but rather a pleasurable experience for them, much like the consumption of spirituous liquids by a human.17

The preceding paragraph may smack of obscurantism and superstition to many, but the accounts from Calama which claim that the night air is rent by the howling screams of dying dogs suggest that this theory is perhaps closer to the truth than any dreams of alien intervention.

Jaime Ferrer, director of the Calama UFO Research center, has not shied away from this possibility, particularly after a conversation he held with a 91 year old desert native from a locality known as Peine. The elder told Ferrer that "his grandfather's grandfathers" were well aware of that these predators existed and that they were, in fact, gods who came to leave messages, adding the curious explanation that in the past, these messages were articulated as complete sentences, but now, they were numerical in nature. When Ferrer pressed him for an explanation, the elder replied: "Seven lowered by one, Thirteen lowered by seven, Four raised by two."

In other words, 666 — the mark of the Beast.

The reader may share the researcher's disbelief at hearing this item of Biblical numerology from the lips of a desert nomad, but Ferrer's written account goes on to mention that these predatory entities were already known as Achaches ("demon-slaves") in the ancient Cunza dialect which predated the current Aymara tongue by centuries, and that the term is still commonly used among the tribal dancers whose performances feature these improbable beings.18

Since 1995, researchers have reached agreement on at least one thing: whatever is draining animals of blood cannot possibly be doing it for its own consumption. Could we speculate that the decline of blood sacrifice in regions where it was once practiced has led to the appearance of an order of beings in charge of collecting it? Certainly the anomalous bloodsucking entities whose trajectory we have followed are drinking many times their own weight in the vital fluids of different animals.

Conclusion

Who or what were these strange deities feared and worshipped by the ancient Atacamans? Their existence has been recorded in a number of cultures ranging from Mexico to Mesopotamia, where blood sacrifices have been carried out at a given point in history. What would occur if the Atacamans neglected to perform the ritual? Did their deities send monstrous minions to collect the blood they appeared to need?

Derided by the intelligentsia as "phantasm of the Hispanic mind", the bloodsucking creature popularly known as the Chupacabras (or the Goatsucker) first emerged in 1995 in Puerto Rico, where its exploits in the municipality of Canóvanas became a matter of legend. But there was no reason why the Caribbean should have a monopoly over such an entity: in rapid succession, the Chupacabras and its kin spread throughout the southern United States in 1996 (southern Florida, Texas, Arizona and California) and began attacking both livestock and humans in Mexico during the same period of time. By 1997, reports were coming in from northern Spain, and the following year Brazil bore the brunt of its depredations. It would seem as if the Chupacabras waited patiently until the landmark year 2000 and saved the best for last—an all out wave of animal mutilations and confusion that persists as of this writing.

1. Schobinger, Juan. Prehistory of the Americas. New York: M.E. Sharpe, Inc. 2000.

2. Correspondence with Dr. Virgilio Sanchez Ocejo, 1/10/01.

3. "El Mercurio de Chile," April 20, 2000.

4. "Crónica", April 30, 2000.

5. "Crónica", April 30, 2000.

6. El Sur, "Mysterious Nocturnal Apparition in Building Courtyard", May 5, 2000.

7. El Sur, "Mysterious Nocturnal Apparition in Building Courtyard." May, 5 2000.

8. Correspondence with Liliana Núñez Orellana, 07/28/00.

9. Núñez, Raul. "Chupacabras in Chile". INEXPLICATA, Summer 2000, pg.

10. Correspondence from Jaime Ferrer, 02/02/01.

11. "Chileans Believe Chupacabras to be a NASA Creation". EFE News Agency, 07/29/00.

12. "Chileans Believe Chupacabras to be a NASA Creation" EFE News Agency, 07/29/00.

13. "Chupacabras Eggs Discovered". Transcript by Patricio Borlone Rojas, 07/14/2000.

14. La Estrella del Loa, "Bombardment Takes Place in Chile's 2nd Region" 07/31/00.

15. "New Vehicle Exchanged for Silence in Antofagasta" Transcript by Patricio Borlone Rojas, 06/09/00.

16. Corrales, Scott. "The Paranormal and Blood Magic" Unsolved UFO Mysteries, Summer 1995.

17. Freixedo, Salvador. Defendámonos de los Dioses. Quintá, 1985.

18. Correspondence with Jaime Ferrer, 01/29/01.

Technology is a remarkable thing. In 1995, while working on the draft of what would be "The Chupacabras Diaries", my first monograph on Puerto Rico's paranormal predator, Sergio Couttolenc, a friend and correspondent in the Mexican city of Coatzacoalcos, sent me a file via e-mail that I was unable to open. Something requiring some obscure piece of software called "Acrobat" that my trusty 386sx did not appear to have, and which dial-up at 9600 baud could not download. So the file was saved to a 3.5-inch disk (remember them?) and placed into a drawer where it rests with hundreds of other 3.5-inch disks laden with UFO and paranormal information from the '90s.

A decade or so later, while burning all the information contained in the little black squares to their descendants – shiny new DVD discs – I found the Adobe Acrobat file that Sergio had sent me, and whose information should have formed part of my project or even "Chupacabras and Other Mysteries" (Greenleaf Press, 1997). Since information is never truly "old" in the field of UFO and paranormal research, INEXPLICATA is pleased to share it with you now. One note: this information predates the start of the Chupacabras wave of 1995 by two years...the pebbles that started the avalanche, perhaps?

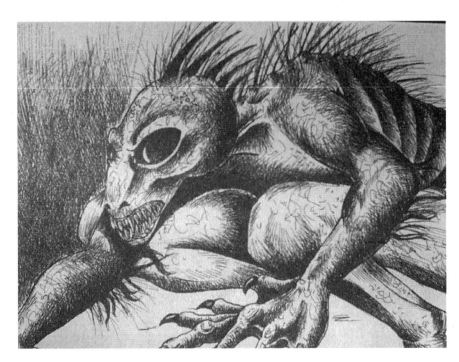

30 Rams Dead with not even one drop of Blood Left.
It drained all the blood from 30 Rams.

ALIEN BLOOD LUST

CHAPTER 16

EL CHUPACABRAS
By J. Felipe Coria
(from Mexico's "El Financiero" newspaper, no date, 1995)

UTUADO, Province of Arecibo, Puerto Rico – June 24, 1993, 03:30 hrs. There is noise in the pens. The sheep are calling out in terror: they are being attacked. Farmer Pedro Cabiya wakes up and is startled. His loyal dog "Emilio" sniffs the air and whines. The dog never barks – rather, it appears to want to bury itself alive rather than go outside. It moves in circles in front of the door, silently, looking straight toward the source of the noise, the sound of murder. It would never dare look outside. The dog is frightened – fear in its pure, raw state. Cabiya looks through the window. The night seems almost solid and deep; a physical, intense darkness. Aside from the sheep, there is no other source of sound. Suddenly they are quiet. He feels a chill. Time goes by – one, ten, thirty minutes. The night suddenly recovers its rhythm. "Emilio" begins barking furiously and bolts out the door toward the sheep pens; Cabiya reaches for his shotgun and a .38 Smith & Wesson, holding a weapon in each hand. He is being propelled by a fear that has crystallized itself into an intense sweat that streams from his brow, and down his back and chest. His t-shirt is soaked through. "Emilio" barks hysterically, leaping about, circling the pens. Cabiya takes a look. The attack is now over: his thirty rams are dead, but not dismembered.

He looks at them closely with a flashlight. No sign of scratching or bruising is evident. Nor does he see a single drop of blood. He does, however, see two perfect incisions at the level of the base of the skull, barely separated by an estimated half a centimeter. At dawn, Cabiya checks his pens again, and not a single drop of blood is to be found. The animal carcasses are free from injury, except for the incisions. He immediately visits Doctor Berg, a veterinary specialist from Utuado, who inspects one of the slain animals. "It was exsanguinated," he says. But before rushing to say that it was a bloodsucking vampire bat, such as the Vampyrum spectrum, an enormous Central American chiropteran (which would be odd in itself: why did it migrate? would it take one or several to finish off an entire flock?), he checks the incisions millimetrically. They are perfect: twelve centimeters and a half deep by three millimeters in diameter. Straight. Symmetrical. Too large to be made by a bat – the bite doesn't match.

The injuries have indeed been made by fangs, but very large and close. A bat would have left scratches and traces of its presence in the bite. Yet it would seem that the intruder, an animal lacking claws and barely the requisite amount of strength, had gently but firmly latched on the sheeps' heads, inserted its fangs, drawn blood and left the exsanguinated carcasses behind.

According to Cabiya's own testimony, there was no sign of a fight. The other sheep were apparently frozen in place by sheer terror and awaited their inevitable death. What Doctor Berg finds startling is that the animals were attacked in the base of the skull, without exception. A bat never does this with such precision.

Since Berg refrains from offering a conclusive answer regarding the assailant, Cabiya heads for Arecibo, the city, to see his friend Frank Cassidy, of mixed Irish and Puerto Rican heritage, a veterinarian graduated from Florida State University. Cassidy listens to him, but also abstains from providing an answer. He promises to look into the incident, but files it away. It isn't until four months later, when Cabiya visits him again, this time in the company of his neighbor Fernando de la Peña, owner of a farm two kilometers distant from Cabiya's. An identical killing terrifies both men: 35 goats, 26 sheep and 13 hens. In this case, Peña fired indiscriminately into the darkness toward his animal pens for over ten minutes, only stopping when he ran out of bullets. But nothing. There was no trace of the assailant.

Cassidy, still unable to offer an answer given the peculiar nature of the attack and the bite involved, believes the culprit to be an unknown animal. He jokes: "I'll send out your goatsucker file to see what we can find out." – He calls it a goatsucker – Chupacabras – because goats represent the largest share of the casualties. He compiles a package with Berg's information, his own necropsies, the official report from the Health department and the farmer's eyewitness account. He sends it to his alma mater in Florida via UPS. The fact of the matter is that he still doesn't know what he's facing.

A web search of veterinarians currently practicing in Puerto Rico does not display either a "Dr. Berg" or "Dr. Cassidy", but these may be pseudonyms employed by the journalist from El Financiero who wrote the article. The intriguing and contradictory claim here is that Dr. Cassidy bestowed the name "chupacabras" – in jest – on the paranormal predator, when in fact it was comedian Silverio Pérez of the Rayos Gamma comedy team who did so; Pérez, in fact, had come up with other funny names to describe strange creatures, such as "el cangodrilo", to refer to the small, hirsute entity reported in central Puerto Rico during the late '80s and early '90s.

ALIEN BLOOD LUST

THE NIGHT OF THE CHUPACABRAS

A small crowed gathered within the narrow confines of a clothing store on San Juan's Ponce de León Avenue to watch the clerks remove armfuls of crisp white t-shirts from nondescript boxes. Colorful serigraphs and silkscreened images depicting the gargoylesque paranormal predator known as El Chupacabras by the media decorated the front of each garment: Chupacabras as lifeguard, Chupacabras as gourmet chef, Chupacabras as straw-sipping vampire. An overweight woman gently took one of the t-shirts and looked at it skeptically. "Eso no puede ser," she said aloud to no one in particular: This thing can't be.

For that was the zeitgeist in the shining star of the Caribbean in December 1995: half-hearted denial of a physical impossibility. A red-eyed nocturnal creature alleged by many to have caused the deaths of countless small animals in rural Puerto Rico since the beginning of the year. What had originally been considered the idle prattle of country cousins was now a subject of serious discussions in thoroughly urban, sophisticated San Juan. Congressmen from opposing sides of the political spectrum now proposed joint resolutions calling for a formal investigation of the problem affecting not only their constituents, but which they themselves had experienced on their country estates.

The madness would soon spread to Florida, then Mexico, then Central America...a paranormal domino theory whose reach would extend as far south as Brazil and across the wide Atlantic to Spain and Portugal. The United States, skeptical and derisive of any supernatural developments outside its borders, would also be brushed by the Chupacabras' dark wings.

ANATOMY OF A PARANORMAL PANDEMIC

WANTED: Chupacabras—the Goatsucker—variously described by witnesses as standing between 4 and 5 feet tall; covered in greenish brown or blackish grey fur; spindly arms ending in claws; powerful hind legs enabling it to jump over fences; a thin membrane under its arms that have been described as "wings"; glowing red eyes; has a crest of glowing appendages running down its back; esti-

ALIEN BLOOD LUST

mated weight at some 100 pounds; has been known to use telepathic powers against human witnesses. Suspect is unarmed but considered dangerous. Contact your nearest police station.

These descriptions, gleaned from dozens of cases in a number of countries, coincide on the details that make this aberrant being a fascinating subject for study. Here we are faced with the ultimate chimaera: a being described as being able to fly or float, but with a body/mass ratio in excess of the size of its wing-like appendages; self-luminous eyes, and perhaps most amazing of all, the resemblance of its head and eyes to that of the so-called "Greys" that have become a staple of contemporary ufology, grafted onto a tail-less, kangaroo-like body. This identikit image was made even grislier by the addition of a proboscis emanating from the creature's mouth, employed to suck the blood out of its victims.

PRE-CHUPACABRAS MUTILATIONS

Eminent Puerto Rican ufologist Willie Durand Urbina offers information concering the mini-wave of animal mutilations which took place in the early 1990's, prior to the appearance of the Chupacabras. The events began in March 1991 and centered around the Lares, P.R. area: residents of Barrio Pezuelas filed complaints with the police regarding the deaths of pigs, geese, chickens and other animals whose carcasses presented fang marks on their throats and had been completely drained of blood. Many of the animal owners told the police that they had seen "a strange animal" hiding in the exhuberant vegetation of the hillside; some eyewitnesses described the alleged perpetrator as an ape, while others insisted that it was much larger in size than a normal dog, and completely black in color. However, Wilfedo Cubero, a director of the Cuerpo de Investigación Criminal or CIC, insisted that no notice of these cases had ever been given to his agency. Nor had any specimens of the mutilated animals been collected by official agencies for formal autopsy purposes. When nine pigs were found exanguinated near the outskirts of Camuy, on the Atlantic shore, Civil Defense Director Aníbal Román would summarily dismiss the case as "the handiwork of a hungry dog."

The benign neglect of the authorities prompted the affected citizenry to take matters into their own hands: like extras from a horror movie wandering through the night with torches, the residents of Barrio Pezuelas armed themselves with clubs and went out to find and liquidate the "vampire" bent on destroying their livestock. Fear spread across the mountainous rural area. Children were forbidden by their elders to walk alone along the country roads or to be out of their homes after seven o'clock at night.

Héctor Colón, a public school teacher, would soon become the spokesman for the terrified residents of Barrio Pezuelas. Himself a farmer, he appeared on radio shows and in newspaper features to stress that the situation experienced by his community was highly unusual. "I'm a farmer and can tell you that these deaths are abnormal," he declared on a radio interview on Lares radio station WGDL on April 4, 1991. He went on to describe the finding of a large boar that very morning which had been completely drained of blood and sported fang-marks on its neck. The aggrieved locals soon began accusing the police of not wanting to look into the matter so as to avoid presenting reports on the high strangeness deaths.

As spring turned imperceptibly to summer, the vampiric activity moved from Lares to Aguada on the Mona Channel, the body of water separating Puerto Rico from the island of Hispaniola. Planters and livestock owners of that community's Barrio Lagunas began experiencing losses in June 1991 to a predator equally in killing animals as in tearing banana trees apart to feed on their succulent tender hearts. The island media soon christened the beast"Comecogollos" — the Banana-Tree Eater.

The jocose moniker did nothing to assuage the fiend's temper. Frightened eye-witnesses described it as a manlike, hairy creature weighing some sixty pounds, strong enough to kill a dog and a goat and tear its way through plantain groves. Manuel Rivera, a planter and businessman in Lagunas, complained to the press that not a single government agency had paid attention to the matter, and that the police refused to respond to calls involving the strange creature. A number of goats slain by the hairy being had to be buried when no official agency turned up to perform autopsies.

In July 1991, officialdom began having a change of heart. Juan Morales, Regional Director of the Civil Defense for the Arecibo area, indicated that the persistence of animal deaths and creature sightings merited careful investigation, while at the same time hestitating to venture any opinions as to their possible cause. The cause of his about-face was almost certainly the unexplained slaying of twenty goats in the Quebradas Sector of Camuy. The twenty lifeless animals all had the same fang-marks on their throats and had been drained of blood.

Their interest had come about too late. By the time elements of the Civil Defense had reported to Quebradas, the dead goats were too far along the decomposition process to subject their carcasses to scientific analysis. But the startling admission that none of the goats had been slain by dogs was made by the same Regional Civil Defense office.

To cap off the high-strangeness events of 1991, government agencies on the offshore island of Culebra, to the west of Puerto Rico, found themselves faced with the appearance of a "mystery cat" — a one hundred and fifty pound feline, grey in color — seen by personnel of the Natural Resources Department and of the Conservation and Development Agency on Culebra's Playa Flamingo. The authorities confessed their bewilderment at how a large feline could have appeared "out of thin air". The outcome of their efforts was never made known to the public.

ALIEN BLOOD LUST

HORROR MADE MANIFEST

After remaining in abeyance for four years, the mutilations started again, this time in the municipality of Orocovis, in the heart of Puerto Rico's mountainous interior. Sickening feelings of deja-vu welled through the hearts of farmers who stumbled upon the silent carcasses of their animals: a new round in the struggle with the unexplained had begun.

On March 21, 1995, word of the strange events replaying themselves in the center of the island was broadcast by the media. The focus of attention was a locality called Saltos Cabra outside Orocovis, Puerto Rico. Reserachers José A. Rodríguez and Federico Alvarez Frank promptly visited the area on March 22, 1995 to inspect the property of Mr. Enrique Barreto, the dead animals' owner. After visiting the municipal police headquarters in search of directions, the researchers arrived at their destination. Mr. Barreto, a lifelong resident of the community and an employee of the Municipality of Orocovis, was considered to have impeccable credentials.

Barreto's testimony indicated that the animal deaths began on March 10, when realized some certain sheep were missing at feeding time. Puzzled as to the situation, he was later shocked to find a consderable number of his flock dead. Saddened but not overly preoccupied, he didn't think to file a police report, ascribing his losses to the predatory activities of some wild dog. But when more animals turned up dead in the days that followed, the farmer was intrigued by the unusual puncture marks on their necks. It was then that he decided to file a complaint with the municipality's police.

Researchers were quick to seize upon the most obvious evidence on the Barreto property — the strange three-toed footprints covering the ground. This fact ruled out a dog or wild cat attack, since canines and felines have four toes. Further analysis proved there was an 18 inch distance between footprints, suggesting that whatever creature they belonged to was bipedal rather than quadrupedal. Its weight was estimated at between 120 and 140 pounds.

Alvarez and his group took Geiger counter readings of the sheep. "The incorrupt sheep," Alvarez notes in his report,"gave off readings of .011 on a scale of 1000 (110 rads, in other words), which is somewhat high [...] The spine of another sheep also produced readings of .011 rads. After the corresponding analysis, the conclusion was reached by one of our experts in nuclear medicine that the radiation emitted by the dead sheep was not irradiated but injected intravenously, judging by the reading found on the dead animal's spinal column. Hence the delayed decomposition process in the carcass."

But although no trace of the mutilator or mutilators were found, a high-strangeness event soon befell one of the investigators, José A. Rodríguez, in the vicinity of a cave, suspected to be the hideout of the creature causing the mutilations.

ALIEN BLOOD LUST

Rodríguez experienced the sensation that something was watching him, and felt mysteriously compelled to head for a nearby gully, falling into it and receiving head wounds. Police officers took the wounded Rodríguez to a nearby hospital to have his injuries seen to.

While animal mutilations continued throughout the remainder of the spring and summer, it was not until August that the creature known as the Goatsucker would finally enter the stage, choosing not landlocked Orocovis but the coastal town of Canovanas for its debut.

Canóvanas is a prosperous community that benefits from its location on Route 3, which handles the heavy traffic between San Juan on one end and Fajardo on the other. The majestic, mist-enshrouded peaks of El Yunque are only a stone's throw away, and the excellent beaches of Luquillo attract thousands of local and foreign tourists. Canóvanas also boasts the spectacular El Comandante, one of the finest race tracks in the entire world. It was this fortunate piece of real estate that the gargoylesque creature called the Chupacabras would select as its own.

Madelyne Tolentino and her husband, José Miguel Agosto, have the distinct privilege of beign the first witnesses to the creature. During the second week of August 1995, at approximately four o' clock in the afternoon on a weekday, Ms. Tolentino looked out a window at her home and saw a young man walking backward with an expression of indescribable fear on his face, as if something horrible were about to pounce on him. She then noticed that a strange creature was approaching the house at a moderate pace, allowing her to take a good, long look at the aberration. Whatever it was stood four feet tall and had a pelt covered in a mixture of colors ranging from brown to black and ashen grey, as if it had been burned. Tolentino added that the entity had gelatinous dark-grey eyes and spindly arms ending in claws. "To me, it couldn't be anything from this world," she would later tell reporters.

Her momentary fascination with the entity came to an end when she realized the enormity of the experience. Shouting, she called for her mother to witness the surreal event. Her mother would later add that it had a coppery plumage running down the length of its back and that it moved in a series of short hops, like a kangaroo, but lacking the marsupial's characteristic tail. The creature ran into an overgrown field, and Ms. Tolentino's husband and other resients of the same street gave chase, but the creature was nowhere to be found.

The supernatural predator appeared to have found an abundance of easy prey in the Canóvanas area and concentrated its attacks there for the next six weeks.

On September 29, 1995 the creature killed an assortment of rabbits, guinea hens and chickens at a farm belonging to Felix Rivera in Guaynabo's Barrio Santa Rosa. A week later eyewitnesses claimed to have seen a beast "hairy like a bear" in Canovanas again: a young man named Misael Negrón allegedly observed the entity for ten minutes from the balcony of his home. He added that the creature appeared to take a great interest in its surroundings and stood up suddenly when it realized that Negrón was watching it. Both creature and human beat a hasty retreat from one another. Misael's brother Angel would claim the following day that he had been pursued by creature after seeing it standing beside a dead goat.

The people of Canóvanas, daunted by their unwelcome visitor, found a champion in a most unlikely source: their own mayor, the Hon. José "Chemo" Soto. On October 29, having organized a citizen militia of up to two hundred people, Soto led a series of nightly hunts for the elusive creature, equipping his posse with nets, tranquilizing dart guns and other non-lethal means. Some decried the gesture as useless, in the face of the powers ascribed to the creature, and others ridiculed the mayor for his gallant effort, but it represented the very first response against the bloodsucking visitor from anyone in an official capacity.

The mayor's plan involved trapping the creature by using a goat as bait. Volunteers crafted a sizeable cage, made out of the welded iron fencing commonly found on the island, and deposited in a field: The Chupacabras, however, was not quite so easily fooled. Its exploits were now being reported from one end of the island to another, causing many to wonder, with increasing dread, if the Chupacabras were not one but many. One case involving a prestigious pharmaceutical company on the island dealt with the inability of the security staff to find guards for its "graveyard shift" since one guard reported seeing three Chupacabras-like creatures on the premises. The terrifying sight prompted the watchman's resignation.

The balance of 1995 was filled with senseless animal deaths and choking feeling of terror among rural residents. Police officer José Collazo would become one of the growing number of citizens having their own close encounters with the non-human attacker. At eleven o'clock at night, as the off-duty police officer and his wife were getting ready for bed, Collazo heard the unmistakeable sound of his car alarm go off in the carport. Fearing thieves were trying to spirit away his new Toyota, he approached the door to the carport with his .357 Magnum in hand. The sight that greeted him would later make him wish that it had indeed been something as mundane as a car thief!

Collazo found his dog growling and keening, engaged in a struggle to the death with what he at first took to be another dog. He then realized that a bizarre creature was overpowering his pet Chow and digging its fangs on the hapless canine's back. Firing a dead-on shot at the creature, Collazo was even more startled to see it roll into a ball—sticking its humanoid head between its legs — and hurling itself against one of the carport walls, bouncing out of the open-ended structure. When asked by reporters if he could have fired another shot and killed the creature, the officer sheepishly admitted that he had been afraid of damaging his

ALIEN BLOOD LUST

new car.

The brief encounter with the unknown yielded a wealth of physical evidence: the creature left behind tufts of coarse hair and samples of its blood on the carport floor and walls. A nauseating reek remained in the air for a number of days.

PHYSICAL EVIDENCE AND SCIENTIFIC NAYSAYING

The growing number of Chupacabras sightings around the island was starting to create a considerable number of physical traces which were being collected and analyzed with unsatisfying results. Dr. Hector García, a veterinarian with the Department of Agriculture's Caribbean Veterinary Laboratory, remained steadfast in his belief that "feral dogs and monkeys" were ultimately responsible for the spree of animal mutilations. After performing twenty autopsies in the last three months of 1995, he insisted that none of the animal carcasses brought to him for analysis presented any perforations in the jugular vein, which would have been the likeliest location for a predator to suck blood. The dead animals, he pointed out, had the amount of blood one would expect to find in carcass, putting paid to the exanguination hysteria. Pneumonia, hepatitis and animal bites were likelier causes for the deaths.

García would soon find his ideological opposite in Dr. Carlos A. Soto, a veterinarian who felt no compunctions about saying that his colleagues were utterly mistaken. Admitting that the island indeed had a problem with wild dogs and feral apes, he was quick to note that the entity performing the mutilations was unknown to veterinary medicine.

Performing autopsies on a number of mutilated rabbits, Soto observed that the puncture marks on their bodies were perfect circles measuring some three to four inches in diameter. If the marks had been made with a scalpel, he argued, there would be irregularites on the edges, which were not apparent. If dogs or apes had been the culprits, there would have been the inevitable tearing of the flesh that is associated with said attacks. The vet went on to remark that the wounds on the rabbits in question appeared to have been cauterized, indicating a heat source; one hapless bunny was missing its trachea and esophagus, although the skin around its throat was intact.

Nor could Soto account for one of the more noticeable characteristics of the Chupacabras attacks: the lack of rigor mortis in its victims. The carcass of a dog slain by the paranormal predator remained flexible five hours after the alleged attack, and no coagulation of the blood was apparent.

Dr. Aracelis Ortiz, a forensic specialist in the University of Puerto Rico's School of Medical Sciences, urged that no responsibility be ascribed to either alien attackers or feral animals until having first established a bite pattern on the carcasses. On the other hand, Jose Luis Chabert, director of the Deparment of Natural Resources' Terrestrial Resources Division, noted that not all the incisions found on

158

the carcasses were alike, adding that it was incorrect to state that the animals had been found bloodless. He explained that many of the victims had in fact been slain by breeders of "pit-bull" terriers, who would show off their animals' prowess to potential buyers by staging nocturnal attacks in desolate fields.

While experts ruffled each others' feathers, the physical evidence continued to gather: on November 16, 1995, Mrs. Santa Ramos Reyes was terrified to see a bony, hairy arm come in through the steel jalousies of her bedroom window. The claw at the end of the arm picked up a teddy bear on a dresser and shredded it before its owners horror-filed eyes. The intruder left behind a piece of white flesh and a thick, goo-like substance which her husband, Bernardo Gómez, quickly collected and put in the refrigerator. Subsequent analysis proved the strange meat "was not beef". The whereabouts of this item were never made clear.

The Chupacabras "drool" was reported and collected in a number of cases. On November 23, 1995, a mongrel dog belonging to Demetrio Rivera was attacked in the home's backyard. The sudden response of its owners caused the assailant to flutter into the darkness. Rivera and his daughter Ivette found the pooch covered in a thick, clear goo which later washed off easily; a number of agonizing rabbits, property of Joel Carrillo and his wife Yolanda, were also found covered in the slimy substance during an attack in Gurabo's Barrio Celada. Elements of the Department of Natural Resources took samples of the substance for analysis but no results were ever circulated.

Experts speculated that the intruder had swallowed the goo-coated rabbit and later regurgitated it.

The powerful and disagreeable odor emanating from the creature was also reported in many cases: in the Collazo case, a Spanish journalist who smelled a sample of the awful stench, collected in a plastic bag, remained physically sick for days after her experience; Madelyne Tolentino, the initial witness in Canóvanas, characterized the unnatural odor as reminiscent of the pesticide Malathion; Efraín Arce, who had a tussle with the creature in Mexico, described it as having the odor of a rabid animal; the ominous smell of sulfur, reported in the April 1996 attacks, was so overpowering that a group of Civil Defense workers and newspaper journalists were sickened by it. Even Mayor "Chemo" Soto described encountering a terrible stench during his nocturnal forays in search of the creature.

THE CONSPIRACY QUICKENS

Lost amid the half-hearted attempts at humor and the Procrustean attempts at making the Chupacabras a space alien, a third alternative was quickly emerging—one which linked the mutilations to U.S. military activity that had been taking place over the course of decades. The events at Canóvanas and the Chupacabras encounters in the towns of Juncos and Aguas Buenas—all of them surrounding the El Yunque Rainforest—led some to believe that creature's point of origin could have been anywhere within the 28,000 acres of dense tropical foliage. Might not, conspiracists reasoned, the creature be the product of some biological experiment taking place within the rainforest?

The framework for this conspiracy theory was somewhat sturdier than many expected. Not only had Agent Orange— the infamous Vietnam War-era defoliant— first been tested at El Yunque, but radiation tests had also been conducted: between February and April 1965, over 20,000 curies of cesium were released in the rainforest, creating a gap in the canopy and affecting the tropical hardwoods growing there. Military activity was prevalent in the area, with the forest periodically being closed to tourism due to exercises. This verifiable framework was buttressed, in the minds of the public at large, by a shakier one linked to the considerable amount of UFO activity over Puerto Rico since 1987—which invariably involved the pursuit of unidentified aerial phenomena by Navy and National Guard fighters, the cordoning off of sites where alleged alien encounters had occurred by shadowy "Federal Agents" issuing vague threats or very real Special Forces types forbidding access to certain locations. It is believed to this day that the large drug interdiction dirigible or "aerostat" moored to a ground station near Lajas, Puerto Rico has a real mission of detecting the approach of incoming spacecraft.

The conspiracy theorist saw matters with much greater clarity than the journalist, the beleaguered Department of Agriculture functionary, or the UFO researcher: the mutilations were simply the next round in the covert relationship between the U.S. government and extraterrestrial intelligences (the large-headed "Greys" so common in '90s ufological lore). Whether the relationship was consensual or hostile was up for debate. Nevertheless, it appeared to be a dangerous dance in which one partner led (the E.T.'s) and the other followed (the chagrined U.S. military). In some scenarios the Chupacabras was an alien creature dumped on earth by aliens for study while the Army Rangers and other Special Forces kept the unwary at bay; in others scenarios, the military turned a blind eye to the creature's depredations possibly in exchange for advanced technology, which was also being tested over the island. It was all part of an emotionally charged scenario in which UFOs were seen to vanish into the premises of the U.S. Army's Camp Santiago in southern Puerto Rico, giant triangular UFOs crossed the skies and "absorbed" hostile U.S. Navy fighters, and casual witnesses to putative extraterrestrial activity or animal mutilations received visits from inviduals in seemingly official capacities, usually bearing cautionary messages or entreating them to remain silent.

ALIEN BLOOD LUST

CHAPTER 18

THE GOATSUCKER — AN INTERNATIONAL PHENOMENON

A case could perhaps be made for paying little attention to the Chupacabras if it had remained circumscribed to the island of Puerto Rico. But in 1996, it (and its cousins) decided it was time to see the world at large.

Miami, Florida, would be the predator's next stop. In February of that year, it killed forty-two animals belonging to Barbara Martínez and exanguinated fourteen chickens belonging to Luis Martin; eyewitnesses in northwestern Miami reported seeing a creature walking erect and covered with thick matted hair at the scene of the attacks. Dr. Virgilio Sánchez Ocejo, who investigated this case and other during the "Florida leg" of the aberrant predatory activity, noted that it ran from February through July 1996.

Mexico's turn would soon be next. On May 2, six goats were found dead along the Rio Grande, their throats presenting the now-characteristic marks associated with the Goatsucker. In the northern state of Taumalipas a taxicab driver reported seeing a five-foot tall creature cross the road in front of his vehicle and effortless hop over the wall of the School of Agronomy, where two dozen goats and sheep were later reported dead.

On May 10, 1996, Mexico's "Primer Impacto" broadcast announced that Teodora Ayala Reyes, a resident of the village of Alfonso Genaro Calderón in Sinaloa, had become the Chupacabras' first human victim—the victim presented what appeared to be "burn marks" on her back, exactly where the creature had clawed her. "It was very ugly," Ayala insisted. "I had my hair up in a bun, and it nearly shredded my scalp." The seaside village was further wrenched out of obscurity after reports of a colossal bat-like creature stalking the area became widespread. All manner of farm animals were being found dead by their owners.

The town of Tlaliscoyan, Veracruz, at the heart of the region's goat-raising area and was also subjected to the mysterious depredatory attacks linked to the Chupacabras' trademark. The death toll quickly rose to sixty slain sheep. Dr. Rafael Lara Palmeros, director of research for Mexico's CEFP, visited the University of

ALIEN BLOOD LUST

Veracruz' Faculty of Veterinary Sciences to find out what measures were being taken deal with the mutilations. He discovered that while authorities had "an awareness of the situation" based on TV and radio reports, the medical establishment was not planning on taking steps to conduct field research of its own.

More human victims began appearing in Mexico: Jose Angel Pulido was the unfortunate recipient of an alleged Chupacabras bite on his right forearm — two deep puncture marks had apparently been inflicted by an entity described as "hairless and gelatinous to the touch." Pulido showed the grievous puncture marks inflicted to his upper arm on Mexico's TV Azteca. He explained: "It leaped on me when I saw it. I slapped it away and turned to run home. I'm not sure if it ran or flew [behind me]. I didn't believe in this at first. Now I can tell you that I did see it, and I do believe in it."

When José Linares' 23 sheep turned up dead with odd puncture marks in Guazguaro, Michoacan, the wheelchair-bound farmer was so shocked that he could only say that something with two fangs had killed his livestock. When a six-hundred pound cow was found dead in similar circumstances, Mexican federal authorities ordered the municipality to perform the necessary autopsy.

The spokesman for Mexico's National Agropecuary Commission, Francisco Gurría, was interviewed by the broadcast media for official comment on the mutilation spree. "We are not talking about the same creature in all cases," he advised. "After autopsies, we have proven that carnivores are attacking goat and sheep populations due to the drought sweeping across our country. This is a perfectly natural phenomenon."

Reports became even more mind-bending as the Chupacabras—or whatever it was— outstayed its welcome in Mexico. Four truck drivers made an effort to earn their place in the history books by capturing a creature which had fallen to the ground after having been entangled in high-tension wires. The truckers tried stoning it to death, but the entity managed to limp away, leaving a trail of slime in its wake. Police officers reporting to the Salinas Victoria truck terminal stated that the eyewitnesses' descriptions corresponded with that of the Chupacabras.

The Mexican government maintained the hard line against the belief that something unnatural could be behind the attacks. Julia Carabias, Secretary of the Environment, decried the destruction of bat habitats by farmers setting caves ablaze in hopes of killing the Chupacabras. Ironically, public opinion believed that the government itself was fostering belief in the creature to distract the public from more pressing concerns.

The infestation was quickly becoming rampant as reports came in from Guatemala, Costa Rica, Honduras and as far south as the Amazon Basin, acquiring suitably mythic proportions: Guatemalan farmer Vicente Sosa thought he had seen a black dog with a long tail that suddenly increased in size, becoming a red-eyed beast with enormous eyes. Dr. Oscar Rafael Padilla visited the site of a Chupacabras attack on chicken coops in the Estanzuela region, and remarked on the high radioactivity readings found in the area.

The southern U.S. soon produced its very own bumper crop of Chupacabras sightings. In mid-May 1996, Sylvia Ybarra went out to her backyard in Texas town of Donna only to find that her pet goat had been killed by three inflamed puncture wounds to its throat. The animal had been felled near its shed.

The story spread like wildfire throughout Donna, although local veterinarians assured the owner that her goat had merely been attacked by a dog, and that the puncture marks had simply become inflamed. As had occured in Puerto Rico, the official explanation didn't wash, and this time there was a good reason for it: the Rio Grande basin had been plagued for decades by sporadic sightings of "giant birds" whose manifestations often coincided with mysterious animal mutilations. A Donna rancher had discovered one of his steers in such a condition as far back as 1970.

On May 1st, 1996, the Tucson police received a phone call from the home of José Espinoza in West Tucson. Apparently, something had broken into the house. Mr. Espinoza would later repeat his story to the media, saying that he'd seen a creature with large red eyes, a pointed nose and shrivelled features within the confines of his home. The mind-bending narration had the Chupacabras entering the home, slamming a door, and jumping on the chest of Espinoza's seven year-old son before hopping out of the boy's bedroom window. Footprints and handprints of all sorts were allegedly left on the walls (most of them corresponded to Mr. Espinoza's three year old son).

Heading ever westward, the wave of perplexing animal mutilations eventually reached California, where a construction worker, Roberto García, claimed that a puncture wound on the back of his hand was the result of falling asleep near an open window.

The Orange County resident told the press that he had been awakened from a deep sleep by the sensation of something tugging on his right hand. Pulling his hand away, he saw a sizeable, shadowy figure moving away very quickly. Adding to the "high strangeness" of this account was the fact that García's third floor apartment opened out to nothing but an alleyway below.

With its depredations in the Americas coming to a close, the paranormal predator somehow crossed the Atlantic Ocean and restarted its activities in northern Spain, decimating flocks of sheep in Aragón, the Pyrenees and the Basque Country. Spanish cattleman Ricardo Bárcena lost over twenty sheep and a mare between mid-1996 and early 1997. He remarked that his dead animals "had a puncture in their necks, about as wide as a button and five centimeters deep and bloodless. They were destroyed inside, as if someone had plunged an awl into the animals, causing damage as it was withdrawn." Other reports mirrored the incidents in the Americas in the most trivial details, and veterinarians noted that the wounds could in no way have been produced by a wolf, dog or insect.

ALIEN BLOOD LUST

CHAPTER 19

YO QUIERO GOATSUCKER

The Chupacabras phenomenon went from relative obscurity during the Puerto Rican phase to global celebrity after the mainland leg of its unholy tour. This gave rise to the another strange phenomenon: the societal impact of the sightings.

In December 1995, a casual television viewer could not watch an hour's entertainment without hearing comic reference being made to the Chupacabras on Puerto Rican television. A memorable TV commercial for a station had a smiling island beatuy simply saying the word "Chupacabras" at the end of a thirty second segment.

Then came the t-shirts, which tried to shoehorn the paranormal predator into the framework of contemporary culture — a grey-colored creature standing beside an all-points-bulletin reading SE BUSCA (Wanted) with the perpetrator's identifying characteristics; a rural family evacuating their home hurriedly as the Chupacabras stages an appearance; chubby, cartoonish Goatsuckers politely refraining from belching after a meal; overmuscled, monstrous depictions of the creature reminiscent of the Balrog from Tolkien's Middle Earth.

More permanent material goods than t-shirts could also be found: a number of eating establishments, even a candy store, dubbed either Chupacabras or El Chupa Cabras materialized throughout the Spanish-speaking communities of the U.S., and even sandwiches named after the unknown entity made an appearance. A Chupacabras "psychic hotline" also made a brief appearance.

Mexico, devastated by the financial depredations of a corrupt administration, produced a wealth of items showing disgraced president Salinas grafted on to the Chupacabras' body. Constant reference was made in the land of the Aztecs to the fact that no bloodsucking could have been more damaging or strange than the one inflicted by the errant politician.

The music industry, always on the lookout for the newest trend to immortalize in song, seized on the Chupacabras' notoriety. A merengue orchestra dubbing itself the New York Band took to the airwaves on Latin-oriented stations with their hit single Chupacabras, a bawdy ditty with few reprintable lyrics. A translated sample follows: "The classy Chupacabras/is fit for any goat/kissing their bodies and necks/inside, outside, what the heck/I'll kiss one goat, two goats/three goats, five or more/I'll never lose the taste/for a lovely little goat, mmm!"

Fans of rap music were not dissapointed either. A song in Spanish by rapper Gaby Meléndez claimed: "At El Yunque with my girl one dark night/we were doing stuff, you know/when this thing came into sight/a shady criter with big eyes and bigger fangs/The Chupacabras came out of nowhere/we were surrounded by its gang..." Chupamania lasted ran its fiercest during the summer months of 1996, dying down by December of that same year.

YES, BUT WHAT IS IT?

Three avenues of thought on the true nature of this predator emerged from the beginning. One held that the being was proof positive of the advanced nature of genetic research and that it had been released into the world to see how it functioned; others claimed that it was an extraterrestrial creature; either an alien probe designed to collect blood from terrestrial livestock or a "pet" left behind by the crew of a passing UFO; still others believed that the Chupacabras was related to black magic. These three viewpoints, of course, were challenged by the skeptics.

The initial urge was to ascribe the carnage in rural Puerto Rico to the activities of Santería practitioners and even black magicians, whose rituals call for blood sacrifice, but the sheer enormity of the slayings soon caused this theory to topple under its own weight. To the contrary, Mexico's Department of Religious Abuses inicated that the bulk of the mutilations were occuring in parts of the country harboring large numbers of satanists and adherents of Santería. Hector Elizondo, a spokesman for this agency, indicated that the mutilations could have been "perfectly orchestrated" by a group of human beings devoted to such religious practices.

Journalistic sources led credence to this belief. Mario Landeros, interviewed by Mexico's El Sol Veracruzano newspaper (5/17/96) stated that the Chupacabras was in fact a giant bloodsucking bat brought to the Americas on a regular basis by a satanic cult known as "Golden Lucifer". An truck accident caused a cage carrying a pregnant female bat to break open, allowing for the chiropterid to fly off into the dense vegetation of the surrounding area. The outbreaks of Chupacabras activity squared perfectly with this event.

The peasantry in the Caribbean and on the mainland believed that only a supernatural creature would be capable of the feats performed by the entity terrorizing their respective countrysides. Some saw it as a sign of the approaching End Times or as the handiwork of a particularly capable sorceror. Religious authorities were quite firm in stating that this belief was not one they shared. Msr. Sergio Obeso, Bishop of Xalapa, indicated that the Church "completely ruled out any supernatural pretentions" when it came to the Chupacabras.

Curiously, the Russian Orthodox Church, far removed from the scene of the events, indicated that the Ebola virus, Mad Cow Disease and the Chupacabras should not be construed as divine punishment, but an "invitation to reflection" upon manmade abuses of God's world.

Greatest attention was given to the propounders of an extraterrestrial hypothesis for the predatory creature's origin, particularly in Puerto Rico, where the Chupacabras was linked to a number of UFO cases. However, this appears to have been the exception, since no anomalous activity of that sort appears to have been prevalent in any of the other locations in which animal mutilations and Goatsucker sightings took place. Mexico's Dr. Rafael Lara Palmeros emphatically stated that no UFO sightings had taken place at Chupacabras attack sites.

The genetic experiment theory captured the public's imagination due to a number of media events that had little to do with the creature itself. One of them was a photograph of a laboratory mouse with a perfectly shaped human ear growing out of its back, appearing in the November 6, 1995 issue of Time Magazine. The story by Anastasia Toufexis indicated that the dramatic photo was "the latest and most dramatic demonstration of progress in tissue engineering." The U. Mass/M.I.T. project involved the introduction of a synthetic structure with human cartilage cells grafted under the mouse's skin. Fed by the rodent's blood, the cartilage cells would multiply and form a human ear. A segment of the popular UFO/paranormal program Encounters: The Hidden Truth discussed the possibility of human-ape hybrids thru gene splicing. The creation of "plantimals"—fusions of animal and vegetable cells— to patented animals, such as the so-called "hupigs"—pigs bred with human genes in order to minimize the danger of rejection during animal to human transplants— led many to believe that the aberrant bloodthirsty Chupacabras could in fact be the grafting of human (or nonhuman) genes onto marsupial stock, accounting for its outlandish appearance.

The genetic experiment hypothesis captured the minds of veterinary experts in Mexico. Dr. Alfredo Villanueva openly expressed his beleive that the Chupacabras was nothing more than a genetic experiment released by accident or design from a research facility in the U.S. or Mexico. Dr. Villanueva used ultrasound to scan the wounds on the animal carcasses; his findings corroborated those of his Puerto Rican counterparts — the puncture marcs extended deep into the animals' vitals. Subsequent analysis proved that said organs had been entirely drained of blood.

Belief in the genetic manipulation scenario was further fueled by the discovery of a "mutant" rabbit during the Mexican events. The newborn bunny, discovered in Veracruz's Ortiz Rubio neighborhood, presented fully developed claws and dorsal muscles which veterinarians thought could be incipient wings. Was

ALIEN BLOOD LUST

some sinister project underway to blend bats and rabbits? Desiderio Aguiar, Secretary of Citizen Protection for the state of Sinaloa (northern Mexico), pointed out that scientists studying the mutilation outbreak in his state believed they were dealing with a "mutation on the cellular level".

CONCLUSION

The events surrounding the Chupacabras' initial eruption into popular awareness are now many years behind us, allowing for a less heated atmosphere in which to debate its origin and even its existence. Episodes involving a nocturnal predator similar to the Chupacabras are still taking place in Brazil, although the animal described in these cases is clearly a canid of sorts—long-eared and quadrupedal—whose wounds on animals and humans alike in no way resemble the perfect, circular perforation marks found on cattle and small domestic animals in the Caribbean, Mexico and Central America.

The material that follows will draw us more into the fray.

The greater part of the naysayers in all countries steadfastly refused to look at the evidence, choosing instead to offer the same tired explanations for the mutilations (feral dogs, apes, satanists) but never explaining the face-to-face encounters with humans or the odd radiation signatures found in Puerto Rico and Central America (which may or may not have been directly linked to the creature). Most certainly, the feral dogs, apes and satanists are still on the scene. Did they choose to stop killing helpless animals all of a sudden, or did these convenient scapegoats vanish along with the mysterious predator?

But the Chupacabras would find advocates—even friends—in a number of different places: renown cryptozoologist Loren Coleman vigorously defended the creature's inclusion among the realm of biological anomalies studied by his field, even speculating that Chupacabras is a fresh-water, land-oriented variety of Merbeing (the hypothetical classification for Mermaids and Mermen alike) . Parapsychologist and lecturer Peter Jordan, who achieved prominence in de-mythologizing the "Amityville Horror" case of the '70s, worked closely with a number of psychometrists and psychics—many of whom have collaborated with U.S. police departments—in finding an answer to the Chupacabras' provenance and motives, producing a wide array of results mostly leaning toward a terrestrial, non-alien origin to the creature.

Space alien, interdimensional wanderer, escapee from a government biological laboratory or denizen from hell — it is almost certain that the creature's origin will never be clearly established. However, no one can deny its impact on our postmodern society and on the ever-turbulent disciplines that dare study the unknown..

Correspondence with Willie Durand Urbina, PRRG, May 1997

.. El Vocero, April 6 1991.. El Vocero, April 5, 1991

ALIEN BLOOD LUST

.. El Vocero, June 26, 1991

.. El Vocero, July 2, 1991

.. El Vocero, n.d.

. Alvarez Frank, Federico. "Report on Unidentified Flying Objects and Animal Mutilations in Puerto Rico." UFOSICPR, 1997. p.1.

Alvarez Frank, Federico. "Report on Unidentified Flying Objects and Animal Mutilations in Puerto Rico." p.3. Pla,

Lucy Guzmán de. Interview with Madelyne Tolentino and Jose Miguel Agosto on March 20, 1996..

Anonymous. La Verdadera Historia del Chupacabras. San Juan: Redacción Noticiosa, 1996.p.14

. El Vocero, November 1, 1995.. Conversation with Jorge Martín, December 21, 1996..

Freixedo, Magdalena del Amo. "Un Monstruo Causa Terror en Puerto Rico." Enigmas No.7 (1996) p.46.

EFE news agency. "Investigan al Chupacabras". November 16, 1995..

El Vocero, February 12, 1996.. Freixedo, Magdalena del Amo. p.48.

Tolentino Interview, March 20, 1996..

El Sol de Sinaloa, May 7, 1996

.. "Research History and Opportunities in the Luquillo Experimental Forest", U.S. Department of Agriculture General Technical Report SO-44, September 1983. p.112-113..

Sanchez Ocejo, Virgilio. Miami Chupacabras. Miami: Pharaoh Productions, 1997..

Lara Palmeros, Rafael A. "High Strangeness: Unexplained Animal Deaths in Mexico — A Preliminary Report."

Nemesis: The Chupacabras at Large. Samizdat Press, 1996..

TV Azteca news broadcast, 1996..

ibid..

ibid..

USA Today, May 15, 1996.. Tucson Weekly, May 30-June 5, 1996..

Cardeñosa, Bruno. "El Chupacabras Ataca en el País Vasco".

Año Cero V-No.74, p.40-42..

El Sol de Toluca, May 9, 1996..

Diario de Xalapa, May 12, 1996..

Ovaciones, May 2, 1996..

Coleman, Loren and Huyghe, Patrick.

ALIEN BLOOD LUST

The Field Guide to Bigfoot, Yeti, and Other Mystery Primates Worldwide. New York: Avon, 1999. p.39

CHAPTER 20

CHUPACABRAS RISING:
THE PARANORMAL PREDATOR RETURNS
Compiled and Annotated
by Scott Corrales

"A psychical investigator can establish the reality of the paranormal beyond all doubt—in private. But as soon as he tries to drag his evidence into the light of public scrutiny, it melts away like ice in the sun. And if in despair he shouts, "Please stop playing games and give me some public evidence!" the practical joker replies blandly, "But of course, my dear fellow—how about this? and presents a proof so preposterous that no one will take it seriously..."

— Colin Wilson, The Occult, 1988

I. Back in The Saddle Again

Only a few days ago, I heard a vulcanologist on National Public Radio discussing the possible eruption of Mammoth Lake in eastern California—a cataclysmic event that would surely be remembered for generations to come. During the course of his interview, the vulcanologist calmly explained the hostility demonstrated toward him by the people whose livelihoods depended on Mammoth Lake's brisk tourist trade. This hostility, said the researcher, reached the extent of having been told at a local restaurant to "stop talking nonsense" about possible volcanic activity at the site, or face the likelihood of having "a bomb" placed in his car.

This impressed me greatly, for you see, I had received, around the same time as the broadcast, what I construed to be a warning regarding my reports on the Chilean Chupacabras. After the initial—and unnecessary—bout of paranoia that ensued, I realized that there are individuals out there whose hostility in fact masks a deep-seated fear of things occurring beyond the control of their laboratory protocols, or perhaps even beyond the scope of their religious beliefs.

ALIEN BLOOD LUST

The phenomenon known as "Chupacabras" has endured efforts at discrediting it and even well-meaning efforts to clean up its unwholesome image by renaming it the SAI (Sporadic Agressive Intruder) and other science-friendly monikers. Its bloodsucking activity has been occurring since 1995 in the most disparate locationsPuerto Rico, Mexico, the U.S., Spain, Portugal, Brazil and now Chile and Argentinaand the physical manifestations of the creature/entity/whatever have been wildly different from one nation to another, according to eyewitness reports. In certain locations it appears to be a phenomenon which repeats periodically: the Puerto Rican outbreak of 1995 mirrors the Moca Vampire outbreak of 1975, and there are indications of similar animal mutilations occurring in the mid-1950s. Walter Cardona, a researcher on that Caribbean location, has uncovered evidence pointing to mutilations as far back as 1819.

The easy solutiondrawn along ethnic lineshas been to dismiss the matter as a phantasm of the Iberoamerican and peninsular Spanish peoples, yet a similar solution is never posited for the Loch Ness monster as a similar phantasm of the Anglo/Celtic mindset. Any such suggestion would be met with hostility, and well it should.

What you are about to read has been drawn from journalistic sources available both in print and on the World Wide Web. I have refrained from including anything that smacks of FOAFtales or other secondhand data (which invariably includes some of the most fascinating and controversial information). The exception to this case are the transcripts from certain Chilean radio programs, since I found such sources to be highly compelling and useful back in 1995, when I began working on The Chupacabras Diaries (Samizdat Communications, 1996).

None of the following would have been possible without the assistance of the friends and members of the Institute of Hispanic Ufology: Gloria R. Coluchi, Patricio Borlone, Ricardo Concha, Liliana Torres Garcia, Lucy Guzmán de Plá and others who made sure that I received text copies and links to the information. I cannot thank them enough!

Background Information

The Republic of Chile is one of the narrowest countries in the world—caught between the towering Andes and the Pacific Ocean. Along its length we find a variety of climates which have made it one of the planet's most significant producers of fruit and vegetables, as well as one of the finest wine-growing regions of the Americas.

Northern Chile is dry and barren, and has enormous salt deserts such as the Desierto de Atacama—one of the driest locations on earth—which has proven a boon to archaeologists bent on finding mummified human remains from many thousands of years ago. Southern Chile presents us with a radically different picture—fertile cropland and woods which give way to dense boreal rainforests covering

172

archipelagoes of thousands of islands all the way down to Tierra del Fuego.

Chile stood alone among Latin American countries for being the only one to have successfully evaded military coups and the ensuing army-led governments...until 1973, when Gen. Augusto Pinochet overthrew the left-leaning government of Salvador Allende and embarked upon a series of atrocities which are discussed to this very day. Pivotal in this coup d'etat were the Carabineros or national police, who were sworn to defend the elected president but sided with the revisionists instead. Unlike state troopers in the U.S., these are true national police forces with broad discretionary powers.

Ufologically speaking, the clear nights of its vast northern salt deserts have provided an array of memorable sightings, causing some Latin American investigators to vote it "the country most visited by UFOs" during the 1970's.

The all-time Chilean classic case is the hair-raising (and beard growing) experience suffered by army corporal Armando Valdés Garrido: in the bitterly cold early morning hours of April 25, 1977, a military patrol of the Rancagua regiment led by Corporal Valdés and composed of soldiers Julio Rosas, Ivan Rojas, Pedro Rosales, Humberto Rojas, Germán Valle and Raúl Salinas, had decided to camp in a rocky, desolate area in the Andean foothills. a few miles east of the city of Putre.

One of the soldiers, who had been assigned sentry duty, rushed back to the corporal to inform him that a red light was hovering above a nearby peak. Suspecting that contrabandists may be at work, Valdés ordered his platoon to ready weapons and extinguish the campfire—their only source of warmth in the near-zero weather. The soldiers moved out toward the source of the purplish-red light, realizing in a matter of seconds that they weren't dealing with illegal activity or lost mountaineers. The light was moving down the hillside, but not on its surface.

Having complained earlier about the frigid temperature, the soldiers were stunned to discover that it was actually getting warmer as the light grew closer, turning into giant oval-shaped object which bathing them in its purplish-red glow.

The object landed some fifty feet away, swathed in a violet fog that stood out in stark contrast to the surrounding darkness. This was enough to cause panic among the young conscripts, but they found themselves unable to move. Weapon in hand, the corporal ventured forward alone into the unearthly fog, adding later that he felt attracted by something within the luminosity, and was standing no farther than nine feet away from his men when the purplish light engulfed him. The corporal stated for the record that his only recollection of the event was a dreamlike vision of falling down a deep well or chasm. He was also left with a feeling that he would meet again with the strange presence.

The truly amazing part of the story follows: the leaderless platoon witnessed the corporal's unexplained reappearance some fifteen minutes later, when they heard him calling for help. Valdés gave the appearance of having been drugged;

his normally clean-shaven face showed dense beard, and his calendar wristwatch indicated that the time was 6:30 a.m. on the 30th of April, when it was still in fact 4:25 a.m. on the 25th. By all indications, the hapless military man had undergone a five day sojourn at an unguessable region of time and space. Hypnotic regression, which would ordinarily have been the procedure of choice in unlocking the "missing time", was expressly forbidden by the Chilean military. Medical specialists agreed that Valdés's panic at the ordeal, as well as the unknown radiation he had been subjected to, could have accelerated the growth of his facial hair, but no explanation was forthcoming about what had happened to his wristwatch.

After crisscrossing Chilean skies for decades, UFO activity dwindled in later decades down to a few unimportant sightings. According to an article from the EFE news agency, more than 400 confirmed sightings took place in the years before 1990. However, the period running from 1990 through 1994 has remained quiet. Not even the truck drivers who cross the Atacama Desert have witnessed any sightings worthy of public attention.

In November 1990, a woman from a small community some 450 kilometers to the north of Santiago was violently awakened by a loud noise while an intense light, as bright as the Sun's, poured into her bedroom. The woman stated that she was filled with dread when she noticed a figure no more than 115 cm. tall standing at the door. It had very large eyes and ears and its skin was illuminated by a strong violet light.

On October 8, 1994 a forest ranger in the Torres del Paine National Park, located in the subpolar Magallanes region, was allegedly chased by a gigantic UFO that hovered in the sky. The forest ranger, who has spent eighteen years in this particular park, was conducting a routine inspection when he was surprised by an enigmatic, spherical artifact that gave off a powerful beam of light.

Visibly upset, the ranger began a frantic race back to the Paso de la Muerte Shelter, some 17 kilometers away. He was pursued the entire distance by the object, which emitted "flashes of light". After gaining the shelter's safety, he was able to alert some comrades, who observed the UFO moving away at a high rate of speed. A driver identified as Arturo Cofre corroborated the forest ranger's testimony, stating that he had also witnessed the giant sphere over the so-called Cuernos del Paine. Carmen Salvat, an employee of the Hotel Explora, claimed to have seen a large luminous sphere moving in a northerly direction as it gave out potent red and violet flashes.

II. Chupacabras Rising
The Activity Begins

Although the year 2000 had started with considerable UFO activity in Mexico

ALIEN BLOOD LUST

(Acapulco and Mexico City), Colombia (an object videotaped over Bogotá), and Argentina (objects reported over the military harbor of Puerto Belgrano and un-explained objects crashing at Santiago del Estero), very little of this activity was occurring over Chile, which had enjoyed a very comfortable southern hemisphere summer in the wake of "El Niño" related problems the previous winter. It wasn't until April 2000 that the first intimations that something strange was happening in the country's northern reaches...

"El Mercurio de Chile" (newspaper)

April 20, 2000

CALAMA (Otilia Huerta). The bizarre deaths of sheep and goats in the rural region of Labanda, El Loa province, led to the summoning of a multiagency meeting to discuss the subject and agree on measures aimed at putting an end to the problem and above all, determining who or what has caused the death of 135 animals(goats, sheep, chickens)and rabbits.)

These events have become the single greatest topic of conversation in the local communities, where the legend of the existence of the Chupacabras is growing apacea mythological monster of possible Mexican origin.

Among the measures agreed by the provincial, agricultural, sanitary and police agencies are the elimination of stray dogs, particularly those living in a semiwild state and occupy the properties adjacent to the municipal dump. Lucas Burchard, chief of Environmental Hygiene and Food Control in Calama, explained that these animals tend to bite each other during fights, inflicting deep bloody wounds, thus developing a taste for the substance. This gives rise to the hypothesis that acting in packs, they now slay animals, and given the difficulty of consuming their flesh, are content to drink their blood. Information obtained from farmers by the Agricultural and Cattle Farming Service (SAG) place the blame on packs of wild dogs. SAG also announced the installation of traps to capture wild animals in a location to be used as a bait area and in which cameras will be placed to record what is going on. Likewise, the Carabineros (state police) will engage in nocturnal vigilance of the area by means of infrared equipment. A forensic specialist shall be in charge of analyzing the most recent kills, in order to determine the type of wounds and the action to which they could be attributed.

Diario "La Tercera" (newspaper)

April 21, 2000

CARABINEROS, FIREMEN AND RESEARCHERS
CONDUCT OPERATIONS IN CALAMA
by Alejando Ahumada/Calama

* Possible Human Intervention in Animal Deaths

* Combing Operation took Place Wednesday Night

ALIEN BLOOD LUST

to Find the Parties Responsible for the Cattle Slayings

Attacks Also Occured in San Fernando

In the community of Talcarehue, near San Fernando in the 6th Region, strange animal deaths have also been reported over the past days. Locals speak of the strange deaths of a hog, a dog, six chickens and some ducks under circumstances which remain unexplained, as well as the presence of footprints for which no explanation could be found.

Unofficial versions spoke at first of only a few animals, but the number grew to around thirty yesterday, spreading fear and uncertainty in the vicinity. Carabineros (state police) from the Aguas Buenas barracks made a formal request to the Agricultural and Cattle Farming Service (SAG) at San Fernando for the presence of a expert at the scene in order to establish the possible causes of death. As of the closing of this edition, the agency's experts at Talcarehue were still conducting initial investigation to establish who or what caused the animal deaths.

Results of the "Combing Operation"

The "combing operation" effected jointly by the Carabineros, Firemen and Researchers of Calama was the culmination of a process which served to gradually awaken the consciousness of a skeptical community. More than 60 agents participated in the operation, which took more than three hours and covered four kilometers on the northern bank of the Loa River in search of the culprit of the deaths of nearly 200 animals, with the possibility of human involvement not being discarded.

Shots Fired

On Wednesday night, the fast, sudden movement of "something" amid the bushes, accompanied by strange howls, alerted police officers who fired a volley of shots into the air in the vicinity of the local cemetery. Nothing was found afterward except for a pair of strange footprints which were taken and sent for expert analysis in Santiago. "The prints were sent to the investigations lab. We cannot say what they are at this time, but at first sight, they are nothing more than dog prints, which tend to expand and acquire strange shapes," stated provincial governor Francisco Segovia.

The public state of alarm unleashed by the circumstances forced the magistrates of the Second Criminal Court to open an investigation of the matter.

"An operation has been conducted, and we want to point out that no evidence of the presence of a strange animal was found, nor of any strange phenomenon which could be the cause of your animals [deaths]. As the SAG indicated, they [the deaths] are attributable to wild dogs searching for food. " The deaths of the last few pigs, however, brought about new background information. According to our pathologist, there was no human participation in this event. It could have been an augertype weapon, or a smallcaliber pistol." stated the governor.

ALIEN BLOOD LUST

Hypotheses

Faced with this new prospect, the Research Commissioner, German Oyanedel,indicated that "it is not possible to discard any hypothesisthey could indeed be dogs or other animals, but they could just as easily be humans taking advantage of the situation. I say this based on the last event, in particular, where the behavior patterns do not match those of the previous attacks."

This morning's inspection helped restore some of the tranquility lost by the affected farmers. But the majority of these find the "wild dog pack" explanation unconvincing. For this reason, they agreed to install a sort of "bait pen" this week-end not far from the last attack site to capture the creature whose name they whisper: Chupacabras.

"CRONICA" newspaper (Concepcion, Chile) May 2, 2000

The Federal Police of the United States decided in 1975, much in the same way SAG has done recently, that the Chupacabras phenomenon has its source in the predatory action of canids. According to the U.S. police agencies, foxes are to blame.

Many are refusing to believe the report issued by the Servicio Agricola y Ganadero (SAGAgricultural and Livestock Service) of the Second Region in regard to the phenomenon known as "El Chupacabras" , which places the blame for the deaths of thousands of animals squarely on packs of wild dogs surviving near the municipal dump of Calama, and which "descended" upon the city when their habitat was jeopardized, as well as the actions of "idle humans". What is more, searches for the mythical animal are still underway in Calama and it is logical that this should be the case, since the feeling of fear permeates throughout the entire city given the possibility that a human might fall prey to the alleged entity. However, the SAG report coincides with others presented by Puerto Rican (where the phenomenon first appeared) and U.S. authorities, as well as those of other countries. The foregoing indicates three possibilities: either scientists in all countries are wrong; their respective governments are engaging in a coverup of what is really going on, or that they are in fact, correct.

In any event, it is worth recalling that the phenomenon of dead animals with punctured necks, rendered bloodless and having lost their soft parts, began precisely in Puerto Rico toward 1970adding up to about 2000 deaths since that time. The strange event moved on to the U.S. (where it is known as "Cattle Mutilation"), then to Mexico and on to the rest of Latin America. In 1975, at the request of several Nebraskan and Californian congressmen the Federal Police of the United States (FBI) undertook an investigation into the subject, analyzing several dozen samples of dead animals, setting up monitoring spots, etc. After this, the FBI issued an official letter (based on veterinarian reports) to the director of said agency , stating that "[the animals] were attacked by other predators, whom we believe to be foxes given the shape of their teeth, which are scissorlike." Another report stated that the absence of soft parts (lips, rectum, genitals, udders, etc.) is an acknowledged thanatological phenomenon, since these are the first parts of a corpse to be subjected to insect attacks.

The foregoing agrees with the SAG report, in the sense that a canid animal is to blame. According to a special report published in "El Mercurio", the lack of blood in the animals found in Calama is due to the tearing of the flesh and not to suction. Furthermore, adds the report, at least three feral dogs were captured while engaging in such activities. The public refuses to acknowledge this fact and insists that "El Chupacabras" is to blame.

In spite of the aforementioned and the calming answers provided by the FBI, a question remains to be answered: Why did said agency classify its report as Top Secret for more than 20 years, and declassified it only a few months ago?

Interestingly, the authorities did not hesitate to trot out that old warhorse: the roving packs of wild dogs engaged in vampiric activity, whose prowess was invoked in Puerto Rico and Mexico (where a drought situation was supposed to have turned the dogs into bloodsuckers). Also of interest was the authorities shielding themselves behind the FBI's Rommel Report, which dismissed suggestions that anything unusual was occurring in the American West during the mid-'70s. CRONICA's story would be followed up by a more direct one:

ALIEN BLOOD LUST

CHAPTER 21

CHUPACABRAS CAUSES MASS HYSTERIA IN TUCAPEL
* Worker claims having seen the "Chupacabras"*

Strange rumors are making the rounds of Tucapel and Huepil about the alleged presence of the "Chupacabras". The authorities have denied the attacks, but an atmosphere of mass hysteria now prevails in the rural areas.

"Are you here about the bird?" is the first question asked by Jose Ismael Pino, 58, when he see strangers approaching the Esperanza Ranch, located 2 kilometers east of Huepil, Bio Bio province, where he works as a farm laborer. He isn't the only one on the lookout for "the bird", as he calls the alleged beast which he claims to have seen last Saturday in the same sector and which many believe to be none other than the mythical "Chupacabras". Pino's boss, Jorge Venegas, owner of the 75 acre farm, carries a loaded shotgun on his shoulder.In recent days, after the strange events which took place in Tucapel two weeks earlier when a large segment of dried brambles were crushed in the wake of a strange luminous phenomenon, many in said community walk around in fear, as well as in Huepil, some 5 kilometers distant. Many stories are told, but almost all of them coincide in that the region's farms were affected by the alleged predator, which has apparently slain four sheep on one farm and a cow on the other. However, both places denied the latter death, although the manager of the Raúl Pérez farm specified that :"years ago we had dog problems. They managed to kill 70 sheep in a single night, but we gave it no further importance at the time."

This resembles statements made on Tuesday by the Santa Fe Carabineros (also in Chile's Bio Bio province) which, as "Cronica" reported, eight sheep, all of them pregnant, were attached by an unknown animal which left them half dead, making it necessary to put them down. The local police blamed it all on packs of wild dogs specializing in mischief.

Subofficer Aliro Valdebenito, in charge of the Santa Fe barracks, further added that a characteristic of said canids is that they are barkless.

ALIEN BLOOD LUST

Gossip, however, states that the landowners are refusing to say what is really happening, although the chief of the Huepil Carabineros (state police), Lt. Walter Koch, pays no mind to it at all. "No, the are no reports about it whatsoever. We don't even have pumas in this sector, and only in the preCordilleran region will you find foxes. The only problems of this type we've had are caused by some Siberian dogs (sic) which have feasted on some chickens,:"he explains, on the verge of laughter.

However, individuals like professor Carlos Villalobos, planter Jorge Venegas and Jose Pino believe in something else. According to Pino, on Saturday (April 29) at around 20:00 hours and under very bright moonlight, his employer sent him to the nearby stream, some 200 meters from the house, to fetch water in a bucket. "There as a lost bull roaming a round. I was walking along when I saw something , and I thought that was it. "Hey, damn bull!" I shouted, and that's when I saw it [the creature]. It hardly moved. It just stood there, looking at me. It stood about 1.50 meters, like a big monkey, with long, clawed arms and enormous fangs protruding from its mouth, as well as a pair of wings. I was so scared that I turned around and ran back for the hounds. I sent them off toward where the Bird was and they chased it. Cachorro (one of the dogs) returned with a bloodstained neck."

He claims not having heard any noise whatsoever and to not have slept a wink that night.

It should be noted that this description coincides with almost all those known at the time, which gives rise to the belief that it is a massive case of collective hallucination, worthy of any school of sociology, or of an alltooreal phenomenon. Venegas, on his own part, insists that all of his employees now leave early, since they are fearful of walking around at night, and he himself stated that since the luminous phenomenon at Tucapel, he sleeps with his shotgun beside him.

"We don't know what we're dealing with here. I'm not so concerned about its attacks on the animals, but I have two children, 12 and 15 years old, and I'm not going to let anything happen to them. In fact, right now I'm out to get a floodlight to see at night, in case something weird shows up." explained the planter, shifting the shotgun's weight on his shoulder.

To Carlos Villalobos, a schoolteacher in Huepil, the phenomenon which has befallen his region is related to a series of anomalous situations which are largely isolated, such as the sheep attack in Santa Fe and the luminous phenomenon in Tucapel. "I think its linked in some fashion to an unknown life form, probably alien in origin, but the problem is that the authorities do not wish to acknowledge it, and this course of action may probably be justified, since a collective panic situation could be unleashed."

Regarding the means by which the riddle could be solved, he added that "the existing human resources will never allow us to know what is going on, since the

It is C A shapeshifter

creature has been pursued for years and all we have to show for it are denials. Moreover, if it is really alien, it's unlikely that we'll be the ones to catch it."

Barkless, vampiric dogs...what greater irony could there be? The early manifestations of the creature were quite similar to the events in Puerto Rico in 1995, but the single most outstanding feature is the fact that the creature descriptions would change from one report to the next, suggesting three possible things: a. that the witnesses were lying; b. that more than one creature or creature-type was involved; or c., that the Chupacabras is a truly protean creature, able to assume shapes that jibe with images drawn from the percipient's brain (a most outlandish notion, but...). For this reason, all eyewitness descriptions will appear underlined in this report.

Meanwhile, the body count continued to rise...

"La Tercera" (newspaper)
35 FARM ANIMALS FOUND DEAD IN PUCON
May 4, 2000

PUCON, Chile (Agencias). 35 farm birds were found dead today in a ranch 12 kilometers away from Pucon, on the route leading to the town of Caburgua, Ninth Region. This new animal attack, attributed to the mythical Chupacabras, presents the same characteristics as earlier ones, since the dead chickens presented bites and scratches on different parts of their bodies. In this regard, the assistant sheriff of the Pucon Carabineros (state police), Captain Roberto Saldivia, confirmed that the animals were found dead within a pen, without a single drop of blood in their bodies.

Orbe (magazine)
FURTHER CHUPACABRAS ATTACKS PUZZLE CHILEAN AUTHORITIES
May 5, 2000

The Ninth Region's Agricultural and Livestock Service (SAG) embarked upon an investigation of the strange conditions in which 35 chickens were slain yesterday morning in the locale of Caburuga, Pucon Commune.

Cesar Hidalgo, the Service's Regional Director, explained that SAG functionaries were on site verifying the claims presented by local farmers and analyzing the dead birds, whose carcasses betrayed the signs of having been attacked by an unknown predator.

"In any case," added Hidalgo, "I personally believe we are faced by a natural activity unrelated to the exploits of the socalled "Chupacabras" seen in other parts of the country."

Over the past two weeks, similar claims have been brought forth concerning situations similar to those of Pucon. In Angol, capital of the Malleco Province, a former Carabinero (state trooper) claimed having seen a giant bat causing depredations in the vicinity of the correctional facility being built in said Commune.

Officialdom's concern over the situation reflected the grim reality that the unknown entity's attacks were now taking place on two fronts—the attacks in Calama and Maria Elena, on the foothills of the pre-Andean cordillera, and another much closer to Santiago de Chile, the nation's capital, taking place in some of the choicest farmland that South America has to offer. While this remark may be disparaging of the authorities, it is a pattern that has emerged again and again—as long as the mutilations are taking place in what we would term "the boonies", officials are quite content to dismiss them as the harmless prattle of rustics. The minute major urban centers are in jeopardy (to wit, the shift of location in mutilations from landlocked Orocovis to coastal Canovanas in Puerto Rico), the "attitude adjustment" becomes manifest. This was certainly case when the mutilations were reported later at the seaport of Coronel...

From "El Sur" (newspaper), Friday, May 5, 2000
MYSTERIOUS NOCTURNAL APPARITION IN BUILDING COURTYARD
Dead dog found later
***Contradictory accounts from witness,
Carabineros and health services***
***Authorities dismiss claims in effort
to lower profile of possible mass hysteria case***
by Carlos Baso Prieto (El Sur Newspaper)
Laguna Redonda, Concepción 01.30 hrs, 03 May 2000

Around 1:30 am on May 3rd, professor Liliana Romero Castillo slept soundly in her apartment located at Laguna Redonda, Concepción, when she was awakened by the howling of the 5 stray puppies she had picked up some time earlier and live in the building's courtyard along with "Black", her large, fierce mastiff. "I crouched and looked through the window. The puppies were whining and Black had huddled against the wall and was motionless. I could see the back of what appeared to be an immense man, standing some 2 meters tall. Its shoulderblades were split, as if it had wings. Its attitude resembled that of a person choking another...that was my impression." says the instructor.

Convinced that a crime was taking place in her garden, she woke her husband, who paid the matter little attention. "I'm not getting up." he said, half asleep.

"In a matter of seconds, I went back to the living room to look at it, but it was gone. It had vanished, " she adds.

ALIEN BLOOD LUST

20:00 hours, May 4th 2000

The following day, Liliana gave the matter little importance until her children went to buy groceries at a nearby shop, using a shortcut located behind their building. Upon returning, they told their mother that there was "a dead dog in the place where the gentleman was being attacked."

Liliana asked her husband to check, and he returned saying that a wooly beigecolored dog was lying on the floor with two puncture marks on its throat. "I don't know if I might be in a suggestive state, but it had two deep holes in its jugular, about as wide as a BIC pen, separated by 5 centimeters between them. What impressed me the most was that it was completely bloodless and was as light as a feather. The dog was incredibly wooly and in fact, I had to move its fur to see the wounds."

22:00 hrs, May 4th, 2000

A truck of the Concecpcion Carabineros, with two subofficers and a lieutenant in charge, reached the site, notified by Liliana. The trio were rather impressed, since the dog had been assaulted in the same manner that the sheep had been at other locations. They called their unit to request the SAG (Agriculture and Livestock Service) to report, but it did not appear. Their headquarters advised them that the carcass would be removed later. The troopers asked for black garbage bags and ordered the family to remain quiet, so as not to spread panic among local residents, "But I'm scared, since I have young children, and I'm afraid that whatever was there will come back," states Liliana. The dog was later transferred to the First Commissariat of the Carabineros and placed in an office near the Prefecture's yard, where many bureaucrats were able to get a good look at it, although they were asked not to create a commotion about the matter. One of the policemen who managed to see the carcass commented that in fact, it had two puncture marks and was "as light as a feather", which left him shaken. "I have considerable experience and have seen many things, but I'd never seen anything like it. Had I not seen it, I wouldn't believe it." he added.

The dead animal remained all of yesterday morning in the same location, where it was filmed and photographed by Carabineros officials, after which it was transferred to the offices of the Concepcion Health Service by a functionary of the Civil Commission and two veterinarians.

The foregoing case remains, in my mind, as one of the most compelling of all the Chupacabras events reported since 1995. The creature reported, again, is not the boilerplate kangaroo-cum-Grey that haunted millions of t-shirts from Miami to Managua, but a towering, possibly winged entity closer more closely reminiscent to West Virginia's "Mothman" (1967) than any other...short of a medieval gargoyle. Skeptics should take note of the painstaking approach of the authorities in this episode: officials visited the site, collected the evidence and transferred it to a suitable facility for analysis. The suggestion that Chupacabras research is conducted by "mystery buffs" or "cranks" simply does not apply here.

Crónica (newspaper), Concepción, Chile
CHUPACABRAS STRIKES IN CORONEL
Monday, May 8, 2000

Four hens died a strange death in a section of Huertos Familiares. In spite of the fact that the henhouse was closed, they turned up dead in the backyard with mysterious incisions on their bodies. The Carabineros have declared dogs to be the culprits in this case.

The discovery of four dead hens yesterday morning alarmed Emilia Parra Campos. It was hardly the first time that animals had died on the premises of Huertos Familiares in the locale of Coronel, where she has lived for 32 years, but the strange manner in which they were found by householder Pedro Conterasoutside the locked henhouse, scattered all over the backyard and with deep incisions on their bodiesled them to believe that something beyond the known was responsible.

"Dogs rip their prey apart and pull the feathers off chickens, "says Emilia, still fearful and trying to explain that canids were not involved. It is worth noting that the henhouse door was locked and the predator only attacked the "mottled" variety of hen, leaving the other six white hens alone. The dead birds had a number of wounds on their bodies.

The penetration marks resembled those made by an ice pick (one per lesion) with slight tearing of the capillaries. Whatever caused the wounds must have been long, since some of the attack victims betrayed the effects of the injury on both sides of the body. None of them was attacked in the throat, although there were wounds on the wings, back and breast.

Nevertheless, Pedro Contreras is not afraid to utter the name of the possible culprit: the "Chupacabras". As he explained, around 9 a.m. yesterday he went to the henhouse to feed his chickens, stumbling upon the nightmarish scene. "It must be [the Chupacabras] or another strange creature, because we have never had anything similar around here." he points out.

He even added that "a neighbor who engages in raising chickens was concerned because we're not dealing with something normal. Animals usually devour their victims."

According to Carabineros (state troopers) in the town of Coronel, who visited the site to inspect the claims, the culprits are dogs which prowl the areas adjacent to urban areas, stating that no one should feel concern in this regard. To insure their safety, the police took the hens to the nearby Lagunillas headquarters, where they remain until the courts wish to see the evidence.

ALIEN BLOOD LUST

The police reportwhich is the same one issued for all the animal deaths occurred over the past week in the areawas reinforced by a neighbor, Salome Salgado, who claimed having seen a black dog at 7 a.m. on top of the henhouse. However, Emilia Parra, expressed her misgivings about a dog being able to climb onto [such as structure], given the height involved and the absence of any means of reaching said heights.

While no images of this carnage were made available on the website they would be redundant for those who have seen similar images from Mexico, Puerto Rico, and Miami, Florida. But the proximity to heavily populated districts would finally prompt an official inquest into the matter—something which did not happen in the Caribbean countries despite entreaties from local legislative bodies.

Diario "El Sur" (newspaper) Concepción, Chile
CHILEAN JUDGE LOOKS INTO ANIMAL DEATHS
Wednesday, May 10, 2000

A claim received at the Third Criminal Court of Concepcion as a result of the strange deaths of seven animals in the Quilacoya sector of the Hualqui Commune forced the courts to open what will be the first inquest into the controversy unleashed by the socalled "Chupacabras". The investigation was initiated by magistrate Flora Sepulveda, who immediately summoned the owner of the animals and ordered the Department of Pathology of the University of Concepcion in Chillan to determine the cause of the massive deaths.

According to a report issued by the Carabineros (state troopers) Headquarters in Quilacoya to the criminal courts, Paula Rodriguez Toledo reported last Thursday that six sheep and a goat on her property were found exsanguinated after having been apparently bit by another animal. Rodriguez's personal opinion is that the sheep and goat were attacked by wild dogs. The animals' owners, however, are not so sure, since the strange event took place during the early morning hours of May 4th, when all members of the family were asleep. "No one seems to have heard or seen anything,"indicate sources at the Quilacoya Carabineros headquarters, whose personnel note that it was not possible to see the animals before the claim for damages was brought forwardthe Rodriguezes had buried the sheep and the goat on their property.

Police authorities note that the in the light of the courtordered investigation, it is likely that the court will order the remains to be exhumed.

Judge Sepúlveda is perhaps worthy of being remembered as the first member of the judicial branch to order an investigation into Chupacabras activity, at least in the Americas. During Spain's experience with an unusual bloodsucking predator (1996), the courts ordered all information sealed, although the disappearance of 200 sheep from an enclosed location prompted a court officer to note, in docket

ALIEN BLOOD LUST

531/96, that the hapless creatures "appeared to have been sucked upward". Even that country's national police, the Guardia Civil, remarked that the vanishing sheep represented "one of the strangest thefts ever investigated."

But Chile's enigmatic visitor wasn't quite done with the country's placid southern regions. It headed south from Coronel to the coastal town of Lebu...

DIARIO EL SUR (Newspaper) Concepcion, Chile
May 14, 2000

Residents of Lebu alarmed

Mysterious animal caused massive poultry deaths

The attacks occurred in two different locations, and in both, witnesses claim having seen a beast with similar characteristics. The attack on two henhouses in the Lebu Commune by an unknown being bolsters the existence of the mythic "Chupacabras" in the area, now specifically in the province of Arauco. In the early morning hours yesterday, in the Lebu Alto sector, two families claimed having been victims of a strange event which caused the deaths of 24 hens. The events, confirmed by the Lebu Carabineros (state troopers), took place at 04:00 hrs on Saturday morning when an unidentified resident (this is due to the fact that background information has not yet been given to the courts) heard a noise in her henhouse. Getting out of bed and going outside, she found her dogs were calmeven fearfuldespite the fact that something was going on in the henhouse. As she approached the site, she told the police, she managed to see a rounded figure which leaped away from the chicken coop and went around the back of a nearby hill. Upon entering, the anonymous witness confirmed that 17 of her 19 hens were dead with visible signs of tearing.

Shortly afterward, the chicken coop at a neighbor's house was also attacked, and another resident (also anonymous) retold a similar account. At 08:00 hrs (approx.) the Carabineros were notified of the events. Police elements reported to the scene and verified the animal deaths. Their carcasses were collected and sent to Concepcion for further analysis.

The authorities indicated that the affected families refrained from presenting a claim for the event. However, given the public alarm that has been raised by these situations, the events shall be notified to the courts. It is worth recalling that the Third Criminal Court of Concepcion is investigating the strange deaths of seven sheep in Hualqui's Quilacoya Sector.

Untitled article from Crónica (newspaper), May 15, 2000

Carabineros is currently in possession of 30 lifeless birds with strange puncture marks in their bodies, found in the early hours of Saturday morning in two

ALIEN BLOOD LUST

dwellings in the urban sector of the commune. This morning, veterinarians from Concepcion, of a state agency not included in the police reportshall perform autopsies on the carcasses of 30 chickens which died under strange circumstances early Saturday morning at Lebu.

The incidents according to Carabineros spokesmen, occured in two dwellings of the urban sector of the commune near Cerro La Cruz. The birds, which in both cases were in locked henhouses, were attacked by an unknown entity which left puncture marks in its throats aside from causing tears in their skin and having rendered them bloodless. This is reminiscent of a case reported by "Cronica" last saturday in Coronel, where four hens suffered a similar fate.

In this case, police officials point out that the event is under investigation and a report is being rendered to the court having jurisdiction, aside from the first measures having been taken.

It is worth noting that last Friday, Radio Pudahuel and Channel 13 transmitted news reports indicating that a family of strange animalspossible "Chupacabrases" had been found by Military personnel in the vicinity of the Radomiro Tomic Mine within the Second Region .

According to information provided by Radio Pudahuel, it was a female, a male and a cuba story which had a harsh ring of "The XFiles" about it and which were delivered to agents of the U.S. FBI agency which arrived at Calama from Santiago (where the U.S. federal police has an office in its embassy). The creatures in question would have been taken to the U.S.

No further mention of this event was made, but police sources told "Cronica" that the capture of the specimens was real and that everything had transpired as originally told. Pure paranoia?

This episode on May 15, 2000 marks the turning point in the Chupacabras wave in Chile—the moment at which readers following the story from a distance with polite interest developed one of two attitudes: either this was going to be one of the most fascinating and mind-bending cases on record, or the whole story was a fabrication.

To be sure, any involvement of a U.S. agency (whether the real NASA or an intelligence agency adopting its identity to benefit from the generally positive opinion Latin Americans have about the space program) would increase interest in the Chilean situation by a level or two—no longer would we be talking about high strangeness playing itself out in the Chilean outback, but an operation worthy of interest by the world's last remaining superpower.

I can no longer refrain from editorializing, so here it goes: the entire creatures-hunted-by-the-military has a decidedly science fictionish air to it and—God forgive me if its true—could have been deliberately planted to tarnish any credibility that the events may have gathered from the outset.

ALIEN BLOOD LUST

"NASA personnel" — and I don't use the quotation marks lightly, in this case — have been seen and reported in many Latin American scenarios, more noticeably in Mexico (Ciudad Valleys, 1991) and Argentina (Metán, 1995) either during UFO sightings or in the wake of putative saucer crashes. During the alleged crash at Metán, the local authorities were advised to step aside and allow the "NASA men" to pursue their activities unmolested: on August 18, 1995, villagers and townspeople reported seeing four wheel drive vehicles manned by English-speaking personnel speeding toward the crash site. According to an anonymous technician at the National University at Salta, the foreign personnel were accompanied by university staffers and technicians from the local nuclear power plant. The foreigners, according to this account, took with them chunks of a thin, metallic material resembling aluminum. The fragments allegedly "assumed a concave shape when joined" and had an unusual consistency. The anonymous university informer claims that all present were instructed to say that fragments of a meteorite had been found, and that pieces of rock should be shown to the press.

Raúl Córdoba, a Saltan journalist interviewed by Buenos Aires' Crónica newspaper on September 1, 1995 stated that "there is no doubt that we have NASA personnel here trying to conceal the truth, assisted by members of the National University at Salta, since it is already involved in the matter but refuses to publicize its involvement."

Another parallel can be found for the Mexican situation: In July 1977 there were rumors that a UFO had crashed near the town of Jopala, to the east of Puebla (due east of Mexico City). Townspeople claimed to have seen a solid craft explode into thousands of sparks, and the witnesses to the event included the local mayor and several schoolteachers who hand managed to recover pieces of what was described as "a rough metal."

But there was a curious aside to the alleged crash. The locals argued that they had only managed to collect a handful of alleged "saucer chassis" pieces because others had beaten them to the punch: a group of persons who arrived by helicopter and were obviously Americans. The news media would later report, as it often does, that "NASA scientists" had visited the area.

In the meantime, things were heating up in the south, for sure, but the mutilations had not ceased in the northern reaches for a single moment...

"El Miami Herald" (newspaper) Miami, Florida
May 20, 2000

CALAMA, Chile 20, (AP) Police officers unsuccessfully combed farms on the suburbs of this town in search of an alleged Chupacabras which has already slain some 200 sheep and which has also attacked pigs in recent days.

Alarmed by recent attacks, the regional government ordered patrols of the outskirts of this desert mining region some 1600 kilometers to the north of Santiago de Chile. Policemen, accompanied by tracking dogs, and under orders to open fire if attacked, combed the farms where the locals maintain small cultivation operations and pens for animal husbandry.

The search, however, has been unsuccessful and no traces of the putative animal were found, although some locals claim having seen it and have described it as having a human/animal shape. The slaughter of sheep and pigs has been attributed not only to the Chupacabrasattorney and ufologist Boris Campos maintains that aliens from space are to blame for the carnage. Meanwhile, reports were received this morning from the southern city of San Fernando about the strange death of some thirty hens, ducks, pigs and dogs in rural areas. Said killings have also been ascribed to the Chupacabras.

The Spanish-language version of the prestigious Miami newspaper was responsible for making this news wire widely known. It is important to recall that Miami, Florida was the Chupacabras' first port-of-call outside Puerto Rico in 1996, and memories of its exploits are still the subject of conversation there.

El Sur (newspaper), June 8, 2000
FOUR CHICKENS EXSANGUINATED AND DISMEMBERED
IN VILLA NONGUEN
by Carlos Basso Prieto

A new case which involved the death of chickens took place in the area, affecting a humble couple in the city of Concepcion's Villa Nonguen sector. As reported in "Cronica" last Monday, when 14 hens perished under strange circumstances at Villa Cruz del Sur, at Talcahuano, the number of affected chickens in this case is four, and they were torn to shreds.

The strange event took place yesterday morning around 4 a.m. while Julio Reyes and his wife Carmen Andrade were still asleep. They suddenly heard a loud noise coming from their home's back yard, a sort of small farm in which they have a henhouse and tomato, potato, "choclo" and pepper cultivations.

"The light outside the henhouse was on. I saw the rooster flapping his wings fiercely while the hens were crowingsomething they never do at that time. That's when I saw the white one (sic) running toward the back. At that time, "Bobby" (the family dog, who slept beside the chicken coop) came out to take a look, but when he reached the back gate, through which the hens had fled, he refused to follow and remained standing still. He then ran toward the street gate and started barking," explains Carmen, who did not witness the events herself out of fear that a burglar might be involved.

" Bobby" became sort of dopey and turned back.. He didn't dare go forward." added the man of the house.

ALIEN BLOOD LUST

Exsanguinated

Around 7:00 a.m, the couple discovered what had transpired. In the very rear of the back yardwhich can be reached by crossing two gates their three hens and one rooster were found dead, completely torn to shreds as if they had been ripped open by the chest cavity and scattered in a 10 meter radius. It is worth noting that the house's entrance is a gate covered in chicken wire. With the exception of "Bobby", who never attacked a hen in his life, none of the neighboring homes has a dog.

Once more, elements of the Carabineros reporting to the location told the householders that dogs had perpetrated the attack. However, based on several paw prints found on the site (twice the size of "Bobby"'s , a half dwarf terrier), the owners were not satisfied by the explanation given the difficulty that a dog would have in getting into the area and second, because the explanation did not consider the total absence of blood in the vicinity. In spite of the fact that the chickens were completely open, there was no blood in evidence anywhere. Not a splash, not a drop, not a clot. Nothing at all.

"Noooo, this is completely abnormal. You see, last year there was a dog who'd appear during the day and steal chickens that would stray onto the street, but that's what he did: he stole them and ate them, one by one. The very same thing happened in the fields: every time a dog made off with a chicken, it would take them one by one," stated Julio Reyes, who added that nothing similar had ever occured in his house, where he has raised poultry for over 25 years. "Besides, if a dog steals an animal, it'll eat it. It won't kill it for the hell of it. Had it been a thief, it would have taken them. In this case, the chicken's racket lasted no more than four minutes. It was all very quick." reasoned the hens' owner.

The other strange thing that occured yesterday is that "Bobby", going against all of his canine instincts, wasn't even approaching the carcasses. There were also deep prints in the surroundingsthe soil is soft and moist which appeared to be those of a dog, with the difference that they were isolated from each other and did not follow the typical sequence of footprints.

Unlike the deaths of the samples at the harbor, where strands of blond hair were left on the fencing that protected the victims, there were no further traces left by the unknown assailant. The householders have no closure in the matter and have stated that they are unsure if the mythical "Chupacabras" could be the culprit.

The Pablo Aguilera Show (Radio Pudahuel), June 9, 2000
NEW VEHICLE EXCHANGED FOR SILENCE IN ANTOFAGASTA
Transcript by Patricio Borlone Rojas

On the June 9, 2000 broadcast of the Pablo Aguilera Show, 11:45 a.m. on Radio

ALIEN BLOOD LUST

Pudahuel, 90.5 FM, a call came in from somewhere in Antofagasta, northern Chile, pointing to a new Chupacabras attack.(H) represents the show's host (C) stands for the caller

Host: I haven't the least bit of doubt, and I state this as a declaration of principles, that there is something fishy about all of this. In other words, this [creature] isn't any known animal, nor a species identified by human beings. Of this I have no doubt at all. In other words, it's something weird...IT IS! Well...it turns out that in a city of northern Chile, and I won't tell you where, a coworker of the person whose on the line...uhh...let's see here...why don't you tell us?

Caller: Look, Pablito, what happened that night [date not specified] is that he says he was asleep in his bedroom and their cat started making noises, waking them up. That's when they saw the alleged Chupacabras. He says that when it saw them, the creature took off at high speed.

H: And what was it like?

C: He says it destroyed their car.

H: What was it they saw, more or less?

C: He says it was about one meter fifty tall and that it upper body was hairy. He says it was like a bat...having the same type of upper body. And it destroyed his car...

H: Excuse me...what did it use to destroy their car?

C: It used some sort of claws to scratch their vehicle.

H: And were any prints left?

C: Of course, and he says they went to

H: Okay, but what happened to the cat? What became of the cat in all of this?

C: It killed it. It killed the cat. He says they got up and went to notify the authorities [the authorities are not specified]

H: I see...

C: That's where they were told that they must remain quiet about the situation, if they wanted to get a new car in exchange for the damaged one.

H: In other words...

C: If they spoke to the press, they wouldn't be given a new car. They'd be stuck with the one they had.

H: In other words, they were asked to trade their silence for a car...

A: Exactly.

H: The hell!

C: So that's how many similar cases have transpired here...near where I live, my sister in law's father is with the authorities, and he's told her that several cases have occurred, and they have nothing to say about what's going on...

H: You mean, not to disclose what they know...nor any larger rumors.. and in the light of all this, didn't the gentleman wind up keeping the shattered car?

C: Exactly...he still doesn't know when the change will be made...

H: They won't be changing any cars now! Ha,ha! We're spreading the news on the air.

C: Of course...but he doesn't know who's calling.

H: Well, very good, my friend.

C: So that's what's going on here...they had told him it was a dog...they had found in a cave...and was supposedly the Chupacabras.

H: Ah...was that the explanation they gave the gentleman, too?

C: Yes...that it was a dog, a Siberian Husky type with a deformed muzzle who was killing the animals.

H: Ah...I see..

C: It came out in the papers.

H: In the local papers?

C: Of course.

H: Well, that's great...Thanks, eh?

C: Sure, Pablito...thanks and so long.

(11:57 A: M:subsequent comment by Pablo Aguilera):

"well, that was a side note I had as part of the daily follow up we're conducting...this happened in Antofagasta...perhaps people living there might have other details to share with us...please call me and we'll compile them. We'll continue on our own with the Court Cases. Background music, please..."

"Diaro El Sur" (newspaper) Concepcion, Sunday June 11,2000

SANTIAGO (EFE) Chilean space researchers announced yesterday that they will ask their government, through the Ministry of Defense, to investigate the alleged responsibility of NASA, the United States space agency, in the manifestations of the socalled "Chupacabras" which has caused the deaths of hundreds of domestic animals in this country.

The "ufologists" pointed out in their press conference that accounts indicating NASA scientists lost control of at least three "genetic experiments" in Chile are growing. Said specimens would be the ones that massacred a variety of animal species in several regions.

A number of animal turned up dead for the first time in Calama and its environs last April, rendered completely bloodless and without having been devoured by the enigmatic predator. Similar killings later took place throughout other southern locations in the country.

ALIEN BLOOD LUST

"Many persons agree that they have seen a kind of ape or mandrill with human features but with very large eyes, who moves very quickly and in a zigzagging manner," stated Cristian Riffo, director of the "Ovnivision" group. According to this researcher, an animal of these characteristics was hunted by the chilean military in the vicinity of the Radomiro Tomic mine near Calama, an operation in which one soldier allegedly died.

For this reason, Riffo stated that they would visit the Ministry of Defense tomorrow to demand a clarification of these accounts. They will also ask the Army to explain if accounts of the death of a soldier during the capture of one of these genetic monsters is indeed true.

Although no further information was forthcoming about Cristian Riffo's efforts at meeting with the Ministry of Defense, the description of the creature in this instance as an apelike entity with large eyes points to one of the very first descriptions ever offered about the creature: on November 9, 1995, Ada Arroyo, the assistant director of a nursing home on the outskirts of Caguas, Puerto Rico, saw a creature which resembled the Chilean entities

"I heard screams similar to those made by a lamb being slaughtered," said Mrs. Arroyo "I went out to the patio and managed to see a strange hairy figure, grayish in color, covering its body with a pair of wings. It had a flattened, vulpine face, with enormous red eyes." Mrs. Arroyo added that the creature held her gaze with its mesmerizing eyes before taking off into the air, vanishing from sight immediately.

The simian aspect is also reminiscent of the descriptions collected by Bruno Cardeñosa and Miguel Aracil during the "Spanish leg" of the Chupacabras's 1996 tour. Aracil goes as far as suggesting that the Catalan word "simiots", referring to nocturnal, supernatural predators going back to medieval times, may be linked in an unsuspected way. This strongly suggests the possibility that the Chupacabras is really a number of entities having different physical characteristics but having the same basic modus operandi — bleed them dry; repeat as needed.

The Pablo Aguilera Show, Radio Pudahuel, June 14, 2000
CHUPACABRAS EGGS DISCOVERED
Transcript by Patricio Borlone Rojas

I reported from Santiago de Chile last night on the story that was conveyed to me by phone regarding the discovery of "Chupacabras eggs" found between the 12th and the 14th of May. Today (Wednesday) Antofagasta's "Diario La Estrella" was discussed on Radio Pudahuel's morning show:

Announcer: "Presence of a strange creature is confirmed. Guards of a security company near the sector claim to have witnessed a strange entity on the prowl, and while they were unable to see it entirely, stated that it moved at considerable speed. According to the descriptions found in the area, which are related to questions made by NASA experts to a guard who was a victim of an attack [by the unknown entity], the theory being circulated is that the creature may be female and in search of a place to give birth."

Comment by broadcaster Pablo Aguilera: "More properly stated, it would be [looking for a place] to lay eggs, because as far as we know, these strange creatures reproduce by means of eggs..."El Gallinero (the Henhouse), that's what the area is called, thus becomes an area meeting all the characteristics for the beast to settle in. You can still find the sediments of the birds that once inhabited this location [Translator's note: in the late 19th century, northern Chile and southern Peru exported coprabird droppingsas part of their economy]. That's why it's known as El Gallinero, because it was something of a hatchery and kept the name long thereafter...

Comment: "The hole discovered in the area could be a nest that the creature was making to deposit its young, a hypothesis proven by the version given by NASA experts, says the newspaper."

Announcer's comment: "Bear in mind that we have already indicated that these creaturesto call them suchwould reproduce by means of eggs..let's see, what else does it [the newspaper] say?"

Announcer: "The scratches found are only samples of the beast's hasty escape when it was illuminated by the floodlights of the security guardsit can be seen in the photo, thereand the footprints found in the sector are the very same which were found in the commune of Maria Elena last week, highlighting the large size and sharpness of the claws. Let's not forget that a listener told us that it might be a hybrid between a nandu [S.Am ostrich] and ape (?)....so that's what it would be all about. Well...unfortunately, I wasn't able to get in touch with my friend from Antofagasta, but I'll keep phoning her , perhaps tomorrow...to get some more details...with all the information she sent me, the rest came out rather blurry. Unfortunately it can't be read all that well. Ah, we'll try to decipher it later...

Tonite, at around 22:30 hours Chilean time, I spoke with my friend Miguel O. by phone from his location in a northern city (I've kept his surname secret at his own request). He told me the following anecdote, which was experienced by a nephew of his who is currently engaged in military service at Calama, precisely in the location where the Chupacabras' activity is taking place.

"A few nights ago (reference is made to a night between May 9th and 11th) while standing guard with his regiment, he had the chance to see a specimen of the socalled Chupacabras and immediately advised his superior. The strange creature took prodigious leaps and bounds and at one point gave the impression of floating in the air (might it have something similar to wings?). He describes it as standing some 1.20 meters tall, halfhairy and somewhat hunched over, but no further details were made out due to the darkness of the night. A patrol was subsequently sent out to capture it and nothing further was heard until a few days later.

Surprisingly enough, the patrol returned with several "eggs" found at the location where the creatures were taken by surprise. He further adds that the patrol managed to kill two and capture one, and that the carcasses were subsequently removed by NASA personnel from the area.

The most extraordinary point of this tale is the emergence of a new player, the "eggs." Do we now change our manner of thinking about how these evil entities or creatures go about reproduction? The true answer is in the hands of those who handle the information on the subject. Why can't the truth be told once and for all?

EFE newswire, Monday, June 29, 2000

Chileans Believe Chupacabras to be a NASA Creation

by Marcial Campos Maza (EFE)

"The gringoes had at least three genetic experiments run away from them and they've only been able to capture two of them," states Dagoberto Corante, a Chilean architect.

Residents of the city of Calama and nearby communities are blaming NASA, the U.S. space agency for the apparitions and attacks of the mysterious Chupacabras, which has caused ruin among farm animals in the region and in other parts of Chile. Several dozen goats, pigs, chickens, rabbits and other animals turned up dead in northern Calama and its environs last Apriltheir bodies completely exsanguinated and undevoured by the mysterious predator.

Among the Chupacabras' alleged characteristics are the ability of leaping over three meter tall walls and walking unmolested among dogs, while police and volunteer patrols who have set out after it only find some scattered footprints which are nearly impossible to identify in the areas desert terrain, some 1500 km from Santiago.

An investigation ordered by the authorities concluded that the slayings were the product of attacks by packs of wild dogs, but no one believed this version while claims of new Chupacabras attacks developed in different parts of central and southern Chile.

According to Dagoberto Corante, one such creature was captured by elements of a local regiment in an operation that resulted in the death of a soldier, but the military have allegedly refused to discuss the matter. "It is said that the captured animal was kept all day at the regiment's [barracks] until NASA experts arrived to take it away." observed Corante, who is well known and respected in the area in which the Chupacabras has feasted on blood and spread fear among the population. "The day that the events transpired, the military even closed the airport for several hours to enable the landing of a helicopter conveying American scientists." he added, "although no one is quite sure why they had to close an airport in order for a helicopter to functionthese are devices able to land anywhere, and the fact has given rise to much speculation and rumor."

* * * * *

Mario Ramos, a respected resident of San Pedro de Atacama, where he owns a butcher shop, largely agrees with the Corante's story and concerns, and while he doesn't care to discuss the subject, agreed that a soldier had indeed perished during the Chupacabras' capture.

The Chupacabras has continued to appear in Chile in spite of the completely unnatural and snowy winter that has affected the southern hemisphereantarctic winds and heavy snow have blanketed Buenos Aires and Santiago, reaching as far north as the Atacama Desert, where it hadn't snowed in human memory. Far from being deterred by the onset of cold weather (as it did in Puerto Rico during one of the island's famous cold snaps (60 degrees) in January 1996, the paranormal predator continues to spread panic throughout the countryside.

The Chilean events have proven to be more divisive than expected: skeptics are responding more fiercely than ever, believers in a UFOrelated origin to the events are willing to do battle with sword or pistol, on horse or on foot to champion their beliefs, and exponents of the paranormal/interdimensional origin are still holding their own. There is no doubt that something is happening in Chile, but true to the Chupacabras's protean qualities, the entity being reported doesn't resemble the ones seen earlier during the Chilean wave, or much less the ones reported in Puerto Rico or in Mexico five years ago.

La Estrella del Loa (newspaper), July 14, 2000
CREATURE STARTLES MOTORISTS

As announced yesterday, this newspaper obtained as an exclusive the intriguing experience of both local residents, who requested anonymity to avoid unpleasantries.

Although they originally planned not to remain beyond midnight at the organization's transfer of power ceremony, they headed home at 1:30 a.m. "Upon reaching the Chuqui checkpoint, a Carabinero (state trooper) was inspecting a vehicle and we drove right past him."

More or less in the vicinity of Puerta Cuatro, the driver flashed her high beams at two intensely yellow "lights" a short distance away. "The other car was about half a block from our own. We were discussing God in a Christian framework when I began to slow down, because the lights remained static. I thought it could be a stranded automobile or a bicycle."

Nerves got the better of the Ford "K"'s owner, who then sustained a hesitant dialogue with her companion in an effort to explain the figure that stood some two or three feet away from the forward bumper. "Is it the devil?" asked one. "Yes, it would seem so," replied the other, while they observed something resembling a dog, but much larger, lacking ears and covered in extremely long grey hair particularly around its neckand having two immense slanted, yellow eyes.

The women and the "thing" exchanged looks for some five to ten seconds, after which the car drove off along the left lane. The "animal" followed their departure with its headan extremity capable of 180 degree turns.

"I felt a terrible panic. I wanted to get out of the car but she [the companion] calmed me down. We saw the two yellow lights again, but this time they lit up the entire road before disappearing. I hit the accelerator and kept up speed until we reached Calama."

Now feeling more calm, both women have tried to rationalize their encounter. "It's from somewhere else," states the driver. Her companion, the professor, still thinks it's "the devil", on the other hand.

Prior to being made known to this publication, the case was only known by friends and relatives, since no records were left with neither the Carabineros nor the Police, in spite of the interest shown by the latter organization."

La Estrella del Loa (newspaper) Monday, July 31, 2000
BOMBARDMENT TAKES PLACE IN CHILE'S 2ND REGION

Last week, two students faced the creature on Galvarino Street. The animal observed them and levitated, but refrained from attacking them. The sightings are increasing as the authorities maintain their silence.

A "nest" where these entities would have reproduced was discovered in an area located to the northeast of the road which joins the Maria Elena Salt Mines office (a town having a population of 8,000) and Pedro de Valdivia (which was abandoned in 1996). According to residents of Maria Elena, who claimed having witnessed the event, a large detonation accompanied by a tremor shook the houses of the commune on July 20, 2000.

All area residents are accustomed to the sounds produced by the explosives operated in the Pampa, and this made them realize that something strange was afoot.

This coincided with the fly-over of a military aircraft over the area since early hours of the morningan event corroborated by several inhabitants. The witnesses are employees of a contractor firm which was engaged in work at a location not far from where the events took place.

According to their testimony, the jet flew past and bombarded an area which had been characterized as a "Chupacabras nest" by men working nearby. [The area] was filled with small hills and mounds which have eroded into caves suitable for use as a shelter by the animal.

A Birthing Location

Researchers of the subject reported a few days ago that the absence of sightings in recent weeks were the result of a period in which the animal was in a reproductive phase, which would require a dark location not far from population centers, since it is indispensable that their source of nourishment be nearby.

The explosionwhich was heard at a distance of several kilometerstook place between 08:30 and 09:45 hours without anyone having produced an explanation for the event.

The Chupacabras staged a reappearance after these events elapsednot only once, but several times and in different parts of the commune. The latest case, and one of the ones which achieved greatest prominence, involved three students from the "Arturo Perez Canto" school who were returning to their homes in the early evening (1900 hours) along Galvarino Street. At that moment, they encountered one of the creatures (which had already been seen simultaneously in different locations). They explained that one of them realized there was a animal on the rooftops, which then jumped off and landed in front of the startled youngsters.

According to their story, the animal did not attack, but they found it impossible to move, largely out of the fear that this event had caused in them. When they tried to react by huddling protectively against each other, the creature levitated some 30 centimeters off the ground, continuing to observe them. Only after less than ten seconds had elapsed were the children able to escape toward their homes, each of them telling their parents about the experience. The elders were unable to calm the terrified students down.

Upon discussing the animal's characteristics they all agreed in that it had large yellow eyes, dense blackandgrey hair [..] of a dense texture and standing approximately 1.50 meters tall. They also recognized a penetrating odor similar to that of ammonia which the animal might employ to paralyze his prey and humans who stumble upon it. In any event, no direct attacks have been recorded on people, giving rise to the belief by researchers of the subject that it was "a genetic manipulation effected by humans and made aware that it should not harm [its creators]."

More Dead Animals

Residents of Maria Elena continue finding dead cats and dogs with perforations similar to those of the first felines appearing in different areas of the commune. Yet they claim having received "thirdparty" warnings urging them to conceal the information. This has caused many to have chosen to take the [dead] animals and deposit them in dump located behind the Las Piscinas sector, where there exist a number of places used as refuse pits. It is worth noting that the creature was seen here a little more than a month ago by a worker from a contractor firm, who also claims having heard the creature scream, a detail reported by this newspaper at the time.

The importance of the events taking place in the Chilean Pampa are evinced by the arrival of Miamibased ufologist Dr. Virgilio Sanchez Ocejo, who is investigating the incidents transpired in Calama and Maria Elena. He indicated that the cases reported in numerous areas, as well as those reported by the residents of other sectors and mining deposits are identical to the cases known in Puerto Rico and in Central America, leading him to presume that it is the same creature or at least one having similar characteristics.

Given that it has increased in strength over time, the notion that the animal reproduces over a brief period of time would explain the increase of sightings in the area, since it would no longer be a matter of one but several "critters" being seen in the area.

In any event, apparitions of the Chupacabrasor whatever the creature might behave grown apace in recent days, thus making necessary an official declaration, or at least an explanation, of what is happening in the area.

III. Remarks

The preceding have only been "highlights" of the torrent of information on the Chilean Chupacabras that have sailed across the Internet since April. While anectdotal, it nonetheless gives us an understanding of the events that are transpiring in Chile even as this is being written.

a. The Creature's Description

An amalgam of the following descriptions appearing herein gives us enough material to build our own identikit image of the creature:

—It stood about 1.50 meters, like a big monkey, with long, clawed arms and enormous fangs protruding from its mouth, as well as a pair of wings...

—[...] a giant bat causing depredations...

—[...] described [...] as having a human/animal shape...

—an immense man, standing some 2 meters tall. Its shoulderblades were split, as if it had wings...

—a kind of ape or mandrill with human features but with very large eyes...

—as standing some 1.20 meters tall, halfhairy and somewhat hunched over..

—it had large yellow eyes, dense blackandgrey hair [..] of a dense texture and standing approximately 1.50 meters tall...

Missing from these descriptions are the quills or spines running from the top of its head down its back, the spindly, almost useless forearms, the thin membranes beneath the arms that would create the illusion of flight (a creature that size would be unable to fly) and most importantly, the proboscis or "sucking apparatus" deployed to conduct the exsanguination — all of these are the trademarks of the initial Chupacabras as described by Puerto Rican witnesses in 1995.

The new entity(ies) described, while fully deserving of the name Chupacabras for the similarity of its slaying technique and blood thirst, more closely match other entities seen during the early part of the Puerto Rican wave, as indicated earlier in this monograph, and the ape-creature apparitions of northeastern Spain.

In his study on the Iberian mutilations phenomenon, Chupacabras: Un Verdadero Expediente X, Miguel Aracil explores the strange simiots which have been a constant feature of Catalan legend since Medieval times. The simiots are described as "strange, hairy creatures having semihuman features" (Aracil, p.87) and a group of woodsmen were attacked by one such entity a few decades ago: the hairy monster engaged in an orgy of destruction, smashing vehicles and forestry equipment, even hurling logs at the terrified tree-cutters (similar behavior has been reported in cases occurring in suburban Maryland during the 1970's). Although Spain's Guardia Civil looked into the matter, they conveniently "cannot remember", as Aracil notes rather dryly in his treatise. A number of armed posses were formed to explore the environs of Peña Montañesa (Huesca) where the events occured, but "nothing was ever found, perhaps due to the large number of immense caves in the area, and the rough terrain." (Aracil, p.88). Medieval statues of the simiots depict them as devouring children or being trodden down by the Holy Mother: while he does not offer specifics, the author mentions that these supernatural entities were allegedly responsible for slaying entire herds of animals and on certain occasions were even responsible for some attacks on humans. Could the simiots have cousins across the ocean?

Reporter Jorge Torrejón, writing in the May 8, 2000 Estrella del Loa, noted that three young men travelling aboard a refrigerator van transporting 20 tons of fish from Lebu to Arica had a close encounter with the creature. Their description is also helpful. Mauricio Correa, an experienced articulated trailer driver, was trying to park his rig not far from the María Elena salt mines assisted by Oscar Robles and Ricardo, an anonymous hitchiker he'd picked up along the route. After parking the truck at 5:00 am, he turned off the engine and the lights and became aware that the vehicle's cab was tilting toward the right, where Oscar was sitting. The vehicle's lights inexplicably began turning on and off. To their horror they noticed that a "very ugly animal, very hairy and black, having a long oval head, fangs and slanted, goggling yellow eyes" was staring at them through the side window. The apparition had pointed ears and "whiskers similar to those of a boar. It was something awful that was stuck to the glass for several seconds."

Recovering from the shock, the driver managed to get the truck going to make a report to the authorities. Oscar, his co-pilot, checked his wristwatch to ascertain the time for the report, but discovered that the digital timepiece had stopped, and later resumed functioning in a haphazard manner.

The drivers did not stop until they reached the vicinity of Victoria, where the frightened men waited for daybreak before getting out of their vehicle at a truck stop, where they had coffee and resumed their journey to the town of Pozo Almonte, presenting their report at the local Carabineros headquarters at 7:00 a.m.

The only evidence of their experience were the prints apparently left by the creature on the back and side of the trailer cab.

Now, contrast that description to the one given to the Carabineros on May 30, 2000 by Cristián Muñoz, who got a closer view of the Chupacabras than he might have bargained for.

The 36 year old man was at home with his family when sounds were suddenly heard. Upon going out to check, he found himself facing a strange, grunting being emanating a nauseating odor. Fortunately Muñoz, there would be a witness to this extraordinary event: Alvaro Terrazas, 14, stood outside his own home at that late hour waiting for a friend, and saw "a black hairy thing" jump off Muñoz's roof and land in front of the startled homeowner—an amazing 30 meter leap.

Young Alvaro told journalists that Cristián Muñoz "appeared to go crazy and was trying to fall to the ground". The youngster added that Muñoz's sudden insanity in the light of what he had just seen persisted well into the arrival of the authorities. "The gentleman was on his knees, asking them, "please believe me, I swear by the Virgin."

The impression of the creature given by Muñoz to the Carabineros differed radically from any other entity reported thus far: ninety centimeters tall, a body similar to that of a horse, a large head, floppy ears, a trunk-shaped muzzle, round eyes, and walking in a semi-erect position.

In short, either all of the Chilean eyewitnesses need new glasses, or a true paranormal free-for-all is taking place in that country.

b. The Creature's Origins

The following have been suggested as the phenomenon's probable origins:

— an induced genetic mutation (i.e., through highly sophisticated genetic engineering)

— an interplanetary visitor (an alien pet, or even an alien crewman)

— an interdimensional entity

— a denizen of the "inner earth"

— a hoax, illusion, etc.

The "genetic mutation" seems to be the one being favored in Chile at the moment, from what we can glean from the journalistic sources. Certainly people trying to maintain a certain degree of "respectability" (whatever that is) are partial to an explanation that can invoke terms like "recombinant DNA" and carelessly throw them around. I expanded on this angle in my book Chupacabras and Other Mysteries (Greenleaf, 1997).

The interplanetary visitor/alien pet is everyone's "pet" theory. The UFO phenomenon's high visibility and ubiquity makes it a perfect companion to the predator's exploits, but even a casual reading of most of the material presented here or available elsewhere on the Internet will go to show that there have been no reports of UFOs in relation to the Chilean Chupacabras, so to invoke the phenomenon as the creature's mode of transportation from one crime scene to the next is unreasonable, at best. The late D. Scott Rogo, co-author with Jerome Clark of Earth's Secret Inhabitants (Berkeley, 1979), also noted that most "manimal" flaps occur when little or no UFO activity is taking place, and even when there is UFO activity present, it is usually not strong enough to tie both sets of paranormal activity (p.162).

The interdimensional entity option may be the only one that seems tailor-made for the Chupacabras and its kin, even though such a concept as higher dimensions or parallel universes is truly the domain of mathematicians, who would probably run the other way from any involvement with such a scabrous subject. There is a common factor in all the cases—from 1995 to the present—aside from the creature's predilection for blood: the glowing eyes. In this matter I take the great liberty of quoting John A. Keel's The Eighth Tower, which should be considered textbook reading for these matters:

Some of our sea serpents, hairy humanoids, and silver-suited spacemen have huge self-luminous eyes. It may be that these "eyes" are the only real things about these entities. The bodies to which they are seemingly attached are often shadowy and indistinct.

(The Eighth Tower, p.124)

And Dr. Berthold E. Schwarz, whose UFO Dynamics is another of the field's heavyweight volumes, also spoke in this regard:

The creature's eye colors seem to be a distinctive feature of many reports [...]. Whatever the origin of the creatures: e.g., if the are materialized, or have existed in dark caves completely undetected, etc., it is amazing that witness accounts seem to be consistent on these points, which conform to an anatomical reality that most witnesses would not ordinarily know about.

(UFO Dynamics, p. 212)

In any event, the world or reality from which these entities would come from, according to this set of suppositions, would hardly be suitable for humans—much like anglerfish at the bottom of Earth's oceans, the Chupacabras and its fellow entities must supply their own light to move about in a world of absolute darkness (very seriously evoking images of Hell) as they go about their unimaginable business. Before we slip off the deep end here, it is perhaps worth asking if such a dark place could exist? Researcher Raymond A. Robinson's The Alien Intent: A Dire Warning (Blandford,1995) offers the scientific concept of several universes having been created by what we term the "Big Bang". Some of these quantum strands which become other universes are too weak to form viable ones, overlapping in bizarre fashion.

Perhaps these Universes exist as a complete opposite of our owen, with anti-positrons and anti-neutrons as particles exchanges constantly take place in a struggle to exist. Such a Universe would be a suffocating, hot and irradiated place where total darkness replaces light and nothing we know of in our Universe could survive.

(The Alien Intent: A Dire Warning, p.95)

If the Chupacabras and its other relatives, like the gargoyles periodically reported around the world (Madrid, 1995 and rural Argentina, 1997), the Mothman and other entities, hailed from such a "hot, suffocating and irradiated place" as Robinson conjures up, could this perhaps explain the radiation signatures left by the Chupacabras in Puerto Rico and in Guatemala during its initial forays in the mid-Nineties?

During the initial Chupacabras outbreaks in Puerto Rico's Barrio Saltos Cabra, researcher Federico Alvarez and his group took Geiger counter readings of some of the mutilated sheep found in the area. Alvarez noted that the carcasses gave off readings of .011 on a scale of 1000—110 rads—which was considerably higher than background radiation. In Guatemala, Dr. Oscar Rafael Padilla and his assistant were made physically ill after inspecting dead animals in Estanzuela, leading the physician to voice his concern that the radiation found at the sites may have been to blame.

Radioactive, interdimensional creatures? Before you throw down this monograph in disgust, at least read what John Keel has to say on the possible "transmogrification" of entities coming into our own reality from another:

In the early stages of creation the transmogrified entities are relatively harmless to us, but when the deterioration begins to occur, they throw off electrons and radiation that can harm humans and animals in the same way that flying saucers can harm us.

(The Eighth Tower, p.101)

In this knowledge, would it be safe to assume that the Chupacabras and other paraphysicals leave radiation traces as their "physical bodies" in our reality begin to deteriorate? That is what Keel suggests in the preceding paragraph.

Chupacabras as a "denizen of the inner earth" is a concept that while laughable at first, and smacking of the 1940's "Shaver Mystery", has been considered by South American paranormalists who openly believe in subterranean communities beneath the Andes, Brazil and the Argentinean plains. Even in Puerto Rico,

Clues

Clues

early descriptions of the creature's furry exterior having a "burned" appearance gave rise to suggestions of the Chupacabras possibly being a subterranean entity damaged by illicit chemical dumping. While this concept is admittedly fascinating, not enough is known about what lies under Chile (except for some oil and gas reserves) to abound on this possibility.

Chupacabras as a hoax, illusion or "phantasm of the Hispanic mindset" is the explanation wielded by two groups of people: the men and women of the scientific community who flatly refuse to have anything to do with the subject, and ordinary citizens who were exposed to the media barrage which followed the entity's original appearance in 1995. Anyone exposed to the t-shirts, inane pop songs and generally silly behavior of people trying to capitalize on the events would be excused for believing it was all a world-class put-on.

But to please our skeptical friends, let us assume that there is nothing more to the Chupacabras phenomenon than human ignorance, and the explanations put forth by the authorities are in fact correct. How come, we may well ask, there hasn't been another outbreak of "one-fanged dog" activity since the Chupacabras phenomenon ended? Or when explanations involving itinerant troupes of monkeys were in vogue, how come these have never seen again? The experts told us that these "solutions" represented, in fact, a permanent condition in the countryside—only farmers didn't pay attention to them until their own livestock was affected. When Mexico's state-employed experts poured cold water over the Chupacabras *Clues* phenomenon by saying that the mutilations were caused by dogs and other predators drinking blood during the '96 drought, how come similar conditions weren't observed during the U.S. drought in '99? Could it be that third-world canids are less sophisticated than their first-world counterparts and therefore likelier to drink blood? Inquiring minds want to know...

Dr. Eugenio González, a Chilean veterinarian, has been moved to remark that "Dogs aren't bloodsuckers: they are essentially blood lickers. Dogs tear at their prey rather than make surgical incisions, and never kill large numbers of animals. A dog bent on sating its appetite will slay one, eat part of it, and bury the remainder in a very disorderly manner, leaving prints everywhere. Dogs prefer meat to blood and never consume more than their own body weight. Our continent does not have packs of dogs like the Australian Dingoes, which have other ways of feeding themselves. The deaths in Calama have nothing to do with dogs..."

c. The Body Count

The following body count of the Chilean Chupacabras' victims has been gleaned from information provided by the country's main and local newspapers: Prensa Austral (Porvenir); Ultimas Noticias (Santiago de Chile); La Tercera (Santiago de Chile); El Día (La Serena); Crónica (Concepción); El Mercurio (Calama); La Estrella del Loa (Calama). Special thanks to Liliana Núñez:

ALIEN BLOOD LUST

04.01.00 Labanda54 sheep, 25 lambs

04.07.00 Calama30 sheep, 40 dogs (killed by authorities)

04.08.00 Calama25 sheep, 5 goats

04.16.00 Calama12 sheep, 12 goats, 45 rabbits

04.18.00 Labanda3 pigs, 200 sheep, 135 goats

04.18.00 San Fernando40 chickens, 4 pigs, 8 ducks, 1 dog

04.18.00 Calama200 head of cattle (incl. 70 pigs)

04.20.00 Labanda90 goats, 20 pigs

04.21.00 La Chimba26 chickens, 1 dog

04.25.00 El Peral16 lambs

04.27.00 Alto Jahuel10 chickens

04.28.00 Toconao1 human attacked, no casualties

05.01.00 Noviciado120 ducks, 17 chickens, 48 ducks

05.01.00 Providencia4 chickens, 1 rooster

05.01.00 La Montaña8 sheep

05.04.00 Angol12 chickens

05.04.00 Caburgua35 chickens

05.04.00 Los Muermos7 pigs

05.04.00 Quilacoya7 sheep, 1 goat

05.04.00 Cobija40 ducks and chickens

05.05.00 La Serena35 chickens

05.06.00 Tocopilla2 rabbits, 4 cats

05.06.00 Un.Campesina1 dog, 15 sheep

05.06.00 Fundo Esperanza4 sheep, 1 cow

05.07.00 Huertos Familiares4 chickens

05.13.00 Lebu Alto24 chickens

05.14.00 Coronel4 chickens

05.18.00 Baquedanounspecified number of rabbits

05.30.00 Quilota1 dog

06.08.00 Concepción14 chickens

06.09.00 Punta Arenas60 dead heifers (+ 40 wounded)

06.09.00 Porvenir100 sheep

06.13.00 Calama1 cat

06.19.00 Calama2 horses, 1 dog

06.29.00 Antofagasta1 cat

07.02.00 Vista Hermosa1 rabbit

07.05.00 Baquedano3 rabbits

As of early July 2000, a total of 1580 animals (including the 40 "stray" dogs destroyed by the SAG as culprits, even though many of them had owners) had been lost to the Chupacabras' depredations. The death toll continues to rise with no end in sight.

A full accounting of the animal deaths in Chile will, of course, be impossible in the light of the private burial of animals by individuals advised to "avoid making a fuss" by the authorities. This doesn't mean that the figures available for other Chupacabras-related massacres are complete, either. For the Spanish wave of slayings, running from 1996 to 1999, guesstimates range between 163 and 700 (including the 200 sheep which simply vanished into thin air). Bruno Cardeñosa cites "2000 animal deaths" in Puerto Rico between 1995 and 1997, whereas a careful tally of the amounts provided journalistically reveals yields 557 — a considerable amount when we take the island's small size into consideration. This figure covers all of the animals slain from March 1995 to the spring of 1996.

Playing the numbers game becomes even harder when dealing with a country the size of Mexico:

Year 1993 State of Guerrero 30 horses

Year 1994 State of Hidalgo 30 sheep

Year 1994 Iztlalmanalcounspecified chickens, cows, sheep

03.06.96 25 de Abril, Nayarit 25 sheep

03.14.96 Altamira, Ver. 43 goats, sheep, chickens

04.01.96 San Antonio, Chia. 20 sheep

04.06.96 Tlalixcoyan, Ver. 3 sheep

04.18.96 Cd.Guzmán, Jal. 20 sheep

05.02.96 Amacueca, Jal. 20 sheep

05.03.95 Tlalixcoyan, Ver. 6 sheep

05.04.96 Los Mochis, Sin. 40 sheep

05.06.96 San Miguel, Coah. 4 sheep

05.06.96 Lagunillas, Quer. 12 goats

05.08.96 Tlalixcoyan, Ver. 8 turkeys and sheep

05.08.96 San Miguel, Mex. 18 "birds"

no date Cuatichan, Mex. 21 chickens and pigs

no date Los Mochis, Sin. 3 goats and a duck

The above is, at best, only a partial tally of the total losses experienced in that country.

DARK VISITORS — PUERTO RICO'S MOCA VAMPIRE

"You're looking for what?"

Perhaps telling the gas station attendant that I was on a quest to find of the ancestor of Puerto Rico's Chupacabras hadn't been one of my better ideas. The paranormal predator had caused enough damage in its short-lived range to cause the locals not to want to hear its name mentioned in jest. Yet here was someone looking for an even shadier entity, in fact, the traditional "scariest monster of them all" – the one that cannot be seen or felt, but whose trail of destruction is all too real and painful.

Waving vaguely in the direction of State Highway 2, the gas station attendant muttered something about a field off the side of a back road. Putting the rented car in gear, I headed down the country road with my photographer in search of the legendary Moca Vampire.

While Chupacabras was a humorous name bestowed upon the creature by comedian Silverio Pérez, it still carried an air of menace. Could the goatsucker suddenly change diet and go for people, becoming the Chupagente? But the Moca Vampire sounded more like a Halloween bakery confection employed to delight children, not frighten them. Yet during its year and a half long reign of terror, the unknown, unseen entity caused a sensation all over the world, despite being all but forgotten almost thirty years later.

The Vampire Awakens

Coinciding with the overwhelming number of cattle mutilations occurring in the United States and in the rest of the world at that time, Puerto Ricans discovered that their livestock was being slain by a mysterious, unseen assailant. They would have been even more distressed to learn that the same situation would replay itself twenty years later, courtesy of the ubiquitous Chupacabras.

In February 1975, a Puerto Rican newspaper ran one of the very first headlines concerning the wave of mysterious animal deaths to occur in the vicinity of the small town of Moca, on the island's western side.

ALIEN BLOOD LUST

The entity, dubbed "The Moca Vampire" by the press, kicked off its killing spree in Barrio Rocha, a sector of the town of Moca, where it took the lives of a number of animals in a grisly manner never seen before. Fifteen cows, three goats, two geese and a pig were found dead with bizarre perforations on their hides, suggesting that a sharp instrument had been inserted into the hapless bovines. Autopsies showed that the animals had been thoroughly relieved of blood, as if consumed by some predator.

On March 7, 1975, a cow belonging to Rey Jiménez was found dead in Moca's Barrio Cruz, presenting deep, piercing wounds on its skull and a number of scratches around the wounds on its body. Jiménez's cow was added to the growing list of victims, which now totaled well over thirty.

As the number of victims grew, the Moca Vampire acquired an identity of its own, much in the same way that the Chupacabras would twenty years later. Speculation as to its nature was rife: many believed it was a supernatural "bird", like the one seen by María Acevedo, a Moca resident who noticed that a strange animal had landed on her home's zinc rooftop in the middle of the night. According to Acevedo's testimony, the bird pecked at the rusty rooftop and at the windows before taking flight, issuing a terrifying scream. Others more readily accepted any suggestion that it was a space alien, an occupant of the UFOs reported on an almost daily basis over Puerto Rico at the time. Some clung to the belief that a gigantic vampire bat had somehow made it from the mainland to the Caribbean, slaking its thirst on the local cattle. Only days later, farmer Cecilio Hernández notified authorities that the elusive Moca Vampire had slain thirty-four chickens on his property at some point during the night. The supernatural entity was by now responsible for ninety animal deaths in a two week period.

A faint ray of hope—soon to be dissipated by harsh reality—appeared during this critical moment in the crisis: another farmer, Luis Torres, became the man of the hour after slaying two enormous snakes (Puerto Rican boas) measuring an unheard-of length of six feet. Torres had captured the snakes as they stood ready to attack a 600-pound heifer. The media hailed this act of heroism as the "solution to the mutilation riddle"; citizens could finally issue a collective sigh of relief.

However, the Moca Vampire had its own agenda. On March 18, 1975, two goats belonging to Hector Vega, a resident of Moca's Barrio Pueblo, were found drained of blood. Puncture marks on the goats' necks were the unmistakable sign that the strange entity causing the deaths was still at large and hungrier than ever: it returned to Vega's farm the following night to finish off ten more goats and wound another seven. The horrified farmer also discovered that ten additional goats had gone missing.

Killer Snakes, Winged Weirdoes and Politicians

The exploits of the greedy vampire finally set the cogs and wheels of government in motion, resulting in official action in the form of a visit from the Senate Agricultural Commission, led by Senator Miguel A. Deynes, police colonel Samuel López and a number of functionaries. Following interviews with the affected parties and local law enforcement officials, Senator Deynes requested that Police Superintendent Astol Toledo "redouble his efforts in getting to the bottom of the situation," as there was no doubt in his mind that no animal could cause so many deaths. (In yet another curious parallel between the Moca Vampire and the Chupacabras of the nineties, the Superintendent of Police 20 years later would be named Pedro Toledo).

Partisans of the "killer snake" theory, which had gained adherents in the wake of Luis Torres' adventures with the boas, had their hopes dashed yet again by Dr. Juan Rivero, a Mayagüez-based herpetologist who unequivocally stated that the Puerto Rican boa, a non-poisonous reptile, was physically incapable of slaying animals as large as a goat, much less a cow. The herpetologist further explained that the snakes' mouths were not adapted to suck blood, ruling them out as potential exsanguinators.

Felix Badillo could not believe his eyes when, on the morning of March 23, 1975, he found a ten pound piglet dead in it pen. The tiny porker was missing an ear and had a sizeable hole on the side of its head. Badillo was haunted by the fact that such a thing could have happened to one of his animals, since his fierce watchdog had neither barked nor growled during the night and there was no sign of a struggle. The pig farmer was hardly comforted by the expert opinion of Dr. Angel de la Sierra, a specialist with the University of Puerto Rico, who noted that the cut on the piglet's ear stump was similar to certain incisions made in experimental surgery to study deafness.

By this point, the Moca Vampire had apparently tired of its monotonous diet and was ready for a little variety. At ten o'clock at night on March 25, laborer Juan Muñiz was allegedly attacked by a "horrible creature covered in feathers," as he would later describe it. Muñiz was returning home to Moca's Barrio Pulido when he saw the unsightly entity. The laborer threw stones at the entity to frighten it away, but only managed to provoke its anger: the creature flew toward him, prompting Muñiz to seek shelter behind some bushes before running to a neighbor's house. An armed band of locals went out to find the winged weirdo, but their efforts were fruitless.

The "vampire" would soon transcend the narrow confines of Moca to embarking on an island-wide spree of animal killings in April 1975. Among its first depredations outside the San Juan metropolitan area was the slaying of a pig on a farm belonging to one Benigno Lozada in Guaynabo, P.R.. Meanwhile, an all-out effort to apprehend the suspected human element behind the mutilations had been set into motion by the police, while on the other hand, the media bent over backward

ALIEN BLOOD LUST

Mind Reading animals

to find a "rational" or "scientific" explanation that would dismiss the strong super-natural air surrounding the unknown predator. When some "odd bats" were discovered in a limestone cave near Moca, hope welled in newsrooms throughout the island. However, it was soon pointed out that the bats were in fact of the ordinary kind, who live on fruit and do not attack animals.

The Night Watch

On April 2, the predator paid a visit to a farm owned by Isauro Melgar in Corozal's Barrio Negro. The Moca Vampire killed eight goats and a dozen rabbits on the property. This loss was particularly painful for the small farmer, since the breeding rabbits had been quite valuable.

Fearing that the unknown entity would stage a return on the following evening, Melgar kept watch all night, spreading poison on the ground to eliminate whatever it was seemed interested in his rabbits. Joined by a group of armed neighbors, Melgar kept watch until three in the morning. The moment the men disbanded, whatever it was returned with a vengeance to slay more animals. This only strengthened the farmers' determination to remain awake all night, if need be.

At half past midnight on April 5th, Isauro Melgar and his companions were startled by a deafening sound that suddenly blanketed the otherwise silent countryside. Amid the unearthly din, the farmers saw a shadowy figure running swiftly through the trees, away from an open pasture. They would later discover that four more goats had been slain. Stoical despite of his losses, Melgar told the press that "whatever killed my goats was definitely not human. I don't believe in vampires, of course, but I really can't say what kind of creature killed my animals."

Official declarations began appearing in the media and in government communiqués two months after the mutilation spree began. Dr. Benedicto Negrón, a veterinarian for the Puerto Rico Department of Agriculture, noted that "the situation was a concern" to his agency, expressing a fear that the uncanny events might unleash hysteria among the population. In an April 9th editorial, the now-defunct El Mundo ran an editorial requesting greater leadership from the government in solving the bizarre mutilations.

A Legendary Researcher On the Scene

The dynamic Salvador Freixedo, who was living in Puerto Rico during the 1975 wave, was able to cover a considerable number of cattle mutilations and interview the thoroughly shocked cattle owners. He was to be one of the first researchers on the scene at Moca:

"During an evening in which UFOs were sighted over the town of Moca," Freixedo says, "two ducks, three goats, a pair of geese, and a large hog were found slain the following morning on a small farm. The owner was going insane, wondering who in the world could have visited this ruin upon him. The animals betrayed the wounds that have become typical of this kind of attack, and of course, they were all inflicted with incredible precision. I did not doubt for one moment who could have been responsible for the crime ... I got in my car and visited the area immediately, and realized what was filling the animals' owner with wonder and fear: there wasn't a trace of blood in any of the animals, in spite of the fact that the dead geese had snow-white feathers, upon which the slightest speck of blood would have shown up immediately.

"Over the next few days, the newspapers continued reporting the growing number of dead animals encountered in the region. No explanation could be found for these mysterious deaths. I visited the rural areas on various occasions to investigate the events firsthand and found that the farmers were as intrigued by their animals' deaths as they were by the enigmatic lights they could see in the nocturnal skies. One of them told me that the lights reminded him of the revolving lights on top of a police cruiser.

"During one of my forays, I was able to see a black and white cow spread out in the middle of the field. I got out of the car and tried to reach the cow, which wasn't easy. The dead beast had characteristic wounds on its neck and on its head. Skin had been pulled back on one side of its head, as if by a scalpel, and the opening to one of its nasal orifices was missing, although there was no indication of rending. In spite of the whiteness of its head, there wasn't a single drop of blood to be seen. The farmer who escorted me could not stop wondering what had caused his cow's death. He related how that very same night he had heard his dogs barking furiously, and that a blind elderly woman who lived on the edge of the field had told him that the cattle, which ordinarily spends the night outdoors, had kept her from getting a good night's sleep due to their frantic, maddened running from one end of the field to another.i

The heat of a tropical summer appeared not to inconvenience the Moca Vampire: On June 25th it killed 25 farm animals outside of Isabela. Fourteen fighting cocks were later exsanguinated by the same predator, this time in Yauco. As the summer wore on, the "vampire", its appetite seemingly sated, diminished its activity before vanishing altogether in August 1975.

UFO researcher and journalist John Keel, in his landmark book The Eighth Tower (Dutton, 1975), makes several observations that can be applied to the paranormal events which occurred in the Caribbean during the '70s and which would repeat themselves years later. One of the reasons for the apparent imperviousness of these so-called monsters to bladed weapons or bullets (the reader will recall the number of Bigfoot cases in the U.S. in which high-power rifles apparently have no effect on these entities) is due to the fact that they are composed of "highly condensed atoms" such as those in plutonium. Keel went on to suggest that if dense, probably radioactive, atoms account for these entities's composi-

[handwritten: atoms must vibrate at specific Frequencies in harmony and softness to Radiation]

tion, it would explain why these manifestations have such brief existences in our material world. When first materialized, Keel suggests, these entities pose no threat to humans, but as their atomic integrity deteriorates, they might easily project lethal radiation. Investigators following the trail of the Chupacabras in 1995, both in Puerto Rico and Central America, reportedly found considerably high radiation readings at the locations in which the entity staged its attacks.

A Startling Revelation

Ufology in particular, and the study of the paranormal as a whole, represent a field of endeavor in which the pieces of the jigsaw puzzle that the researcher hopes to piece together sometimes do not emerge for many years. This too has been the case with Moca's best-known citizen. Although it would be a source of enormous satisfaction to be able to say that the solution to the riddle of who or what was the Moca Vampire has been found, the best we can do thirty years later is to learn that a government-mandated cover-up was in effect at the time.

On May 1, 2004, at a UFO event organized by researcher Reinaldo Ríos and held at the Guayanilla Public Library in southwestern Puerto Rico, retired police officer Marcelino Pérez told his story to an audience of over 400 people who crammed into the library's auditorium.

In 1974, Pérez explained, he held the rank of lieutenant in Puerto Rican Police and became involved in the Moca Vampire's depredations during the course of his police work. His supervisors in the island's police force had issued the order that any and all mutilations ascribed to the unknown predator should be classified as the work of feral dogs. According to this secret memorandum, the retired officer added, avoiding a panic was of the essence, and anyone discussing the subject in terms of space aliens or monsters should be openly ridiculed as a liar or madman. This was the fate of a certain journalist who wrote certain stories about the unknown mutilator for one of the island's newspapers: the reporter was accused of hoaxing the stories and even worse, of being responsible for the animal mutilations.

On the average, according to Marcelino Perez, the Moca Vampire would appear and disappear with three-month lapses in between each spate of activity. The police investigated over a hundred cases in all—cases in which he would arrive on the scene and proclaim in a loud voice that the mutilations had been the work of wild dogs. Given his rank in the police, he explained, people believed him and returned to the homes with their feelings slightly assuaged. It is his belief that his willingness to go along with the directives issued by his higher-ups resulted in his promotion to captain shortly after—a rank with which he retired from law enforcement.

[handwritten: Same as Selling your Soul.]

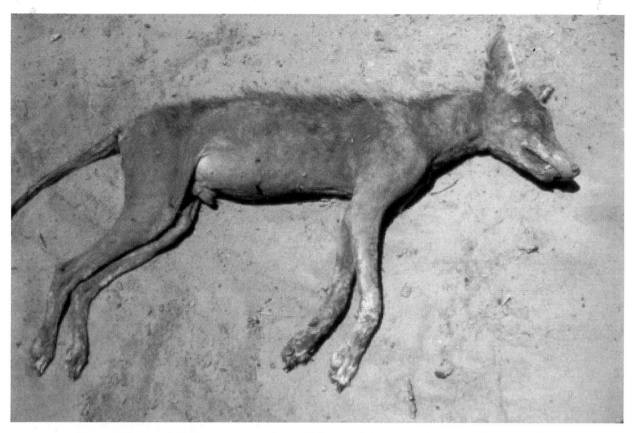

Thought by locals to be a chupacabras, this varmit turned out to be a diseased dog.

Books and blogs celebrating the blood-sucking chupacabras abound.

ALIEN BLOOD LUST

CHAPTER 23

GARGOYLES OF THE OUTER DARKNESS
By Scott Corrales

The story begins with a telephone call, as do many great adventures and experiences. The year was 1997 and Willie Durand Urbina, director of the PRRG (Puerto Rican Research Group) had phoned me with information about the Chupacabras for a book on the subject that would appear later that year. During our conversation, Durand mentioned the fact that a curious, self-published book on the subject of Puerto Rico's paranormal predator had already appeared, but the author was a complete unknown in UFO/paranormal circles.

"But that's not all," he added. "I read the book and the author suggests that they're some sort of gargoyles. Worse yet, it's an accursed book."

"What do you mean, an accursed book?" I asked. "How so?"

"Well, the book ends with an imprecation against any and all researchers who look into the subject of the Chupacabras, cursing them for trying to unravel the mystery of the gargoyles."

I paused to consider this. Certainly enough attendant phenomena had surrounded the Mothman sightings in the late '60s. That someone would try to bring about a "curse of the Goatsucker" wouldn't be at all new.

And that's where the matter was allowed to rest until now, when sightings of strange winged creatures unequivocally described as "gargoyles" appeared in newspapers in the northern Chilean city of Arica, on the Pacific Ocean.

First of all, it is necessary to understand what is meant by "gargoyle". Anyone who grew up watching repeated showings of the movie The Gargoyles on television during the 1970s doesn't need an explanation as to what these creatures look like—or at least what the human mind has imagined them to be. Parents of younger children have probably also seen Saturday-morning cartoon depictions of these entities in a heroic setting. But what are gargolyes? Why is there so little information on them, and why do we speak of their existence so naturally?

Stemming from the medieval French word gargouille or "throat", a clear indication of their nature. Gargoyles were fearsome human or animal figures projecting from roof gutters to throw rainwater at a distance from the building they were attached to. Cathedrals made prominent use of them as spouters of rainwater but also to protect the structures against evil (fighting fire with fire, to a certain extent). Some particular gargoyles have become world famous, like Notre Dame's pensive "vampire" who looks over the city from his vantage point on Ile de la Cité. No one, however, seems to have a convincing explanation as to what inspired their creation, although it is universally agreed that they are protective spirits, perhaps "denizens of the lower airs" who were placed in bondage by a medieval cleric-magician, their evil natures subverted to the purpose of Good.

But this is only speculation: gargoyles existed long before the first medieval mason ever cut a stone to lay the foundations of the cathedrals at Chatres or Reims. Greek and Roman temples were protected by similar figuras that served the dual purpose of warding off unseen evil spirits and reminding the faithful that they were entering a sacred spot protected by unimaginable forces at the service of the respective deity. Known to antiquarians as apotropaic figures, they suggest the existence of a force that is considerable and often hard to control. "The ancient gods," writes one source, "are turned into demons, acknowledged for their power and admirable respect, yet tamed and relegated to servitude at the temples of the new religion. These spiritual forces, able to induce either fear or reverence, are confined to the perimeter of the holy site, forever frozen and protecting a place which they themselves can never enter."

And on that poetic note, we put the ancient texts behind us to face the unfettered gargoyles that seemingly appear in our midst…

Gargoyles in the High Desert

A family drive is stressful enough without having to face the paranormal.

In the close confines of the family vehicle, sibling rivalry can reach critical proportions and the monotony of the landscape can drive even the most patient passenger to ask if the intended destination is any closer. Carlos Abett and his wife Teresa, riding in a pickup truck between the family home in Pozo Almonte, a military community attached to the Fort Baquedano facility, to visit relatives in the city of Arica, were almost surely accustomed to these flare-ups and worse, but nothing, not even many years of driving the same road under a variety of conditions, could have prepared them for the event they experienced in July 2004.

At 9:00 p.m., some twenty kilometers south of Arica, in a wilderness known as Pampa Acha, the Abett family's vehicle, containing the couple, their three children and a nephew who had come along for the ride, came across what they would later describe to news reporters as four "dog-faced kangaroos" that floated slowly in the night air.

Carmen Abett, the family's eldest daughter, offered the most vivid description from her vantage point at the backseat window. "I was ridingn the backseat with my brothers, talking, and suddenly everything went dark. Then I told my brother what I was seeing and he told me to keep quiet, because Mom gets nervous. Later I looked through the window and saw some things that looked like birds, with dogs' heads and backswept wings. My father said they were like gargoyles. We were speechless for some 10 minutes and my Mom told us to react, and then we started discussing what we'd seen," she explained.

The flying entities were quite large, an estimated two meters (6 feet) long although it was impossible to estimate their wingspan, since these were "moved toward the back" as the eyewitness described them. Two of the entities classified as gargoyles by Carlos Abett flew over the car, while another two would later "leap" in front of the moving vehicle only minutes later.

But it was Abett's wife Teresa, riding shotgun, who would get the best view of the flying oddities through the windshield. The creatures, she explained, appeared to be moving slowly over the car at first, but somehow matching the vehicle's 100 kilometer per hour (65 mph) speed perfectly – a characteristic shared by West Virginia's Mothman.

Nervous beyond words, the Abett family simply prayed that they could make it to Arica before long and see their relatives, putting the whole incredible ordeal behind them. Upon arrival, they promptly shared the experience with other family members, and were later considerably nervous about having to make the return trip to the Fort Baquedano area, forcibly traversing the area where the encounter occurred. Carlos Abett, an Army subofficer at the military facility, wisely kept quiet about the incident, not wishing to become the butt of jokes among his fellow men in uniform. The family would break its silence a few weeks later, however, when two men – coincidentally, another Army suboficer – would have an encounter with "dinosaur-like" creatures on the same stretch of road.

Is there something about Chile that attracts these winged entities we have come to identify with medieval gargoyles, perhaps because there is something comforting about being able to give them a name?

Five years ago, on May 3, 2000 in the city of Concepción, college instructor Liliana Romero – usually a sound sleeper – was wakened by the howling of a number of stray puppies she had picked up from the street a few days earlier. The five puppies shared a space in her building's courtyard with Romero's large mastiff. Checking the time, Romero saw it was one thirty in the morning and feared that a break-in might be taking place. Crouching by the window, she looked outside. What she saw made her wish that it had indeed been a burglar...

"The puppies were whining and Black [the mastiff] had huddled against the wall and was motionless. I could see the back of what appeared to be an immense man, standing some 2 meters tall. Its shoulderblades were split, as though withwings. Its attitude resembled that of a person choking another...that was my impression."

Romero, horrified, was convinced that someone was being murdered by an improbable creature – some kind of animal she had never even dreamed could exist. She tried to get her husband to wake up and witness the event to no avail."In a matter of seconds, I went back to the living room to look at it, but it was gone. It had vanished, " she adds. The next day, the Romero family's children returned home through a shortcut that brought them across the courtyard where the strange entity had been seen. They promptly told their mother that there was "a dead dog in the place where the gentleman was being attacked."

Liliana asked her husband to check, and he returned saying that a wooly beigecolored dog was lying on the floor with two puncture marks on its throat. "I don't know if I might be in a suggestive state, but it had two deep holes in its jugular, about as wide as a BIC pen, separated by 5 centimeters between them. What impressed me the most was that it was completely bloodless and was as light as a feather. The dog was incredibly wooly and in fact, I had to move its fur to see the wounds."

Only a few nights before Liliana Romero's sighting, two farmhands from the town of Tucapel, Jorge Venegas and José Pino, were taking advantage of the bright full moon to fetch a bucket of water from a local creek. Walking cautiously out of concern for a stray bull that was roaming the fields, Pino saw a dark shape moving among the moonlit vegetation, which he took for the stray bovine. Only later did he realize that it wasn't the bull, but a nightmare creature he described as "a big monkey with long, clawed arms and enormous fangs protruding from its mouth, as well as pair of wings." In terror, the farmhand ran back toward the farmhouse to unleash the mastiffs. One of them, Cachorro, came back with a bloody neck, testimony to the encounter with the unknown figure. From that night onward, Pino never ventured into the darkness without a shotgun slung from his shoulder.

But what happens when a firearm isn't available, and one must venture into the darkness? For that is exactly what happened on Tuesday, July 23, 2003, when the Calama UFO Center informed the world of a mind-bending case involving still another gargoyle-like entity.

Diego, a young student from the city of Calama in the Chilean high desert, had gone to visit his grandfather in the town of San Pedro de Atacama, accompanied by two close friends. The three young men enjoyed visiting this wilderness area during their school recess and helped Diego's uncle herd his goats. On the fateful evening in question, the three youths were getting ready to sit down to a meal of bread and tea in the rural home, which lacked electricity. At around nine o'clock at night, they heard the odd wheedling and howls made by the dogs on the property; fifteen minutes later, a series of violent raps were heard on the door, followed by scratching sounds that filled the three visitors with fear – enough that the three friends huddled against a wall and parapeted themselves with a matress and blankets against the unknown quantity.

A few minutes later, the rattling and scratching ceased. Regaining confidence, Diego and his companions decided to step out into the cold night air for a look— something they might have preferred, in retrospect, not to have done.

For there it was: amid a stand of pear trees some fifteen meters away from the door was a creature they described as "horrifying", standing a meter and a half tall and with outstretched wings measuring an incredible three and a half meters.

The description of the creature offered by the three witnesses to the Calama UFO Center was a detailed one: "It was covered by glossy black skin, very clean and hairless," reads the report by Jaime Ferrer. "It appeared as though it had recently emerged from the water, but without being wet. It had a large head and a small beak, presenting a sort of crest which was apparently missing a piece from a fight. Its eyes were immense and completely black, but sparkled brilliantly. They thought it was a prehistoric being, since its wings had a strong resemblance to those of pterodactyls or bats, featuring bone-like protubreances which form the skeletal frame of the wings. Its legs were sturdy and had powerful claws like those of a carrion bird, but much stronger."

But this gargoyle of the Chilean wilderness had no interest in the three youths. Instead, it shook its enormous wings and flew off into the darkness.

There have been other occasions on which the gargoyles have taken a violent interest in hapless humans intent on their own business. One such case occurred during Chilean creature sightings in the summer of 2000, but is no less impressive or terrifying than the more recent event mentioned above.

Walking home at midnight on the 7th of May of that year, Guido Canales was possibly more concerned about catching pneumonia from the fall chill (the seasons being inverted in the southern hemisphere) than worrying about supernatural terrors. Far from the mysterious northern deserts of his country, Canales dwelt in the verdant, wooded part of Chile known for its near-European beauty and climate. His town of Codao, south of the nation's capital, was a peaceful rural community among massive, fairy-tale quality trees.

Within sight of his home, Guido Canales was attacked by a massive bird-like creature whose strength toppled him to the ground. Stunned, he realized that far from being a condor or any other raptor known to him, his assailant was a creature best described as a gorilla with wings, golden eyes and emitting a nauseating, rotting stench. Fearing for his life, the young man managed to recover the flashlight – fallen to the ground during the attack – to shed light on the creature. The entity, either harmed by the flashlight's beam or repelled by it, took an enraged swipe at Canales, clawing his back. In desperation, Canales screamed for his neighbors to help him. One good samaritan responded to his call and turned on the front porch light before going outside to render aid. The porch light sufficed to cause the winged aberration to fly off into the dark. The victim would later tell his family that judging from the way the creature had grabbed him during the struggle, it was trying to exsanguinate him.

His skin scratched, dazed and unable to speak, Canales' relatives took him off to the doctor. The five scratches, running from his left shoulder to his neck, were treated with antibiotics and anti-rabies vaccinations.

But the Canales story does not end there.

Ramón Nava Osorio of Spain's IIEE group, author of La Verdad Oculta (Madrid: IEEE, 2003) visited Chile and managed to interview members of the family who were quite willing to discuss the ordeal. After the attack on Guido, his brother Luchito and other friends decided to venture into the darkness and avenge the victim, armed with shotguns. Their valor and righteous rage was rewarded by an encounter with the winged "ape", which was sititng on a high tree limb. Luchito pointed at its chest and fired the twelve-gauge shotgun, which should have brought down a horse easily. Seemingly unaffected, the creature merely flew away into the cold night

Gargoyles in Spain

Leaving the Andean region and its many mysteries behind, we follow the gargoyle's flight to Spain, where aeronautics researcher Francisco J. Máñez describes a strange story that befell a close coworker. The co-worker, who knew of Máñez's interest in the unknown and was aware of his stature as a writer and radio personality, agreed to recount his childhood experience only if he could remain anonymous.

The witness in this case was a 5 or 6 year old boy living in Barrio del Carmen, a neighborhood of the city of Valencia on the Mediterranean Sea. The event would have taken place in the late Sixties, and even with the passing of decades, he claims that his recollection of the high-strangeness occurrence is still crystal clear.

One cold November morning, the young protagonist of the event asked his mother for permission to go out and play on the sidewalk with his toys as he did every weekend. For some unknown reason, his mother refused and told him to go to the house's upstairs terrace and play there. Obediently, the boy picked up his toys and headed up the staircase.

The terrace was a broad and uncovered area from which the rooftops of neighboring buildings could be seen. Upon opening the door leading to this expanse, the boy was surprised by a strange "bird" perched silently on the terrace railing, quietly surveying the city from his vantage point. Fascinated by the large bird, the boy approached it quietly. It was about the size of an eagle, he told Máñez, with wings like a bat and completely featherless.

At some point, the "bird" must have heard the boy's footsteps and turned its face around to look. What the boy saw was completely incredible and it caused him to freeze in his tracks: the bat-winged entity had a nearly human face. Its body was also manlike, ending in sharp talons. The creature immediately leaped into the air, soaring away gracefully on its outspread wings, vanishing somewhere over the city.

The boy was too young to have ever heard of gargoyles, and it wasn't until years later, when he saw one sculpted high above a church, that the memories of his strange event flooded his brain. "That bird," he told Francisco Máñez without any hesitation, had a human face and body, and no one can make me think other-wise."

The Kitchen Gargoyle's Story 5.5.

It isn't often that researchers of the paranormal get to have a close look at their subject of interest, and whenever there are exceptions, these tend to be signifi-cant. One such case involves the director Mexico's Fundación Cosmos, A.C., Ing. Marco Reynoso, a distinguished UFO researcher and MUFON state director for Nuevo León. In the fall of 1979, Reynoso was a harried engineering student trying his best to deal with a heavy course load and work on his dissertation. One night, leaving the university earlier than usual, he arrived at his parents' house – a ram-bling, high-ceilinged old manse of the kind common in Mexico – whose kitchen can be clearly seen from the main entrance.

All was dark; Reynoso's father never got back from work before ten o'clock and his mother was out visiting neighbors. The only light came from a single bulb in the kitchen, casting enough light to show the kitchen table, which was located next to a window covered by a curtain.

Making his way to the kitchen to grab a bite to eat, the future ufologist noticed movement behind the curtain, but thought it was the normal action of the wind blowing through the open window. Then suddenly, a figure stepped out from be-hind the curtain: it was a humanoid figure, covered in glossy black hair and stand-ing some thirty centimeters tall with outstretched bat wings. The curtain partly covered its face, so Reynoso was unable to make out any features. Fearlessly, he thought to use the curtain as a means to ensnare the strange apparition and pin it down, but the cloth drapes were suddenly sucked toward the open window, top-pling objects on the table surface, and the bizarre creature vanished. Running out to the courtyard, he tried to see if he could find the intruder to no avail.

That's when fear crept in: "I was completely certain that it was no optical illu-sion," says Reynoso, "nor any known animal. The contrast ebtween the kitchen and its contents, which were all white, and the blackness of the creature, left no mistake as to what I had seen. That event changed my life completely, since it highlighted the interest for the unknown I'd had since age 8." The experience prompted him to join his first UFO research group, in whose files he found another case similar to his own, witnessed by a woman from another Monterrey neighborhood.

A Forgotten Chupacabras Case from 2005

As the year 2006 draws to a close, our colleague Raul Nuñez of the IIEE –Chile organization has forwarded the following report of a strange animal-mutilating entity from the 9th Region of Chile. The story somehow eluded the media and has only been made known thanks to the diligent efforts of researcher Raul Gajardo Lepold. The following is INEXPLICATA's translation of Mr. Gajardo's work:

On November 18, 2005, Mrs. S.T.C., age 59, married, illiterate, but able to make her mark, was alone in her rural property near Angol, since her husband and son had gone into this city. At around 2:00 p.m., she was returning home after fetching the family's ten cows, which had been taken to drink water from a stream 30 meters downhill from the house. One of the cows, accustomed to this routine, got ahead of the others. When Mrs. S.T.C. came within 3 meters of the stream of water, she allowed the animals to continue alone and walked back to her house. It was at that moment that one of the cows began to bellow, and the woman ran back to see what was amiss. At that moment, she saw a very strange animal attempting to bite both the front and hind legs of the cow, which was already bleeding from one of its front legs. The strange creature surrounded the cow, attacking it on all sides, making small jumping motions and running with its two very large legs, which grew outward from the body at an angle and ended in four long toes with hard, black claws. Mrs. S.T.C. came within 4 meters of creature; in her despair, she ran back to her house to fetch a stick with which to beat the intruder. At no time did the entity try to attack her.

She found a stick but never managed to strike the creature with it, as it ran toward the body of water, jumped in, and skittered under a large bush at the site, which was later removed and the site remains clear to this day. The animal ran away clumsily, in an erect position, on its two legs, but with considerable swiftness.

The first time that she was close to the creature, at a distance of some four meters, the animal issued powerful whistling noises—some three or four continuous blasts—only to quiet down and resume again, all the while attacking the cow. Mrs. S.T.C. had never seen as strange a creature as this one and has never seen it again, nor have there been similar reports from other residents of her rural community. She only shared her story with her children and relatives.

The following is a description of the creature observed by Mrs. S.T.C.:

The entity measured approximately half a meter tall, some 25 cm. around, covered all over with green and pale red spots. There was something strange resembling wings growing out of its sides, starting at its shoulders, but these were kept folded. It was covered by some kind of short brown fur; the head was dog-shaped with large, slanted and protruding eyes, almost surely black in color, as Mrs. S.T.C. was unable to get a closer look. Its muzzle was elongated and flat, measuring some 20 centimeters, which it could open very wide to display long teeth. The witness estimates that it had two rows of them, judging by their number and whiteness. She did not notice if the entity had nasal passages or a tongue, but its front teeth were longer than the rest.

The creature's head was elongated and a sort of wavy crest grew out of its forehead, reaching down to the bottom of its back. Short, thick and firm neck. Cream-colored spots appeared on its abdomen.

When it attacked the cow, it did so with a series of very small leaps, raining bites on the animal while it emitted whistling sounds. On its back, where the protruding crest came to an end, there were brown bristles and the body ended with a short, 10-cm. tail with a blunt tip. It lacked upper claws or legs. But it moved its shoulders upward as it attacked, without ever losing its upright position. At one point the witness saw it on the ground, felled by a kick from the cow, which fought off its assailant gamely. The claws were covered with dark brown hair as well as scales (sic). No ears were reported.

INEXPLICATA wishes to express its gratitude to Mr. Raul Nuñez and the members of IIEE Delegación Chile for bringing this case to our attention.

Some witnesses claimed the chupas had wings like a bat or pterodon.

ALIEN BLOOD LUST

CHAPTER 24

THE CHUPACABRAS DIARIES
An Unofficial Chronicle of Puerto Rico's
Paranormal Predator
By Scott Corrales
A Reissue of the 90s Classic

Contents

I. The Opening Rounds

For over a century now, the Puerto Rican peasantry has fervently sung: ¡Líbranos, señor, de este terrible animal! ("Deliver us, Lord, from this terrible beast!"). It is a song accompanied by the syncopation of numerous drums called tumbadoras, and the percussion instruments available in the rural reaches of the island at the time. Folklorists almost surely dismiss the possibility that there might be anything to these lyrics other than an ardent Christian urge to be delivered

from the devil, who is described in bestial terms. But Puerto Rico's long history of paranormal phenomena can lead even the sternest doubter to read between the lines of this peasant song.

For decades, Puerto Rico has experienced paranormal phenomena beyond the amount usually felt elsewhere in the world. Major documentaries like *Ovnis Sobre Puerto Rico: Documento Confidencial* alerted the world to a situation in which bizarre creatures, UFOs and their occupants, and religious phenomena played out on the same stage, or in different rings under the same tent. Animal mutilations presided over the weirdness of the early 1970s, mirroring the Stateside UFO wave of 1972-73, while at the same time people disappeared at the rainforest known as El Yunque. Men in Black walked into business offices, and presumably alien craft crossed the skies with impunity--one of them even pausing to be picked up on a TV commercial for a rum distillery while the camera was left running all night in order to capture a perfect sunrise from the top of a building in the heart of San Juan.

But that was then.

The modern age of weirdness kicked off with the alleged crash of a UFO in El Yunque Rainforest in 1987. Soon after, a massive underground detonation would rock the southwestern tip of the island, attracting the attention of the military. Amaury Rivera would have his controversial abduction experience--a controversy which threatened to destroy the ufological community in both Puerto Rico and Spain, and has indeed left it badly divided--in the same area a year later.

1989 kicked-off with sightings of the enigmatic, repulsive "vampire birds" which appeared in many different parts of the island simultaneously. Naysayers came forward, alleging that they were common island birds with rooster spurs grafted into their beaks. This improbable statement seemed to quell the incipient furor, but the fact of the matter is that government officials confiscated not only the birds in private hands, but even film that was being developed at a Fotomat store.

1990 and 1991 witnessed the return of the UFO phenomenon and its attendant manifestations to the Adjuntas area, a mountainous region famous for its coffee-growing plantations and as a source of high- grade copper (still unexploited). It was at this time that Laguna Cartagena, an unremarkable, kidney-shaped body of water near the towns of Boquerón and Cabo Rojo, became the alleged entry/exit point for a subterranean/submarine base that reputedly exists deep below the lagoon's surface.

The outrage over the UFO sightings reached such extremes that the mayor of Adjuntas, perplexed by the viewings, and doubtlessly irritated by the sheer volume of sightseers pouring into his normally quiet town, demanded from then-President Bush an investigation into the heavenly phenomenon accosting his constituency. It is unknown if his request ever made it to the White House.

ALIEN BLOOD LUST

The 1992-94 period witnessed an intensification in the number of UFO sightings, encounters, and abductions. A mysterious "aerostat" — a kind of barrage balloon tethered to a ground station — was flown by Federal authorities not far from Laguna Cartagena, ostensibly to help win the war against drugs, but in the process, raising countless suspicions that the aerostat was being utilized to detect UFO activity in the area.

The appearance of triangular UFOs, such as the ones reported over the Hudson Valley in the mid- Eighties, intensified during this period. 1994 ended with the strong likelihood that a diminutive alien corpse--the mortal coil of a creature shot and bludgeoned by farmers who placed it in a freezer for years--was in fact the strongest physical evidence collected on the island to date. The obstacle, however, was the unwillingness of the party in possession of the cadaver to relinquish it for study, mainly out of fear that it would be confiscated by Federal authorities.

But no one could have imagined what was being heralded by the lull in sightings and unusual activity shortly before New Years, while thousands engaged in revelry and the joys of a tropical Christmas...

II. The Merry Month of May

Jorge Martín's message on the answering machine on the afternoon of May 17th carried a certain ring of urgency. When I returned his call, the first thing he said was, "Do you have any idea what's going on down here?!"

For the next forty-five minutes, Jorge and his wife Marleen briefed me on what had been going on during their investigations in the central region of Puerto Rico's mountainous interior. Since March, animals of all shapes and sized had been mutilated in the municipalities of Orocovis and Morovis. The authorities were stumped and no clue as to the perpetrator's exact nature had been found.

This new wave of mutilations that disturbed the normally peaceful Puerto Rican springtime was different in many respects from the classic 1975 wave investigated by Salvador Freixedo, who lived on the island at the time. Only a few cases presented the extrusion of organs that characterized the "mutes" of the American Southwest (admirably documented by Tom Adams). These new gruesome developments left animals entirely bloodless through a single neat perforation found on some part of the body.

The Orocovis mutilations were first brought to light by Arnaldo García, a radio show host and journalist with Radio Cumbre, and an affiliate of San Juan's WKAQ. While the popular perception remains that these events began in March, they had in fact been taking place in scattered locations over a period of time. One year earlier, for instance, a number of deer at the Mayaguez Zoo had been found mutilated and bloodless. At the time, it was considered prudent to conceal this fact from the public.

The mutilation "wave" also had a strong component of "high strangeness" in the form of bizarre humanoids resembling the so-called Grey aliens popularized by Stateside ufology. One of these creatures, in fact, was the first to be reported during the Orocovis flap. A police officer investigating a dead sheep on the property of Mr. Enrique Barreto suddenly became aware that "something" was staring at him from the shadows. The "thing" was generally humanoid in appearance, some 3 to 4 feet tall, and with orange-yellow eyes. Ordering his partner to stop the squad car they were in, the police officer jumped out and pursued the creature. But a truly perplexing thing happened next: the policeman was engulfed by a sense of nausea accompanied by a pounding headache when he tried to go after the creature. He was rendered so helpless that his partner had to come to his rescue.

At six o'clock in the morning on March 26, Jaime Torres encountered a similar creature in the field where Mr. Barreto's sheep were kept. Torres, an avid UFO enthusiast, had come to the area the previous evening in the hopes of learning more about what was going on. He and his brothers had repeatedly seen UFOs since December 1994 from their home in Orocovis' Barrio Gato. A nocturnal skywatch, he felt, represented a good chance at seeing more UFOs.

In the early hours of the morning, Torres realized that a round-headed creature with elongated black eyes, a fine jaw, and small mouth, was resting on a tree limb not far from his position. This unusual being had chameleon-like pigmentation, alternating from purple to brown to yellow, while its face was a dark greyish tone.

According to the lone witness, the creature made a curious gesture, moving its head from side to side, and producing a sibilant or hissing sound that caused him to feel faint. Overcoming the sensation, he managed to see the creature drop from the tree-limb and rush off into the dense foliage. Torres decided to abandon the site as well—quickly.

José Vega (pseudonym), a neighbor to the Barreto property, claimed seeing a similar creature at a distance, keeping watch from a tree limb as journalists and investigators covered the terrain where the slaughtered sheep had been discovered. Vega confessed that although he had been looking at the creature through binoculars, it left him deeply shaken and made him feel ill.

The news division of TV Channel 11 in San Juan reported that on the night of May 11, a gargoylesque creature had been reported by a policeman and other individuals waiting at a bus stop in Santurce—the hub of metropolitan San Juan. Armed with his truncheon, the policeman struggled bravely against the five foot-tall creature outside the building which houses the Water and Sewage utility (Aqueductos y Alcantarillados). The nightmarish creature had allegedly been devouring a rat before squaring off with the policeman. It flew straight into the air, snatching the billy club out of the policeman's hand with its claw. (A similar creature was allegedly seen flying over the De Diego Expressway by drivers

Chick It out

caught in an afternoon traffic jam. Many of them, no doubt, must have envied its freedom of movement.)

Reports issuing from the Fajardo area, where the El Conquistador Hotel complex is located, indicated that local residents were concerned by chilling screams and howls heard in the night skies, seemingly produced by something flying over the area. On May 15, 1995, Jorge Martín interviewed Mr. Dolores Torres in the mountain community of Barranquitas. According to the gentleman's testimony, he had stepped out to his backyard momentarily to cut some fresh plantain bananas for dinner when everything around him became brightly lit in shades of yellow, orange, red and white. When he looked up to locate the source of the polychromatic display, he was stunned to see a transparent cylindrical object, less than two feet long, suspended from a cable which vanished into the sky.

The next thing Torres became aware of was that a large black shape was flying or floating toward the cylinder. He was able to distinguish a grey-faced humanoid figure, sheathed in a black outfit. The figure, whose eyes had the curious detail of being shut, approached the farmer, who took a few swings at it with his machete. The cylinder and the black-clad figure disappeared, leaving Torres badly shaken and in need of medical treatment. During his interview with Martín, he declared: "Look, people have come here to tell me that the thing I saw was the Chupacabras that's been killing all these animals. Others tell me it's the devil. They're both wrong. These creatures are extraterrestrials...what use could the devil have for a cylinder with a cable attached to it? Something's definitely wrong here."

Mr. Torres was not alone in his speculation regarding an extraterrestrial origin to the entire situation. The strangeness of the animal deaths in Orocovis' Barrio Saltos had many wondering if the federal government would step into the confusing and frightening situation to investigate, particularly after it was learned that a representative of the U.S. Department of Agriculture had inquired into the situation, and that his superiors in Washington had developed interest in the matter as a result of media items issuing from the island.

By now, both the farmers and townspeople of Orocovis were convinced that they were faced with an extraterrestrial menace in the shape of the Chupacabras. Fifty goats had been slain in the town of Comerío, south of Bayamón, and the creature had been identified as three feet tall and hairy. The means by which the animals had been slain was common to all others on the island—incisions around the neck through which blood had been extracted, and in some cases, the absence of certain organs, such as the heart and the liver.

On May 19, 1995, the inhabitants of the beautiful lake town of Patillas were dazzled by a UFO that flew over the Valle Real urbanization. According to Moisés Picart, the vehicle lit up the hillsides and disappeared shortly after, and did not correspond to any known commercial or military craft. Amazingly bright objects had been reported over the neighboring communities of Comerío and Barranquitas, where another "high-strangeness" event had transpired.

Earlier that same week, an elderly sugarcane cutter, hard at work in the fields, suffered a heart attack after fending off an attack by a monstrous winged creature (which may or may not have been the Chupacabras) in broad daylight. A police report indicated that the man had been carrying out his work at Barrio Palo Hincado when the "bird," for want of a better description, assaulted him from behind.

Don Francisco Ruiz, a cattleman in the town of Humacao on Puerto Rico's eastern shore (south of the Roosevelt Roads Naval Facility), was stunned to discover, on the morning of May 22, that three of his goats and their young lay dead without a drop of blood in their bodies. Officer Stephen Alvarez, a spokesman for the police department, said that the dead animals were found in the Punta Santiago section of Humacao. Puncture marks were discovered in the goats' necks, foreheads, and lens.

The results of Mr. Ruiz's crude autopsy on his animals, performed on the spot, demonstrated beyond any doubt that the carcass had been completely emptied of blood. This was the first case to take place outside the mountainous central municipalities of the island, and it would by no means be the last.

III. Junebugs, or How much is that doggie in the window?

As the month of June began, the media seemed to lose interest in the Chupacabras and in the constant animal slayings. There was the threat of another water shortage on the horizon (Puerto Rico was very nearly left waterless in 1994, when excellent weather produced no rainstorms to replenish cisterns and reservoirs). Political intrigue between one party and another, and the very real threat posed by the discovery that the U.S. Navy intended to build a huge radar array in the southwestern corner of the island. Such concerns understandably drove the Goatsucker to the back burner, but the brown mailer deposited into my mailbox on a sunny Saturday contained a cassette which proved that the critter was still at large. Only now it was the skeptics' turn to have their say.

Perhaps emboldened by the success of a "UFO" conference held at the University of Cupey on June 3 by former ufologists-turned-skeptics and disbelieving zoologists and psychologists, the skeptics felt that they could make their case on the national airwaves.

The cassette began with the obvious disappointment in the voice of José Valdez—my uncle and correspondent for my SAMIZDAT newsletter in Puerto Rico. He warned that it had been a mistake to tape the live call-in show because the guest speaker obviously didn't have the first idea of what he was saying. An hour later, I was forced to agree with my uncle.

The host, parapsychologist José Enrique Acosta, announced in a somewhat affected tone that the subject of the evening's broadcast was to be that of the "vampires" afflicting not only the island but the rest of the world. His guest, zoologist Edwin Velásquez, had apparently studied these cases in Mexico, Brazil, Thailand, etc. However, unlike what was the case in these countries, certain interests had tried make an issue out of the mutilations, alleging extraterrestrial intervention and other supernormal conditions.

The zoologist stated that his study of Puerto Rico's "vampire" problem went back twenty years, when he was employed with the now defunct Safari Park zoo. He had been invited by the media to decipher what exactly had caused the mutilations in the Moca region during the 1975 wave. Apparently, after a search of mountains, valleys, hills and dales, no cause that couldn't be attributed to dogs was ever found.

At this point, I could feel my interest in the recording rising.

Even cats and mongooses, he promptly added, were responsible for the mysterious killings. The slain animals were neither desiccated nor bloodless, as had been alleged: blood was still in evidence within the organs. The signs of attacks to the muzzles of beef cattle were indubitably caused by canine assaults.

In an incident investigated in Toa Alta, the death of a number of heifers had been attributed to an itinerant mandrill. The zoologist pondered this, and decided that if dogs hadn't caused the carnage, a mandrill would constitute a fitting replacement indeed, since mandrills are carnivorous, and the configuration of their teeth is that of a carnivore.

The host asked his guest why these things appeared to come about every two, three years or so, providing UFO believers with the theory that when lights are seen in the nighttime sky—particularly in Mexico—dead cattle usually litter the ground the following day.

Pausing for a moment, the zoologist replied that if one notices closely, it can be found that there is a refractory period between the so-called waves, the last one being the Adjuntas sightings of 1993. This time span could be understood as a period of catharsis or release that the popular mind demanded in order to cope with worldly tribulations. Belief in UFOs could best be seen as a safety valve of sorts, and people who would ordinarily never consider visiting the mountains of Orocovis were now doing so as a means of "escape."

Host: many people have said that the creature drags itself along the ground, lives in caves...is there anything to this belief?

Zoologist: Not everyone can describe a creature they see at night, and their imagination fills the blanks by association with other things. It happens very often in the Laguna Cartagena region, where feral monkeys escaped from a research institution. A person seeing one of these apes in twilight would believe they had seen a little man, thus confusing the real for the fantastic.

Host: [...] people must learn to banish their fears, as can be witnessed by the situation created around vampires, bloodsuckers, and an entire array of creatures.

Zoologist: This is dangerous, because when the humble, ignorant people of our rural areas hear that there is a bloodsucking creature on the loose, they believe it. Hysteria sets in. We should not be so sensationalistic. The media, for whatever reason, only gives one part of the story rather than the whole story.

After a commercial break, the host returned with another guest on the line: Arnaldo Ginés of Channel 11 on the telephone. The reason for his having been invited on the show was that he had of course investigated the Orocovis "vampires."

Journalist: Who said they were vampires?

Host: The callers to our show who've been saying that vampires or extraterrestrials are to blame...but since you're a scientific journalist, we'd like you to tell us exactly what transpired.

Journalist: Well, I always try to produce an objective report by having people say exactly what it is they've seen. I cannot testify to something I haven't seen, or that my cameraman hasn't filmed. All I can say is that there were indeed dead animals with wounds on their bodies which can be attributed to any creature, in all the time that we've been going to Orocovis. We did see a bull die before our very eyes, which was a very impressive sight, but aside from that, I can't lay claim to having seen anything unusual. Some of the people who've agreed to be interviewed before our camera claim, allege, having seen something strange and have even produced a number of drawings of what they saw.

Host: But your cameraman hasn't picked up anything strange?

Journalist: Not at all. We have gone out at night with infrared film in the camera and haven't come up with anything.

Host: What about these strange marks on the animals' bodies? Do they appear to have been made by dogs? Journalist: Well, that's where I draw the line, because I'm in no way well-versed in the subject. I understand that a when a dog bites, it tends to tear at the flesh, but I'm not by any means an expert in their behavior. It is curious, however, that the dead bull and the dead sheep had wounds that were similar to each other, and the animals that were wounded but didn't die displayed the same wounds.

Host: [...] Our guest Edwin Velásquez has some questions for you...

Zoologist: Yes, I would like to know if the persons in the regions remarked that there were dogs in the area, or if the wounds could be attributed to feral dogs.

Journalist: Well, at least one witness says that wild dogs could have been responsible, particularly around the property belonging to Quique Barreto, where the dead sheep were found. There is a waste dump in the area where wild animals of all kinds could have bred. It's possible, therefore, that dogs could be involved. I think in fact that Tito Chávez from Natural Resources has said that dog bites or bites caused by some other animal are more than likely the explanation, as opposed to some extraterrestrial creature as some parties have tried to make it seem.

Host: What about the dead heifer? Was it ill before it died? Was its owner treating it with some medication?

Journalist: I really don't know if it was sick. I understand that, as in Don Quique's case, when they found the animals lying there, they were injected with substances at the recommendation of a veterinarian. I suppose the same happened with the bull. It's possible that a reaction or overdose brought about the death--but I'm speculating. I understand that lab results are being expected. I would like your listeners to know that I enjoy this kind of reporting and that when it is an unusual matter, it is highly attractive for purposes of the print media and television. I become concerned, though, when hysteria begins to spread, for which reason I made a report twelve days later showing that no animal deaths had taken place. We cannot say the witnesses are lying, but it cannot be denied that something has been seen causing the attacks.

Zoologist: There is always possibility that an exotic animal is on the loose and has caused these deaths. It could have been released accidentally or on purpose, causing the damage in question.

Journalist: Well, what matters is that there have been no more attacks over the past 12 days, and the people of Orocovis can begin feeling calmer about the situation. Trust that the authorities will clear up the matter...I recall that in Camuy, a few years ago, certain pigs died mysteriously, and I'm not sure if it was ever cleared up. For many years people spoke about the Moca Vampire, but I understand that it was all a hoax...

Host: It was a hoax...

Zoologist: It was fabricated...

Journalist:...they took a bat and inserted false fangs into its mouth, or something like that.

Host: No, the fangs were inserted in a bird that was photographed in the newspapers, and it allegedly sucked blood. It turned out to be a guabairo, a bird native to Puerto Rico, into which the spurs used by fighting roosters had been inserted.

Journalist: Now, during all my time in Orocovis, no one has told me anything about animals being bloodless or having their blood removed.

Host: Of course, of course, and you've just made an interesting point. Blood specimens were drawn on the dead animals.

Journalist: Sure.

Host: But the story is that the extraterrestrials landed and left them without a single drop of blood, and this isn't true.

Journalist: Correct. No one has told me that they have no blood. I believe that there are people here and around the world who believe in extraterrestrials and have studied the matter for years, there are folks in different parts of the island and of the world who allege having seen strange lights and animals. I respect these peoples' beliefs, in the same way I respect religion and politics. But as a journalist I must stay objective, even though I have my own point of view of this situation. But I can tell people that it is a UFO only if I've captured it in my camera lens. For this reason I insist that these deaths could have been produced by an exotic animal, and that the people of Orocovis were unable to describe an animal they had never seen before...not so long ago I went to Cabo Rojo to report on some apes that were on the loose, in an area where there are no apes to begin with.

Zoologist: They're still there, you know.

Journalist: Its a highly complex matter, and the problem is that the people of Orocovis have taken it very seriously, and it has affected many local children. They can't go to school, they're restless in their sleep, and I feel that although we have a responsibility to inform people about what's going on, we're also responsible for urging them to remain calm, without having to cause an alarm.

Host: That's how it is, and Arnaldo, we would like to thank you for being on our show...everyone knows the serious and scientific approach you've taken in all your stories.

Journalist: You're very welcome. Good night.

Host: We will now begin taking phone calls on the line, only calls related to tonight's subject. Noti-Uno, hello?

Caller #1: Hello, good evening. This is Tita Mercado calling...

Host: Doña Tita, excuse me for a minute...aside from the callers already on the line, I'm inviting our listeners from Orocovis to call us as well. I feel they deserve every chance to comment on what's going on in their community. Please go ahead, Doña Tita.

Caller #1: As I'm talking to you, The Learning Channel, I think it's Channel 30, is showing something on flying objects, UFOs, and there's a Harvard professor who alleges that they exist, and a whole lot more. My question is this: where do the UFOs seen over Orocovis fit in? Where do the...

Host: Excuse me, Doña Tita, who said anything about flying saucers?

Caller # 1: Well, according to the reports...

Host: There were no reports, photos, films, or any evidence or proof.

Caller #1: I'm sorry, but I heard on WKAQ that there are two witnesses who did see flying objects. I'm not making this up as I go along.

Host: No, no, I understand. Scientifically, there is no proof that any sightings have taken place, only sightings of lights, which are common...

ALIEN BLOOD LUST

Caller #1: And the decomposition [process] of the animals, which didn't take place, was something I also found strange. Furthermore, all I could say—and Don Edwin knows that I know quite a bit about animals...

Zoologist: Yes.

Caller #1: Do you remember, Edwin, the Tasmanian Devil that escaped from el Monoloro? [defunct zoo] Zoologist: The one in Carolina, you mean?

Caller #1: No, not the Monoloro, the other one...

Host: Safari Park?

Caller#1: That's the one! That was years ago, and it's the only thing that could...I'm looking at this objectively, but the flesh didn't rot with the tremendous heat we've been experiencing. Once, I took two geese which had been found in Cabo Rojo, with no blood and puncture marks, to a vet, who was well known here. He did the autopsy and everything, but after it was done, he refused to sign the autopsy protocol. The geese didn't have a drop of blood between them.

Host: I'm going to jump ahead of Edwin here. I'm not a scientist or a doctor like he is...

Caller #1: I think that the protocols or the Federal paperwork granted to veterinarians or importers, people having to do with fauna and flora, are afraid to receive a sanction from Federal authorities, but I'm sitting here watching extraterrestrials on channel 30, and I'm wondering what's going on?

Host: Well, you can have anything you want going on, But let me tell you from experience that I'm not an authorized embalmer, but I have done embalming of bodies during years, and blood is the first thing to decompose. When something has bled to death, there is little blood to be found. With no blood in the body, the decomposition process takes longer to come about. I imagine that the same applies to animals. Edwin can challenge me on this point if it isn't so.

Zoologist: It is so, and both the climatological and soil conditions play a role in determining this matter. Many animal corpses do not show the decomposition one would expect after many days.

Caller #1: I'd like to add that a few years ago, along with 42 other people at the Caguas Drive-In, I saw a mothership which was later featured on the first page of the old El Mundo newspaper. Among the witnesses there were judges, psychologists...

Host: I'm not saying extraterrestrials don't exist, but the animals are the subject tonight. I have to let you go, since the board is full. Noti-Uno, hello?

Caller #2: Good evening. Do they [extraterrestrials] exist or not?

Host: Look, the subject tonight isn't whether extraterrestrials exist or not, and I still haven't met anyone who has photographed them or filmed them. The day that happens, I'll do like my friend Arnaldo Ginés and respect the person who took the photo or film, which I would then present to you. I don't doubt it. My concept of extraterrestrial is different from that of most people. Someday we'll do a special program on the subject. To me extraterrestrials and Marian apparitions are the Gods which have been deified over the centuries.

Caller #2: But my question has to do with tonight's...

Host: No. As Dr. Edwin Velázquez has said, the wounds are caused by dogs. Got it?

Caller #2: So now it's dogs.

Host: No, it's not a matter of "now it's dogs." It has always been dogs that attacked the animals because the waste dumps were close. Wild dogs were seen in the area. There are no extraterrestrials in Orocovis. It isn't true.

Caller #2: Well, now there's a neighbor saying they saw dogs, and it's really confusing...

Host: No, no. There were people who claim having seen an animal skulking about, another [person] was performing a biological necessity and saw an animal climb up a tree...

Caller #2: And he made a drawing of it...

Host: Aha. Why didn't he make a drawing of it before? We're just going through a period of collective hysteria, fear. If we were living in the Puerto Rico of the 1920's, I would have believed the man who appeared on the newscast, but in the age in which we live, with toilets available, anyone who tells me they went into the woods to defecate, I can't believe...these cases are entirely different. They are not the same. [break in dialogue]...We cannot compare what happened in Mexico or in Canada with what happens here in Puerto Rico, specifically what's happening in Orocovis. Do you understand?

Caller#2: Ummm.

Host: Okay? Thanks for your call and good night. Noti-Uno, good evening?

Caller#3: Good evening, this is Jorge Berrios from Bayamón.

Host: Yes, what is your question for Doctor Edwin Velásquez?

Caller#3: My question is: why, if he categorically states that we're dealing with dogs, did the same dogs not attack in the same area earlier?

Zoologist: These things have always occurred. Dogs have always attacked animals and the people who live in the area and have been interviewed can attest to it. However, in this matter, for whatever reason, there is a lapse of a few years and new wave of stories emerges about UFOs or attacks on animals. It's a seasonal affair. It just so happens that now it's in Orocovis...

Caller #3: Okay, but what I'm saying is that with the sheer volume of dogs that we have in Puerto Rico, it just so happens that the dogs from Orocovis are the ones going after steers?

ALIEN BLOOD LUST

Zoologist: It isn't a coincidence. It happens every day.

Caller #3: With the same characteristics?

Zoologist: With the same characteristics. In other words, it's nothing strange. What's strange is that there are people who want to give it connotations of an unknown phenomenon.

Caller #3: But I ask you again: have you gone to the area?

Zoologist: Orocovis? Yes, I've been in Orocovis. And I've been to many other places on the island.

Host: Don't forget, friend, that Dr. Edwin Velásquez is a zoologist and independently from this, the government has hired him to perform this kind of work over the past 20 years. For that reason I asked him to come on this show: not just to tell you that dogs were responsible, but to give you faith in that it's a scientific matter, OK?

Caller #3: I know, but excuse me: Noticentro Cuatro just interviewed a biologist, and the man said that in no way could vampire bats have caused such damage to the animals.

Host: We're not talking about vampires here. We're talking about dogs.

Caller #3: In closing, I would like him to tell me what kind of exotic animal can cause wounds of that nature, and bring about an animal's death?

Zoologist: Well, there are several kinds of carnivores that can cause that kind of damage. What do you want me to tell you? There are felines, and we're not talking about lions or tigers here..

Caller #3: Who won't tear their prey?

Zoologist: You have to have a certain amount of knowledge. When a feline attacks its prey, it doesn't tear at it. It suffocates it by crushing it, leaving two neat fang marks. Therefore, there is no rending of flesh.

Caller #3: Then what's the purpose of inflicting the wounds and nothing else?

Zoologist: Well, the wounds...

Caller #3: Excuse me, but when an animal attacks it's because it's hungry.

Zoologist: Usually. But these attacks by packs of dogs don't always eat the animal. For some reason, they kill the animal, become frightened, and leave the area. They don't always eat the kill.

Caller #3: Well, you haven't convinced me, but all right.

Host: But friend, I urge you to find more information at [name of bookstore]

Caller #3: But in that case—what's your name?

Host: José Enrique.

Caller #3: In that case, José Enrique, I would have to ask you to do the same. If there is no proof about UFOs, then what proof is there about what you're saying?

ALIEN BLOOD LUST

Scientific proof on the subject.

Host: You know what happens? No UFO was ever seen, but the dogs were seen.

Caller #3: No, no, I mean about the subject you're dealing with.

Host: Well, the subject we're dealing with tonight... Caller #3: What scientific proof is there?

Host: Well, visual [proof], for one.

Caller #3: I mean about your field, parapsychology. What proof is there?

Host: Hey, we can talk all you like about it. I've been a year and a half on Noti-Uno and have 28 years of experience behind me regarding the powers of the mind and the psyche. It's nothing religious, just the mind.

Caller #3: But I mean scientific proof.

Host: Well, the scientific proof would be proof that I've been a year and a half with Noti-Uno, have 28 years experience, and I have a really, really professional office, and I'm doing really well for myself.

Caller #3: Well, okay then. Thank you.

Host: The reason I'm telling you this is that I'm good at what I do, you know?

Caller #3: Great. Thanks again.

Host: I'm at your service whenever you'd like to stop by my office, and I'll give you all the proof you want...The reason I'm saying this to the caller is because there are many people who try to say: what proof do you have? But as you've said, Edwin, it's something real, something that has been proven, these animals are dogs. And it's our subject tonight. Good evening, Noti-Uno?

Caller #4: Good evening.

Host: What's your question, please?

Caller #4: My name's Ricardo...

Host: Quickly, because we're running out of time.

Caller #4: I'm not a zoologist, but I've been bitten by dogs.

Host: Aha.

Caller #4: There's an observation I would like to make. I'm concerned that someone who hasn't seen these bite wounds is saying that it's a dog. I didn't go to Orocovis, but I recorded everything with great care because I'm a medical photographer. I've seen the bites of many animals, including humans.

Host: What does a medical photographer do, friend?

Caller #4: A medical photographer photographs everything having to do with medicine in order to show it to students.

Host: Do you work for some agency?

Caller #4: I'm employed by the College of Medicine. There's an observation about animals I'd like to make. Animals--if you've ever seen a documentary on hunters--that bite other animals respond to their self-preservation instincts. Bulls have one of the strongest self-preservation instincts. This bull allowed itself to be bitten, yet did not respond to the attack by its aggressor. This is a concern for me, that a zoologist hasn't explained up to now why this didn't take place.

Host: Well, look here, friend--Edwin is going to answer your question.

Caller #4: But before he answers, let me ask him a question...

Host: Let him answer you first, then you can ask the second question. Don't go away.

Zoologist: Yes, in the bull's case, it did not display any particular type of wounds or punctures, except in one of its legs. Therefore, we can't really say that it was even a bite, and I would say that it had stepped on a nail or something similar. There wasn't even a bite, in the case of the bull in question.

Caller #4: But I'd like to give you a detail provided last night by the Director of Parque de las Ciencias, who performed an autopsy with some biologists and veterinarians on the bull.

Zoologist: Yes.

Caller #4: This bull had certain incisions on its neck, and had other incisions reaching down to its lungs, okay? After eight days, the dead animal was entirely flexible, it wasn't stiff. Those who raise cattle for commercial sales know that after eight days, no animal is going to be flexible. That's the first surprise...

Zoologist: Let me ask you something. Was the autopsy protocol...who was the person who performed the autopsy, did you say?

Caller #4: I don't recall the name, but I know that it was authorized by the mayor of Bayamón at Channel 4's request.

Zoologist: Yes, but is there an autopsy protocol? Does one exist?

Caller #4: Sure it exists.

Zoologist: And who has it?

Caller #4: The director of Parque de las Ciencias in Bayamón.

Zoologist: The director of Parque de las Ciencias performed an autopsy?

Caller #4: Yes...

Zoologist: To the best of my knowledge, the director of Parque de las Ciencias isn't a vet.

Caller #4: Well, he went there with a biologist and a veterinarian.

Zoologist: Ah.

Caller #4: I heard these words from his own mouth in a recording featured on Jorge Martín's program last night. It was aired with his own words. They got there, they opened the animal, they checked its heart, noticed the animal had died in agony, there were blood clots, eight days later the animal's blood was still liquid, and it was flexible when it shouldn't have been. They even thought, before laying a hand on the animal, that the temperature had kept it from decomposing, but at midday the heat became unbearable. I'm sure they'll communicate the results [of the autopsy] to the people in their own time. It's not normal.

Zoologist: I think that the person whom you're describing is a friend of mine, the vet at Parque de las Ciencias, Dr. Bientot. If the autopsy protocol exists, you can be sure that I'll examine it, and I'll talk to Dr. Bientot to see what's really behind all this.

Caller #4: Honestly, you should really inform yourself well, because talking without having visited the site, is a bit...

Host: But friend, what you're trying to do is—sorry for interrupting you—is make it seem as if what our friend Jorge Martín says...and I've heard his show...is that these are extraterrestrials...

Caller #4: No, I'm not talking about extraterrestrials...

Host: You're trying to create the impression that...

Caller #4: For a human to have done that would require...

Host: It's that you, you--the autopsy you're referring to is impossible. Its impossible to make such determinations in a split second. You're giving us conclusions that you yourself don't have in your hands

Caller #4: Yes, but it's evident. There is no aggression, there's nothing...

Host: But this isn't...

and...

Caller #4: Look, when a dog bites it tears...have you ever been bitten by a dog? I've been bitten by dogs.

Host: It's not the same thing to be bitten by a dog as by a human.

Caller #4: Look, a dog has teeth...

Host: Aha.

Caller #4: It'll stick its fangs into you and the other teeth as well.

Host: If you listened to the show from the beginning, you heard Edwin Velásquez comment that the bull may have been ill to begin with. Its death was not necessarily caused by a dog bite.

Zoologist: In fact, the animal's owners remarked to someone who was present that the animal had indeed been sick around that time, and that many of the owner's animals had been sick and were being medicated. Possibly one of the medications given to it brought about death.

Caller #4: But did you see the puncture marks on it? I've got tapes with close-ups showing that it was an animal that bites with a single fang. There are no one-fanged animals.

ALIEN BLOOD LUST

Zoologist: Yes, but keep in mind that these farm animals can scratch themselves against barbed wire...

Caller #4: You mean to say all the animals, so many cows and goats?

Zoologist: Tell me why can't it be so?

Caller #4: They'd better get the nail out of wherever it's stuck!

Zoologist: But tell me why can't it be so? Why can't it be barbed wire? Why?

Caller #4: Because how are you going to drive barbed wire down to the lungs? He said this himself, and you can ask him if he's your friend, that whatever pierced down to its lungs didn't damage any viscerae, which surprised him. How could something pierce a body without...

Host: Let's do something, friend. Let's--

Caller #4: I'm only asking that...

Host: Let's take up this matter with Dr. Bientot, so that Edwin can talk to him this week, discuss the autopsy, and then next Friday we can comment on it, all right?

Caller #4: Sure, of course.

Host: We're running out of time. Thanks for your call.

Caller #4: So long.

Host: Our last call. Noti-Uno, good evening?

Caller #5: Good evening.

Host: Your question, please.

Caller #5: Yes, I had the same thoughts about the Orocovis situation since it first started, and I've been against anything having to do with extraterrestrials, vampires...

Host: We should always look for the scientific aspect first.

Caller #5: To me, it has to be a dog...either a dog or a lion. There's nothing else.

Zoologist: Yes, well...an animal, you're correct.

Caller #5: A wild dog or a lion.

Host: It may be, but we can't rule out extraterrestrials so as not to offend our friends, like the one who just called, claiming that he has photographs, and wholeheartedly believing in extraterrestrials. The history of the gods discusses extraterrestrials as backward spirits who live off the blood of human beings or animals. However, the lungs were extracted from the bodies and burned...for this reason, the aspect he wanted to discuss and insinuate as extraterrestrial just because Martín said so, I feel is incorrect. The day Jorge Martín sees an extraterrestrial I hope he'll come here and show me photographs, because he's simply a scholar of these matters; and I respect him greatly for it, but he is neither a contactee nor has he ever seen an extraterrestrial. He's merely a scholar, of course, and he has a magazine, and if he's gone as far--which I doubt--as to conclude that it was an extraterrestrial who caused the situation he is very wrong, and both myself as a parapsychologist and Dr. Edwin Velázquez as a veterinarian invite him to tell us the contrary. All right?

Caller #5: Well, I only called to tell you that.

Host: Thank you for your call.

Caller #5: I've always thought that it was a wild animal like Armando said...was that his name?

Host: Arnaldo Ginés, correct, from Channel 11. As Arnaldo said, the people he interviewed spoke about wild dogs. The problem is that if one goat is killed, it soon becomes ten, or twenty. Like our friend the caller said, he exaggerated that there were twenty goats when it wasn't true. The owner of the farm has gotten in touch with Edwin and the animals were ill, you know? But, thanks for your call.

Caller #5: Bye.

Host: It'll be until next...the board is still loaded, but we're out of time...

* * *The recording ended abruptly. I rewound the tape and played it once more, this time in the car, on an hour-long journey to a nearby town. I played it once more on the way back, and still couldn't believe what I was hearing.

Translation is my profession, and transcribing tapes from one language to another to produce a written record is a routine task. In preparing the transcription you have just read, I couldn't help wondering if the skeptics realized that they had been pinned against the ropes from the very first call (NOTE: I have gone over the tape once more after the transcription to insure fidelity. I deliberately omitted ad-libs for the sake of felicity in communication and because of the numerous overlaps in conversation between host, guests, and callers. I understand Drs. Acosta and Velásquez's points of view, and hope they realize no disrespect is intended).

The "feral dog" theory in the Chupacabras wave would soon become the equivalent of "swamp gas." As has been observed elsewhere, the thought of one-fanged, bloodthirsty Fidos roaming the countryside is enough to make the most snowbound tourist cancel a planned and paid vacation to the Continent of Puerto Rico, as the ad agencies call it. Contradictions, which can be observed in the transcript, were forcibly invoked to support the dog bite theory; last-minute solutions (the animals being sick) sought to rescue the skeptics from the deepening water in the radio studio. As Frank Herbert has Muad'Dib say in the memorable banquet scene in Dune: "I never saw a man drown around a dinner table before."

The callers represented a cross-section of the island's demographics. Caller #1 was a middle-aged woman, obviously knowledgeable about the subject of unidentified flying objects, but quite willing to concede that animals such as the legendary Tasmanian Devil could cause such havoc among bovines. The host and guest mounted an ineffective defense when they sought to deny that any UFOs had been reported in the Orocovis area, when the networks had been broadcasting such testimony for over a month.

Caller #2, another middle-aged, soft-spoken woman, triggered the skeptics' defenses in a spectacular way, prompting the host to become just a touch discourteous. The insistence that it had never been anything but dogs (with sharp canines, excuse the pun) behind the Orocovis slayings became a mantra rather than a theory. The situation fell apart with the ultimate non-sequitur concerning the existence of latrines in rural Puerto Rico.

Caller #3, a middle-aged man, asked the sensitive question regarding the reason why dogs, feral or otherwise, hadn't caused similar damage before. Rather than limiting himself to answering the question, the zoologist took the offensive, challenging that the belief in UFOs, previously described as a safety valve or mental alibi for a distressed population, caused these periodic manias. The pitfall lay in the fact that no mutilations were ever reported during the refractory periods when people weren't "hallucinating Martians," so to speak. The host responded to the demand that he furnish proof of the validity of parapsychology by making an arrogant remark aimed at putting the caller down.

But the coup-de-grace clearly belongs to Caller #4, the medical technician who challenged the zoologist's expertise by saying that a televised autopsy had prompted experts to say that something was definitely unusual about the bull that remained both uncorrupted and free from rigor mortis. Reeling from the verbal punches, there was nothing left to do but issue a vague threat of verifying the story with the veterinarian who performed the autopsy.

Caller #5, a grandmotherly woman, appeared to be the only caller to go along with the pooch- oriented scenario the skeptics had set up, only to whimsically add that "a lion" could have made the single puncture mark. Chagrined, the skeptics were forced to agree with her, but took advantage of the conversation to direct a few blows against believers in any extraterrestrial intervention in the Orocovis scenario.

We do not know if Dr. Acosta revisited the subject on the next installment of his show. Only Arnaldo Ginés' statement that the killings appeared to have abated in the Orocovis region rang true. After a brief lull, the killings would begin anew.

IV. Stalking the Beast

There are no hard and fast rules for monster hunting. Certainly, cryptozoologists can indicate the most suitable equipment to take on an expedition, but every researcher, from Heuvelmans to Lara to Chorvinsky, has his own method. Some might opt for a "photo safari" approach, hoping to capture photos of the elusive critter. Others might consider carrying firearms in case there should be a replay of the Goatman incident, where a cornered entity began hurling tires against his pursuers with the ease of a frisbee thrower. Certainly the method of Mayor Soto and his unarmed cadres, using a cage built from welded iron fencing and with a goat as bait, constitutes another option.

Some of the cases were fascinating: the industrial complex that couldn't find any security guards to work the graveyard shift, because three "Goatsucker"-like creatures had been seen at the same time; the people waiting for the bus in broad daylight who saw the Chupacabras walking down the street; the driver waiting at a stoplight who thought "a dog" was crossing the street in front of him, only to realize that it was a creature he had never seen before; the woman who looked out the window in the midst of Hurricane Luis only to see the Chupacabras standing at a distance, impervious to the rain, wind, and lightning; the man with the machine gun who fired a hail of hot lead against the creature, but was too scared to report his case on account of his illegal firepower.

Flashback: The Moca Vampire

During the 1975 wave, Freixedo observed that the smallness of Puerto Rico allowed any investigator to hop into a car and drive to the scene of the events in an hour or two—something that would be difficult to do in his native Spain, much less in the United States. It was this closeness that enabled him to be one of the first people on the scene at Moca.

"During an evening in which UFOs were sighted over the town of Moca," Freixedo says, "two ducks, three goats, a pair of geese, and a large hog were found slain the following morning on a small farm. The owner was going insane, wondering who in the world could have visited this ruin upon him. The animals betrayed the wounds that have become typical of this kind of attack, and of course, they were all inflicted with incredible precision. I did not doubt for one moment who could have been responsible for the crime...I got in my car and visited the area immediately, and realized what was filling the animals' owner with wonder and fear: there wasn't a trace of blood in any of the animals, in spite of the fact that the dead geese had snow-white feathers, upon which the slightest speck of blood would have shown up immediately.

"Over the next few days, the newspapers continued reporting the growing number of dead animals encountered in the region. No explanation could be found for these mysterious deaths. I visited the rural areas on various occasions to investigate the events firsthand and found that the farmers were as intrigued by their animals' deaths as they were by the enigmatic lights they could see in the nocturnal skies. One of them told me that the lights reminded him of the revolving lights on top of a police cruiser.

"During one of my forays, I was able to see a black and white cow spread out in the middle of the field. I got out of the car and tried to reach the cow, which wasn't easy. The dead beast had characteristic wounds on its neck and on its head. Skin had been pulled back on one side of its head, as if by a scalpel, and the opening to one of its nasal orifices was missing, although there was no indication of rending. In spite of the whiteness of its head, there wasn't a single drop of blood to be seen. The farmer who escorted me could not stop wondering what had caused his cow's death. He related how that very same night he had heard his dogs barking furiously, and that a blind elderly woman who lived on the edge of the field had told him that the cattle, which ordinarily spends the night outdoors, had kept her from getting a good night's sleep due to their frantic, maddened running from one end of the field to another."

The benefit of twenty years hasn't added much to the investigator's arsenal. Researchers of the paranormal still stand over the carcasses of bloodless, mutilated animals wondering what explanation might satisfy the pleading look on the rancher's face. Can the ufologist, cryptozoologist, Fortean investigator or paranormalist really "level" with the animal's owner, who has just lost a valuable investment or a beloved pet, and start spouting wisdom about EBEs, killer UFOs, interdimensional beings that need blood for their sustenance, and other standbys of the occult? On the other hand, can the skeptic tell the same distressed farmer that an "archetype" or figment of the popular imagination just put a finger-sized hole through an animal's throat?

Avians and Aliens

Is the Chupacabras merely another of the winged weirdos -- ranging from pterodactyls to Mothman-like creatures -- that have characterized the Fortean nature of Puerto Rico's cases? Apparently, the winged monsters retain a fondness for their old stomping grounds in the mountains, as exemplified by the following case.

Georgie Quiñones, a citizen of Naranjito, a community located in the island's interior, reported how his mother had run into a being she at first thought was a child, because its height and build resembled that of a three year-old boy. The being was standing next to some hedges, and upon closer inspection of it, Mrs. Quiñones realized that she was in fact staring at something that she had never seen before--it had a large head and eyes, a flattened nose, and a delicate jawbone that appeared to be connected to the creature's body.

Creature and woman held each other's gaze, until the latter began feeling faint and nauseous. Taking advantage of her discomfiture, the being abandoned the area with stunning speed. The small intruder apparently belonged to the same order of beings seen earlier in Orocovis. Prior to this encounter, Mr. Quiñones' mother had also witnessed a flight of "gigantic" birds passing over the area two weeks earlier. One of the immense birds was described as having a "hump" on its back. Being familiar with eagles and the native guaraguao (a kind of hawk), she assured her son that the birds did not resemble either of these. One of the birds landed on the branches of a nearby tree, causing it to bend on account of its weight.

Mrs. Quiñones also found forty-seven of her chickens dead on her property, which added a touch of horror to a strange situation. One of the dead hens had a considerable puncture mark on it, large and deep enough that a finger could be stuck into it. A neighbor of Mrs. Quiñones' had an encounter with a small humanoid that allegedly "jumped him" and caused him to flee in panic.

The Canóvanas Sightings

The summer brought sporadic sightings and reports of the Goatsucker, while UFO activity remained constant. The situation did not pick up again until the focus of activity had shifted from Orocovis to the coastal town of Canóvanas.

Canóvanas is a prosperous community that benefits from its location on Route 3, which handles the heavy traffic between San Juan on one end and Fajardo on the other. The majestic, mist-enshrouded peaks of El Yunque are only a stone's throw away, and the excellent beaches of Luquillo attract thousands of local and foreign tourists. Canóvanas also boasts the spectacular El Comandante, one of the finest race tracks in the entire world. It was this fortunate piece of real estate that the gargoylesque creature called the Chupacabras would select as its own.

Residents of Canovanas' Lomas del Viento neighborhood were treated one evening to a rather spectacular UFO sighitng. One of them, Victor Rodríguez, told Jorge Martín that around 11:45 p.m. on the night of the event, he became aware of a scintillating object that descended upon a group of trees. The light, described as "round and brilliant," took off from the area as if it had been spotted.

Lucy Batista, residing in the Alturas de Campo Rico neighborhood, commented on the curious noises associated with the Chupacabras—inhuman screams resembling the combined sounds of a cat yowling and a goat's bleating. Not only did it cause her to feel fear, it also caused all of her animals to panic. One night, she heard the sound of an animal running behind her house. At first she thought it was a horse, until the terrifying cackle filled the air, causing her to fear for the safety children in her household.

During her interview with Jorge Martin, Mrs. Batista expressed her belief that a link existed between the creature or creatures known as the Goatsucker and the lights seen entering and leaving El Yunque, which faced her development. Her husband and her son had also witnessed the brightly-colored lights that maneuvered above the mountain rainforest.

Believing at first the lights belonged to National Guard helicopters on nocturnal maneuvers, Mrs. Batista soon realized that the lights were executing a number of senseless maneuvers every single night-- standing still, ducking, flying in circles--that no helicopter is able to do. Motivated by curiosity, her husband and son drove up the tortuous mountain road to El Yunque, proceeding on foot to avoid detection by patrols. An encounter with Forestry Service workers put their expedition to an end, and both were turned back. She now believes that the lights correspond to what are commonly called flying saucers.

ALIEN BLOOD LUST

"The creature being seen everywhere in Canóvanas must be an extraterrestrial," she told Martín during the course of the interview. "The drawings that are going around show a combination of extraterrestrial and terrestrial animals. This is the conclusion that we've reached, and the conclusion of the people who've seen it." Other residents of her area refer to the creature jokingly as "The Rabbit" on account of the shape of its hind legs, or "The Kangaroo," for its ability to take prodigious leaps with its powerful legs.

In the light of all the commotion the creature's antics caused in Canóvanas, many of the locals were surprised that no agencies aside from members of the Civil Defense had chosen to look into the matter. "The Department of Natural Resources was called, but no one was sent to investigate. Perhaps they thought this situation was something cooked up by the townsfolk," one local grumbled.

The fact of the matter is that the witnesses were subjected not to the negative influence of MIBs or hostile government agents, but to the scorn of their own peers. A young woman named Mariane, interviewed by Martín, indicated that her husband's co-workers had taken to teasing him by calling him Goatsucker all the time. Other members of their family who had also expressed their belief in the existence of this creature, or had seen it with their own eyes, had also been subjected to ridicule. "This creature isn't a joke," she said angrily. "I didn't make it up, either. It's real."

Undoubtedly, one of the foremost witnesses of the Canóvanas sightings, whose credibility was never an issue, was a pious gentleman named Daniel Pérez who was well-regarded in his community. Mr. Pérez had encountered the Goatsucker not once, but twice.

Interview with Daniel Pérez

Martín: We're here with Mr. Daniel Pérez of the Campo Rico sector, which has been affected by the appearance of the mysterious creature that has been seen in the area over the past couple of weeks. Don Daniel, we understand that you've had the opportunity to see the creature on two or three occasions in very important circumstances, because you saw it by daylight and were able to distinguish certain important features. We would like to ask you what you saw, what meaning it holds for you, and what you think about the situation?

Pérez: Well, it was around a quarter to seven in the morning...I heard a kind of moan, something going: "Oooooo," something strange, so I got up and went to the window, and saw nothing at all. When I was about to close the window, I heard a buzzing sound [makes buzzing sound], which prompted me to look out again. At that moment, the creature descended, apparently flying. Yes, it came down, and it alighted on a large stone that is on my property, some twenty feet away from where I stood. As soon as it made contact with the stone, it gathered impulse again, rose into the air, and cleared the trees ahead without touching a single leaf. It's a crea-

impressed mind inspired to multiply more of them

ture measuring some three feet in height, I'd say, when it isn't erect, but when it stands straight, it must be some five feet tall. Its hind legs are long, its forelegs are short, it's somewhat cute, has a little belly, and...from the top of its head all down its back it has some sort of fins that move. When it was about to take off, the fins moved in the direction it was headed. I really didn't see its eyes, but its head is large...the eyes are big, but I couldn't see what color they were. Its face is small and pointy. The following day, at the same time, I saw it heading back in the opposite direction. It's skin is squirrel-colored and I can't describe it properly...

Martín: Why's that?

Pérez: Because I can't describe it as actual fur or skin per se. It's something that causes a rather strange sensation. In fact, my first impression upon seeing the creature was to remain silent. In other words, well, I...

Martín: They tell us that you were deeply impressed and affected by the creature's presence.

Pérez: Well, I thought it would be best to keep quiet and not tell anyone, but then I told my wife, and she told the neighbor lady, and it took off from there. I originally thought about keeping it to myself, feeling that if I tried explaining it to people, they wouldn't believe me. As far as my personality is concerned, I have no mental reservations whatsoever about there being creatures in other parts of the universal system...to my understanding, this in no way contradicts the Scriptures, because God, in his immense labors, has things we've never seen nor heard of.

Martín: You're telling me this because...it seems that you felt that it could be some sort of alien life form.

Pérez: I think so.

Martín: And why's that?

Pérez: According to the way I see it, a creature that flies without having enormous wings...

Martín: Didn't you see it fly?

Pérez: I didn't see any wings as such. It does have some sort of fins that apparently help it glide...

Martín: What do those fins look like?

Pérez: They're triangular in shape, but sometimes, when it's in the air, they can be mistaken for hair, perhaps because of the speed with which it moves them, they could be interpreted as hair, but not to my understanding.

Martín: But you're saying they're not very big.

Pérez: They're some six to eight inches long. They protrude from its spine.

Martín: Six to eight inches...how many do you think there are? We've been told that it has a kind of crest.

ALIEN BLOOD LUST

Pérez: They're not all the same size. They go from medium-sized, mix in with the larger ones on its back, and then diminish. Honestly, I can't say if it had a tail, or I didn't see a tail as such. Maybe those who've seen it have pictured the fins that run downward to be part of a tail, but to me they ended on the creature's back.

Martín: The majority of witnesses have described spines or quills coming out of its back.

Pérez: I had the same impression when I saw it flying, coming in. But I'll tell you again--it moves them so fast that it makes it seem that they're hairs, but as soon as it stopped, I didn't feel they were hairs, as such.

Martín: [garbled] Were you able to make out the shape of its eyes?

Pérez: Its...Its eyes were rather large, but I honestly didn't see the color. Now, the shape--

Martín: Basically we're talking about an eye looking like this--

Pérez: Two inches, more or less.

Martín: Ahhh, we've been told that the eyes are slanted--

Pérez: Yes, inclined--

Martín: Almond-shaped?

Pérez: Inclined upwards...like so.

Martín: Um...the hands. Could you see its hands?

Pérez: The hands are tiny.

Martín: Tiny?

Pérez: Yes.

Martín: How many fingers, if any?

Pérez: I honestly didn't see...

Martín: What are its legs like?

Pérez: The legs are rather, rather long. When he landed, he did this: He came down...

Martín: Bent its legs...

Pérez: Exactly, then he took off. I think that he doesn't fly as a result of impulse--he flies by nature.

Martín: But what has to be seen...what you're describing, and what others are describing, in regard to the spines or fins on its back, just wouldn't be enough to impel a body of that size.

Pérez: That's what I found so strange. According to what I could see, he uses the fins to guide the direction of his flight, but when he's in the air, he apparently crosses them. They buzz [makes buzzing sound] and many have perhaps confused the fins with hairs, since they move so quickly.

Martín: So it flies with those appendages?

ALIEN BLOOD LUST

Pérez: With those appendages or whatever [they are]. But he also uses them, apparently, to orient himself.

Martín: When you saw it the second time around, and you heard the buzzing, you were looking at it from where?

Pérez: I was at the, the...the window of my house, looking out. He was heading toward my house, and I thought he was going to land on the stone, but he turned when he reached the gate and turned upward.

Martín: In other words, you didn't see where it was coming from?

Pérez: No, no I didn't.

Martín: You saw it when it went by at the moment.

Pérez: That's correct, yes.

Martín: You're a religious man...you're well-liked in the sector, and you're seen as a very serious person. And I congratulate you on that, because everyone we've spoken to holds you in very high regard. But...you were telling us a short while ago that you feel this doesn't contradict...it's having a relationship with something extraterrestrial...this doesn't contradict the Scriptures?

Pérez: [unintelligible]

Martín: I know, I know, but if this is so, and what we're dealing with isn't terrestrial, what implications would this have for you?

Pérez: Well, for me...ah, it would confirm what, what I've always believed, that there could be life elsewhere in the universe. And it would mean that God is even greater than I previously imagined, and as I said earlier, in the course of his immense works he may have ordained life elsewhere, which shouldn't alarm us or surprise us. I understand that these are the things the Bible tells us are reserved for the eyes and ears of the faithful, and that...well, much in the same way we're trying to get to the Moon, and we send ships to Mars and to other countries (sic), they may be trying to reach us, as we've found drawings of extraterrestrial beings, or whatever you want to call them, made by human beings who lacked the intellectual powers that we have today. These things are there...they're facts that can't be denied.

Martín: Is there anything you would like to add, or to say to the people who may be listening to this interview, something you may want to tell them based on your experience?

Pérez: Well, I urge people not to be alarmed, as far as I know he hasn't attacked any human beings, and...if they should see him, well...take it as naturally as possible, um, they're going to be somewhat surprised, but it's only natural, and not to create fantasies about it or treat it as a joke. If there's something I've come to learn it is that these things should not be taken in jest. The fact that one hasn't seen it...shouldn't make you disbelieve it. But most importantly, don't think it's some sort of "goof," as they say...

* * *

The transcript of Martín's interview with the religious Canovanan was proof that educated, perceptive members of the population—immune to the sensationalist press--were providing highly detailed accounts of their experiences with the elusive creature.

Pérez's testimony was vital for an important reason. First and foremost, he was privileged to have seen the "monster" twice--on its way to and from an unguessed-at location--and was able to contain whatever fear or concern he may have had for his safety or that of his family, thus allowing him to take a long look at the entity and study its peculiar characteristics.

The creature's identikit image, which had been featured on the first page of San Juan's El Nuevo Día newspaper, was revised on the basis of the Pérez testimony. The "spikes" running from the creature's head down its back were apparently fin-like appendages that vibrated so quickly it made them seem like hairs to other witnesses, particularly those who did not stick around to take second look.

Nonetheless, Pérez' testimony created an added complication. Where it had been believed that the entity merely took prodigious jumps from one location to another by means of its powerful hind legs, it was now capable of wingless flight by means of these buzzing appendages. While the wings of a hummingbird are theoretically too small to support its weight, eppur si muove!, as Galileo would have said. Could this be the case with the Goatsucker? Pérez also corroborated descriptions of the creature's head, eyes (though not their color), arms, and legs.

V. Into the Realm of Beasts

Perhaps no single area in the realm of paranormal studies evokes more reactions —positive and negative-- than the appearance of strange beasts, ranging from winged entities and oversized felines to grotesque, hairy simian creatures. They elude police and hunters, yet become plainly visible to suburbanites emptying the trash; they have been seen hurling fifty gallon drums at their pursuers, yet also appear to have a ghostly, insubstantial aspect which allows them to vanish almost instantly; they have been reported in every single location possible, from the tropical rainforests and high mountains to the heavily congested streets of our metropolitan areas.

Researchers have shunned research into these apparitions; it is as a sure-fire way to achieve disrespectability, even among fellow investigators of the unknown. The scientific and academic establishment scoffs benignly at these reports, confident in that what isn't known to them isn't knowledge. Meanwhile, to this very day, thousands—perhaps hundreds of thousands--of witnesses around the globe continue to report encounters with physical entities that defy explanation.

In the restless years between the two world wars, journalist H.P. Wilkins visited the Belgian city of Bruges, and looked into a most curious story regarding an ancient monastery, once occupied by members of the Dominican order. At the turn of the century, Wilkins' host told him, the monastery had been turned into a boarding house for the use of students and tourists. However, in many cases paying guests refused to stay the night because of an apparition, described as "damned inhuman" and emitting a foul odor.

The owner of the monastery turned boarding house did not relish the prospect of losing any more customers, and contracted a crew of builders to break up the stone floor of a cellar which was believed to be the root of the problem. Nothing was found underneath the cold medieval stones, but when the cellar walls were broken, the builders discovered an alcove containing bones which were not in the least bit human. A pathologist was summoned to examine the bones. After carefully observing the disquieting find, the pathologist declared that they belonged to an adult rather than an infant. Aside from that, he was unable to say much more on the monstrosity. The journalist was told that once the bones were removed to the Belgian Medical Museum, no further disturbances were reported. Wilkins ends his treatment of the subject by speculating whether the remains were those of a creature resulting from "some nasty amour of the unnatural type denounced in the books of the Pentateuch, or the remains of some horrible thing teleported to Bruges from some world in space."

This quasi-Lovecraftian account may be dismissed as a fanciful Gothic anecdote related to a visitor to a foreign country, but could those bones, lying in the dusty ossuary of some European medical establishment, be the only physical proof of the existence of non-human creatures which slip in and out of our world?

Perhaps the man-apes known as Sasquatch, Yeti, Ucumari, etc. constitute the greatest and best known variety of mystery creature, and the only kind whose study has received a tacit nod from officialdom. Anthropologists have even gone as far as establishing its identity as the Gigantopithecus, an anthropoidal creature which may have survived into modern times by keeping clear of homo sapiens. The historic record contains mentions of these beings, such as that they were used by the ancient Medes and Persians as ferocious battle animals, and that Nearchos, Alexander the Great's admiral, encountered communities of these creatures on the barren shores of the Persian Gulf, living in crude huts made out of whalebones. Medieval bestiaries faithfully included them under such headings as Woodwose, Wild Man, Vampires, and other demihuman categories. Bigfoot may have given rise to the Nordic myth of giant Trolls. All this appears to point to an elusive physical being which has been repeatedly encountered throughout the centuries.

Argentina's Salta region has been the focus for a number of hairy hominid sightings for many years. This rugged, mountainous region could not differ more from the Sasquatch's forested Pacific Northwest: arid, desolate landscapes meet

ALIEN BLOOD LUST

vast salt deserts, such as the Puna de Atacama, where rainfall is almost nonexistent.

Dr. Rafael Lara Palmeros, Director of Research for Mexico's CEFP, provides the following information: In 1957, Dr. José Cerato and geologist Claudio Spitch discovered the footprints of a Bigfoot-like creature at an elevation of almost 16,000 ft. The prints, according to Spitch, were so large that they precluded the possibility of having been made by a human being. A month later, José Santolay ran into the alleged maker of the footprints, a large, fur-covered creature that emitted sharp cries which terrified the onlooker. Authorities looking into Santolay's claims surmised that it could have been the Ukumar Zupai described in the legends of the Coya inhabitants of the region.

Seventeen years later, Benigno Hoyos, a worker in the vicinity of the Arízaro salt desert, had a face- to-face encounter with one of these creatures, firing upon it with his gun. According to anthropologist Silvia Alicia Barrios, hunters have successfully apprehended live specimens of Bigfoot's southern cousin. One such case involves the capture of a family of Ukumaris--a mother and two offspring—by Andrés Olguín. The two young Ukumaris were allegedly turned over to a Paraguayan zoologist.

In late December 1993, there were repeated Bigfoot incidents in New Mexico, among them, sightings of a large hairy creature near a major highway; a white Bigfoot; another similar creature stalking a herd of elk; and, more amazingly, a report of a large man-ape that hurled a dog over a six-foot fence. The Bigfeet were also active in Pennsylvania during January 1994, causing a flurry of excitement for a number of days.

Pennsylvanian researcher Stan Gordon's files include a 1995 case in which a young man, home alone in a part of the state notorious for its manifold Bigfoot sightings, ran barefoot across a freshly-tarred driveway to get away from a screaming creature prowling in the vicinity. Unlike its counterpart on the Pacific coast, the Pennsylvania Bigfoot has shown an inclination toward appearing in suburban areas and closer to human habitation.

But what about other simian creatures of a slightly less substantial nature? Noted authors Jerome Clark and Loren Coleman discuss the appearance of one of these man-beasts at a séance in Poland during the 1920's. According to the testimony of Colonel Norbert Ochorowicz, witness to one of these apparitions, the ape-like creature often caused fear among the sitters, but did not have an evil disposition and expressed "goodwill, gentleness, and readiness to obey."

Among the Pennsylvanian sightings mentioned earlier are some which border on the paranormal: three-toed creatures seen in the proximity of UFO's, others which could be pierced by flashlight beams as if not really there (holographic projections?), and the classic case of a woman who heard the sound of raccoons or a dog rattling through the cans on her porch, and upon going outside to inspect, was confronted with a seven-foot tall hairy ape. The woman fired almost point-blank at the creature, which "just disappeared in a flash of light...just like someone taking a picture." Gordon notes that many of those involved in UFO/Bigfoot cases have experienced phenomena such as strange presences in their homes and other occult manifestations.

During the earlier wave of cattle mutilations in the mid-'70s, which shall be referred to throughout this work, Puerto Rico was also visited by the ubiquitous big hairy monsters. Many witnesses to these Bigfoot-type creatures agreed that they ranged in height from 4 to 7 feet, with black or brown fur, presented a generally humanoid appearance, and had a penchant for destroying plantain and banana trees, tearing them open to extract their nutritious sap. One witness managed to fire his pistol at one of these rampaging creatures, with no apparent effect. An issue of ¡ENIGMA! magazine featured a photograph taken of this apparently vegetarian "smallfoot," who was christened el comecogollos (roughly translated as the "Banana Tree Eater," a most unwieldy monicker) by the irreverent island media. The creature's existence and exploits, however small, became a regular feature in certain local comedy shows.

The Comecogollos' apparently placid nature and vegan ways did not mean that the other hairy hominids under investigation were equally sanguine. A document obtained by researcher Jorge Martín deals with a preliminary investigation into one of these cases, in which a Bigfoot-type entity embarked upon a spree of raids against animals kept in henhouses, pens, and hutches in the community of Trujillo Alto. The Alamo family, who witnessed one such raid on their property, described the hairy intruder as having glowing blue eye, and greater proportions than the Comecogollos.

Another manimal nearly caused a resident of Rexville, a suburb of San Juan, to have a heart attack in the summer of 1991. Eduardo Velasco stepped out to his backyard one day only to discover that the eighteen rabbits he kept in neat hutches had been ripped to pieces by the fury of some powerful unknown entity. "It" had torn its way right through the resistant wire of the hutches to reach its prey.

Winged Wonders

To many, winged humans and humanoids belong strictly in the realm of myth (Daedalus and the Garuda, respectively) or in the literary domain of magic realism, as exemplified by Gabriel García Márquez's A Very Old Man with Very Big Wings or Pedro Prado's Alsino. Cryptozoologists and Fortean researchers, however, know these flights of fancy are firmly grounded in sightings of weird, often hostile anthropomorphics which move through the air with wings entirely too small for their size and apparent weight.

The Caribbean island of Puerto Rico is the heavyweight champion of apparitions of these strange winged wonders. Some cases go as far back as the turn of the century, while others have occurred -- too close for comfort -- in this very day and age.

On April 23 1995, Reynaldo Ortega, a resident of Naranjito, P.R. (where Georgie Quiñones' mother had an encounter with winged oddities in Ch. 4), saw a gigantic "bird" standing on the roof of his house. Ortega had gone out to look for a small goat on his property, since the epidemic of animal mutilations on the island was at its greatest virulence. Ortega described the winged oddity as a creature between three and four feet tall, with the body and dense black plumage of an eagle, a thick neck, and piercing eyes. The nightmarish raptor had an even more peculiar characteristic Ortega would never forget: it had a wolf-like muzzle instead of a beak.

This "griffin," for want of a better description, did not harm the terrifed onlooker, but others were not quite so lucky. A worker in a sugarcane field near the town of Patillas was allegedly assaulted in broad daylight by a huge flapping "thing" that toppled him to the ground.

During the early Nineties, residents of the communities surrounding the controversial Laguna Cartagena reported seeing a ghastly bird-like creature perched on a metal fence. The grotesque avian had leathery wings, scales, and a horned head. The witnesses produced sketches of what they had seen, which to all extents and purposes resembled a pterodactyl.

Pterodactyl-like birds, curiously, have been reported elsewhere on Puerto Rico at different times. One witness recalled that during her high-school years, while walking down a street with friends in broad daylight, she experienced the sensation of "time" slowing down around her: this bewildering effect made it seem as if her companions were speaking and walking in slow motion, and made the air appear rarified. In the clear sky above, she saw a large winged creature flap its wings and issue a cry that was apparently not subjected to the time-lag effect. Once the bird had flown out of sight, time resumed its normal "speed."

Surprisingly enough, the protagonist of this singular experience had no knowledge or interest in Prehistory. It was a considerable time later when she realized that what she had seen a pterodactyl, after learning about them in school. The experience has remained in her mind forever.

A number of hypotheses have been put forth to account for the persistent reports of unusual animals in a small but environmentally-varied island such as Puerto Rico. Rationalists, such as distinguished political thinker J.M. García Passalacqua, have put it down to the island's uncertain political status, which, he believes, generates subconscious anxiety. In his opinion, this political anxiety translates into apparitions, both religious and otherwise. The problem with this hypothesis is that UFOs, monstrous beings, and religious apparitions occur in many parts of the world where there is no particular anxiety over political identity (to wit, the U.K., Spain, the U.S., etc.).

VI. An Incredible Month

The tail end of the summer of 1995 was dominated by the controversial and lifeless protagonist of the Roswell Alien Autopsy aired by the FOX television station in the U.S. and by TELEMUNDO in Latin America. Many high-ranking UFO investigators had already viewed the debatable footage earlier, but the democratic transmission allowed everyone to join the fray. The large-headed, immobile "spaceman" stole whatever headlines were being commanded by the alive and kicking Chupacabras.

At this point, the newspapers began to give the Goatsucker regular coverage, with at least some of the latest exploits of the bloodthirsty being recounted in the daily papers.

It becomes necessary to make an explanation at this point. Puerto Rico has four newspapers serving the needs of its 2.7 million inhabitants. Foremost among them is El Nuevo Día (The New Day) which remains the public's choice for information. It is followed by the English-language The San Juan Star, a well-produced tabloid formerly belonging to Scripps-Howard, with fine international and domestic coverage.

The rest of the market is occupied by two radically different newspapers: the weekly Claridad (Clarity), a government watchdog that advocates independence and espouses nationalist causes, and El Vocero (The Town Crier), a tabloid whose headlines, in bright red uppercase letters, often surmount a grotesque photograph of a murder or auto accident. Unlike Stateside tabloids or Mexico's Ovaciones, it provides little or no celebrity coverage.

The first three have traditionally handled any supernatural material gingerly. El Vocero, however, has always rushed in where angels fear to tread, developing consistent UFO/paranormal coverage as the situation demands it. Julio Víctor Ramírez, a respected journalist, brought a degree of maturity and professionalism to the "saucer beat" throughout the early '90s and up to the present; Rubén Darío Rodríguez covered the fanged bird which caused a sensation in 1989, and so forth. Many have chosen to disregard these facts and simply dismiss the UFO/paranormal coverage along with the sensationalistic car crashes, homicides, crimes of passion, and other matters that fill El Vocero's pages. This is not an effort at portraying this newspaper in a better light, only to stress that not all aspects of it should be condemned. Unless stated otherwise, the following diary entries reflect events which appeared in El Vocero.

Tuesday, October 31, 1995

Halloween was never like this. At best, I recall the antics of a few boys, like my friend Toti Troia, who would take advantage of the cover of darkness to throw eggs against anything in sight -- homes, cars, neighbors he disliked -- but nothing ever matched the supernatural madness produced by the Chupacabras, particularly on a night like this.

Mayor José "Chemo" Soto and his band of cammo-clad hunters made it clear than not a single member of their 200-man militia had been armed during their latest foray into the tropical night in pursuit of the Goatsucker. Looking to all the world like a Recondo leader from the Vietnam War, Mayor Soto made it clear that the small arms fire heard that night had issued from the weaponry in the hands of fearful citizens.

Mayor Soto was clearly pleased at the response elicited by his nocturnal patrols in search of the winged intruder: news of the Chupacabras and its nefarious deeds had made worldwide headlines. According to the mayor, one of his constituents had described the beast as a creature some three feet tall, which could increase its height suddenly, and was endowed with either a crest or horns on its head. It also had large hind legs resembling those of a kangaroo. This matter, stressed Mayor Soto, was a very serious one, and that his patrols served the added purpose of calming the citizens of Canóvanas. His political opponent, Melba Rivera, who expects to unseat Soto in next year's elections, has gone on record saying that the incumbent mayor is doing his level best to discredit the city by his ridiculous antics.

Wednesday, November 1, 1995

What a way to start the month. The Goatsucker, as it is called, or its peers, is crisscrossing the countryside, laying waste the small animal industry that had characterized rural Puerto Rico for decades. This time, the predatory gargoyle descended upon the community of Sábana Grande, located near UFO-haunted Laguna Cartagena.

A report filed by police officer Abraham Báez of the Sábana Seca police noted that a Nubian goat belonging to José Vega Lugo was found in a lot adjacent to Route 167, which leads to Barrio La Torre. The officer's report states that the animal was found missing an eye and displayed a curious wound on its neck. The carcass gave no indications of having been attacked by dogs, but the goat's innards were outside its body. The animal had also been rendered bloodless by it nameless attacker.

José Vega Lugo discovered at 3:00 p.m. that his goat had been slain in a lot near his property. Neighbors found several black hairs entwined in a barbed wire fence.

Lt. Medina, the interim chief of the Sábana Grande district, noted that the wounds inflicted on the hapless goat "were precise and without any rending." Perhaps to keep at bay the more fanciful explanations for the goat's demise, he promptly added that there had been reports concerning the presence of feral monkeys in the area. Three years earlier, an unknown assailant had decimated a flock of sheep belonging to a doctor from the nearby city of Yauco. The dead animals presented the same throat punctures and had inexplicably lost all their blood.

Mayor José "Chemo" Soto's paramilitary antics may have been scorned by his political opponents in Canóvanas, but they were hailed as pro-active by Carlos De Jesús, manager of "Junker Correa," an auto salvage lot located on the main highway running from Caguas to Rio Piedras. Mr. De Jesús insisted that the course of action taken by the mayor of Canóvanas was neither foolish nor futile.

De Jesús' junkyard had just been the Chupacabras' latest lunch stop. Upon opening for business at 7:00 a.m., De Jesús was puzzled that the five sheep and four geese he kept on the premises had not come out to greet him, demanding their morning meal. Manuel Correa, the junkyard's proprietor, accompanied De Jesús in search of the animals, only to find they were all dead.

"The Chupacabras is a serious matter, not a cause for levity. The government should pay greater attention to this weird situation. Right now, only farm animals are being killed, but in the future, it could well be our own children or grandchildren," De Jesús declared emphatically to reporter Rubén Darío Rodríguez from El Vocero.

Thursday, November 2, 1995

The Chupacabras or Goatsucker has hit the big time. No, it hasn't decided to kill circus elephants or giraffe -- an Associated Press writer has apparently picked up the story and broadcast it on the newswires.

This time, it was residents of Ponce who had the dubious pleasure of the visit. The Chupacabras feasted on four cats and five dogs in the Lajés and Bellavista neighborhoods of the city.

Angela Lajés told the press that she woke up in the morning and found that her dog, who had been put outside in perfect health the previous evening, was dead. As well as showing a trickle of blood around its anus, the dog was described as being desiccated and with a few viscera exposed.

Mrs. Lajés ran to her neighbor, her sister Angela Santiago, who told her that two cats on her property had been found entirely dry, as if they had nothing inside them. "I heard the sounds of a fierce fight last night, but I felt afraid to come outside, but the fact of the matter is that a number of animals have been slain without any explanation whatsoever."

Other reports continue coming in from the Halloween spree embarked upon by the seemingly supernatural Chupacabras. Today's newspaper reports that twenty parakeets—hardly containing enough blood for a creature the size of the Goatsucker--had been found slain in the coastal town of Yabucoa, down the road from the prestigious Palmas del Mar resort. Not satisfied with killing the parakeets in their cage, the bloodthirsty creature topped the night off by relieving five goats of their vital fluids.

Mr. William Rodríguez's five goats were inspected by Officers Lozada and Ortiz of the Yabucoa precinct, who noted that the animals had been slain in a manner identical to the other deaths reported all over the island.

Melba Rivera, the politician who hopes to unseat Canóvanas' Mayor Soto in the '96 elections, has asked Illeana Carlo, the Commonwealth's Controller, to look into the possible misuse of funds, personnel and equipment by Mayor Soto during his patrols in search of the Goatsucker. Rivera's letter to the Controller stated unequivocally that Mayor Soto "had embarked upon yet another propaganda act characteristic of his administration. Not satisfied with placing Canóvanas in ridicule, Chemo Soto has also taken advantage of the situation to squander public funds which could well be used to help our needy townspeople...the hunt for the Chupacabras resembles something lifted from the old "Fantasy Island" episodes. Undoubtedly, a need for public recognition has caused the Mayor to resort to the ridiculous, to the great embarrassment of his constituency."

Monday, November 6, 1995

So far it's only been animals, but the fear behind every single mind on the island was that the Goatsucker would get it into his head to give human hemoglobin a try. Two fishermen who had cast their hooks by the banks of the Canóvanas River almost became an entree, according to Obed Betancourt, a writer for El Vocero.

The two men had been fishing buruquenas (a sort of Caribbean shad or sunfish) in the early evening (7:30-8:30 p.m.) in the Barrio Palmasola section of Canóvanas, when they suddenly became aware of a sound in the vegetation behind them.   Luis Angel Guadalupe and Carlos Carrillo, his brother in law, were convinced that the thing which interrupted their nocturnal fishing was none other than the Chupacabras itself. Guadalupe observed that it was "horrible--like the devil himself," proceeding to describe the creature as a having large ears, oval and luminous eyes which alternated between orange and read, claws, and wings. The nightmarish intruder stood anywhere between four and five feet tall.

This close encounter prompted both men to run faster than either of them had ever run, while the Chupacabras pursued them flying above the treetops. Upon reaching his house after the mad footrace, Guadalupe availed himself of a machete and turned around to see the Goatsucker, ready to pounce, perched on a nearby hutch. But battle wasn't joined--the gargoyle jumped to the ground, leaving deep prints in the earth, and dashed back into the woods, tearing down the hutch, fences, and other structures in its path.

Perhaps it wasn't hungry. It was later learned that earlier that evening, the winged terror had slaughtered fifteen peacocks and a heifer belonging to one Miguel Domínguez.

ALIEN BLOOD LUST

Mayor José "Chemo" Soto and thirty of his "Ramboes" -- the militia-like posse of fearless Goatsucker hunters-- patrolled the areas in question in search of the creature. Mayor Soto expressed a belief at one point that the Chupacabras prowls the riverbanks to drink water after killing its prey.

Tuesday, November 7, 1995

The Chupacabras strikes again: this time it has chosen to add a cat to its monotonous goat and lamb diet. Striking at a junkyard, it killed a cat, a sheep, and apparently swallowed an entire lamb, since the third animal being kept by the junkyard owner never turned up again.

The junkyard, known as "Junker Tito", is located on Route 1 between Caguas and Rio Piedras, a heavily- trafficked urban corridor. Perhaps the solitude that reigns over these used auto parts cemeteries is perfect for the creature's depredations, since this is its second strike at a junkyard. "Junker Correa" and the sheep it held were victims to the Goatsucker a few days earlier.

Victor Ortiz, owner of "Junker Tito", had this to say to the press: "We have no idea if it all happened on Sunday night or in the early morning hours of Monday. When we opened for business on Monday morning, we were surprised that the animals hadn't come looking for us as was their custom. A short while later, we found the dead cat, two almost-dead sheep and a missing lamb."

Ortiz went on to add that in spite of the muddiness of the junkyard's terrain, there were no footprints to be found anywhere. However, there were signs that a fierce fight had ensued between the animals and the attacker, who vanquished them in the end. The dead animals had the characteristic circular puncture marks around their necks.

Wednesday, November 8, 1995

The Chupacabras, now believed to be merely one of many creatures, continued its killing spree throughout the island's central municipalities, this time leaving fifteen guinea hens completely bloodless. The dead birds exhibited bizarre stinger marks, as if they had been attacked by a swarm of bees. This event transpired in the locality of Cidra, at a body shop owned by Juan R. Colón.

A few days earlier, a Cidra mechanic had seen a veru strange creature land on a tree branch. Not willing to risk ridicule, he confided his experience to a cousin. The mechanic repeatedly stated that he had never seen anything similar in his life, and believed that he had quite possibly seen the notorious Chupacabras.

The undercurrent of fear caused by the Chupacabras spread throughout the city of Caguas and its outlying suburbs as a result of the mind-bending killing of a large horse and four goats belonging to Efraín Rojas, Jr..

The animals, kept at Mr.Rojas' property off Route 183, which links San Lorenzo to Caguas, were found with deep incisions in their chests, one of them leading directly to the heart. No stains of blood spillage were found on the ground, nor

Has Hypnotic Eyes

ALIEN BLOOD LUST

was any blood left within the carcasses.

Jonathan Rojas, a high school student, claims to have woken from a deep sleep at 2:30 a.m. after hearing the noise made by the horse kicking the door to its paddock. Upon taking a quick look through his bedroom window, he was amazed to see an odd, pyramidal object some sixteen feet tall by twenty feet wide floating amid the heavy fog.

Rojas added that the object seemed to have a sort of entrance or doorway, and was hovering over a small brook some three hundred feet away from his house, as if supplying itself with water. He fell asleep once more, awakening at five in the morning to see the same object in place. This time he alerted his uncle, who was only able to distinguish an intense glow departing from the area as he looked out the window.

Thursday, November 9, 1995

Mrs. Ada Arroyo, identified as the assistant director of the Mount Sion Nursing Home outside Barrio Turabo Arriba in the city of Caguas, fell victim to a nervous breakdown after seeing the infamous Chupacabras. According to the story, the event took place at 7 p.m.. Mount Sion is a peaceful and inviting facility, equipped with a large and modern swimming facility.

Mrs. Arroyo was quoted as saying: "I heard screams similar to those made by a lamb being slaughtered. I went out to the patio and managed to see a strange hairy figure, grayish in color, covering its body with a pair of wings. It had a flattened, vulpine face, with enormous red eyes." Mrs. Arroyo added that the creature held her gaze with its mesmerizing eyes before taking off into the air, vanishing from sight immediately.

It was later learned that the noises identified by the nursing home director came from a herd of cattle downhill from the place where she spotted the winged oddity. No dead animals were discovered.

Other animals in Rio Piedras weren't so fortunate: two sheep, a goose, and a turkey were found dead the following day. It was rumored that the Chupacabras had been active in the area only days before, when a 150 lb. sheep was found dead and drained of all its blood. No footprints were found around any of the victims.

Friday, November 10, 1995

Word on the streets has it that the Chupacabras is hiding out in the vast natural cave systems that riddle Puerto Rico like a piece of Swiss cheese. Hundreds of residents of the town of Aguas Buenas, famous for being the birthplace of Luis Muñóz Marín, the Commonwealth's founder and first governor, believed that the famous, bat- infested caves of their region were providing shelter for the Chupacabras.

Mayor Carlos Aponte, taking a page from Mayor Soto's book, decided to or-

Gun control ✗
Vermont

ganize a posse and go after the creature, which had already left its calling card in Aguas Buenas. The entity appeared in broad daylight and killed a rooster and two hens at a private farm located at Barrio Camino Verde, before being scared away by the screams of local residents who witnessed its deeds. Those selfsame residents allegedly saw it enter the gloomy caves. The police, members of the Civil Defense, and dozens of townsfolk headed to the cave area, but none dared venture into them for fear of cornering the creature.

Saturday, November 11, 1995

Gun control is a non-issue in Puerto Rico. Not only is it a citizen's right to bear arms, but it is safe to say that one of every three island residents owns a weapon, registered or not. This freewheeling ownership of sidearms enabled farmer Elliot Feliciano to open fire against a nocturnal predator which turned out to be the hellish Goatsucker.

According to Feliciano, a large animal jumped the fence surrounding his home, prompting the armed response. While he cannot say for sure if he scored a hit, the farmer believes that the sizeable creature may well have been the Chupacabras. He described the beast as being some 3 to 4 feet tall, endowed with large eyes, and with what appeared to be wings.

Police report 95-5-050-15435, filed by police officers Gonzalo Tubens and José Toro, states that an animal making a noise that the complainant could not identify was shot at on the property. A search by both officers revealed no trace of the Goatsucker.

The El Rosario sector, located between Mayagüez and San German, has been gripped by fear since the first sightings of the gargoyle-like creature began, prompting farmers to safeguard their animals. UFO sightings over the mountainous region of Maricao (a notorious materialization point or "window area") have done nothing to assuage these concerns.

Two locals claimed having seen a brilliant, round object flying over the Sábana Grande area. The following day, elements of the local police found an eighty-pound goat which had been killed by means of strange wounds to its throat, and rendered bloodless.

Monday, November 13, 1995

The possibility that the mysterious Chupacabras could well be an extraterrestrial force was reinforced by a very strange occurrence which took place in the town of Vega Baja.

Although five chickens were found entirely drained of blood in the backyard of the property owned by Julio and Julia González, the most spectacular event appears to have been the strange mark placed upon the forearm of the couple's daughter this past summer.

Oralis González, 5, was marked with a tatoo-like impression which read OJO-

ALIEN BLOOD LUST

10-OJO after an alleged account with nonhuman entities. While the child is reluctant to discuss what exactly transpired, and her parents discouraged mention of it for fear that it would affect her studies, it is generally acknowledged that this supposed event has triggered the child's IQ, causing her father to describe her as a prodigy.

Little Oralis'experience came to light while police officer Pablo Robles interviewed Mr. Gonzalez about the dead poultry found in the backyard. The chickens were found lying in a perfect row, giving the impression that they were "sunbathing." This charming notion was soon put to rest when it was discovered that the animals were dead and drained of their blood.

Tuesday, November 14, 1995

The UFO question rears its ugly head again. An anonymous resident from Aguas Buenas claims to have seen fiery spaceships shooting "elevators" of light against the ground, primarily at sites where bloodless and mutilated animals have been found. In this anonymous witness' opinion, the dreaded Chupacabras is simply a being from another world in space. The man, age 37, insists on the need for anonymity out of concern for his wife and children. He lives near the renown Aguas Buenas cave system.

When asked to describe the luminous elevators, he explained that they resemble "cones" of opaque light whose interior cannot be seen. He theorizes that some kind of suction must lift whatever is on the ground toward the unidentified object above, whose dimensions cannot be made out due to the alternating green, red, and yellow lights surrounding it. By tying loose ends, the Aguas Buenas resident believes that the recently slain ox and two goats found near his home could have been sucked upward to the vehicle, had their blood extracted, and then been deposited back on the ground when discarded.

Other residents elaborated upon this theory, surmising that the Chupacabras may have been a creature "lowered" to earth from a spaceship which was then unable to retrieve it due to some technical difficulty, thus leaving it to roam the countryside in search of sustenance.

Wednesday, November 15, 1995

A society raised on Friday the 13th movies, the exploits of Freddy Kruger, and splattergore films is usually immune to monster stories, but what happens when a creature that could well be an escapee from one of these celluloid nightmares sticks an arm through an open window?

Ask the wife of Bernardo Gómez, who saw with her own eyes how a clawed hand belonging to a long, thin, hairy arm entered through her bedroom window just as she was getting ready for bed. The claw seized a teddy bear sitting on a counter top and shredded it in seconds. Mrs. Gómez hurled a coffee cup at the sinister appendage, which withdrew immediately. She managed to see a single red eye and the left side of the intruder's face, who promptly vanished into the heavily wooded area behind the house.

These events took place in the city of Caguas, directly south of San Juan. Agents of the police, Civil Defense, and the Municipal Guards responded to the emergency phone call, finding a slimy substance deposited against the torn window, as well as an unidentifiable piece of flesh that had apparently been left behind as the creature beat a retreat.

The Technical Services Division of the local CIC agency dusted the window for fingerprints, but were unable to find any. A thorough search of the nearby wilderness failed to reveal any sign of the mysterious intruder.

Thus far, city dwellers had felt safe from the attacks of this elusive creature or creatures. Yet the same evening that Mrs. Gómez underwent her harrowing experience, two hens and their chicks had their blood drained by a Chupacabras-like entity in the heart of San Juan's Puerto Nuevo neighborhood, a heavily built-up area filled with shops, restaurants, and main avenues. The owner of the slain hens had gone to nearby Dorado for the day, and returned to find the hair-raising scene.

Thursday, November 16, 1995

The long-suffering citizenry has decided to fight back. Neither monster, nor alien, nor gargoyle will ever crush the human spirit: the residents of Barrio Caín Alto in the town of San German chased the Chupacabras away as it was poised to kill three fighting roosters belonging to one of the neighbors.

This foiled attack took place in the afternoon, when the people of Barrio Caín Alto heard the commotion taking place in the area where the cockfighting roosters were kept. Three of the neighbors ran into the nightmarish attacker, who appeared to hesitate at the sudden appearance of the humans, whose fear was overcome by intense rage: they began throwing stones at the Chupacabras, who rose to its full height and sprang upwards into the air, flying off in the direction of a nearby hill.

The three rockslinging witnesses described the intruder as being a grayish brown simian creature with large, almond-shaped eyes, an oval face, and small hands protruding from its shoulders.

In his regular column on UFOs, Julio Victor Ramírez, who reported most of the UFO incidents taking place during the 1991-92 sightings, observed that area residents did not link the Chupacabras with UFO activity. He pointed out that farmers in Western Puerto Rico linked the Goatsucker with giant vampire bats which may have been introduced deliberately or not from their habitats in South America.

Wednesday, November 22, 1995

Rubén Darío Rodríguez observed in a column that elements of the Department of Natural Resources had completed tests on a number of dead rabbits which betrayed deep puncture marks. They returned a stunning verdict: the wounds on

ALIEN BLOOD LUST

the hapless bunnies could not have been produced by anything native to Puerto Rico.

The investigators thought it strange that the dead rabbits had been found outside their cages, which showed no signs of having been forced open. One of the rabbits had punctures in its paws and was covered in a slimy substance (which would later be found at a number of sites). The slime also underwent analysis, but no report on the findings was ever issued.

Coincidentally (but perhaps not), the rabbit killings took place in the town of Gurabo, where the vampire bird had been discovered in 1989.

Thursday, November 23, 1995

Reason enough to panic, yet no one did: The Chupacabras' depredations are coming closer to the urban sprawl of San Juan. This time it struck in Carolina, a municipality bordering the island capital. A small mongrel dog belonging to Demetrio Rivera was found dead.

According to Mr. Rivera's testimony, his dog was tied out in the backyard, as was customary, when it suddenly began barking furiously. But the barks soon turned to pitiful moans, as if something were suffocating the small pet. This prompted Demetrio and his daughter Ivette to turn on the patio lights and take a look. The allegedly heard the strong fluttering of a winged thing flying away: their dog, near death, was covered with a strange slime, like the one found on the Vega Baja cattle.

The canine was so terrified by what it had seen and experienced that it refused to let its owners come closer. After a while, the Riveras were able to pour water on their beloved pet and remove the curious "goo" that covered it.

Maribel Arroyo, a resident of the same neighborhood as the Riveras, also had a visit. Mrs. Arroyo, who runs a chicken farm, stated that she heard the cries of large birds over her farm. The following day she discovered that thirty of her hens had been slain and rendered bloodless. The unfortunate fowl had puncture marks in their throats and bellies.

The puzzling slime, reminiscent of the substance made famous by the film Ghostbusters, was also found on the window of a home in the Cañaboncito sector of Caguas, where "something" introduced a long, hairy arm into the window of the house and shredded a teddy bear that happened to be within its reach.

Friday, November 24, 1995

The very real possibility that witchcraft could be at the root of these mysterious killings was aired in the media for the first time, just as a UFO connection to the Chupacabra situation was reinforced by a close encounter near Toa Baja.

A resident of this town, less than half an hour from San Juan (in good traffic, that is) told the media that he had a close encounter with a small, 4 ft tall creature shortly after residents of the city of Arecibo were treated to the sight of a "saucer" crossing their skies.

A slight whiff of high strangeness accompanied this case in Toa Baja: policeman José Matos, sent to investigate, found a number of dead heifers lying in a perfect row down the middle of a lonely road in the Hoyos sector of Toa Baja. The oddity was that no heifers of the kind slaughtered can be found anywhere for miles around the area. No one claimed the carcasses, leading to the belief that they were slain elsewhere and deposited in Toa Baja for some reason.

The eerie disposition of the carcasses was captured in a photograph taken by Baltazar Vázquez of El Vocero. It led many residents of the area to speculate about the possibility that a warlock or witch was making use of the animal's blood.

Saturday, November 25, 1995

It was a matter of time before the lunatic fringe chimed in, ready to drop its two centavos worth on the Chupacabras scare. This time, the fringe was embodied by Brother Carmelo, a clairvoyant from Caguas who wanted to describe the creature and the best methods to capture it.

Brother Carmelo was quick to state that the Goatsuckers (note the plural) were definitely extraterrestrial. "These creatures are vampires who nourish themselves on the fresh blood of their victims. They are purplish grey in color, have fiery red eyes, are equipped with a short tail and could have two small, horn-like protuberances on their heads. These beings can only come out at night, and they spend the day in places where the vegetation is extremely dense or else in deep caves."

Brother Carmelo, in his infinite, supernatural wisdom, added that: "Not everyone can capture one of these beings. To do so requires the use of laser beams or a silver bullet."

Need any more be said?

Monday, November 27, 1995

The Chupacabras (whether singular or plural) appeared this time in Rincón, a small seaside town which may have been Columbus' landing site during his discovery of PR in 1493 (an honor disputed by the neighboring cities of Aguadilla and Mayagüez).

Five goats, described as "costly" by reporter Tomás de Jesús Mangal, were found comatose and bloodless out of a flock of 29 such animals. One of the goats died, but as of today, the other four remained between life and death. A local veterinary had kept them alive by means of judicious injections of a coagulant known as Azium, which stanched the bleeding caused by the creature's trademark single puncture to the animal's jugular. The owner of the flock, Edwin Lorenzo Féneguez, was beside himself at his considerable loss.

Things took a darker turn when elements of the pseudo-UFO research group

ALIEN BLOOD LUST

NOVA appeared on the scene. The leader of this cultlike organization declared that the remaining goats, the ones that had not been attacked by the Goatsucker, would die anyway. His explanation? They had been injected with a poisonous substance that would bring about death within a matter of days. This hardly comforted Mr. Féneguez. The elements of the NOVA group aired their utterly unfounded theory that the bloodsucking creature was one of twenty which had descended to Earth to conduct experiments with human blood in order to produce blood viruses aimed at eliminating humanity.

An official from the Commonwealth department of agriculture, Hector López, visited the Féneguez farm and asked the distraught owner to touch neither the dead goat nor the 4 dying ones until his agency had had an opportunity to run a number of tests on them.

On a lighter note, a young student theater from the José Julián Acosta School, Daynalee Cardona, has written a prose poem on the Goatsucker which could become the basis for a stage production on this phenomenon.

Tuesday, November 28, 1995

Proof of the Goatsucker's existence? Hardly. The papers reported the discovery of a footprint or handprint -- the very first found since this rash of animal mutilations began—at the site of an attack near Vega Baja. Photographs showed a splayed, six-fingered (or six-toed?) print in the clay-like ground. More impressive was the viscous slime left around the neck of a wounded cow.

The bloodsucker was only steps away from becoming a victim itself. Police sergeant Jesús Medina Montes regretted not being able to steal a few shots against a "being" shaped like a bird and which fluttered while making a loud noise with its mouth. The Chupacabras would have paid dearly for the wounds inflicted upon a number of steers, among them a large Zebu bull.

Sergeant Medina told El Vocero that a local landlord, Anselmo Rodríguez, toured the property after the Goatsucker's attack, only to discover that much of his heard was bleeding from their humps. Some of the beasts were covered by a slime that could not be properly described. Irene Mercado and her 9 year-old niece allegedly saw the creature "fly away" from the area that night.

VII. The Infiltrators

Webster's Dictionary defines an infiltrator as one who "enters or becomes established gradually or unobtrusively." We speak of infiltrating enemy lines, of James Bond's infiltrating into the archvillain's stronghold, and many other references. The UFO community, a Hydra-like entity whose heads are always snapping against each other, has been howling in protest since the late 1950's that it's been infiltrated--like the labor movements earlier this century--by government operatives, outside agitators (echoes of The Graduate), and agents aimed at the spreading of disinformation. NICAP was infiltrated by these types, APRO probably was, and MUFON possibly is. From reading the vast corpus of saucer literature that has piled up over the decades like stacks of National Geographics, we can infer that the mission of these putative agents has been to drive ufologists mad by providing false leads, tantalizing evidence, and above all, impressive- looking documents like the MJ-12 papers, which have the effect of splitting up an already divided community even further. The Internet, the modern equivalent of the Roman Forum, contains thousands of postings which "name names" in real or imaginary efforts at unmasking the moles lurking in ufology's mainstream.

The infiltrators--whose existence is undeniable—have honed their techniques over the past thirty years, leading to the development of a bold new technique: rather than taking the trouble to infiltrate the UFO organizations, why not create their own cadres of UFO "researchers?"

The first of these shadow organizations surfaced in Puerto Rico earlier this year. They appeared at mutilation sites, places where witnesses had experienced encounters of every single kind, and at the homes of the witnesses themselves, sporting impressive ID cards and fully outfitted with gadgets designed to persuade interviewees about their professional status. Forsaking the gas-guzzling limos and Caddys of the legendary Men-In-Black, they drove around in government-issue Fords and Chevys, which were also eminently easier to drive on the tortuous backroads of the Puerto Rican interior.

These pseudo-organizations first appeared during research conducted by CEDICOP (Center for UFO and Paranormal Study and Dissemination) into the Orocovis situation. Subsequent information received by CEDICOP indicated that the members of these shadow organizations were in possession of "directories" with the names of witnesses to the mutilation phenomena and UFO activity. Their modus operandi consisted of interviewing these witnesses and offering them membership in their organizations, promising to provide them with special means of identification which would allow the holders access to areas restricted by the police or similarly important agencies.

At this point, we may well wonder if this equivalent of the All Access backstage pass is merely a delusion aimed at ensnaring the unwary. The power to cross police lines would be reserved for agencies like the FBI (á la Mulder and Scully), DEA, and other Federal agencies. How could an allegedly civilian UFO study group acquire such clout?

Efforts at discrediting serious UFO research also took a high-tech approach. Items disseminated on the Internet created the impression that a UFO had crashed on the island during the month of July, creating a brief flurry of electronic messages from one researcher to another. This untruth was "substantiated" by the clever distribution, from an unknown source, of promotional materials (glossy photos) from a cable TV special depicting the bodies of dead aliens found at the

ALIEN BLOOD LUST

Roswell, N.M. crash site. The special's cleverly fabricated corpses were circulated as the real thing among UFO aficionados on the island. These shenanigans prompted a response by Evidencia Ovni in the form of an editorial denouncing these efforts at deception. Photos of the special effect dummies, clearly identifying them as such, accompanied the editorial.

The shadow organizations increased their visibility to parallel the rise in Chupacabras activity. One of them, calling itself NOVA, operated out of the western shore of the island. Another, dubbed UFO, wore black caps with the unimaginative name of their organization stitched on them. As featured in an earlier section, these groups expressed a belief that the Goatsucker was one of two dozen beings whose task was that of depopulating the earth, leaving it open for alien colonization efforts. They also claimed that the Goatsucker was "the source of the AIDS epidemic" and was unstoppable (perhaps they should have tried Brother Carmelo's silver bullets).

Aside from casting a pall of ridicule upon the entire situation, and discrediting any clear-headed investigations underway, the groups clearly had a dark side: they claimed to have been endowed with such broad powers as to be unstoppable by the FBI or Puerto Rico State Police, and had offered membership in their ranks to a number of people, even a prominent Political Science professor at the University of Puerto Rico at Río Piedras. These activities were discussed openly on Jorge Martín's radio program, Ovnis Confidencial, in a conference with Argentinian ufologist José Aldonati and other local researchers. After their activities were denounced on the air, the phantom groups went into hiding--one of them even eliminated its trademark black outfits.

What can we make of the seemingly infantile yet dangerous behavior displayed by the phantom groups? Only that someone is interested in keeping control of UFO information emanating from Puerto Rico at any cost.

Friday, December 1, 1995

The Chupacabras has chosen the Caguas suburb of Bairoa as its latest stomping ground, feeding off rabbits kept in outdoor hutches throughout the area. Rafael Ortiz, one of the individuals affected by these mysterious depredations, found two of his rabbits slain by means of holes in their necks. Another four were removed from their cages. According to Ortiz, he had heard some noises coming from the backyard area in which the hutches are located, but much to his regret, didn't pay very much attention. At daybreak, he was confronted with the sight of the dead animals, and noticed the others were gone.

On the southwestern corner of the island, in the picturesque city of San Germán, a pair of ducks, a rabbit, and two chickens were added to the Chupacabras' tally of slain animals. As has happened in all the other cases reported in these diaries, owners find their animals in the morning when they are getting ready to feed them

ALIEN BLOOD LUST

(recall the number of junkyard cases in November).

Some of San Germán's residents claim having seen a strange being standing some three feet in height, brownish-grey in color, with slanted eyes, small hands, and equipped with what appeared to be wings. This creature was allegedly responsible for the death of a goat in Barrio Caín Alto. Nonetheless, the Police and other government agencies have chosen to dismiss the matter as a joke.

The city of Guánica, site of the landing of U.S. forces during the Spanish-American War of 1898, was also chosen by the Chupacabras for something other than its beautiful bay and fine beaches. A police report filed by Lt. Noel Quiles states that two goats and thirteen roosters were found slain with peculiar marks on their bodies at Barrio La Montalva. Officers responded to a call by an unidentified resident who had found that all his black hens had been slain by strange perforations, while all the white hens had been shredded by the claws of a predator. Lt. Quiles was hesitant to say that the Chupacabras had been at work here. He circumscribed himself to saying that the birds had been slain by an unknown assailant.

A second complaint was filed by Reinaldo Serrano, who found two goats dead upon returning home at 6:00 a.m.. According to Serrano, the goats had been alive and healthy when he left for work earlier that evening. Although neighbors admitted to having heard strange noises, none saw the intruder.

Friday, December 8, 1995

Six sheep were left bloodless by a mysterious attacker, according to a police report issued by the Homicide Division of the Carolina Municipality Center for Criminal Investigation. The locale was none other than Barrio Campo Rico, the Chupacabras' regular feeding ground. The police report did not rule out the strange creature as the "perpetrator" of the incident.

At around 4:00 a.m., neighbors were wakened from their sleep by horrifying noises. A local man who happened to be walking by the place where the Chupacabras' attack took place was so frightened by the feral screams that he dropped his lunch box and broke into a run away from the area. Police officers reporting to the location found five dead sheep, and a sixth one with an unusual wound on its head. It did not recover.

The Chupacabras was not blamed for another bloody killing in which two dozen cockfighting roosters were torn to pieces. To the relief of local law enforcement, the crime was readily attributable to a pack of wild dogs. Edwin Velázquez, of Yabucoa, lost all of his fighting cocks, a misfortune estimated at almost four thousand dollars.

Tuesday, December 12, 1995

As if the loss of the six sheep only a few days ago hadn't been enough, the residents of Canóvanas' Barrio Campo Rico are now being mocked by the Chupacabras, which has taken to running at a blinding speed after cattle and other animals. According to a police report, the mystery beast spent the weekend chasing frightened animals from one field to another, and even managed to steal a piece of meat that had been left out as bait.

Lt. Jorge L. Rivera, who has been in charge of police response to the citizenry's complaints about the creature, observed that the creature emanates a smell resembling that of paint thinner. The local newspaper, El Vocero, quoted him as saying: "There is a great deal of concern here [in Canóvanas]. This isn't a joke or a humorous situation."

Last month, when one of Lt. Rivera's men fired against a strange animal he thought was the Chupacabras, a small sample of blood was secured and sent for analysis. An anonymous veterinarian who handled the tests declared that the samples were neither human, nor canine, nor belonging to any known species. These samples have since been consigned to a Stateside laboratory, and no results will be available until after the holidays.

(We broached the matter with investigator Jorge Martín during our stay. He added that the results had yielded levels of proteins and acids that did not correspond to any member of the animal kingdom, but that the blood also contained strong traces of chlorophyll!)

Wednesday, December 13, 1995

A curious vigilante movement has arisen as a result of the Chupacabras' depredations, and possibly in imitation of Mayor "Chemo" Soto's posses. These armchair "regulators" have the distinct advantage that they merely conduct their nocturnal watches from the comfort of their own homes, most often sitting on their back patios, terraces, on their rooftops, and even in "duck blinds" located amid the branches of massive tropical trees. A respected professional from the town of Juncos explained that around nightfall, he sits in a chair with his back to the wall, wielding a hunting rifle and in the company of a German Shepherd, hoping to "get lucky" one night and bag a Chupacabras.

Other armchair vigilantes have conducted their silent watches of the warm tropical night from the slopes of El Yunque to Orocovis. One of these self-appointed sentries has apparently discovered a correlation between the phases of the moon and the Chupacabras' attacks. It would seem that the elusive creature takes advantage of moonless nights and of the waning moon to pursue its hunting activities.

Thursday, December 14, 1995

Seers and mystics continue to proliferate as the situation becomes more and more complex. Aside from "Brother Carmelo" and his Lon Chaney-inspired silver bullet theories, there is now "Brother Serafín" who claims to have plotted the trajectory of the Chupacabras' flights over the island. On an island a hundred and ten miles long by a scant forty five miles wide, the trajectory put forth by the seer

matched many of the places where killings have occurred, such as Naguabo. *Check*
Brother Serafín boasted of employing "sensory waves and vibrations" (!) to find
the Chupacabras' lair, conveniently located at the heart of El Yunque. Unlike the
earlier mystic, Brother Serafín had complete confidence in his psychic gifts, stating that he had been chosen in his youth to do good and to make predictions about
the future. His TV set-like ability to capture waves and vibrations enabled him to
learn that the Chupacabras comes from another world within our own galaxy, and
that its kin are slowly dying out due to genetic reasons.

Serafín's "vision" of the creature(s) describes them as being hideous, having
a pestilent odor about them, hair-covered wings, as tall but not very strong, and
with the ability to "charm" their prey until they suck out their blood. He added that
the creature sleeps during the day and moves about at night, and that the creature
will soon go into "hibernation," perhaps in underground caverns.

A resident of Naguabo, José Luis Oyola, discovered that a number of the rabbits he owned had been bled dry by a creature leaving vampiric puncture marks
on their bodies. This attack had a distinguishing feature: many of the rabbits were
missing, as if the attacker had first chosen to slake its thirst, and then take other
bunnies "to go." In this case, the victim believed neither in apes nor aliens--he
was firmly convinced that the mysterious deaths were brought about by evil forces.

Tuesday, December 19, 1995

The bloodthirsty Chupacabras struck again after laying low for a period of
time. This time, residents of geographical locations as disparate as Naguabo (south
of San Juan) and Guayanilla (on the island's Caribbean shores) experienced the
loss of chickens and rabbits.

Undaunted by their losses, local residents have managed to find some grim
humor in their predicament: a number of citizens of Caguas suggested that the
Chupacabras' name be changed to that of the Gallinejo (a contraction of
"gallina"--chicken--and "conejo"--rabbit), since according to their tabulations, the
nocturnal predator has slain a greater number of those two animals than goats or
larger creatures.

Nemesio Vargas of Guayanilla lost a dozen chickens to the Chupacabras on
the previous evening. Grimly, he estimated his losses -- attributed to the
Chupacabras' supper -- at less than a hundred dollars, and denied that dogs of
any breed could have caused the strange deaths of his birds. While he refused to
say that the mystery beast had been the culprit, he observed that the punctures in
the necks and backs of his fowl corresponded to the Goatsucker's modus operandi.

As if not to be outdone by his new rival, "Brother Carmelo" staged a return
to the scene after the Chupacabras killed five rabbits at the home of Valentín
Rodríguez. The alleged clairvoyant called the newsroom of El Vocero to explain

the reason for the Chupacabras' preference for animal blood (as opposed to human, hopefully!): the strange being has chosen to feed on the beasts of the field because their blood exhibits a greater purity than human blood, being free from the toxins that pollute humans. In the clairvoyants' philosophy, "the uncontrolled ingestion of fats, alcohol and nicotine by humans have made our blood unsuitable for these creatures."

(I'll have fries with my double cheeseburger, please...)

VIII. On-Site

The winter holidays have a stronger hold on Puerto Rico than on any other comparable location in North America. Anglo-Saxon traditions--the singing of carols, wreaths of holly, and the ubiquitous Santa Claus—blend imperceptibly with the thundering beat of Christmas plenas, the melodious singing of jíbaro holiday songs, and the serene majesty of the Three Kings on their way to visit the Christ-child. At a local mall, we were treated to the sight of an army of plena singers—beating their chimeless tambourines and singing litanies--wearing the red caps associated with Santa Claus. This revelry continues past Christmas and into New Year's, then for another week into the Three Kings' Day, and for another eight days after that as part of the octavitas--well into mid-January.

Yet all this holiday fervor did not hold the Chupacabras at bay, nor did it comply with the skeptics' cherished belief that Christmas cheer would drive the phenomenon back into the dungeons of the imagination. From the moment we arrived in San Juan, the Chupacabras was foremost in everyone's mind, even if only as a figure of fun: one saw a TV beauty leering saucily into the camera and tauntingly calling out "Chupacabras!" at the viewer; the endless comedy show sketches in which any damage done on the island was promptly blamed on the terrifying creature; cartoonish T-shirts depicting the intruder as a lifeguard from the "Baywatch" TV show, others showing it sipping blood out of a dead bovine through a long straw, and still others which depicted the creature debating the right kind of condiment to apply to his next kill.

A fleeting hint of paranoia crossed our minds. Could the aura of hilarity bestowed upon the Chupacabras have been encouraged by officialdom in an effort to defuse a potentially critical situation? The ruling New Progressive Party (NPP) had already chastened one of its representatives who had urged a formal investigation into the matter, and another had already "lost" his reelection bid. Would the gallant "Chemo" Soto also be unseated as a result of his participation in the Chupacabras crisis? Only the future held the answer, and our crystal ball was hazy.

The fact remained that in spite of the initial concern caused by the Chupacabras, the population was unconcerned with its activities or with the doom-filled assumptions put forth by the phantom UFO groups in their statements to the newspaper. This point is certainly worth stressing: in spite of its well- deserved reputation as the island which harbors every single kind of supernatural or ufological phenomenon, Puerto Rico's population remains unaffected by the possibility that non-human entities are sharing their living space. If and when a formal announcement is ever made declaring that aliens (extraterrestrial or otherwise) are indeed visiting the island, or are established on it, the man on the street will not perceive any "loss of self" or enter into a panic as a result of a "shattered paradigm." This resilience is perhaps characteristic of island-dwellers around the world, who are accustomed to seeing unusual visitors pulling in aboard ships or landing in airplanes, silent testimony to lands beyond the horizon. Any visiting non-humans would merely be a continuation of this pattern. Jorge Martín has speculated that this tolerance toward the unusual, the spiritual, and the unknown could in fact be the reason that has impelled the government to use P.R. as a testing ground for human reaction to the revelation that--as has been stated so dramatically over the years--"We Are Not Alone."

An Early Morning Drive

Leaving San Juan on the main artery leading eastward, Route 3, gives the visitor an idea of how congested the island really is, and how the so-called Metropolitan Area, which stretches far beyond the municipal limits of San Juan, is growing exponentially every few years, spreading out like an ink stain on a tablecloth. However, the urban environment with its garish neon signs and unescapable traffic jams ends abruptly at a given point just short of El Yunque, giving the tourist a glimpse of what life must have been like before the onset of the industrial age: cattle graze by the roadside where vendors sell maví and guarapo — derivatives of sugarcane — while horses roam freely without any fear of the increasing traffic. The rural bliss is already being marred by giant Wal-Marts and shopping malls popping out in the midst of the rural communities, yet there is enough vegetation to conceal an army of Chupacabras—and of what lurks under El Yunque, who can tell?

Canóvanas prides itself on being a growing municipality, and the main entrance to the town off the highway boasts a monument depicting a Taíno chief and his spouse. Large letters spell out: Canóvanas, Ciudad de los Indios (Canóvanas, the City of Indians) as a well-paved street runs past the single-story concrete homes which constitute the Puerto Rican equivalent of the American tract house. But bypassing the more modern part of the city we come to the narrow, busy streets of Canóvanas proper. Navigating through hair-raising traffic, the Town Hall (Casa Alcaldía, in Spanish) is finally within view. Our plans for speaking with Mayor Soto, however, are thwarted when two beige-clad municipal guards inform us that the Town Hall is closed in preparation for a holiday performance to be held in the placita, the square directly outside the municipal building. We catch a glimpse of a platform and drive off, following a street which leads us out to the rural surroundings.

ALIEN BLOOD LUST

The fertile plains on either side of the Espíritu Santo and Loíza Rivers have been prime grazing land for cattle since the Spaniards arrived in the 16th century. They have also proven to be a magnet for the Chupacabras -- a great number of attacks have taken place in this littoral, where cows are allowed to sleep in the open at night.

As we drive farther eastward, toward Fajardo, where hair-raising screams were heard coming out of the sky earlier this year, we appear to come inexorably closer to the baleful mass of El Yunque, access to which is closed as a result of a shutdown in the Federal government. Despite the blue skies and fine sunshine, clouds cling to the mountain like cotton candy, giving it only the slightest hint of menace. With palm tree-covered Luquillo Beach on our left, the imposing bulk to the right conjures up Tolkien's descriptions of cloudy Mordor as seen from the fair valleys outside its mountains. If a similar Dark Lord commands El Yunque's lofty, verdant heights, then there is more truth to the old Taíno legends of Yukiyú than believed before.

The next town along the road is Río Grande, and the mountain rainforest is still at hand. The Navy radio towers on Pico del Este, one of the El Yunque complex's summits, can be seen through the enshrouding fog. The inspiring sight of man's triumph over nature is promptly replaced by more immediate doubts: is the U.S. military using the rainforest as a laboratory to produce mutant species of some sort or another? What of the gigantic radar complex projected for the Lajas area on the island's southern shore, bearing more in common with Alaska's project HAARP than with any other Over The Horizon radar? The flow of questions is disrupted by a road sign indicating the kilometers remaining for Ceiba and Humacao, farther down the highway. Ceiba is the municipality containing the vast Roosevelt Roads Naval Installation -- one of the foremost U.S. naval bases. The presence is strong enough to be felt at this distance.

We finally reach Fajardo, the easternmost point on the island, a thriving community looking out to the Lesser Antilles and providing ferry service to the smaller island-municipalities of Culebra and Vieques. This area has had its own share of unusual activity: not too long ago, UFOs were reported plunging into the ocean and emerging once more, and local fishermen and yachtsmen reported objects causing upboilings of water around their craft. Perhaps no other incident describes Fajardo's reputation as a strange location better than the controversial Garadiávolo. Twenty years after a book on the subject appeared, heated discussions regarding the creature's true nature still take place. A respected professional who visited Laguna de San Juan, a large lagoon on a promontory jutting out into the sea to the north of Fajardo, discovered a most unusual amphibian during one of his trips. The diminutive creature was able to walk on spindly legs and even climb up trees. The man captured the specimen and brought it home, after which it soon caused a sensation in the press. Unfortunately, it was confiscated in the dark of night by

ALIEN BLOOD LUST

men who claimed to be with the U.S. government. It has been argued that the Garadiávolo was simply a common sea-ray sliced in half -- an old "sea monster" known as a "Jenny Haniver" to cryptozoologists. I can attest to the fact that samples of this Garadiávolo were sold for the affordable price of $7.95 at my mother's store in San Juan under the name "devilfish." Yet others who saw the original creature first hand insist that its cat-like face, eyes, and fangs could not have been the product of any hoaxing, like the "Jenny Hanivers."

The magnificent El Conquistador Hotel crowns the peaks above the fishing village of Las Croabas. Its terraced parking lot provides a spectacular view of El Yunque that cannot be fully captured by the camera. As noon approached, the fog around the mountain was dispelled by the sun's heat, lifting the veil that conceals the rainforest from the looks of the average curious mortal. Within the halcyon environment of the hotel, we asked an employee of one of the dozen boutiques on the promenade if the Chupacabras had been seen in the area. "I think people exaggerate too much," she replied with a smile.

The Investigators

We had the pleasure of being invited to Ovnis Confidencial, their radio program on the NOTI-UNO network, which has repeater stations throughout the island and even, I believe, in New Jersey. Jorge had recently completed the tremendous show in which the proverbial whistle had been blown on the phantom groups described in the previous chapter—an act which led him to add, ruefully, at the end of the broadcast, that it might cause his show to be yanked off the air. To his surprise, he not only received strong support from station management, but also caused the phantom groups to tone down their activities, at least for a little while.

The best segment of any radio program is very often the call-in portion. This is certainly true of Ovnis Confidencial. Half an hour into the broadcast, when this author had spoken about all and sundry with the host, an interesting phone call concerning our discussion on the Chupacabras came in. The caller, who had earlier been given the pseudonym of "Julio Marín," had been a former military man whose involvement in certain sensitive operations had provided him with an insight on the situation. Among the items discussed up to the moment had been the Aberdeen Proving Grounds' alleged role as a harbor for strange beings, and the greenish blood that had been recovered from a Bigfoot-like creature, along with other instances around the world in which chartreuse-green blood had been reported.

[Ovnis Confidencial, December 21, 1995 — 10:30 - 11:30 p.m.
Partial transcript of caller testimony]

J. Martín: Well, we have a caller on the line who is going to be making use of the alias "Julio Marín" in view of the information he'll be passing on tonight. The subject we're discussing this evening is rather sensitive--the strange creatures currently being seen, and the link they seem to have with the UFO situation. Therefore, let's go to Line 1. Good evening! To whom are we speaking?

Caller: This is Julio Marín.

J. Martín: Good evening, Don Julio.

Caller: I heard you discussing the Aberdeen Proving Grounds. I've been there--that's where weapons, including biological weapons, are tested. However, certain things cannot be tested there, which is why they have to make up wars overseas to test them out there. That so-called peace treaty [sic] in Bosnia includes Puerto Rican soldiers who don't even speak the local language. If you look closely at a photo of these soldiers, at their rifles--

J. Martín: Yes.

Caller: Certain weapons are designed, and since they can't be tested here, there has to be a conflict--

J. Martín: They take advantage of those opportunities?

Caller: Precisely. They take advantage of those opportunities...there are other sites in the U.S. where aircraft are tested, such as Nevada and Utah, which are flat, and...Arizona, which is inaccessible, having mountains some nine thousand feet tall, and has valleys in spite of these mountains. It is a large state, yet among the least populated ones. There are many [Indian] reservations, and within these reservations one finds--there's no better way of putting it-- other reservations. It's very hard to reach them. The roads aren't always paved...to reach these places might even jeopardize the lives of those who make the attempt.

J. Martín: Excuse me, Don Julio--What's the importance of these valleys?

Caller: The importance is that these valleys house structures in which experiments of different kinds take place...call them animals or creatures or whatever you like...the Indians who live on these reservations are sheep farmers.

J. Martín: Yes.

Caller: If you notice, the Indians there are sheep farmers, and suddenly we get a creature called the Chupacabras...

J. Martín: So what you're trying to tell us, in fact —

Caller: ...if you put one and one together, you understand? The climate out there is, well, slightly colder...it gets cold, but still--

J. Martín: It's a warmer climate.

Caller: Yes. I remember reading that this creature seems to prefer tropical climates.

J. Martín: Don Julio, let me ask you something. Please answer only if you feel comfortable doing so, because we're aware of your position. You were once linked to an area that was dedicated to researching these strange creatures, but from the

ALIEN BLOOD LUST

military intelligence standpoint.

Caller: Yes.

J. Martín: This is the reason you cannot use your real name tonight, correct?

Caller: Well...[unintelligible].

J. Martín: What moved you to call us tonight?

Caller: I've been hearing your show, and I've been hearing things that aren't true.

J. Martín: Such as?

Caller: Uh, well the blood...the chartreuse-green blood...just can't be. It's not ordinary blood.

J. Martín: But that's precisely the reason we're discussing it tonight on our show. There have been a number of situations and cases here in Puerto Rico which we believe may be related to experiments conducted in this field. You told me confidentially a few programs ago about your knowledge that creatures matching the Chupacabras' description...had been seen in the late 1950's and were known to exist by the U.S. government, who even had some of them in captivity at the time. Is there any truth to this at all?

Caller: It's very true. These were creatures quite similar to what has been described here [in P.R.]. If you take a kangaroo, cut off its tail and a bit off its legs, it would look similar to it, but it has spines running down the length of its back.

J. Martín: Where did you see this, Don Julio?

Caller: I saw it at a place in...in...gosh, I really can't recall...

J. Martín: What sort of facility?

Caller: I remember travelling from Kansas to a state near Texas or Mexico...

J. Martín: New Mexico?

Caller: Yes, New Mexico...

J. Martín: And where in New Mexico would this have been?

Caller: It was in New Mexico, but I can't recall now...I know that there was a [unintelligible] and we went past a town called Flagstaff.

J. Martín: And I ask you, Don Julio, why did you have to be the one to see this?

Caller: Well, because I had a Top Secret clearance at the time, and I would volunteer to do what's known as "riding shotgun." Remember the Old West? They still use the term to refer to the guarding of the merchandise.

J. Martín: Don Julio, since we don't want to reveal too many details that might give your identity away...did you in fact get to see one of these creatures related to the Chupacabras in that place?

Caller: Yes, but I want to add that this creature is completely harmless.

J. Martín: How so?

ALIEN BLOOD LUST

Caller: The creature is very intelligent, and is capable of distinguishing between a human and an animal.

J. Martín: Are you sure of that, Don Julio?

Caller: Of course.

J. Martín: Why?

Caller: Once in Vietnam...if you go to Vietnam, you'll find the climate is...identical to Puerto Rico's. In fact, when you touch down in Vietnam you'd think you're landing in Puerto Rico. As I told you the last time, when I saw that "thing", I forgot to tell you that a light came out from under it, and two human-like beings came down to the ground. They were humans. We saw them through the binoculars, which was hard, because the light was so brilliant

J. Martín: For the benefit of our listeners, you are now describing an incident that you and your comrades witnessed in Vietnam.

Caller: My companion and myself [saw it] during a New Year's Eve.

J. Martín: This was in Vietnam?

Caller: Yes, and he was an American whose name I can't recall. We didn't notify the authorities when the event took place because we were afraid of being ridiculed.

J. Martín: Now, Don Julio, so as not to digress: in what circumstances did you see these creatures now described as the Chupacabras in Puerto Rico at this secret U.S. facility in New Mexico? What year?

Caller: This creature is a sort of pet, to put it that way. There's a radar currently being built in Lajas with the purpose of detecting aircraft.

J. Martín: With drugs?

Caller: This not only picks up aircraft but also any...any aircraf.

J. Martín: Including the unidentified objects seen in the area.

Caller: Anything flying five to seven feet off the ground

J. Martín: But let's go back to the subject, because we're out of time. Under what circumstances did you see these creatures at this secret U.S. facility in New Mexico?

Caller: They were caged.

J. Martín: Why?

Caller: I don't know...they were being studied, and evidently, their sex could be distinguished...there was a male and a female, and...

J. Martín: And what happened?

Caller: Well, she was getting bigger and bigger--her stomach was--and, and they realized she was pregnant. And they "put her to sleep" as they say in order to study her.

277

ALIEN BLOOD LUST

J. Martín: They sacrificed her?

Caller: They opened her up and found another creature within, just like her. They procreate.

J. Martín: Did this creature at any moment try to attack you or any of the people working at that facility?

Caller: No. These creatures looked at you pleadingly with their sad eyes, and they inspire pity. They appear to be lost on an unknown world.

J. Martín: What kind of personnel was working with those creatures at the site?

Caller: They wore those outfits that cover the entire body, and changed garments from one room to another, discarding them as they returned. Decontamination room to the showers, discarding clothing once more and burning it.

[...]

J.Martín: Don Julio, please forgive the interruption, but time is of the essence. Feel free to answer only if you can. I understand from what you told me during your call a few programs ago that you were alongside these creatures, which according to you may have been brought to Puerto Rico as part of an experiment, is this so?

Caller: No, they brought creatures similar to the ones which appeared in an autopsy a few years ago...they were three, one of them was a female who died from a wound to the thigh--

J. Martín: You're referring to what appeared in the [Roswell] movie.

Caller: The other creature died carbonized, no one knew what it was, and the third was wounded, stayed alive. I think it died of old age. This isn't the only [vehicle] to have crashed or to have been knocked out of the sky. It's all very secret, and right now I'm putting myself at risk by calling you.

J. Martín: Don Julio,...I'm concerned about something you said earlier about your days as part of this special intelligence service where some of these creatures seen in Puerto Rico were kept. These creatures seemed harmless to humans, contrary to what is being circulated by some groups in Puerto Rico. Are you certain of what you're saying?

Caller:Y es, I'm sure...they're harmless. The problem is that since they're ugly and different from us, people become afraid. They are like lemurs or those sloths that dangle from trees, only that they have a terrible odor and are quite ugly. Anyone would be afraid.

The pseudonymous caller had played hard-to-get throughout the length of the call, wandering off to other subjects and giving out as little information as possible. Naturally, he made a few mistakes, such as placing Flagstaff in New Mexico rather than Arizona, but his completely unverifiable story had an undeniable ring of truth to it.

ALIEN BLOOD LUST

After the program was over, we discussed "Julio Marín" with Jorge and Marleen at a local restaurant. The caller claimed to have really been an intelligence officer during the '50s and '60s, and had been subjected to harsh treatment when he attempted to speak out about the things he had seen during his career. Throughout the conversation, his voice sounded muffled, as though he were using a handkerchief to disguise his identity. The most outstanding feature about his story, had it been a concoction of bad science fiction films (and we all agreed about this), was his conviction that the creatures were harmless. Anyone trying to make up a story would have gone for the flashier "dangerous" creature á la Alien or Predator, as the phantom saucer research groups had done. His story, told in the slow, deliberate voice of a man who'd experienced a great deal of suffering, remained present in our minds for a long time after. But as we accompanied the Martíns on some of their cases, we realized that tantalizing stories were, in fact, legion.

The Dog that Got Away

Suki the pup looked like a dog sprung from a cartoonist's pen: an elongated black-and-white body surmounted by a floppy-eared head with gleaming eyes—the product of a dachshund and the hardy island mutt known as a sato. The spunky three-month old was a celebrity and didn't know it. It, among all the animals in Puerto Rico, had held off the Chupacabras with its sharp barking and thus avoided getting "goatsucked." Suki's tale of canine bravery (or good luck) could not have been recounted in a better location: her owner's rural home, overlooking the southern slopes of El Yunque near the town of Juncos.

Mrs. María de Gómez, a housewife in her mid-fifties, a resident of Barrio Valenciano Abajo on the outskirts of Juncos, told us how her pooch's barking alerted her to the fact that something was wrong on the high terrace overlooking her backyard (which is in fact a plantation spanning several acres of exuberant vegetation) at 7 p.m. a few nights before our visit. When she went to check on the cause of the pet's excitement, she was startled beyond belief: an ash-grey creature, weighing some seventy-five pounds and standing some four feet tall, loomed over the defiant animal in silence, as if trying to browbeat it into submission.

"It was the ugliest thing I'd ever seen," Mrs. Gómez explained. "All that stood between me and it was the screen door leading to the kitchen. A baseball bat, which my husband leaves here in case a prowler should come around, was all I could have used against it."

But something as remarkable as the puppy's defiance happened next. The housewife's eyes met those of the inhuman creature and stared it down, as she thought aloud: "If you're the Chupacabras, you're a pretty sorry excuse for a creature," promptly adding the abusive word pendejo to her thought. The gargoylesque entity then slowly covered its pointed face with its wings, as if hurt by her rebuff. It moved away from its position, slinking against a wall and half-hiding behind a washing machine. Eventually, the chastened Chupacabras took a few awkward steps toward the railing surrounding her terrace, jumped on it, and flew off into the dark sky.

Mrs. Gómez was able to add a curious detail to the story: the creature's eyes were somehow able to light the entire terrace with a clear, whitish light like that of a bulb. She had no problem in making out all the physical details which had been included in her testimony. But other strange events that had transpired on the Gómez's property were no less fascinating: a black, hairy Bigfoot-like creature had been seen through the trees on the plantation only a few years earlier, and Mrs. Gómez had seen small, silver-suited "Greys" jump over a fence on her property while escaping from a watchdog, holding hands as they did so.

Beyond the tree-covered plantation, she explained, was a pond or small lake which had been used to dump chemicals by a local industry. It was eventually used to dump every single kind of waste, to the point that it would have been impossible to sit on the terrace we were on without being nauseated by the odor. It was at this point that the strangeness began. While tending to the vegetable gardens at the far end of the property, Mrs. Gómez and her daughter had seen "Greys" running toward the vicinity of the contaminated pond. This detail was interesting for the following reason. As the Martíns research has proven, many cases involving supposed alien activity on the island revolve around environmental and ecological issues, a concern for how humans seem hell-bent on polluting and destroying their own world. Could this case have followed the pattern?

The mystery birds which have made Puerto Rico's cryptozoological fauna so rich had also been seen in the trees close to the Gómez property. Mrs. Gómez pointed toward a tree where a creature looking like an owl with a tremendous wingspan had rested on a branch before spreading its wings and soaring off toward El Yunque. Her personal opinion, she told us, was that these creatures, lock, stock and barrel, came from the mountain rainforest.

Hand-to-Hand Combat

We took our leave from Mrs. Gómez and drove down the twisting mountain road leading from Barrio Valenciano down to the plains, heading for the nearby town of Gurabo. The community came to mind immediately as the place where the fanged mystery bird of 1989 had made its debut, causing the sensation which filled newspapers locally and overseas.

The Chupacabras had also been seen in Gurabo, and many had experienced losses, Mr. Jesús Sánchez among them. A devout man belonging to one of the many Protestant churches which are claiming an increasing number of followers in this traditionally Catholic country, his experience with the creature could be described as nothing but hand-to-hand combat.

Our arrival at the Sánchez household coincided with a private Christmas party, so the awkwardness of discussing a questionable subject in a religious household was doubled by the reproving looks of the guests, who went by the Scriptures as far as the Chupacabras was concerned, and had no illusions at all about it.

"I'm still affected by what happened," Mr. Sánchez confessed. "I haven't been myself since the encounter, and my wife and daughters can testify to that."

The bloodthirsty predator had landed in his backyard one evening and killed the rabbits Mr. Sánchez raised there, opening the cages one by one and leaving the characteristic puncture marks on their bodies. Fearing that the creature would stage a return, since attacks were still being reported throughout Gurabo, he decided to mount a watch in hopes of overcoming it and capturing it. His wish came true: the repeat visit came at 4 o'clock in the morning only days later. The homeowner apparently blinded it with a light bulb, causing the creature to seek shelter from the light behind a tree. When the light was turned off, the predator raced past him out of the darkness, allowing only enough time for a terrified Sánchez to deliver two stiff blows with his machete against the creature's skin. Shuddering at the recollection, Sánchez added, "aquello sonó como un timbal" -- the blow sounded like a hit on a drum.

In spite of the state in which his close encounter with the Chupacabras has left him, Sánchez is guardedly hoping that the creature will come back for more. He has already promised himself to capture the creature, despite a threat levelled at him by an official with the Department of Natural Resources, who warned him that this agency would prosecute him if he killed a "protected" creature. The defiant Sánchez riposted that a creature that is said not to exist cannot be protected by anyone, and that any action taken by the agency will only point to its complicity in the hundreds of animal killings which have plagued the island since the beginning of the year.

Not wanting to keep him from his guests, we said goodbye to Mr. Sánchez and headed back to San Juan. The expression on the witness's face as he recounted the frightening seconds when the creature rushed past him left no doubt in anyone's mind that he had experienced something utterly unnerving, and that the tropical twilight engulfing us housed a creature that could not possibly be dismissed as an rogue ape or dog.

Bigfoot Enters the Stage

Human nature is curious. Many of us prefer to carry out certain tasks at different times from others; therefore, no one should be surprised by the urge to wash a car at 2:50 a.m., which is exactly what Osvaldo Rosado was doing on December 23 — just hours after our visits to the Gómez and Sánchez residences.

Rosado, a resident of the city of Guánica, where the Chupacabras had already made its presence felt earlier in the month, had allegedly finished hosing down his vehicle and getting ready to disconnect the hose when as strange hairy creature approached him from behind and gave him a bearhug so strong that wounds appeared on the victim's abdomen. Rendered speechless by panic, Rosado was finally able to scream and struggle with the entity until he managed to break the deadly embrace. Turning to face his assailant, he was doubly shocked to find that it was a simian creature, much taller than his own six-foot height. The shaggy embracer turned tail and ran away from Rosado's backyard. Neighbors responded to his screams, and eventually took the badly shaken victim to a hospital in Yauco to have his wounds treated.

Conflicting stories circulated for a while. One newspaper blamed the incident on the Chupacabras, but the victim claimed never having spoken to the reporter who wrote the story. The creature in no way matched the descriptions given of the Goatsucker, and was certainly not winged--Rosado believed that the assailant must have been at least two feet taller than himself.

This landmark encounter would have been the first time that a full-sized Bigfoot creature—similar to the kind regularly seen in the Laurel Highlands area of Pennsylvania—had been reported on Puerto Rico, which had characterized itself for the activities of man-sized or smaller mystery apes, jokingly dubbed "Smallfoots" in English.

Incident at the Lovers' Lane

Far from observing the holidays on the 24th and the 25th of December, the Chupacabras killed a number of small animals belonging to residents of Piñones, a scattered community of homes and businesses pegged between the Torrecilla and Piñones lagoons on one side and fantastic unspoiled beaches on the other, long considered a lovers' lane. In Rio Grande, Raymond Frías, manager of a horse farm, found that an eighteen year-old horse on the property had been killed by a creature originally taken to be the Chupacabras, but the strange marks found on the dead animal's body did not correspond with the neat punctures that had become synonymous with the mystery prowler's bloodletting activities. Furthermore, the dead horse's anus had been cored and removed in the fashion typical of cattle mutilations in the American West. Was another creature at large?

The Bahía Beach Plantation and The Berwind Golf Course, some fifteen miles away from Piñones in the municipality of Loíza, had also been visited by the Chupacabras, who was apparently unimpressed by the well-manicured fairways and greens. Groundskeepers had become accustomed to seeing weird creatures and UFOs over both golf courses over the years, and there was a story circulating that the Chupacabras had chased the herons found in the vicinity of the numerous water hazards on the course. Without skipping a beat, the pro shop at one of the courses ordered a number of pricey golf club covers to be made in a comical likeness of the mystery creature--a sable critter made out of plush, with little felt bat- wings. The sheer size of both links, and the density of the tropical vegetation

ALIEN BLOOD LUST

they contained, was not only enough to discourage any player from chasing a ball into the rough, but could have easily hidden an army of strange bloodsucking animals.

A Public Figure Comes Forward

The last days of 1995 had not been heavy in Chupacabras activity, but the fact that Latin Americans from Mexico to Argentina consider December 27th--Day of the Holy Innocents--to be their April Fools' Day, references to the mystery prowler were too good not to use.

In the town of Cabo Rojo, a man had strapped a loudspeaker to the top of his car and driven through the streets warning townspeople to get themselves and their animals to safety, as the Chupacabras was reportedly in the neighborhood. Pandemonium ensued, and it remains unclear if the driver was ever charged with inciting a panic.

A radio announcer observed gravely that the Chupacabras had just killed several goats, mares, and other animals. Allowing the incredible tally of kills to sink in, he promptly broke into a sweet voice, informing his listeners that they'd been "had."

One true story among the many humorous ones appearing at the time was that Fernando Toledo, the president of the Puerto Rico Agricultural Association, had publicly expressed a belief that the Chupacabras could not be from this Earth. "I think that if we already know that it's not an ape, we must then be dealing with an extraterrestrial," he said candidly during a Christmas Day radio interview on NOTI-UNO. Toledo reasoned that if our solar system only has a dozen known planets, there must be other star systems in the galaxy with worlds capable of supporting life. This "thing"-- as he called the Chupacabras--must come from one such point of origin.

Toledo's statement, which did not appear in any of the major newspapers, represented a landmark moment in the Chupacabras wave, as a major public figure was willing to concede that the extraterrestrial hypothesis--the butt of jokes and popular derision--was now being taken into consideration in solving the riddle posed by the creature which had caused havoc among Puerto Rican livestock.

"It's in the Trees—It's Coming!"

December 28th, 1995: a significant night for Ovnis Confidencial and for local ufology. Before the show was even ready to go on the air, phones had been ringing with callers wanting to report UFO activity taking place over San Juan and recent Chupacabras encounters. A woman from the residential suburb of Guaynabo was observing a motionless object hovering over the power lines; a man from Cayey, where another military radar was being built, had found a number of his ducks slain by the Chupacabras and wanted to turn the carcasses over to a reputable veterinarian; in short, the silence into which the Chupacabras reports had fallen, by official decree or not, had been circumvented by direct reports from people experiencing the sightings and situations.

Minutes into the broadcast, shortly after my wife and I had given our impressions on the Chupacabras situation, a call arrived at the switchboard from Cuco Rodríguez, a UFO researcher on the southwestern corner of the island, with an update on the Bigfoot "attack": the creature that attacked Osvaldo Rosado had been seen by many other residents of the area of Guanica in which the attack had transpired. These eyewitnesses had been able to corroborate the size and description of the attacker, and more importantly, had been able to compare it with the smaller Chupacabras, which they had also seen. Hairy creatures, though not quite as tall, said Rodríguez, had also been seen around the Aerostat Installation in Laguna Cartagena.

IX. Some Final Thoughts

The totally unexpected furor caused by sightings of the strange entity dubbed "el Chupacabras" (the Goatsucker) by residents of rural Puerto Rico raises some serious items for debate. What should be our response, as commonsensical (as opposed to skeptical or prejudiced), educated individuals?

Skeptics have dismissed these events as hallucinations or worse. People do not hallucinate the deaths of their pets or their livelihoods (in the case of small animal farmers). The person whose livelihood depends on a computer does not wake up one morning, arrive at the workplace, finds his/her computer smashed to bits and say: "I'm probably hallucinating." There is extensive photographic evidence available-- to all who care to see it—displaying the thoroughly unnatural means of slaughter employed by this unknown being. These animals died as the result of a single puncture mark, found on some part of the body, which apparently drained them of blood. One particularly graphic photo shows a Siamese cat with a single puncture mark right through its skull.

In the face of all the cases and situations presented here, the skeptics' knee-jerk reaction has been a steadfast insistence on blaming these deaths on (a) dogs, (b) feral monkeys, (c) vampire bats, (d) other exotic beasts. Let us examine these possibilities one by one.

(a) A plague of single-fanged, bloodsucking dogs is probably a more terrifying thought than a carload of Goatsuckers. Nonetheless, veterinarians have stuck to this unlikely possibility, regardless of the fact that dogs rend their prey and eat them, rather than extracting their juices. To date, there are no reports of mastication on any carcass found.

(b) Puerto Rico harbors a number of military animal research laboratories. The Caribbean Primate Research Center's La Parguera facility lost a number of rhesus monkeys in the 1970's, and these fugitive apes have allegedly been proliferating throughout the island. Jesús Rodríguez, a veterinarian interviewed by the

San Juan Star (11/19/95) stated that monkeys are notoriously messy eaters and would have left four holes and scars rather than the single puncture that has become the Chupacabras' trademark.

(c) Local tabloid El Vocero echoed the possibility that giant vampire bats had infiltrated the island in cargo shipments proceeding from South America. Eyewitness reports in no way describe a batlike creature, and normal-sized bats are fairly common in the Caribbean, so witnesses would have a good point of reference for their descriptions.

(d) The possibility of exotic pets imported by wealthy dilettante zoologists has been dear to many skeptics on the island. However, no one can imagine what kind of reptile, simian, bovine, etc. could fit the bill of a creature answering the Chupacabras' description. Furthermore, the USDA has a very effective control of anything—animal or vegetable-entering or leaving the island. Tourists to P.R. are familiar with the obligatory USDA inspection at the airport prior to leaving the island.

Naysayers have found it convenient to blame the entire situation on Puerto Rico's particular political status. Neither a state of the U.S. nor a free country, sociologists have long debated that this political limbo has affected people's minds. Prominent politicians have gone on record saying that as 1998 approaches—commemorating a century of U.S. occupation of the island—the greater the mental stress regarding this political status to be experienced. The fact of the matter is that strange creatures are not exclusive to the island: the U.K. experiences phantom felines and lake monsters; the northwestern U.S. has Bigfoot; the northeastern U.S. is home to a number of enigmatic beings, ranging from three-toed "Bigfoot"-like creatures to even more unusual life-forms, Argentina's lake Nahuel Huapi contains a "Nessie"-like creature seen by hundreds over the years. There is clearly no "political status" question affecting the minds of the citizenry of these countries (this was discussed earlier in the book). Are we dealing, in fact, with an extraterrestrial situation? Here we are venturing into truly uncharted waters which have produced the biased reactions of many.

Puerto Rico is famous for its myriad UFO sightings, as well as encounters with strange--presumably alien—beings. As Jorge Martín of CEDICOP, the only organization conducting responsible research on the island, has stated many times, we can only deal with the human aspect of the phenomenon--witness testimony--since the other aspects of the phenomenon are closed to us. For this reason, ufology all over the world is more properly the realm of the social scientist, psychologist, anthropologist, etc. rather than the physicist or the chemist. Since the descriptions given of the Chupacabras portray it as having the head and torso of one of the creatures known as "Greys" in UFO research, one working hypothesis has linked it to ufology. Some of the other working hypotheses include:

ALIEN BLOOD LUST

Genetic manipulation by human agencies. TIME magazine recently featured a photo of a mouse with a human ear growing out of its back, showing the advanced development of the genetic sciences at the dawn of the 21st century. It would not be unreasonable to suppose that a level of competence has been achieved that would enable the fabrication of a hybrid being such as the Chupacabras.

The possibility of a paranormal origin. For many decades, a number of investigators have postulated a "paranormal" origin for beings such as the Chupacabras. The word "paranormal" triggers a number of flags in people's minds, since it has been used to describe everything from Zenner card tests to poltergeists. Suffice it to say that this paranormal theory postulates entry into our "dimension" or "reality" by creatures that are not native to it by means of materialization. Before dismissing this working hypothesis as science-fiction, recent advances in physics comfortably accept the existence of other dimensions, and geometry has accepted the existence of several million dimensions. Whether these dimensions are populated by exotic creatures or not is an entirely different matter.

No one should feel "railroaded" into accepting any of these working hypotheses as gospel: we should, however, not slam the door on the witnesses (who stand little or nothing to gain from their stories) by holding our noses and demanding "evidence." Under our system of justice, thousands are convicted on eyewitness testimony. If eyewitnesses are good enough for the courts, why can't their integrity be trusted in this matter?

There is a very real danger, however, in the proliferation of pseudo-UFO research groups whose efforts seek to spread panic among the population. One of these irresponsible organizations, calling itself "Nova," has its members going around dressed in black (like the notorious Men-In-Black who were a staple of early UFO stories) and spreading the news that the Chupacabras heralds the end of humanity. They ascribe to it "the origin of the AIDS virus" and the capacity to destroy mankind and all its works without damaging the planet (a kind of "organic" neutron bomb), thus rendering it habitable for alien settlers. This kind of activity is both irresponsible and wrongheaded.

Adding insult to injury, a news crew from the "Inside Edition" TV tabloid visited Puerto Rico early in December 1995 to cover the Chupacabras story for its program. Although "Inside Edition" has covered other unusual situations remarkably well, they chose to mock the witnesses it interviewed and managed to anger Mayor José Soto of the city of Canóvanas, who has led the only organized effort by an elected official in getting to the bottom of the Chupacabras situation. Perhaps the antics of the "Nova" group, "Brother Carmelo," and other colorful characters led them to believe that it was it was all a joke.

Conclusion:

Real animals belonging to real people are being slaughtered by a being which is not native to the Puerto Rican ecosystem. We should constrain ourselves from passing judgement on its nature until we have a better idea of what we're up against. This advice goes for both skeptics and "believers" in UFOs and other unknown quantities. Alas, time did not permit a fuller round of interviews with witnesses who had encountered the creature face to face, like Mrs. Gómez and Mr. Sánchez, nor a trip to the southwestern corner of the island. These individuals, and thousands like them, stand beside us as we turn elsewhere in search of answers.

Friday, January 5, 1996

Two goats were slain by the Chupacabras in Caguas' Barrio Cañaboncito. Police officials reported to the scene after being alerted by Wanda Rivera, who discovered her two young goats dead within their concrete and wire cage, which was still closed and gave no signs of having been forced.

Three sheep were also bled dry at the residence of Jose Ramos Aponte in Aguas Buenas. According to the owner, he rose early on Thursday morning to find that his animals were agonizing from their puncture wounds.

Tuesday, January 8, 1996

The Chupacabras attacked a farm in Canóvanas, killing a pair of sheep belonging to Monchito Colón. Police officers Orlando Marín and Rosa Santiago reported to the site. Just as the police reached the area, another call was received from José Febo, who had allegedly just seen a creature with pointed ears, a strange profile, and a shaven head. Febo encountered the creature as it rested on a tamarind tree. When it noticed the human, the entity jumped off the tree and ran "like a gazelle."

Thursday, January 11, 1996

Mayor José Soto of Canóvanas, who led expeditions in search of the elusive Chupacabras back in November

'95, made a formal request from Police Commissioner Pedro Toledo to help him obtain the resources needed capture the creature. While the commissioner met with Mayor Soto, no allocation of police resources was made.

The creature attacked the Canóvanas area once more, killing a sheep and a rooster belonging to Tomás Santiago Lopez. The sheep was badly wounded and was later put down by a local veterinarian. Mayor Soto visited the Santiago farm, located in Barrio Cambalache.

Monday, January 15, 1996

Two sheep found dead on a farm in Lajas, P.R.. Wisbel Ayala, head of the Civil Defense, looked into the matter, declaring that a veterinarian identified only as "Dr. Ruiz" had offered to analyze the carcasses which had been "attacked by the monkeys which live in the area." The possibility that the carcasses will be frozen and shipped to the CDC in Atlanta hasn't been ruled out.

18 mouths
Lure

CHAPTER 25

CHUPACABRAS UPDATE

If reality resembled the world of fiction more closely, monsters would be put down with the finality of Lieutenant Ripley purging the hideous alien xenomorph out of an airlock, consigning it to vacuum of space. The sense of finality and justice delivered by a wooden stake through the undead heart of a cinematic vampire imparts catharsis, but we find none of that with the monsters and visions that persistently manifest themselves in our reality. After eighteen months of depredations in West Virginia in 1966-67, the Mothman disappeared into legend and the uneasy dreams of those whose encounters changed the course of their lives. Hunters and scientists emerge from forays after the elusive Bigfoot with little to show for their efforts, save the tell-tale strands of hair and plaster casts that have become a trademark of their avocation.

18 mouths

The same can be said for the Chupacabras. The protean creature manifested for the first time in Puerto Rico in the mid-90s, followed by a rash of sightings throughout Latin America, each time described a little differently than before. Media burnout and the trivialization of the subject by popular culture – the cascade of t-shirts and bumper stickers, rap and ranchero songs, cheap plastic memorabilia sold in marketplaces – resulted in a loss of interest in the creature's exploits in Brazil and Chile later that decade.

But the Chupacabras keeps coming back like a prize fighter, unmindful of the fatuous pronouncements of skeptics, efforts at fitting it into the UFO totem-pole by researchers bent on seducing the media once more, their prize a conference invitation or the lure of a television show. The demon is triumphant.

Lure

So it was that the Puerto Rican media approached the subject of the paranormal predator again in 2012, when reporter Yaritza Santiago wrote an article for El Nuevo Dia about the entity's return to the scene, this time in the island municipality of Vieques. "A strange wild animal prowls the verdant fields and communities of this island municipality. This is the only way to explain the discovery of dead horses, hens and rabbits in situations that terrified Viequenses have ascribed to a panther that allegedly escaped from an American tourist's possession. Others say it is a jaguar; still others speak of the return of the Chupacabras, whose existence they do not question for a second."

Thirty chickens met an untimely demise on the property of José Martínez and his wife Jeami in Barrio La Hueca. The couple had gone off to a birthday party on the previous night, returning home an hour before midnight. They went to bed and Mr. Martínez woke up at half past five in the morning to feed the family animals. In cold glow of his flashlight, José was startled to find the roosters dead in their cages, with deep puncture marks on their backs, drained of blood. The couple told reporters that they had not heard any abnormal sounds in the night.

José, 26, and Jeami, 21, described the massacre of their animals as "a battlefield" where the unknown assailant had operated at leisure. She remained convinced that the perpetrator was none other than the mysterious being that spread fear throughout Puerto Rico during her childhood. "It wasn't a dog. I think it could be the Chupacabras."

Reporters from El Nuevo Dia found "sort of animal print" at the location as well as poultry carcasses and metal cages scattered around the premises. Mr. Martínez filed a complaint with the municipal police, which in turn referred the case to the Civil Defense and Emergency Management Bureau. Police chief José Belardo, however, was unmoved by the carnage at the Martínez household, citing a lack of specific evidence or physical proof. He did, however, manifest to El Nuevo Día's reporters his awareness of a "radar image" of a strange creature taken by a U.S. Marines radar, and that fear among the island's population was quite real. Unlike Mayor "Chemo" Soto's gallant efforts to capture the Chupacabras in the mid-90s, law enforcement on Vieques was not planning any grand gestures.

On main island of Puerto Rico, news organizations were covering the "gargoyle" that supposedly haunted the vicinity of Guánica, the city with the magnificent bay on the Caribbean Sea. This nightmarish vision had attacked not only animals, but allegedly humans as well. Its patterns of attack resembled those of the Chupacabras, but not exactly the same entity. "Some identified it with the Chupacabras, but others believe it was a different creature, a sly and sinister one, using the ruins and tunnels of the [abandoned] Central Guánica sugar mill as its lair," wrote Pedro Bosque in an article for El Nuevo Dia. It was in this warren of half-flooded, weed-choked tunnels that the skeletons of its victims were reportedly found.

Despite its predilection for lovely Guánica, the "gargoyle" had reportedly been seen in Lajas and San Germán, communities in southwestern Puerto Rico that acquired notoriety in the late '80s and throughout the 1990s as paranormal hotspots. And unlike those relatively distant years, eyewitnesses were reluctant to share their names with the media, particularly when it came to the attacks on humans.

ALIEN BLOOD LUST

These incidents were discussed in hushed tones. One witness interviewed by the press claimed seeing injuries on a man's belly, produced by an "animal with large wings" whose claws had torn at his flesh "to the extent that his fat could be seen." The unnamed witness spoke soberly of seeing the victim – nicknamed - lift his t-shirt to display the wounds received in his own backyard.

Police officer Miguel Negrón, on the other hand, admitted to hearing "a loud sound of flapping wings" while patrolling the abandoned sugar mill. Was an unknown avian taking off from the rusted cranes of the old mill? According to the officer, the "gargoyle" had been described by some as a very large bird reeking of sulfur or rot (hydrogen sulfide?), feeding on live animals such as dogs, cats and horses by exsanguination.

Four Thousand Miles Away

While the Chupacabras staged a return to Puerto Rico, its sinister kin were making news in Chile, where the national media latched on to a story that was as sensation as it was bizarre: while attacking a henhouse in Paine, on the outskirts of the city of Santiago, the predator had allegedly suffered what was described as a "miscarriage".

Cristián Solís was sleeping peacefully when the frantic clucking of his hens woke him up at four o'clock in the morning. He ran outside to find fifty dead hens, arranged in circles, presenting no visible injuries, but without a drop of blood in their carcasses. Shocked and dismayed though he was, Solís was bowled over by what he found next.

He described the find as "embryos of something I had never seen before". Describing them as miniature dinosaurs measuring some 30 centimeters long, they had hairy backs, thick, hard tails with sharp tips, arms shorter than their bodies, suggesting bipedal motion. "They were rather horrible," he was quoted as saying. "I think the dead hens were attacked by the mother of these embryos, who must've had a miscarriage due to the strain of the attack."

The specimens were turned over to SAG (the notorious Agriculture and Wildlife Service that hindered research into the Chilean mutilations wave of the year 2000). The ministry reported that it had been unable to determine the species to which the specimens belonged as they were "too dehydrated to be properly analyzed."

Chupacabras activity had gone into abeyance for a number of years in these latitudes, with the most recent cases dating to 2007, when reports of attacks in world-famous Viña del Mar appeared in the press.

During the month of May of that year, the Ugalde family had its own close encounter with the unknown at four a.m., when a loud noise woke up the entire household – the sound of something very large and heavy suddenly landing on the roof, dragging its wings. The chickens behind the family property erupted in chaotic

2013

noises, extinguished one by one.

According to an article in the La Estrella newspaper, Mrs. Ugalde ran out into the darkness to save her poultry farm and face the unknown intruder. "I went to the backyard and I saw it. It was like a large bird, standing about a meter, with the bearing of a dwarf. It has feathers, wings and left footprints like those of a goat. It was looking for food, and I think it must've been hungry," she explained. The entity had already broken the henhouse door and helped itself to the farm animals. Upon being surprised by the woman, it flew off toward the hills.

Seven hens were lost that evening, and the family did not hesitate to place a call to the Carabineros (the Chilean state police) to report the attack. "They told us it was that (the Chupacabras) and that they had never seen anything like it. They were overwhelmed as well," Mrs. Ugalde added.

When the strange animal passed over the roof and reached the backyard, it broke the henhouse door and extracted the birds one by one, for a total of seven. When he was surprised by the homeowner, the Chupacabras took off, flying toward the hills.

Argentina, Chile's neighbor on the opposite side of the towering Andes Cordillera, was not free from these strange attacks and sightings. In March 2007, El Ciudadano (www.elciudadano.net) reported on seven mutilated and exsanguinated bulls in Santiago del Estero, decrying the fact that farmers and ranchers had automatically leaped to ascribing responsibility for the killings to the Chupacabras. It is true, however, that there are significant differences between Chupacabras attacks and the "traditional" cattle mutilations, characterized by their fine incisions and the removal of certain internal organs, as was the case in the Santiago del Estero incidents.

A Mystery in Spain

On 23 February 2013 – as this article was being written – news arrived from Spain regarding a bizarre goat mutilation in the northwestern region of Galicia, specifically in the town of Fene. The story, which appeared in La Voz del Ferrol, described the mutilation and exsanguination of the goat as the work of "parties unknown". The animals owners, understandably irate, ascribed responsibility to a "satanic cult", stressing that "a number of people must have been needed to carry away all of the goat's blood."

No mention of involvement by the Chupacabras, of course, but a reminder of the long and silent history of encounters with the paranormal predator that have occurred in Spain since the '80s, resulting in the deaths of thousands of animals. Traditionalists blame wolves, especially in the Pyrenaic region between France and Spain, but reports and investigations carried out by the judicial system invariably mention the presence of aberrant entities, sometimes described as mandrills, baboons, or giant canids.

ALIEN BLOOD LUST

We must defer to the extensive work carried out by Ramón Nava Osorio and members of his Instituto de Investigaciones y Estudios Exobiológicos (IIEE) whose Chilean branch – spearheaded by Raúl Núñez – has become known to readers of INEXPLICATA over the years.

In March 1996, writes Nava Osorio, a shepherd in northern Spain by the name of Guillermo Miral Cordesa had an unexpected encounter with a strange animal as he led his flock from one mountain slope to another. "That day," explained Miral, "I had left the flock on high and was headed downhill with two magnificent dogs. I descended quietly and normally and suddenly found myself confronted by an animal I had never seen before, and whose description I'd never heard from other shepherds. It was neither a wolf nor a dog. It looked like a huge dog, an unknown mixture, but it's an unknown creature in the end. Neither a mastiff nor a wolf....I cannot describe its eyes, but I did focus on the enormous width of its muzzle (describing it as flat and nearly square), and for that reason I can tell you it wasn't a wolf. It was an unknown animal with large flat ears; its fur was grey and spotted, with abundant short hair. A short tail, large paws and looking like a dog, yet not a dog. It didn't run. It took two impressive leaps and vanished."

While clearly a predator, the entity did not growl or bear its teeth. Miral's own dogs followed the intruder, only turn back after traversing a brief ten meters' distance.

In his study on the Iberian mutilations phenomenon, Chupacabras: Un Verdadero Expediente X, Miguel Aracil explores the strange simiots which have been a constant feature of Catalan legend since medieval times. The simiots are described as "strange, hairy creatures having semi-human features" and a group of woodsmen were attacked by one such entity a few decades ago: the hairy monster engaged in an orgy of destruction, smashing vehicles and forestry equipment, even hurling logs at the terrified tree-cutters (similar behavior has been reported in cases occurring in suburban Maryland during the 1970's). Although Spain's Guardia Civil looked into the matter, they conveniently "cannot remember", as Aracil notes rather dryly in his treatise.

A number of armed posses were formed to explore the environs of Peña Montañesa (Huesca) where the events occurred, but "nothing was ever found, perhaps due to the large number of immense caves in the area, and the rough terrain." Medieval statues of the simiots depict them as devouring children or being trodden down by the Holy Mother: while he does not offer specifics, the author mentions that these supernatural entities were allegedly responsible for slaying entire herds of animals and on certain occasions were even responsible for some attacks on humans. Could the simiots have cousins across the ocean?

Navia Osorio contributes a "high strangeness" detail to the situation that raises the stakes: the possibility that the anomalous entity (or IEA, the Spanish acronym for "Spontaneous Aggressive Intruder") had been brought along by a human or humanoid presence, unleashed at selected locations. Also in October 1996, José Miguel Trallero, a member of the IIEE, appeared on a local television program in the town of Barbastro to discuss the mutilation crisis. In the wake of the broadcast, a local woman approached him to tell him about a sighting near Barbastro's shrine of Pueyo: she had seen two figures, described as "atypical", with a very strange dog between them. The two figures had "greyish skin" and their arms were longer than usual.

February 20, 1996

According to SAMIZDAT correspondent José Valdez, the unusually cold weather conditions Puerto Rico experienced during January 1996 kept Chupacabras activity to a minimum. He speculates that the creature may have gone into some sort of hibernation for a period of time. The fact of the matter is that the elusive creature is back, and has even been reported on the island of Vieques — 20 miles off the Puerto Rican mainland.

January 12, 1996

The police seems unable to protect even its own. Police colonel Agustín Cartagena, who owns a farm near Caguas, P.R., received a visit from the Chupacabras. The intruder killed 22 animals--an assortment of ducks, chickens, and guinea hens. This incident apparently took place just days after six sheep were killed on the property of police lieutenant Jorge Rivera, whose farm is located in Canóvanas.

January 18, 1996

The Chupacabras turned its thirst for blood against five ducks, slaying four and leaving one mortally injured. However, it found its match in the fierce flock of geese kept by Mrs. Luz Bonilla in her Guaynabo backyard. Even the Chupacabras meets its match now and then, it seems.

According to Mrs. Bonilla, the geese made a racket in the wee hours of the morning. Upon venturing to her backyard to see what had happened, she was faced with the sight of the dead ducks. Mrs. Bonilla added her voice to a growing number of citizens demanding a serious investigation by the Commonwealth government into this matter.

On the other side of the island, reports came in from a number of sources reporting a flurry of UFO activity. Police officials confirmed receiving distressed phone calls regarding this unusual activity. The sightings allegedly took place over the Costas, Sabana Yeguas and Candelaria sectors of Lajas. The objects were described as triangular in shape and moving at prodigious speed across the night skies from south to west. Curiously enough, the UFO reports coincided with the arrival of several squadrons of jet fighters from USAF. Local residents were awakened to a deafening sound, only to find the fighters making low-level runs over

ALIEN BLOOD LUST

their homes. The police could not speculate as to why the Air Force had chosen to embark on practice runs in the area.

January 19, 1996

A professor from the University of Puerto Rico at Mayaguez, Dr. Juan A. Rivero, has become part of the scientific task force which is currently investigating the puzzling deaths of animals throughout the island-- deaths attributed to the creature known as the Chupacabras.

Dr. Rivero expressed his support for the theory that the animal deaths caused throughout the island have been caused by Rhesus monkeys which were brought to Puerto Rico's offshore islands for research purposes. A Harvard graduate and director of the Puerto Rican Zoological Society, Rivero suspects that most of the strange animal deaths which took place during 1995 were caused by the Rhesus, which has been known to kill for the sport of it.

January 25, 1996

Julio Victor Ramírez, staff writer for El Vocero, described the strange disappearance of a Siberian Husky and the death of a number of animals belonging to Antonia Rodríguez García, a Mayaguez housewife who notified local authorities about the incident.

According to the report filed by police officer Carlos Rivera, the victim reported the loss of a pair of rabbits and one of her dogs. One of the rabbits had curious incisions on its neck, while the other showed signs of ripped flesh. The animals gave the appearance of having been drained of blood. The mutilations appear to have taken place at 3:00 a.m., and the police report indicates having discovered chunks of raw meat mixed with fur from Mrs. Rodríguez's missing dog.

The dog engaged in a fierce encounter with the intruder, which tore off a clump of the Husky's fur during the fray. The report did not speculate if the rabbits had been killed by the Chupacabras or by a more mundane creature.

January 26, 1996

A dead pet is a cause for great sadness in any family, but a beloved pet found shredded by an unknown force, perhaps a supernatural one, inspires sheer terror.

Julio López and his family can attest to this, having experienced it themselves on the evening of January 23, 1996 when they returned to their home in Urb. Las Carolinas near Caguas. The pet in question—a rabbit belonging to Mr. López's youngest daughter--was found torn to bloody shreds in cage, which showed signs of violent destruction. Some kind of dark excrement—different from that of cows, horses, dogs or apes--was found on the site. It was suggested that the darkness was the result of having ingested blood.

Mr. López was quoted by San Juan's El Vocero newspaper as saying: "The shape in which the cage was left was incredible, being built out of metal tubing and linked

wire...they took out the rabbit, killed it, and tore out its heard and other entrails."
López added later: "This is the work of a supernatural agency--neither a dog nor
an ape nor a snake could have done such a thing.

Ironically, Mr. López works as a butcher for a Caguas butcher shop. He expressed understanding what people throughout the island have felt when they discover their beloved animals have been viciously slain. His twelve year-old daughter still weeps uncontrollably over her dead rabbit.

February 3, 1996

The authorities have sought solace once more behind theories of ravenous monkeys and one-fanged dogs--the Nineties equivalent of "Swamp Gas". A turkey belonging to Herminio García, a beekeeper from the Mayaguez area, had the dubious distinction of being the first animal of its kind to be slain by the Chupacabras. The gobbler was found dead with claw marks on its neck.

The interagency task force led by Wisbel Ayala, entrusted with the task of analyzing the spate of mysterious deaths around the island, took the dead animal away for autopsy purposes. Ayala expressed the belief that although there were no witnesses, a monkey attacked the turkey. The owner did not have time to see the assailant, since by his own admission, as soon as he heard the sounds made by the attacker, he ran to grab a shotgun in hopes of defending his animal, but arrived too late.

Of a total of nine confirmed cases in western P.R., four have been submitted to forensic analysis with inconclusive results. The cases remain officially open.

February 8, 1996

Mayor José Nazario of Lajas has never seen a UFO despite persistent sightings over his municipality in southwestern Puerto Rico. He belittles the importance of the phenomenon, but did not wish to engage in argument with local ufologists on the matter. Mayor Nazario's position on the matter differs significantly from that held by Humberto Ramos, Mayor of Adjuntas, the mountain community where UFOs became an everyday occurence in the early 90's. Unlike his colleague, Ramos has seen the maneuvers of unknown lights in the skies over his municipality.

February 8, 1996

The Chupacabras returned in full force to the Quebrada Negra sector of Canóvanas, killing at least two sheep and mutilating an unspecified number of other animals. The incidents occurred around 3:00 p.m. in a farm owned by Mr. Elias Reyes, who told authorities that his dead livestock had puncture marks on their necks and bellies, as well as torn flesh in their hindquarters, through which inner organs were apparently extracted. Mr. Reyes refused to believe that apes or wild dogs could have committed such a horrifying act, and called upon Governor Pedro Roselló to show some leadership concerning this distressing situation.

ALIEN BLOOD LUST

CHAPTER 26

SOME PARTING THOUGHTS FROM THE PUBLISHER

In "Alien Blood Lust" we have covered a very taboo topic that seldom – if ever – gets any attention. We are known for our provocative probing of a subject that is so strange that even the researchers in the field tend to want to tread lightly for fear of ridicule whenever the least little controversy is brought up.

In the last few months we have published "Screwed by the Aliens," which tackles the subject of sex between humans and Ultra-Terrestrial beings. And prior to that, "UFO Hostilities: The Evil Alien Agenda." To say the least, we fully expected – and intended – to cause a bit of a stir, and we think it did.

Scott Corrales should be praised for his intentions, which are to push forward the science of UFOlogy. He is determined to piece together a puzzle that incorporates a variety of puzzles.

We welcome you to join us on all future journeys as we explore the bizarre, the strange and what can only be considered the paranormal.

—Timothy Green Beckley

A single-minded group of aficionados believe the chupacabras are dropped off by ETs.

ALIEN BLOOD LUST

BIOGRAPHIES

TIMOTHY GREEN BECKLEY — Fifty years and fifty bursting file cabinets later, Tim Beckley is well deserving of the status of a true pioneer in the UFO/paranormal fields. In addition to having founded as a teenager his own niche publishing company, Inner Light – Global Communications, (with over 300 volumes in print today), Beckley says he must have been duly influenced by all the strange goings on around him. His grandfather was frightened by a headless horseman, his life was saved by an "invisible hand" at age 3, he lived in a house that was haunted and has had three UFO encounters, the first at ten years old.

Beckley started his writing career early on. His published articles have appeared in Fate, Beyond Reality, Saga, UFO Report. For many years he served as a stringer for the Enquirer and edited over 30 newsstand publications, including "UFO Universe," which lasted for over 11 years before almost everything became digital. He has appeared on a multitude of radio and TV shows going back as far as the Long John Nebel program, in the 1960s, and recently on William Shatner's "Weird or What?" program. Currently he is co-host of the podcast "Exploring the Bizarre." He has also produced several horror movies as "Mr Creepo."

ALIEN BLOOD LUST

Tim has traveled extensively, going to many UFO landing sites, speaking for hours with credible witnesses about their experiences, and was even invited to speak before a British House of Lords UFO group in the early 1980s. At age 70 he is "semi-retired," publishing on the average of a mere three new books a month.

An early believer in the ET Hypothesis, Tim now believes that the UFOs are more likely to originate from other than interplanetary sources. He is open to a variety of concepts and theories which will be discussed as well as his belief that not all UFOs are piloted by "warm and fuzzy" ETs, but instead the craft and their occupants have shown a heightened degree of hostility toward humanity over the years, bringing down aircraft, zapping humans, causing them to vanish from the face of the Earth, and, in some cases, incinerating them.

Timothy Green Beckley trying to catch a ride with a friend in Sedona, Arizona.

ALIEN BLOOD LUST

SEAN CASTEEL

Sean Casteel is a freelance journalist who has been writing about UFOs, alien abduction and many other paranormal subjects since 1989. Sean's writing appeared in many UFO- and paranormal-related magazines, including "UFO Magazine," Tim Beckley's "UFO Universe," "FATE Magazine," "Mysteries Magazine," and "Open Minds Magazine," most of which are now defunct but were a major part of a thriving UFO press in their heyday. Magazines in the UK, Italy, Romania and Australia have also published Sean's work.

Sean has written or contributed to over 30 books for Global Communications and Inner Light Publications, all of which are available from Amazon.com. Sean's books include "The Heretic's UFO Guidebook," which analyzes a selection of Gnostic Christian writings and their relationship to the UFO phenomenon, and "Signs and Symbols of the Second Coming," in which he interviews several religious and paranormal experts about how prophecies of the Second Coming of Christ may be fulfilled.

To view and purchase books Sean has written or contributed to, visit his Amazon author page at: http://www.amazon.com/author/seancasteel

Tim R. Swartz — is an Indiana native and Emmy-Award winning television producer & videographer, and is the author of The Lost Journals of Nikola Tesla, America's Strange and Supernatural History, UFO Repeaters, Time Travel: Fact Not Fiction!, Men of Mystery: Nikola Tesla and many others. As a photojournalist, Tim Swartz has traveled extensively and investigated paranormal phenomena and other unusual mysteries from such diverse locations as the Great Pyramid in Egypt to the Great Wall in China. He has also appeared on the History Channel's programs "The Tesla Files"; "Ancient Aliens"; "Evidence"; "Ancient Aliens: Declassified"; and the History Channel Latin America series "Contacto Extraterrestre." His articles have been published in magazines such as FATE, Strange, Atlantis Rising, UFO Universe, Flying Saucer Review, Renaissance, and Unsolved UFO Reports. Currently, as well, Tim Swartz is the writer and editor of the online newsletter ConspiracyJournal.com; a free, weekly e-mail newsletter, considered essential reading by paranormal researchers worldwide. Tim is also the host of the webcast "Exploring the Bizarre" along with Timothy Green Beckley, kcorradio.com

www.ConspiracyJournal.com - www.TeslaSecretLab.com

ALIEN BLOOD LUST

NIGEL WATSON — has researched and investigated historical and contemporary reports of UFO sightings since the 1970s. He is the author of Portraits of Alien Encounters (VALIS, 1990), Phantom Aerial Flaps and Waves (VALIS, 1990), Supernatural Spielberg (with Darren Slade, VALIS, 1992), editor/writer of The Scareship Mystery: A Survey of Phantom Airship Scares, 1909 - 1918 (DOMRA, 2000), The UFO Investigations Manual (Haynes, 2013), UFOs of the First World War (The History Press, 2015). For the UneXplained Rapid Reads e-book series he wrote; UFOs: The Nazi Connection, Spontaneous Human Combustion, UFO Government Secrets, The Great UFO Cover-Up and Ghostships of the Skies (all 2015). He has also written for numerous books, publications and websites, including Magonia, Paranormal Magazine, Fortean Times, Wired, Flipside, How It Works, All About Space, Fate, Strange Magazine, Beyond, History Today, Aquila, Alien Worlds, UniLad, The Unexplained, Flying Saucer Review, UFO Magazine India and UFO Magazine (USA). In the 1980s, he gained a BA degree in Psychology (Open University) and a BA (Hons) degree in Film and Literature (University of Warwick). He has recently contributed to several books publisher by Tim Beckley including, UFO Hostilities and Screwed by the Aliens. He has also appeared on the podcast Exploring the Bizarre with Tim Beckley and Tim Swartz.

SCOTT CORRALES

A prolific writer and investigator of UFO and paranormal events in the Hispanic communities worldwide, he is one of the most respected names in the global world of UFOlogy with contacts in South and Central America, Mexico, Spain and the Caribbean. The Institute of Hispanic Ufology was established in October of 1998 with the appearance of the first issue of Inexplicata. The organization currently has representatives and contributing editors in over a dozen Spanish-speaking countries. Director: Scott Corrales http://inexplicata.blogspot.com/.His research into sightings and hair raising encounters with the Chupacabras are the inspiration for this volume's fascination with the lust for blood by the Ultra-terrestrials.

ALIEN BLOOD LUST

HERCULES INVICTUS

Hercules Invictus is a Lemnian Greek, a proud descendant of Argonauts and Amazons. He is openly Olympian in his spirituality and worldview, dedicated to living the Mythic Life and has been exploring the fringes of our reality throughout his entire earthly sojourn. For over four decades he has been sharing his Olympian Odyssey with others.

Having relocated the heart of his Temenos to Northeastern New Jersey and the Greater New York Metropolitan Area, he is now establishing his unique niche locally and contributing to his community's overall quality of life. Hercules is also recruiting Argonauts to help him usher in a new Age of Heroes.

Hercules currently hosts **The Elysium Project**, **Pride of Olympus** and **Voice of Olympus** e-radio shows on the **Spiritual Unity Radio Network**. He currently writes for **The Magic Happens**, **Mysterious Magazine** and **Paranoia Magazine**, has published two e-books on Kindle **Olympian Ice** and **The Antediluvial Scrolls** and has been contributing to Timothy Beckley's awesome anthologies. Hercules founded or co-founded **Mount Olympus LLP**, **Olympian Heroic Path**, **Olympian Shamanic Path**, **Cosmic Olympianism**, **Mythic Atlantis**, **The Order of the Golden Fleece**, **Living Theurgy**, the **Regional Folklore Society of Northeastern PA** and the **Center for the Study of Living Myth** here in NJ. He also spearheaded many of the real-world Age of Heroes initiatives and the fictive Mythic Adventure tales. For more information please Friend him on Facebook or visit his website: http://www.herculesinvictus.net

Independent Publisher Of Alternative Titles Since 1965

Timothy Green Beckley's
Conspiracy Journal
bizarre bazaar
US $3.00

Incorporating Inner Light / UFO Review

Promoting Free Speech and Individuality
Opposing The System, Censorship, Death & Taxes

IN THIS ISSUE: Strange, Amazing, Rare and Exotic Items From Worldwide Sources

Photo by April Troiani

COMING DOWN THE ROAD WITH TIM BECKLEY PLEASE STOP AND SAY HELLO!

Well it has been awhile, but we're still alive but not so well — hope we don't have to send out a medical bulletin through Face Book.

I know some of you have been with us for years.

We started this little publishing venture in 1965 with a mimeograph machine and a darling mother who vanquished me to the back porch as there were ink spots all over the house making it look like a crime scene with my fingerprints in black instead of red, on the refrigerator and the walls.

Over the decades we went through some hot and cold spells where books were being moved from our sorry ass storage container with no lights, heat or AC. But we were selling all over the world to several hundred independent bookstores and metaphysical centers as well as to wholesalers like New Leaf (still active and still getting our books out there to shops in this genre that remain open). And both customers and retailers were clamoring for more titles and so we increased our production into different areas — all

the while I was editing numerous newsstand magazines and producing a movie or two. I was a busy young man. The James Dean of the Paranormal!

But then the bubble burst with the advent of the internet. Amazon became king of the hill and stores lost their customers as

rent and salaries and insurance went up for the most part and we, too, had to lay off people and cut down on our activities.

However, in the last few years we have risen like the Phoenix and now have over 300 titles to whet your appetite. We can't afford to put out a printed catalog more than twice each year, but we still issue about 3 new books a month and have remained a pretty popular small press, while others have folded due to retirement (Yes! we are now in our Seventies having started around age 14 — and Carol Ann is still with us!) . We thank Tim Swartz , William Kern, Sean Casteel, Maria D' Andrea, Peter Bernard, Helen Hovey, Charla Gene, April continued on Page 2>

HENCHMEN
Tim Beckley, Publisher/Editor
Associates: Tim Swartz; Brad Steiger; Sean Casteel; Carol Ann Rodriguez
Layout, Graphics & Typesetting: William Kern (Adnan)
CONSPIRACY JOURNAL GLOBAL COMMUNICATIONS
Payment For All Merchandise To Timothy Beckley
Box 753, New Brunswick, NJ 08903
MRUFO8@hotmail.com • PayPal Orders Preferred
All Other Methods Accepted—732-602-3407
FREE VIDEOS on our YouTube Channel
"Mr. UFOs Secret Files"
Tim Beckley

continued from Page 1

Troiani and Earl The Cat for their ongoing support — and we miss you Brad Steiger. And love all our writers and honored guests on our podcast, who are just too numerous to name in this small amount of space.

But let us go so you can thumb through this issue and hopefully send us an order. The printer ships most of the books and they come well packed and in a reasonable amount of time. New titles include: "Screwed by the Aliens," "UFO Hostility, "Project Magnet," "Occult Secrets of the Third Reich," "The Black Pullet," "The Miracle of Nikola Tesla's Purple Energy Plates," "Nikola Tesla Journey To Mars — Update!" —

And we have increased the number of kits and "bizarre" products we carry. So don't forget us, and we promise not to forget you!

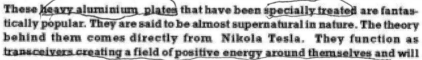

ALIEN BLOOD LUST

ALL KITS AND PRODUCTS SOLD FOR EXPERIMENTAL USE ONLY

NIKOLA TESLA MAN OF MYSTERY
NEW – NIKOLA TESLA JOURNEY TO MARS UPDATE

With Shocking Photos That Show Evidence Of Life On Mars!

Thanks to technology developed by the "wizard Nikola Tesla," Mars is no longer the Mystery Planet! What is the truth about a supposed Secret Space Program outside the jurisdiction of NASA?

For centuries astronomers have peered through their telescopes for signs of life on the Red Planet. Some thought they saw canals or strange lights that roamed the surface. Jules Verne — and other early pioneers of science fiction — wrote what were then considered to be far-fetched stories about the exploration of the moon and the planet Mars. They based their classic literary works not just on their own fertile imaginations, but on "wild rumors" circulating that such voyages had already been made, accomplished by a group of scientists — all members of the same secret lodge or society that had tapped into an unknown power source, using it to facilitate the birth of flight, years before the Wright Brothers were able to leave the ground.

Contacted by this secret fraternal order, Nikola Tesla is said to have furthered their cause, coming up with his own method of interplanetary travel, soon to be stolen and used by Hitler and perhaps the New World Order.

Here is proof that scientists and engineers regularly travel back and forth between colonies that have been set up on the Martian surface and deep underground. *Update* is all part of a super-secret space program that the public has been told nothing about. ☒ Large format. $15.95

OTHER TITLES OF INTEREST

☐ TESLA AND THE INCREDIBLE TECHNOLOGIES OF THE NEW WORLD ORDER — Does Area 51 hold the key to many modern day mysteries? — $15.00

☐ MEN OF MYSTERY - NIKOLA TESLA AND OTIS T. CARR — A ship to get us off the planet was constructed in the 1950s. Suppressed Plans — $20.00

☐ NIKOLA TESLA FREE ENERGY AND THE WHITE DOVE — Was Tesla a space man or a time traveler? Here are the suppressed stories and rumors. — $18.00

☐ THE EXPERIMENTS, INVENTIONS, WRITINGS AND PATENTS OF TESLA - 396 large format pages for serious students who want to view hundreds of his papers and documents. - $27.00

☐ THE LOST JOURNALS OF NIKOLA TESLA - Tim Swartz uncovers Time Travel, Alternative Energy and the secret of Nazi flying discs. - Large Format, $21.95

☐ NEW — THE MIRACLE OF TESLA'S PURPLE ENERGY PLATES — The plates are said to be almost supernatural. — $10.00 (add $25 for one 4x5 plate).

ALL BOOKS AS LISTED $120.00 + $10 SHIPPING

Timothy Beckley, Box 753, New Brunswick, NJ 08903 (Available via PayPal - mrufo8@hotmail.com)

310

ALIEN BLOOD LUST

225 Large format pages – $19.95

CRYPTOZOOLOGY – MYSTERIOUS MONSTERS

They Stalk Our Land In The Darkness Of Night As Well As In The Daylight Hours. Their Reality Is Debated But We Have The Evidence They Actually Exist!

☐ **NEW! – WEIRD WINGED WONDERS: THE TWILIGHT WORLD OF CRYPTID CREATURES**

Here are dozens of the creepy-crawly narrations – backed up by the strangest of photographic evidence – of bizarre and unknown flying cryptids who frolic in our sky as if they have not a care in the world. Theories abound as to their origin(s) and nature and their overall grip on our perceived reality. The Jersey Devil is said to be a demon who flies near the Pine Barrens mainly in the dead of night, while the Thunderbirds are massive creatures with wingspans of more than 30 feet.

● – Dragons are thought of as beings rooted firmly in mythology and the stuff of movies such as "The Hobbit" and popular cable TV shows such as "Game of Thrones." Yet sightings of these aerial demons known to spit fire have been seen worldwide and are part of every culture – past and present – from Europe to the United States, and every continent in between.

● — Even more eerie are the flying and floating "alien" humanoids and witchy "brohaus" observed widely in Mexico and South America.

ALSO AVAILABLE

☐ **CRYPTO CREATURES FROM DARK DOMAINS**

Legions of dogmen, devil hounds, phantom canines and horrific werewolves of fact and folklore are described in detail. The bloody beasts come in various sizes and apprently even have the ability to shape-shift into a even greater variety of hideous creatures of their occupants.
236 Large Format Pages – $19.95

☐ **TIM BECKLEY'S AUTHENTIC BOOK OF ULTRA-TERRESTRIAL CONTACTS**

Don't think that this is just another book on UFOs – it isn't! Here are reports of their occupants so weird that they could not possibly exist – but they do! There are the Flower People: and Alien Pods. – The flying "Tin Cans." Hairy creatures from hell. Space Monsters galore.
Large format – $15.00

SPECIAL – ALL 3 BOOKS ABOVE: $42.50 + $6.00 S/H
TIMOTHY BECKLEY, BOX 753, NEW BRUNSWICK, NJ 08903
Best way to order is through PayPal to mrufo8@hotmail.com

AND THE TRUTH SHALL SET YOU FREE!

New Show Weekly
THE PARACAST
Your Host GENE STEINBERG
200 + Shows Archived FREE!

ALIEN BLOOD LUST

FEAR FACTOR – DARK SIDE OF UFOLOGY

Not all Ets are our friends. There are apparently a variety of beings visiting from space, other dimensions and the other side of the veil. These works are guaranteed to keep you up all night worrying that we may not be alone!

☒ SCREWED BY THE ALIENS: TRUE SEXUAL ENCOUNTERS WITH ETS

The Sexterrestrials are here – and they want to mate with you! Since the beginning of time otherworldly entities – no matter how you wish to identify them – have been pillaging and plundering our planet, raping our women, probing our bodies in an ungentlemanly manner, and ostensibly creating a "master race" of alien hybrids by removing the fetuses from artificially inseminated females who have been abducted by UFO occupants around the globe. The aliens then raise the "children" as their own. These are the anal probes, the kidnapping and removal of men, women and couples from the planet for evil, inhuman purposes that often involve molestation and torture. Some of those abducted have literally been branded and physically scarred for life. "Tattoos" have been placed on their skin, and horrific scratch and claw marks can be found on their chests and stomachs, arms, legs and breasts. Some of these markings can only be seen under florescent lighting; others can be viewed with the naked eye because they are so obvious. Seventeen researchers provide the evidence. Here are historical as well as some of the most recent cases of copulation with Reptilians, the handsome Nordic "Space Brothers," the Greys, insectoids, and a host of other intergalactic stalkers – the real invaders from "Mars" – as taken from the files of seventeen top researchers of our time. To paraphrase Cindy Lauper's 80s smash pop single, there are a few space aliens who it seems are coming here because they "just want to have fun!"

330 Large Format Pages – $24.00

29,67 Usul Bookstore Price (handwritten)

☐ UFO HOSTILITIES AND THE EVIL ALIEN AGENDA: LETHAL ENCOUNTERS WITH ULTRA-TERRESTRIALS

Secret Government Findings Claims There Is A Valid "Alien Threat" — - UFOS COULD DOOM LIFE ON EARTH! Here is irrefutable proof that UFOs could be perilous to your well being and could doom all of humanity. Here is evidence that UFOs profoundly alter the consciousness of those exposed to it and is surrounded by deceptive activities. HERE ARE CASE HISTORIES OF UFO ATROCITIES – FROM STRANGE DISAPPEARANCES TO BIZARRE DEATHS: ** From the "Foo Fighters" who dogged our fastest planes of WWI and II, to the battalions of well-armed soldiers who walked into a strange ground level cloud cover never to be seen again, global conflict seems to bring out the most hostile manifestations of the UFOs. From time to time America's bravest have been seen marching into oblivion. Many top secret aerial skirmishes have victimized pilots and passengers; some planes have "gone down" without a trace; hundreds have been killed – including famous Hollywood celebrities!

** There have been terrifying incidents of flaming destruction that have incinerated individuals or rendered them helpless. In one case UFOs left a military fort and its sentries smoldering, while entire coastal towns in Brazil have been "burned out," by what are called by the locals chupachupas. ** Learn about a cursed "Lethal Lake" in Texas where dozens of people have mysteriously died, while other vacationers have vanished completely on land and underwater. Entire towns have been known to disappear in association with UFOs, while unsuspecting individuals have walked off wilderness trails in front of onlookers only to slip into a parallel universe inhabited by hobgoblins, men-in-black and other cross-dimensional terrors. ** Alert yourself to paralyzing episodes of alien acts of aggression that have blacked out power systems, erased memories and crippled human beings. **448 Large Format Pages — $21.95**

continued next page>

TIMOTHY G BECKLEY, BOX 753, NEW BRUNSWICK, NJ 08903

313

ALIEN BLOOD LUST

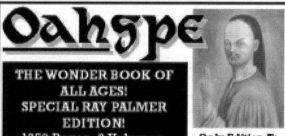

ALIEN BLOOD LUST

MOST TITLES AVAILABLE FROM AMAZON—PRINT AND KINDLE EDITIONS

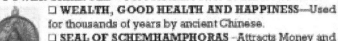

319

Book
The Eighth ~~Tower~~ Tower
John Keel
Dutton 1975
$26.04

Made in the USA
Columbia, SC
12 March 2019